Morte

Sams **Teach Yourself**

Microsoft®

Expression™
Web 4

Second Edition
Updated for Service Pack 2—
HTML5, CSS3, jQuery

in **24**
Hours

SAMS

800 East 96th Street, Indianapolis, Indiana, 46240 USA

Sams Teach Yourself Microsoft® Expression™ Web 4 in 24 Hours, Second Edition

Copyright © 2012 by Pearson Education, Inc.

ISBN-13: 978-0-672-33590-7
ISBN-10: 0-672-33590-5

5571 9842 08/14

Library of Congress Cataloging-in-Publication Data

Rand-Hendriksen, Morten.
  Sams teach yourself Microsoft Expression web 4 in 24 hours / Morten Rand-Hendriksen.
    p. cm.
  "Updated for Service Pack 2, HTML5, CSS3, jQuery."
  ISBN 978-0-672-33590-7
  1. Microsoft Expression Web. 2. Web site development. 3. Web sites—Design—Computer programs. 4. Web sites—Authoring programs. I. Title.
  TK5105.8885.M525R36 2012
  006.7'8—dc23
                          2012003376

This product is printed digitally on demand.

First Printing April 2012

Trademarks

All terms mentioned in this book that are known to be trademarks or service marks have been appropriately capitalized. Sams Publishing cannot attest to the accuracy of this information. Use of a term in this book should not be regarded as affecting the validity of any trademark or service mark.

Warning and Disclaimer

Every effort has been made to make this book as complete and as accurate as possible, but no warranty or fitness is implied. The information provided is on an "as is" basis. The author and the publisher shall have neither liability nor responsibility to any person or entity with respect to any loss or damages arising from the information contained in this book or from the use of programs accompanying it.

Bulk Sales

Sams Publishing offers excellent discounts on this book when ordered in quantity for bulk purchases or special sales. For more information, please contact

U.S. Corporate and Government Sales
1-800-382-3419
corpsales@pearsontechgroup.com

For sales outside of the U.S., please contact

International Sales
international@pearsoned.com

Editor-in-Chief	Greg Wiegand
Executive Editor	Loretta Yates
Development Editor	Todd Brakke
Managing Editor	Kristy Hart
Project Editor	Betsy Harris
Copy Editor	Bart Reed
Indexer	Lisa Stumpf
Proofreader	Kathy Ruiz
Technical Editor	Kathleen Anderson
Publishing Coordinator	Cindy Teeters
Book Designer	Gary Adair
Senior Compositor	Gloria Schurick

Contents at a Glance

Table of Contents

About the Author

Morten Rand-Hendriksen is the owner and creative director of Pink & Yellow Media, a boutique-style design company providing digital media consulting and creations for individuals, businesses, and broadcast television. He was awarded the Microsoft MVP (Most Valuable Professional) Award for his work with Microsoft Expression in 2008, 2009, 2010 and 2011.

In addition to Microsoft Expression Web, Morten is considered an expert on the publishing platform WordPress and he has published numerous articles and videos and done public speaking engagements on both topics.

Sams Teach Yourself Microsoft Expression Web 4 in 24 Hours is Morten's fourth published book. He is a regular contributor to the official Microsoft Expression newsletter and has been published in international design magazines. You can find more tutorials, articles, and other design-related musings on Morten's blog at www.designisphilosophy.com, and you can follow his rants on Twitter under the name @mor10. Also, you might run into him in different forums and newsgroups throughout the Web, usually using the same handle.

If you have any questions relating to this book, contact Morten through the website dedicated to this book, which can be found at http://expression.pinkandyellow.com.

Dedication

*I dedicate this book the crew of Expression Web MVP Award
recipients over the years:*

*Kathleen Anderson
Steve Easton
Tina Clarke
Chris Leeds
Ron Symonds
Ian Haynes
Yoshie Kohama
Patricia Geary
Minal Agarwal
Cheryl D. Wise*

...and a special thank you to Steven Guttman—the man who made it all possible.

Acknowledgments

On the shelf next to me sit three volumes of my *Sams Teach Yourself Microsoft Expression Web in 24 Hours* series: the original, the rewrite, and the update. And here I am, once again on my couch with my trusted laptop on my lap, putting the final touches on the fourth edition. You'd think this would be superfluous; four versions of the same book about the same software, and the last one a rewrite for a mere service pack no less. But no. The fact that four editions were warranted is a testament to the work done by the Expression Web development team to take the application from its meager beginners as a reboot of Microsoft's venture in the front-end web development market to a state-of-the-art, future-friendly application with more tricks up its sleeve than a seasoned magician at Hollywood's Magic Castle.

This fourth edition came about because the release of Service Pack 2 for Expression Web 4 marks such a fundamental change to the application that new tutorials and new information were needed. Whereas service packs regularly see bug fixes and simple updates, this service pack was in many ways a reboot of the application, introducing whole new dimensions of functionality, clearing out a lot of old rubbish, and bringing Expression Web into the future. We're talking a dedicated Code Snippets panel, full HTML5 and CSS3 support, and even code support for JavaScript and jQuery. All this combined with a more stable core and long-sought-after features like custom toolbars and configurable and savable work-spaces meant that what was covered in the original Expression Web 4 book just wasn't enough.

Acknowledgments

You may have noticed that I chose to dedicate this volume to my fellow Expression Web MVPs. I did so for a reason. Were it not for this eclectic group of people of which I am honored to be counted as a member, the Expression Web you see before you today would not have been the same. The Expression Web team at Microsoft lead by Steven Guttman made an early decision to involve the community through the Expression Web MVPs at every level of the design and development process of the application. This meant the application was built around real-life usage scenarios, and bugs and features were reported, requested, and included on a running basis. There are several features in the application, and especially in the new Service Pack 2, that members of the Expression Web MVP group can point to and say "I came up with that" or "That was my suggestion." And it was the same group that beta-tested the application in real life and helped shape the application into what it is today.

Don't misunderstand me: I am not saying we built the application. The honor and respect for that should go to Steven and his amazing team of developers. What I am saying is that this application is the fruit of an unprecedented interaction and collaboration between the development team and the people who use the application the most. And for that, everyone involved deserves a tip of the hat. So to my dear friends who label themselves xWeb MVPs, I salute you.

I can't wrap this up without expressing a big thanks to the people who made this book possible. For the second time in a row I was lucky enough to have my fellow Expression Web MVP Kathleen Anderson sign on as technical editor ensuring that everything I wrote actually made practical sense so that I wouldn't lead you astray. On the development and editing side, Betsy Harris, Todd Brakke and Bart Reed have to be credited for making my sometimes archaic language and run-on sentences make sense.

On the practical side, a big thanks goes out to the Expression Web development team, and in particular to Steven Guttman, for providing unrestricted access to and influence on the application months before it was in its final version. I also want to thank my friends Paul LaBerge and Simran Chaudry from Microsoft Canada for their continuing support and assistance and for supporting my fourth Expression Web MVP Award nomination. Receiving the award four years in a row was an honor, and I can only hope I am living up to it.

There are countless others involved in both the pre- and post-publishing process I have not mentioned, and they should all be gravely offended for not being named by name. Without their contributions, this book would never have made the journey from my mind to the hands of the readers, and they should be acknowledged for their invaluable work.

We Want to Hear from You!

As the reader of this book, *you* are our most important critic and commentator. We value your opinion and want to know what we're doing right, what we could do better, what areas you'd like to see us publish in, and any other words of wisdom you're willing to pass our way.

You can email or write me directly to let me know what you did or didn't like about this book—as well as what we can do to make our books stronger.

Please note that I cannot help you with technical problems related to the topic of this book, and that due to the high volume of mail I receive, I might not be able to reply to every message.

When you write, please be sure to include this book's title and author as well as your name and phone number or email address. I will carefully review your comments and share them with the author and editors who worked on the book.

E-mail: feedback@samspublishing.com

Mail: Greg Wiegand
            Editor-in-Chief
            Sams Publishing
            800 East 96th Street
            Indianapolis, IN 46240 USA

Reader Services

Visit our website and register this book at informit.com/register for convenient access to any updates, downloads, or errata that might be available for this book.

Introduction

About This Book

Because you have opened this book and started reading the Introduction, I assume that you are interested in learning how to create websites using Microsoft Expression Web 4. If so, I congratulate you: By choosing this application as your platform, you are already well on your way to creating functional and well-designed sites based on web standards. In other words, unlike me, you are putting the proverbial horse before the cart and starting at the beginning rather than learning things the hard way.

Expression Web 4 is the fourth version of a web design and development platform that sees Microsoft take a whole new approach to the concept of web standards. The application you work with throughout this book produces standards-based websites right out of the box without requiring any tweaking or custom coding. In fact, using Expression Web 4, you can create advanced standards-based websites with lots of fancy interactive features without ever writing a line of code. And with that, the threshold for learning, understanding, and creating websites that look and behave the same across all browsers and platforms is lowered to a level anyone can manage.

This book is the fourth revision of my first book, *Sams Teach Yourself Microsoft Expression Web 2 in 24 Hours*. Well, actually, it's an update of rather than a revision of the third edition, *Sams Teach Yourself Microsoft Expression Web 4 in 24 Hours*. This new edition covers the many enhancements introduced by the Service Pack 2 update, including a new Code Snippets panel and full support for HTML5, CSS3 and jQuery among other things.

Since the publication of the first book, I have received a lot of feedback from readers, and I've taken all of it into account.

When I started writing this book, I spent a lot of time thinking about you, the reader—more specifically, how to ensure that after reading this book, you would walk away with not only an understanding of the application, but how to use it to get from an idea to a finalized product. The result of my ponderings was a website called MyKipple.com that showcases many of the basic and more advanced functions available in Expression Web 4. By following the tutorials in this book, you build the MyKipple.com website from scratch and, in the process, learn how all the different elements come together and how to get the most out of the application. When you finish the last hour and the site is complete, you will have both the tools and know-how to build your own websites using Hypertext Markup Language (HTML), Cascading Style Sheets (CSS), and the many other functions that Expression Web 4 offers. You will also have a basic understanding of how the application deals with more advanced coding languages, such as PHP, and you'll learn how to embed external content like YouTube videos.

Accompanying this book is a small website that contains information about the book itself along with the lesson files for each hour and, in time, a wiki or a forum for you to get more information and showcase your work. The website is located at http://expression.pinkandyellow.com.

Who This Book Is For

Opening this book, you are probably wondering, "Is this the right book for me?" So, I guess I should tell you who this book was written for. The answer, though it might sound silly, is that I wrote this book for myself—or rather myself 15 years ago.

When I started building websites in the 1990s, I really had no clue what I was doing other than a vision of what I wanted to create. And when I looked around for help in the form of books or tutorials, I couldn't find anything that spoke to me. What was available was either too technical or too superficial. No matter where I looked, I could find only basic algorithms on how to perform simple tasks, never detailed explanations of how to get from point A to point B. As a result, I ended up teaching myself how to do things. Needless to say, I learned the true meaning of the term "taking the long way around."

So, when I signed up to write this book, I had one main goal in mind: to write the book I was looking for and really needed when I started out—a book that took me all the way from a basic sketch on a napkin to a fully working website and taught me how to use the application at the same time.

As a result, this book is written with the novice designer in mind. No, let me rephrase that: As a result, this book is written in a way that I think a novice designer can understand and learn from. I make this distinction because, even if you are a seasoned designer or developer, I am certain you can find lots of useful information inside these covers.

Being introduced to Expression Web has had an enormous impact on my business because it reduced what used to take hours or days to only minutes. In particular, I am talking about the application's excellent CSS features: More than just a design and development application, Expression Web 4 is a tool that helps you learn, understand, dissect, and modify style sheets with unprecedented speed and accuracy. Getting a firm grasp on these tools and understanding how to use them in real-world scenarios can almost certainly make your work with CSS more efficient and productive, regardless of whether this is the first time you've encountered the term *style sheets* or you are a seasoned professional with years of experience.

So, without further ado, I wish you a pleasant journey and hope you come out on the other side with the skills, understanding, and confidence to take on the wild and exciting world of web design.

Lykke til!

—Morten Rand-Hendriksen, February 2012

HOUR 1

Getting to Know Microsoft Expression Web 4 Service Pack 2

What You'll Learn in This Hour:

▶ What Expression Web 4 is and what you can use it for

▶ How to navigate and customize the workspace layout

▶ How to open and close toolbars and panels

▶ How to reset the workspace to the default settings

After opening this book, you probably want to jump right in and start creating websites. However, before you start, it's a good idea to familiarize yourself with the program. Whether you are a first-time user or a seasoned web designer, Expression Web 4 has something new to offer you. And because you'll be spending a lot of time with the program, learning it before you start working on projects can save you both time and frustration. If you are impatient, you can always jump ahead to Hour 3, "A Website Is Really Just Text: Build One in 5 Minutes," and come back here later. But, as my father always told me, "If you want to bottle an elephant, you better read the manual first." Getting to know your tools before you use them makes your life easier in the long run.

Introducing Expression Web 4

Expression Web 4 is a complete web-publishing suite bundled into one program. It's an HTML editor, a WYSIWYG editor, an authoring tool, a code debugger, a Cascading Style Sheets (CSS) generator, and a file-management tool all wrapped up into one convenient package—a one-stop shop for putting content on the Web.

Whether you are a designer with no previous code experience, a developer with no previous design experience, or somewhere between the two, Expression Web 4 can help you work faster and more effectively.

By the Way

WYSIWYG (What You See Is What You Get) is an acronym used for visual web-editing applications in which the user can view and edit the page as it appears in a browser rather than simply viewing and editing code.

As you will see when working with web design, this name is a bit misleading: The fact that a web page looks a certain way in a WYSIWYG editor doesn't necessarily mean it will look the same when viewed through an actual web browser. Also, different kinds of content cannot be displayed in WYSIWYG editors, such as Silverlight applications and dynamic web content. You will be introduced to these components and learn how to deal with this problem later in the book. In spite of this, the WYSIWYG editor is a powerful tool that gives you a fairly accurate picture of what your design will look like on the Web.

Expression Web 4 is a new link in a long chain of web-authoring tools. What makes it unique is that it gives the user the ability to create 100% standards-based sites even without knowing what the term *standards based* means. Expression Web 4 is, in many ways, a shortcut that opens the world of standards-based code, previously accessible only to the web developer elite, to anyone using it. And because creating standards-based sites is (or should be) the ultimate goal of any web designer, Expression Web 4 gives you a huge advantage. Of course, that doesn't mean your sites will be perfect, but you will spend far less time picking at finicky code and solving browser incompatibilities.

With Expression Web 4, you can create new pages and sites from scratch or from templates; view, edit, and alter existing pages and sites; and build new server-based applications with ASP.NET (Active Server Pages .NET) and PHP (PHP: Hypertext Preprocessor; its name is recursive). In short, Expression Web 4 is a complete package for creating and publishing websites whether on a local computer, a network, or the Web.

By the Way

The terms *standards based* and *web standards* refer to the formal standards and technical specifications set out by the World Wide Web Consortium (W3C) to describe how the World Wide Web works. If you follow these standards, your web page *should* look the same in all web browsers. (I emphasize *should* because not all web browsers follow these standards.) By creating standards-based websites, you avoid many of the problems associated with browser incompatibilities and build clean and functional websites accessible to people with disabilities and anyone on slower connections or older computers. The terms refer to a website's coding, not what it looks like. So don't worry: A standards-based website does not have to be boring or ordinary, just built properly. If you want more information on web standards, a good place to start is the W3C website: www.w3.org.

Getting and Installing Expression Web 4

Expression Web 4 was launched in June 2010, and it is available through most software retailers or through the Microsoft Expression website (www.microsoft.com/expression). The application comes bundled in the Expression Studio 4 Ultimate and Expression Studio 4 Web Professional packages. If you are a web developer and you are not going to dive into Silverlight and Windows 8 HTML5 applications, the Expression Studio 4 Web Professional package is the right option for you. If you haven't already, consider purchasing the software as a download from Microsoft rather than through a retailer. Not only is it much quicker than going to a store or ordering from an online retailer, but you save the planet from all the unnecessary waste created in the production and shipping of the product. Just remember to back up the software installation and save your activation code in case something goes wrong somewhere down the road.

If you are new to the field and unsure of whether you want to use this program, from the same site you can download a fully functional trial version that gives you 60 days to make up your mind.

Expression Web 4 is designed for the Microsoft Windows platform and works on Microsoft Windows XP Service Pack 2 and 3, Windows Vista, and Windows 7, as well as on Windows Server 2003 and 2008. It also works on a Mac running the aforementioned Windows operating systems either as a dual boot via Bootcamp or in virtualization software such as VMWare Fusion or Parallels.

Installing the software, whether it's from a download or from a DVD, is straightforward. If you purchased the software in a box from a vendor, your activation key is inside the box. If you purchased the software from the Microsoft Expression website, you received your activation code during the purchase. If you are using a trial version, select the Trial option the first time you run the software.

Did you know?

If you have any problems with the installation or the program doesn't work after you install it, troubleshooting tips, FAQs, and forums on the Microsoft Expression website can walk you through the troubleshooting process and get you up and running. There is also a known issue in which licensing and activation occasionally don't work. If you run into this problem, you can find a fix at http://support.microsoft.com/default.aspx?scid=kb;en-US;2635101.

Getting and Installing Service Pack 2

Since its release in the summer of 2010, Expression Web 4 has seen the release of two Service Packs, aptly titled Service Pack 1 and Service Pack 2 (referred to as "SP2" from here onward). More than general software updates, these service packs introduced support for new and updated code languages, new features and functionalities, as well as user interface upgrades. The difference between the application itself when shipped and the application with SP2 installed is so different that we decided to release this update to the book to cover all the changes. These changes will be addressed throughout the book.

To take full advantage of all the features in Expression Web 4, you need to install SP2. After installing Expression Web 4 itself, go to the Web 4 Service Packs and Add-Ins page on the Microsoft Expression website (http://www.microsoft.com/expression/service-packs/Web.aspx) and find and click the Download Web 4 SP2 button. This takes you to the Microsoft Expression Web 4 Service Pack 2 (SP2) page in the Microsoft Download Center. From here, follow the instructions to download and install Service Pack 2.

After installation is complete, open Expression Web 4, click the Help option on the far right of the main menu, and select About Microsoft Expression Web from the drop-down menu. This opens the application dialog for Expression Web 4, which shows among other things the version number and licensing information. If SP2 was installed correctly, the first line should read "Microsoft Expression Web Version 4.0.1303.0 SP2," as shown in Figure 1.1.

FIGURE 1.1
The Expression Web About dialog.

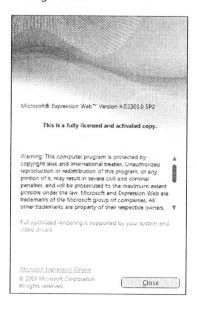

Getting Acquainted with the Workspace

When you open Expression Web 4 for the first time, it presents several views, panels, and toolbars containing tools and information (see Figure 1.2). In the middle, the Code view and the Design view show you the current page. Together, these panels and toolbars give you a complete picture of the project you are working on and multiple ways of working with and editing that project.

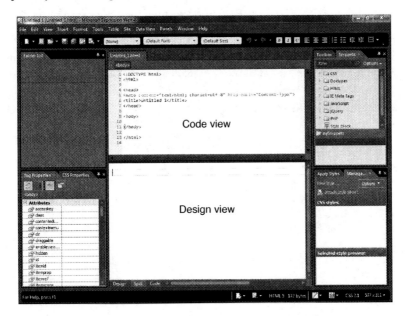

FIGURE 1.2
Expression Web 4 as it appears when first opened.

The Program Bar

The address and name of the current file you are working with appear at the top of the workspace. In Figure 1.2, this is "Untitled 1 (Untitled_1.html)." When you open the program for the first time, it displays this default empty web page. Later, you learn how to decide what the program displays when it opens.

The Menu Bar

The menu bar is directly under the address bar. This bar is familiar to anyone who has used a computer program. The menu bar is the program's control center from which you can access any tool, feature, or functionality. Clicking a menu item reveals that item's drop-down menu. Sliding your mouse left or right displays the drop-down menus for the selected menu item. Some drop-down menu items have an arrow icon to their right. Hovering your mouse over the arrow reveals additional submenus. We cover each option in later hours. To collapse the menus, simply click anywhere outside the drop-down menu.

▼ **Try It Yourself**

Use the Menu Bar to Close and Open Design View and Code View

If you have never used a web design application such as Expression Web 4 before, the window with all its menus and panels and views might seem intimidating. However, when you understand how to use and manipulate them, you will see that they are there for one reason only: to help you get your job done faster and more efficiently.

At the center of the page is the View panel. By default, it is split in half horizontally with the Code view on the top and the Design view on the bottom. These views will be explained later, but for now let's look at how you can use the View menu shown in Figure 1.3 to change them to see only what you want.

FIGURE 1.3
The View menu with the Page submenu open.

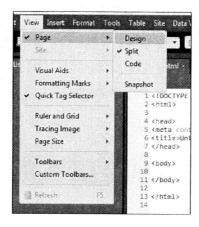

1. View the Page item and then hover the mouse pointer over it.

2. Select Design in the submenu that opens to the right (see Figure 1.3).

3. Notice that the middle of the workspace now shows only Design view.

4. Repeat step 1 and click Code in the submenu. You now see only Code view.

5. Repeat step 1 and click Split. Notice that doing so restores the workspace to what it was when you started.

▲

Common and Other Toolbars

The Common toolbar is under the menu bar (see Figure 1.4). This toolbar contains the most commonly used functions in the program, such as New, Open, Save, Font, Alignment, and so on. In addition to being an excellent tool for quick access to frequently used functions, the Common toolbar also displays information about your current selections.

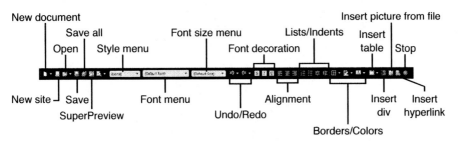

New document

Save all   Font size menu   Lists/Indents   Insert picture from file

Open | Style menu   Font decoration   Insert table | Stop

New site — Save | Font menu   Alignment   Insert   Insert

SuperPreview   Undo/Redo   div   hyperlink

Borders/Colors

FIGURE 1.4
The Common toolbar holds the most commonly used tools for easy access.

In addition to the Common toolbar are numerous other toolbars that serve different functions (see Figure 1.5). You can activate these toolbars by clicking View on the main menu and selecting Toolbars or by right-clicking in the empty area to the right in the Common toolbar and selecting the new toolbar from the pop-up menu. When you open a new toolbar, it docks directly under the Common toolbar (or whatever is the lowest visible toolbar).

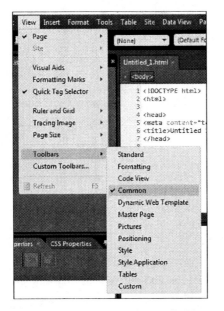

FIGURE 1.5
The different toolbars are accessible from the Toolbars submenu under View.

When you hover your mouse over a button or function throughout the program, a small ScreenTip appears that explains what the button or function does and, in some cases, gives you the shortcut for that action. Learning shortcuts not only speeds up your work, but it also prevents muscle and joint problems caused by excessive mouse use.

By the
Way

Code, Design, and Split View

As you work on your pages, you need to switch back and forth between the different views. To make this as easy as possible, the View panel comes equipped with three buttons to toggle the different views on and off, as shown in Figure 1.6.

FIGURE 1.6
The Design, Split, and Code buttons can be found at the bottom of the View panel.

As its name suggests, Code view displays the code (or backend) of the file in which you are working. In reality, all web pages are just code documents, and Code view gives you a behind-the-scenes look at the inner workings of your page. Code view has many features to help you in your work—from color coding and line numbering to IntelliSense and snippets. You use this view not only to inspect the code Expression Web 4 created for you, but also to make alterations and add your own code. If you work with a strict code file (.css, .php, .js, and so on), this is the only view available.

Did you Know?

> When you open a page in your web browser, you are actually looking at the browser's interpretation of the code in the file. Web pages are written in a markup code language that, when interpreted, turns into what you see in your browser. What you don't see is that many of these pages actually consist of several different files, and some of these contain only programming code. These are what I refer to as "strict code files," and they are an important part of functional web design. By placing code in a strict code file, you can use this one file as the code source for multiple pages and thus make sweeping changes to all the related files by editing just one. In this book, you learn how to use one such strict code file, known as a Cascading Style Sheet (CSS), to control the look and feel of multiple pages at the same time.

Design view is the WYSIWYG editor. This view emulates a web browser and (at least in theory) displays your files as they will appear in a web browser. This is probably where you will do most of your work. In Design view, you can visually edit HTML and other markup files by dragging and dropping content, editing text, and moving borders in much the same way you would work in word-processing software such as Microsoft Word. It also features visual aids to help you see how the page functions. Design view provides a much less intimidating approach to web design, and people just starting out often prefer it to Code view.

Split view gives you the best of both worlds: Code view on the top and Design view on the bottom. In Split view, you can see, in real time, how changes in one view affect the other. For a beginner, working in Split view can greatly enhance the learning process, whether you come from a coding background or a design background.

Left and Right Panels

On the left and right sides of the workspace are four panels, described in the following sections. These panels contain tools, information, and content you can use in the design process.

Folder List (Top Left)

The Folder List panel shows the folder and file tree in the project or site you are working within (see Figure 1.7). New in SP2, the folder or filename, file size, and associated application are shown in the top of the panel. In the case of PDF files, the first page of the file is previewed.

FIGURE 1.7
The Folder List panel with a HTML file high-lighted. The browser default is set to Chrome.

Tag Properties and CSS Properties (Bottom Left)

This panel contains two tabbed subpanels. The Tag Properties panel (see Figure 1.8) and CSS Properties panel (see Figure 1.9) display the current tag or CSS properties of the selected object. Clicking different parts of the code in Code view shows how the tag properties change depending on the code you click. We cover both panels in more detail in later hours.

FIGURE 1.8
Tag Properties
panel.

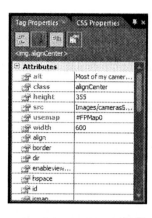

FIGURE 1.9
CSS Properties
panel.

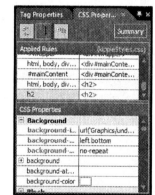

Snippets (Top Right)

The Snippets panel, shown in Figure 1.10, is a new feature introduced with SP2. It enhances the code snippets function in Expression Web 4 and provides an easy way to insert code in a variety of languages and even create your own custom snippets. The Snippets panel is further explored in the new Hour 16, "Using Code Snippets."

FIGURE 1.10
The new
Snippets
panel.

Toolbox (Top Right)

The Toolbox panel contains code segments and tags frequently used while editing in Code view (see Figure 1.11). The Toolbox panel is made up of two main sections, HTML and ASP.NET Controls, and each section has multiple subcategories. By clicking the arrow icons, you can explode and collapse the categories to see what they contain.

FIGURE 1.11
Toolbox panel.

Apply Styles and Manage Styles (Bottom Right)

This panel contains two tabbed subpanels. The Apply Styles panel displays the CSS styles available to the current page and enables you to apply styles to objects in Design view (see Figure 1.12). The Manage Styles panel has similar functionality with the addition of a preview area where you can see what each style does to your content (see Figure 1.13). Both panels give you the ability to apply styles and create new styles.

All the panels are intelligent; they learn from how you use the program. If you use a particular item often, it moves higher on the list to become more accessible. A rarely used item moves down on the list. The panels also help you by turning currently unavailable functions gray so that you don't waste time trying to do something impossible.

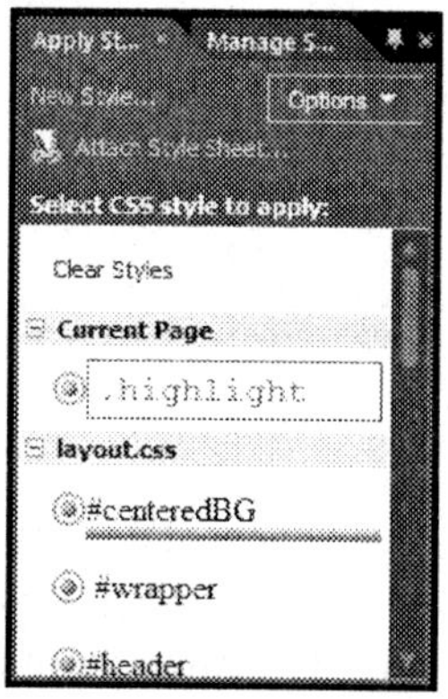

FIGURE 1.12
Apply Styles panel.

FIGURE 1.13
Manage Styles panel.

Status Bar

The status bar appears at the bottom of the workspace (see Figure 1.14). It provides information about the program itself as well as general information for the page you are working on, such as file size and overall settings (the code format you are using, for example). In addition, the status bar has tools that warn you if there is invalid or incompatible code in your page. If you want to close the status bar (not something I recommend), click Tools, Application Options and then uncheck Show Status Bar under General.

FIGURE 1.14
The status bar appears at the bottom of the workspace and gives you constant and current information about the file you are working on.

Changing and Customizing the Workspace

Depending on what you are doing, you might want to have a certain panel or menu more prominently featured, or you might want to open a new panel with more functions. In response to user feedback, the service packs introduced new and powerful features to the Expression Web 4 user interface, making it possible to create and save a custom toolbar and custom workspaces. As a result, you can now customize your workspace to fit any working scenario and change it at any time.

Using the Custom Toolbar

In addition to the predefined toolbars in Expression Web 4, of which there are many, you can now create your own custom toolbar that contains the features and functions you use the most. This was a much requested feature from users like myself, who only use a small number of functions on the default toolbars and want more focus on frequently used tools. You can create as many custom toolbars as you like.

Try It Yourself ▼

Add and Configure Your Own Custom Toolbar

A custom toolbar can contain any of the elements found in the other toolbars in Expression Web 4. That means you can consolidate the features you use the most into one toolbar and hide the rest for when you need them.

To use the custom toolbar, you first have to activate it.

1. On the main menu, go to View, hover over Toolbars, and select Custom from the bottom of the pop-out menu. This adds a new toolbar to the top of the workspace with the text "Edit…" (see Figure 1.15).

▼

FIGURE 1.15
When activated, the custom toolbar appears as an empty area with an Edit button below the Common toolbar.

2. To add a new button to the custom toolbar, click Edit. This opens the Custom Toolbars dialog (see Figure 1.16).

FIGURE 1.16
The Custom Toolbars dialog, from which you can create your own custom toolbars.

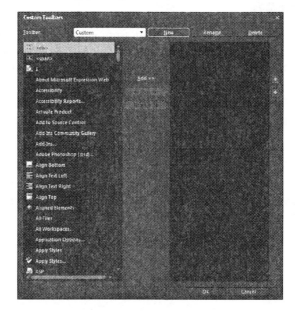

3. Click New to open the New Toolbar dialog. Here, you can give your custom toolbar a descriptive name (see Figure 1.17). Note that the name has to be a single word with no spaces.

FIGURE 1.17
Custom toolbars can be given custom names.

4. To add a new item to the toolbar, select the item in the left panel and click the Add button. This moves the item to the right panel (see Figure 1.18).

FIGURE 1.18
New toolbar buttons are added from left to right.

5. To remove an item from the toolbar, select the item on the right side and click the Remove button.

6. When you are done adding buttons to the custom toolbar, click OK and the buttons appear.

Once a custom toolbar is created, you can toggle it on and off using the Toolbars menu found under View, Toolbars.

Using Default Workspaces

One of the core user experience features in Expression Web has always been the flexible workspace. To accommodate the different needs of different types of developers, Expression Web's workspace is modular with panels that can be sized, docked, and moved around to fit most needs. Even so, users were asking for more flexibility. Most importantly, users had only one workspace to work with, and the only function was to reset it to the default. What was needed was the ability to configure and save custom workspaces. And with the release of SP2, that feature was included.

The workspaces can be configured and switched from the Panels option on the main menu (see Figure 1.19).

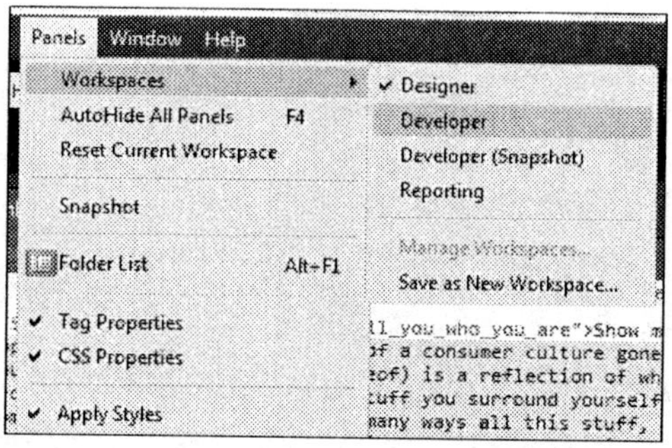

FIGURE 1.19
Workspaces
are controlled
from the
Panels,
Workspaces
menu.

By default, Expression Web 4 SP2 ships with four preconfigured workspaces: Designer (default), Developer (Toolbox, Manage Styles, and Snippets pinned to the left side), Developer (a Snapshot panel is added to the bottom of the view panel), and Reporting (a panel with the five reporting options is added to the bottom of the View panel). In addition, you can create your own custom workspaces.

Modifying the Workspace

To accommodate modifying the workspace, the workspace is now completely customizable: You can grab any horizontal and vertical border within the workspace to make a panel smaller or larger. You can also grab panels and move them around both by repositioning them within the workspace and by undocking and floating them on top of or outside the window (see Figure 1.20). This technique is particularly useful if you use a dual-monitor setup because you can dedicate the main window to Code view and Design view and leave all the tools on the other screen.

As you saw previously, each panel can contain several subpanels. Each subpanel becomes accessible through tabs. Expression Web 4 groups related subpanels together for convenience, but you are free to move them around in any way you like.

The Panels menu on the menu bar controls the panels (see Figure 1.21). From here, you can select what panels are active (indicated by a check mark). If you click one not currently featured in the workspace, the program adds it to the relevant panel. You can remove a panel from view by clicking the small X in its upper-right corner.

Expression Web 3 introduced the ability to pin the panels to the sides of the workspace. This feature allows you to keep the panels handy in the workspace without them taking up much-needed real estate. To pin a panel to the side of the workspace, simply click the pin icon at the top-right corner of the panel (see Figure 1.22).

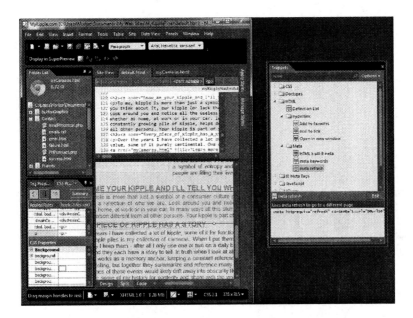

FIGURE 1.20
The Snippets panel floating outside the workspace.

When a panel has been pinned, the panel name is written vertically down the side of the workspace. To access the panel, simply hover your mouse over the name of the desired panel, and it "pops" out to cover your workspace (see Figure 1.23).

FIGURE 1.21
You can turn all available panels on and off from the Panels menu.

FIGURE 1.22
You can pin any panel to the side of the workspace by clicking the pin icon in the top-right corner of the panel.

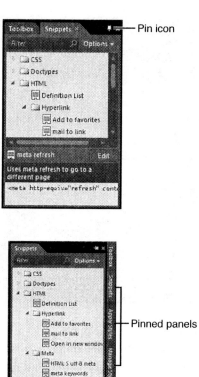

Pin icon

FIGURE 1.23
The pinned panel pops out to cover the workspace when you hover your mouse over the name.

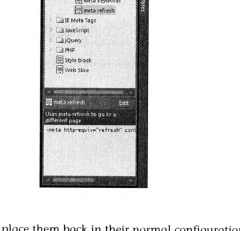

Pinned panels

To unpin the panels and place them back in their normal configuration, simply click the horizontal pin in the top-right corner of the currently active pinned panel (refer to Figure 1.23). If you want to quickly pin all the panels in your workspace, go to Panels on the main menu and select Hide Panels. To unpin them again, go back to the menu and uncheck the same function.

Try It Yourself ▼

Create and Save a New Workspace

As you perform different tasks while working on a page or website, your needs will change in terms of what tools and information should be prominently displayed and what can be hidden. For this reason, Expression Web 4 gives you complete control over what panels are available and where they are positioned at any time.

1. Hover your mouse over the vertical line that separates the Code and Design views from the right panels.

2. Click and drag the separator to the left to create more space for the panels.

3. Use the pin icon in the Folder List panel to pin the folder list to the left side of the workspace. When the Folder List is pinned, the Tag and CSS Properties panel shifts up to fill out the space.

4. Pin the Tag and CSS Properties panel to the side to free up space for the View panel (see Figure 1.24).

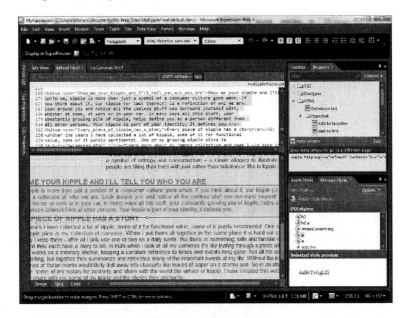

FIGURE 1.24
You can customize the look of Expression Web 4 to suit your specific needs.

5. When you are happy with the look of the workspace, go to Panels on the main menu, hover over Workspaces, and select Save as New Workspace (see Figure 1.25).

▼

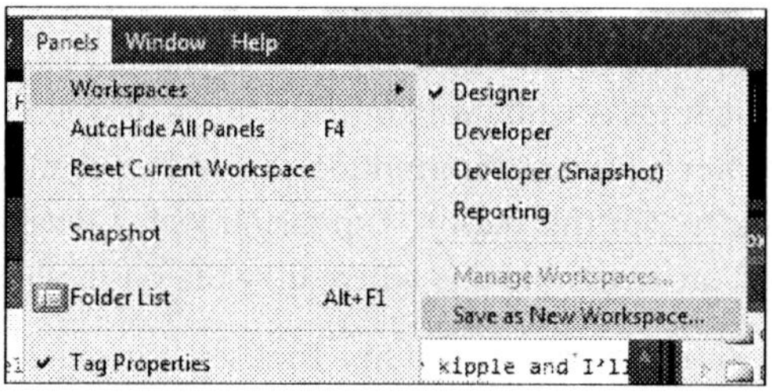

FIGURE 1.25
Saving the current workspace as a new workspace from the main menu.

6. This opens the Save as New Workspace dialog. From here, give your new workspace a descriptive name (see Figure 1.26). Note that the name can have spaces but cannot end with a space or a period).

FIGURE 1.26
Setting a name for the new workspace.

7. Click OK, and the new workspace is saved and appears on the Workspaces pop-out menu (see Figure 1.27).

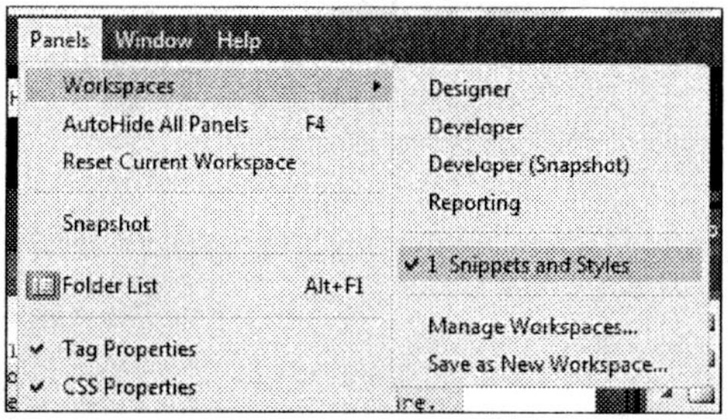

FIGURE 1.27
The new workspace appears on the Workspaces menu.

Following this exercise, you can see that creating new workspaces is easy, and there is no "right" or "wrong" in terms of workspace layout: Whatever works for you is the right layout.

But what if your workspace gets too "messy," or you accidentally close a panel or lose it altogether? To simplify the process of cleaning up your workspace, click the Panels button on the menu bar and select Reset Current Workspace to restore the current workspace to its original configuration.

Summary

In this hour, you learned how Expression Web 4 works and how you can customize it to suit your needs. To some readers, this information might seem rudimentary or even redundant. However, as you progress through the next 23 hours, you will see that having a solid understanding of the program makes a world of difference when you encounter new challenges. By knowing the basics, you'll find it easier to understand the more advanced issues. And because you'll be spending a lot of time with this program, it's worth your time to get to know it properly first.

For convenience, this book uses the default workspace and panel layout. However, now that you know how to customize them, feel free to organize their layout any way you see fit.

Q&A

Q. *The Common toolbar looks a lot like the Formatting toolbar in Microsoft Word. Does that mean that it works the same way?*

A. Yes and no. The Common toolbar has many of the same functions as Microsoft Word's Formatting toolbar, but when you click a button on the Common toolbar, a change happens through the addition or modification of a snippet in the code or hypertext rather than in the text. (The program refers to these code snippets as *styles*.) So yes, they look similar, but no, what happens when you click a button is different.

Q. *If I accidentally close a panel or a toolbar, will I be able to open it again?*

A. All the panels are accessible from the Panels button on the main menu. If you accidentally close a panel, you can always open it again from there. Furthermore, you can always reset the original layout of the panels by clicking Panels, Reset Workspace Layout. All the toolbars are accessible by clicking View and selecting Toolbars.

Workshop

The workshop has quiz questions to help you put to use what you just learned. If you get stuck, the answers to the quiz questions are in the next section. But try to answer the questions first. Otherwise, you'll only be cheating yourself.

Quiz

1. What is the proper way to create a web page?

    A. Using only Code view

    B. Using only Design view

    C. Using Split view

    D. None of the above

2. How many panels can you have open at one time?

    A. 8

    B. 14

    C. As many as you like

Answers

1. **D.** None of the above. There is no right or wrong when it comes to how you create a web page. Some people create spectacular sites using only Notepad, whereas others create just as spectacular sites without ever seeing a line of code. To get the most out of this book, use Split view as much as possible. That way, you get to see what happens in Code view when you make changes in Design view, and vice versa. In the end, though, what works best is up to the individual user.

2. **C.** In theory, you could fill your entire screen with panels and toolbars, but if you did, you would find it hard to get any work done. With that said, however, you are free to set up your workspace any way you please.

Beginning at the End: A Walkthrough of the Finished Project

What You'll Learn in This Hour:

▶ How to import and work with a completed website in Expression Web 4
▶ How to preview a site in your browser
▶ How this book is laid out
▶ How to use the different tools in Expression Web 4 to explore a website and learn how it works

When I start to read a book like this, I always want to see the end result of all the lessons before I start so that I know what I'm getting myself into. So, rather than making you go through all the tutorials to see what you can build in just a few hours with Expression Web 4, I start at the very end by showing you the site you will build throughout these lessons and use it to showcase some of the many features available in this application.

Because websites consist of many different files linked together, it is important to keep everything organized. But, to do this, you first need to understand what the different elements are and how they work and relate to each other. By looking at a completed website and using the tools available in Expression Web 4, you can get a firmer grip on how everything comes together.

The methods you learn in this hour will be useful to you down the road. In fact, when you finish Hour 24, "Publishing Your Website," I urge you to come back to this hour for a second look. Because you'll come back with a better understanding of how the website works, you'll have an entirely new perspective on the different lessons in this hour.

Working with a Completed Website

To work efficiently in Expression Web 4 (or any web design application, for that matter), it is important to understand how the application handles files and file relationships. By working with a completed website, you can experiment and learn how Expression Web 4 works with you to keep everything functioning properly as you edit and reorganize the different elements. That way, you get an early start developing techniques and understanding that usually comes only much later in the learning process.

The Import Site Wizard is a helpful tool that saves you a lot of time when you need to work on a website built in a different application or by a different designer. Therefore, you will probably use it frequently.

▼   **Try It Yourself**

Importing a Completed Website

A website is actually just a folder with a group of files linked together. What makes it a *website* is that the files within that folder can be viewed using a web browser. You get a more thorough explanation of this idea later in this book. By creating a new website in Expression Web 4, you tell the application that the main (root) folder is the bottom line or foundation and that everything in it relates back to this folder. When you publish your website, the domain name replaces the root folder.

To start, use the Import Site Wizard to import the finished project into the application as a new website. You can use it to import sites from your local computer or network and from external web servers or even directly from the websites themselves.

    1. Go to this book's website at http://expression.pinkandyellow.com and download the lesson files for this hour to a central location on your computer.

    2. Unzip the lesson files using your operating system's native file-extracting function or an application such as 7-zip. Place the lesson files in a central location on your computer (for example, on your desktop).

    3. Open Expression Web 4.

    4. Go to Site, Import, and then select Import Site Wizard. This opens the Import Site Wizard dialog, as shown in Figure 2.1.

    5. Select the File System option and use the Browse button to navigate to the location where you placed the unzipped lesson files for this hour. Select the folder called MyKippleFinal. With the address set, click Next.

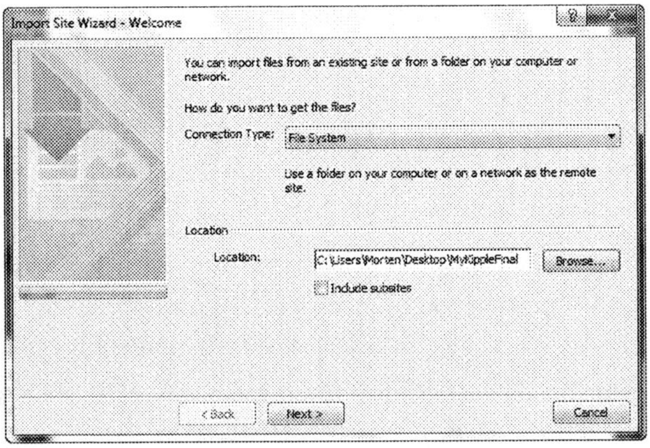

FIGURE 2.1
The Import Site Wizard dialog lets you import an existing site from a multitude of different sources both on your computer and on the Web.

6. On the next page (see Figure 2.2), you are asked to define where the local copy of the site should be created. You need to select a folder different from the one the files are in right now. It is always a good idea to keep all of your website projects in one location on your computer so that they are easy to find. Many people use the My Web Sites folder under Documents. Browse to the location you want the new website to be created in, create a new folder called MyKippleFinal, and select it. Click Next.

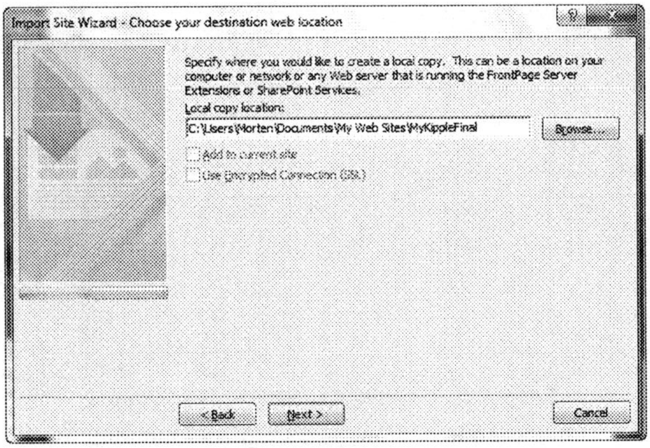

FIGURE 2.2
The second page of the Import Site Wizard lets you define where you want the new website project placed on your computer.

7. Expression Web 4 will most likely flash two warning messages at this point: The first one tells you that there is no site at the location you defined in step 4, and the second message asks you if you want to set up a site in that location. Click OK to both. The final page of the Import Site Wizard tells you that the website has been set up and that you can now start importing files. Click Finish.

Now that you have defined a location for the new website, Expression Web 4 opens in Site view, and you see all the files in the remote location (the folder you downloaded the lesson files to) on the right and your new site location on the left. To begin with, the left side is blank. To populate your new site with the files from the finished project, select all the folders and files on the right side and click the blue left-pointing arrow between the two views. This button publishes the existing files to your new site. This might seem odd, but if you consider a scenario in which you were downloading files off a web server, it makes sense.

When the transfer is complete, you see a view like the one shown in Figure 2.3. This view shows you the local website on the left and the remote website on the right. This is your site management window from which you can synchronize two locations or move files and folders between the local and remote locations either one by one or in groups. Expression Web 4 keeps tabs on what files have been moved and what files have been modified in the program, and whenever you come back to this view, it tells you what files need to be updated on either the local or remote location.

FIGURE 2.3
The second page of the Import Site Wizard lets you define where you want the new website project placed on your computer.

Local website address   Remote website address

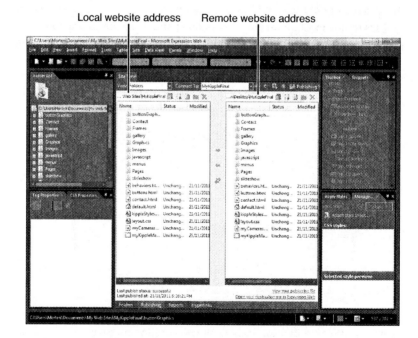

You have successfully imported the new website when you can see that the local and remote websites are identical in terms of files and folders and that the Folder View panel shows all the files and folders. You can now click the disconnect button (a power plug with a red bar next to it) to sever the connection.

By the Way

Don't Be Confused by the Names "Local" and "Remote"

As you saw in the preceding lesson, Expression Web 4 separates the website you are working with from the one you are publishing to by referring to them as *local website* and *remote website*, respectively. However, these names can easily be confusing. In the example you just saw, it can be argued that *both* websites are local.

Expression Web 4 considers the website you open in the application as the local website and the one you are publishing the files you have worked on to as the remote website, regardless of the actual location of either. This can lead to some interesting and confusing results: If you want to, you can set up a website so that the files you are working on are on a web server (technically, a *remote* location) and publish these files to a hard drive on your computer (technically, a *local* location). In that case, the web server would be considered the *local* website and placed on the left, whereas the folder on your hard drive would be considered the remote website and placed on the right.

If you are ever confused about which location is defined as remote or local, you can always check the address bars at the top of each folder tree in Site view (refer to Figure 2.3).

Previewing the Site in Your Browser

Now that you have set up the MyKipple website in Expression Web 4, look at how the site works in real life. One of the most important habits you need to establish when working with web design is to constantly test what you are doing in one browser (or preferably several browsers) to see that everything is working as it should. For this reason, you have the ability to preview a page in your browser from anywhere inside the application.

To see the new site as it would appear for any visitor when it is on the Web, go to the Folder List panel, right-click the default.html file, and select the current preview browser (prefixed by a browser icon) from the pop-up menu (see Figure 2.4).

This opens the default.html page of the MyKipple website in your browser. The default.html page is the home page of the website, and from here, you can navigate through all the different pages that have been created.

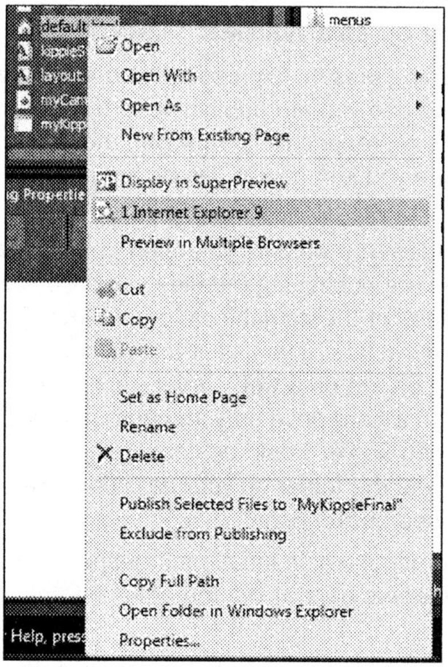

FIGURE 2.4
You can preview
any page in your
website by
selecting a
browser from the
right-click menu.
In this case, the
default browser
is Internet
Explorer 9.

The website itself serves as a good introduction to the different sections of this book. The following sections describe the different functionalities and when you will learn them.

Setting Up a Website and Building Pages

All websites consist of a group of web pages. These pages can contain anything from text to images to interactive elements such as Flash movies or Silverlight applications. In Hour 3, "A Website Is Really Just Text: Build One in 5 Minutes," and Hour 4, "Building a Home Page: A Look Behind the Curtain," you learn how to set up a new site and build simple pages.

Hyperlinks

On the MyKipple website, you can see that several segments of text are highlighted in blue. These are hyperlinks that point the browser to different pages either within the website or in external websites. You learn how to create and manage hyperlinks in Hour 5, "Getting Connected with (Hyper)Links: The Cornerstone of the World Wide Web."

Images

If you scroll down to the last paragraph and click the link with the text "my collection of cameras," you are taken to a new page with a large image of a collection of cameras. Images are an important part of web design and can serve both as content, such as the camera image; as functional elements, such as buttons; or even as design elements. You learn how to insert and manage images in Hour 6, "Getting Visual, Part 1: Adding Images and Graphics," and Hour 7, "Getting Visual, Part 2: Advanced Image Editing, Thumbnails, and Hotspots."

Tables

At the bottom of the camera page, you find a standard HTML table. In the past, tables were heavily used as design elements to structure the contents of web pages. However, this was never an ideal situation, and it caused a lot of problems for designers and the people visiting their sites. As a result, designers are moving away from using tables as design elements and now use them only for their intended purpose: to display tabular data. Because the focus of this book is to learn how to design standards-based websites with Expression Web 4, you learn how to use tables to display only tabular data. Tables are covered in Hour 9, "Getting Boxed In, Part 1: Using Tables for Tabular Content."

Styling the Content

Go back to the home page by clicking the Home button, and you see that the text in the page has many different styles (see Figure 2.5). The heading is big, uppercase, and gray; the paragraph text is smaller, darker, and justified. There are subheadings that look different from the main heading, links, a sidebar with a text box and links,

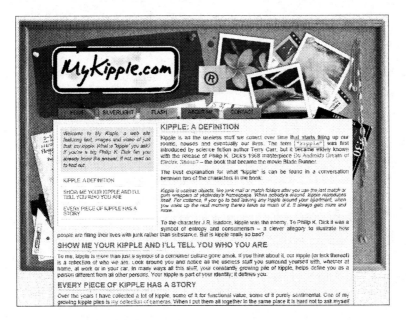

FIGURE 2.5
The home page of the MyKipple website features many different text styles defined by CSS.

and so on. If you were working in a word-processing application, you would have applied these different looks or styles to each of the sections. But in standards-based web design, you create an external set of styles that define how the different elements look and behave. These styles are created with a code language called Cascading Style Sheets (CSS), and Expression Web 4 is an excellent tool for both learning and working with this language. In Hour 10, "Bringing Style to Substance with Cascading Style Sheets," you learn how to create and manage these CSS styles to give your content more identity.

Page Layout

As you just learned, designers used to use tables to create page layouts, but this practice is on the way out. In its place, designers are now turning to CSS as their primary layout tool. In addition to changing the look and feel of text and other content, CSS can build containers or boxes that wrap the content. Using this technique, you can group different elements together and create styles and substyles to define how these different elements should look and behave. With the proper use of CSS, you can create visually stunning and easily approachable web layouts that look the same across all browsers and platforms. Hour 11, "Getting Boxed In, Part 2: Knee Deep in CSS," and Hour 14, "Harnessing the Power of CSS Layouts," show you how to create, modify, and apply styles using the built in CSS functionalities of Expression Web 4 and by editing code directly. In these hours, you learn how to use CSS to create advanced layouts for your sites and how external style sheets can control the look and feel of multiple pages from one central location.

Buttons

Buttons are a subgenre of the common hyperlink in which the hyperlink is attached to a visual element, such as an image or a text box. Because there are many different types of buttons, there are many different ways to make them, and each serves its own purpose. In Hour 15, "Buttons, Buttons, Buttons," you learn how to create several different types of buttons and when to use them.

The Main Menu

Aside from the content itself, I would argue that the navigation is the most important feature of any website. There are many ways to create functional navigation, and some ways are better than others. One of the most intuitive and visually exciting navigational tools you can put on your website is the image-based menu. As with everything else, there are several different ways you can make such menus, and each has advantages and drawbacks. In Hour 17, "Building a Functional Menu," you learn how to create several different CSS-based menus, including a drop-down menu. All these menus are highly functional and are used heavily throughout the Web.

Contact Forms

The Internet allows for a two-way conversation between the website owner and the visitor. To facilitate this type of communication, a large group of tools, known as forms, is built in to the main code language of the Internet, HTML. Using forms, you can create anything from a simple email form to advanced forum, blog, and even e-commerce functionalities. If you click the Contact button on the main menu, you are taken to a page with a contact form. In this book, you learn how to make this contact form work using two different server-based technologies: FrontPage Server Extensions (FPSE) and PHP. In Hour 19, "Getting Interactive with Forms," you learn how to build and configure web forms and use the built-in functionality in Expression Web 4 to create a contact form based on FrontPage Server Extensions. However, this form works only if your web server has FrontPage Server Extensions installed. As an alternative, you learn how to build an identical email form using a different code language, called PHP, in Hour 21, "Beyond the Basics, Part 1: PHP in Expression Web 4."

Watch Out!

The Email Forms Don't Work!

If you try to use the email form, you immediately notice that it doesn't actually work. This is not because there is something wrong with the forms or you have done anything wrong on your end. Both FPSE and PHP forms use *server-side scripts* to generate emails. And, as the name suggests, server-side scripts need to run on a server to work. When you preview your pages in your browser from Expression Web 4, you are not using a web server, but just looking at your local files.

In Hours 20 and 22, you will be introduced to an application known as Expression Development Server and learn how to use it to preview the functionality of the email forms. If you want to see a fully working version of the email forms right now, go to www.mykipple.com.

Flash and Other Embeddable Content

On the main menu is a button named Flash. In Hour 20, "Working with Flash and Other Embeddable Content," you'll learn how to include Flash movies and other embeddable content in your pages. Flash movies are created using a dedicated application, and you can use Expression Web 4 only to insert them into your pages and configure their data files. In that hour, you get a glimpse into the world of Flash and how that technology works and interacts with your website. You also learn how to insert, or "embed," advanced HTML5 and Flash content from sites such as YouTube in your site.

Exploring the Website in Expression Web 4

Back in Expression Web 4, you can use the different features to explore the website and understand how it works. The application comes equipped with a set of tools to help you get a quick overview of the different elements the site is made up of and how everything is put together to work.

On the bottom of the Web Site view, you have four tabs: Folders, Publishing, Reports, and Hyperlinks. These are four different ways to view your website:

▶ Folders gives you a regular browser view of the files and folders in your website. In other words, it works the same way as the Folder List panel.

▶ Publishing gives you a view of the local and remote websites side by side and lets you transfer files between the two locations either one at a time or in groups. This is where you actually publish your site to the Web. (Publishing your site is covered in Hour 24.)

▶ Reports gives you a rundown of all the assets in your website and the status of each of these assets. From there, you can see, for example, how many hyperlinks are in the site (and how many of them are broken), how many images it contains, and how many files are *unlinked*—meaning they can't be accessed by the visitor.

▶ Hyperlinks creates a visual map that looks a lot like a mindmap, showing your files and how they relate to each other through hyperlinks. This tool makes it easy to understand how the site is organized.

Click the Reports button to see the stats of the new website you imported. Expression Web 4 produces a list of all the different assets grouped in specific categories, as shown in Figure 2.6.

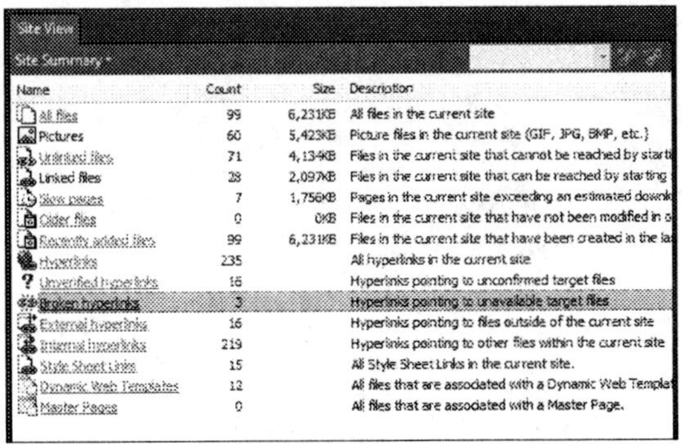

FIGURE 2.6
Reports gives you a complete overview of all the assets on your website and how they relate to each other.

Two of the most important items on this list are Slow Pages and Broken Hyperlinks. The Slow Pages report gives you a list of all the pages estimated to take more than 30 seconds to load on a 56Kbps connection. This report is important if you expect a lot of visitors with slower connections and shows you whether any of your pages is unnecessarily large or heavy to load. You can change the default connection speed the report tests for by going to Tools, Application Options and then selecting the Reports View tab.

When you click Broken Hyperlinks, the Hyperlinks report opens displaying all the broken and unverified hyperlinks. By default, all external links are considered unverified until they are verified by the application. When you open the Broken or Unverified report, Expression Web 4 asks whether you want it to verify the external links for you. The application goes to each hyperlink location to ensure that it is valid. If so, the hyperlink is checked off as valid. If not, it is checked off as broken.

▼ **Try It Yourself**

Fix a Broken Hyperlink

After running the report, you should see one broken hyperlink pointing to a file called Contact/confirmed.html. You can fix broken hyperlinks right from the report without even opening the page itself.

1. Right-click the broken hyperlink and select Edit Hyperlink. This opens the Edit Hyperlink dialog (see Figure 2.7).

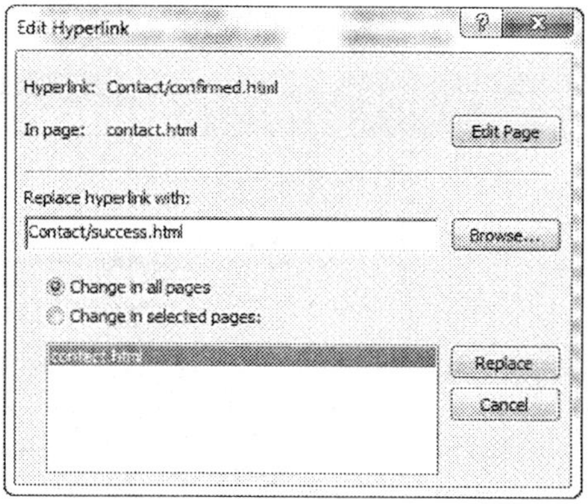

FIGURE 2.7
You can fix broken hyperlinks from the Reports view without opening the pages themselves.

2. From here, use the Browse button to find the correct file. It is under the Contact folder, and it is called success.html.

3. Click the Replace button and the hyperlink is automatically updated in all the pages where it is featured.

▲

Keeping Your Pages Functional

As you previously learned, a website consists of a group of files and folders that are linked together. That means for the individual pages of the site to work, all the links between them have to be correct and up to date. One of the many important features of Expression Web 4 is that it keeps tabs on your files for you, making the necessary changes throughout all of your files when something is changed.

As long as you make the changes to your pages, files, and folders inside Expression Web 4, the application makes all the necessary changes to the links within related files to make everything run smoothly. Therefore, if you want to move a file or folder into or out of another folder, always use either the Folder List panel or the Folder view, and the links to your files and folders will be updated automatically. A short example puts this into context.

Right now, the root folder (main folder) of the website contains two files: kippleStyles.css and layout.css. These two files (known as *style sheets*) contain all the CSS or styling code for all the pages of the site, and as a result, every page has a link to them. To make the style sheets easier to find, you want to put them in their own folder called Styles:

1. Switch to Folders view and click the folder icon in the upper-right corner to create a new folder. Give it the name **Styles**.

2. Drag and drop the kippleStyles.css and layout.css files into the new Styles folder.

3. A dialog briefly appears, telling you that the files are being renamed. This means that all the links that point to these two files from all the pages are being updated to reflect the change in location. When the dialog disappears, preview the default.html page in your browser again to make sure nothing changed.

When you preview the pages in your browser, it appears as if nothing has changed, but in fact, the links to the external style sheets have been changed in every page. If Expression Web 4 hadn't changed all the links to the two files you moved, all the pages would have appeared as regular text without the backgrounds and different styles. By using this drag-and-drop technique, you can move any and all files inside your site and be certain that Expression Web 4 updates the links that point to them so that everything keeps working as it should.

Watch Out!

Never Move Your Files Outside of Expression Web 4

A common mistake of new web designers is moving files or folders by using the regular browser window in their operating system rather than inside Expression Web 4. If you move a file or folder that way, the hyperlinks that tell the browser where these files are when the pages are displayed will not be updated, and as a result, you end up with a page that doesn't work properly. If you want to move a file from one folder to another, always use the Folder List panel or Folders view to ensure that all your hyperlinks are updated accordingly.

Summary

Expression Web 4 is a powerful web design and management tool that lets you easily build and publish advanced websites based on web standards. In this hour, you explored the final product that you will end up with after following all the tutorials in this book and used it to learn how Expression Web 4 works to help you manage your website.

The ability to import an existing website gives you a quick-and-easy way to pick up an old project or take over an existing project from someone else. In this hour, you learned how to import an existing website and move the necessary files from a remote location to your website's folder. You also learned how to use the Reports view to manage the files and folders in your website and track any problems or errors that are present. Expression Web 4 is set up in such a way that you can find and fix problems, such as broken hyperlinks, without actually having to open the pages and make changes there. This ability is a huge timesaver and gives you intimate control of the site even without knowing or understanding exactly how it works.

Finally, you learned how to use the Folder List and Folders view to rearrange the files within your website without breaking the many links between them by letting Expression Web 4 handle all the details for you.

What you saw in this hour is just the beginning. In the coming hours, you learn how to build the MyKipple website from scratch and, through that, learn how to get the most out of Expression Web 4.

Q&A

Q. *When I preview the MyKipple site in Internet Explorer, a bar appears on top of the page saying that, to protect my security, it has blocked the page from running scripts and ActiveX controls that would access my computer. Does this mean I have a virus or that there is something dangerous in the MyKipple website project?*

A. Internet Explorer is a little overprotective when it comes to previewing local websites. By that, I mean if the same pages were loaded from the Web, you wouldn't be getting that message. You can safely click the bar and select Allow Blocked Content. There is nothing in the MyKipple website project that would harm your computer in any way.

Q. *The contact pages don't work at all! There's something wrong with these files.*

A. The contact forms work by utilizing server-side scripts. When you preview these pages directly from Expression Web 4, the scripts cannot run. If you want to test these pages properly in your browser from the local location, you can do so by triggering Expression Development Server. For more information on this, check Hour 20 for the FrontPage Server Extensions form and Hour 22 for the PHP form.

Q. *When I try to use the Import Site Wizard, it says that the folder with the files is not valid (or is empty or won't open).*

A. The #1 reason you might encounter problems with the Import Site Wizard is that you are trying to import files from a zipped archive. Before importing the site from the lesson files, make sure you have extracted the files from the zipped archive so they reside in a normal uncompressed folder.

Exercise

Open the Hyperlinks view by clicking the button on the bottom of the view and then select any of the pages in the Folder View panel to see how it relates to other pages and files. You see that all the pages that link to the page are placed on the left and that all the pages the selected page links to are placed on the right. You can also click any of the other icons in the view to see how these files relate to further files.

A Website Is Really Just Text: Build One in 5 Minutes

What You'll Learn in This Hour:

▶ How to create a new website

▶ How to create a new page

▶ How to create and edit simple text content using Design view

▶ How to test your first web page in multiple browsers

▶ How to use SuperPreview to test your pages against Internet Explorer and other browsers

Now that you have seen what this program can do, it's your turn to make your own project. You start at the beginning with a blank site and one Hypertext Markup Language (HTML) page, and work your way from there to the fully functional site you saw in Hour 2, "Beginning at the End: A Walkthrough of the Finished Project."

Creating a New Website

As you saw in Hour 2, a website is a group of related files and folders under one main folder. In fact, a website such as www.designisphilosophy.com is little more than a folder on a server you can access through the Internet. By creating a new website in Expression Web 4, you tell the program, "This folder is where I will put all the text, images, and other files I want to share with everyone in the world when they visit the website. Please keep track of them for me." In response, Expression Web 4 keeps tabs on what you do and makes appropriate changes to your files to reflect the changes you have made in related files and keep the website working properly. It does so by creating a set of hidden metadata files that describe the site and its contents. That way, the information about how your site functions is stored even if you delete the program from your computer or hand over the project to another Expression Web 4 user.

The first thing to do when you start a new project is to create a new website. You can do this from the Site menu or from the New Site icon on the Common toolbar. This opens the New Site dialog, which displays the different options available (see Figure 3.1).

By the Way

Expression Web 4 makes a deliberate separation between sites and pages through the use of the New Site button on the Common toolbar and by placing the New Site, Open Site, Recent Site, and Close Site functions under the separate Site menu.

From the New Web Site dialog, you have the option to make a basic website with no content, create one from a template, or import an existing site using the Import Site Wizard. Under General are three more options: One Page Site, Empty Site, and Import Site Wizard. The One Page Site option creates a website with a home page file called default.html. The Empty Site option creates a website folder with no files. The Import Site Wizard lets you import an already existing site from a local folder, a network folder, or the Web.

By the Way

Don't take titles such as One Page Site and Empty Site too literally. People often think of computer programs as rigid and inflexible and start to worry when they see definite descriptions like these. A common question that arises when people open the New Site dialog for the first time is, "What option do I choose if I want to create a site with *more* than one page?" It might seem like a silly question to those well traveled in the world of web design, but this confusion is understandable in much the same way that my high school teacher could never understand that the computer casing was not the hard drive. It's all a matter of perspective. In reality, programs are (at least for the most part) flexible, and titles such as these are merely general descriptions. Using a One Page Site template in

Expression Web 4 just means that you start with a folder with one file. In fact, strictly speaking, a one-page website isn't a website at all—it's just a single web page. Likewise, an "Empty Site" is a website folder that starts with no files in it with the expectation that files will be added later.

At the bottom of the dialog is the suggested location for your new website. The suggested location varies depending on your computer's operating system and setup. To avoid confusion, always create a new folder with the same name as your project and use it as your website folder. You can use the Browse button to select any folder on your hard drive, on a local network, or on an external server, such as your website or root folder, but keeping your files on one of your local hard drives is usually the best solution.

It's a good idea to have a central location where you keep all your websites. Expression Web 4 suggests you use the My Web Sites folder located under Documents, but you can use any folder you want. This book uses the My Web Sites folder as the central location for all projects.

Try It Yourself ▼

Create a New One-Page Website

Creating a new website should always be the first step when starting a new project. In this task, you create a new website with one HTML page.

1. Click the New Site icon (second from the left on the Common toolbar) or click Site and select New Site from the main menu.

2. In the New dialog, select General and One Page Site.

3. Click the Browse button next to the Location box at the bottom of the dialog and navigate to the My Web Sites folder under Documents. Create a new folder and name it MyKipple.

4. Click the MyKipple folder to highlight it and then click Open. The Site Name setting automatically matches the folder name you created, unless you want to give the site a different identifying name.

5. Make sure the Add to Managed List box is checked and then click OK. ▲

By the Way

Beginning Where You Left Off

When you start Expression Web 4 again after closing it, by default the program opens the last project you were working on. This function is great if you are working on only one project, but it can be annoying if you have several projects going at once. If you want the program to start without opening a website and create a blank web page instead, you can change the settings under Tools, Application Options.

Expression Web 4 has now created a new site with one page called default.html (see Figure 3.2). This is the blank canvas you work with from here on out.

As you make changes to the files in the website, Expression Web 4 keeps tabs on what you do and makes sure your hyperlinks are up to date, even if you change them, to keep everything working properly.

FIGURE 3.2
The MyKipple site as it appears after creation.

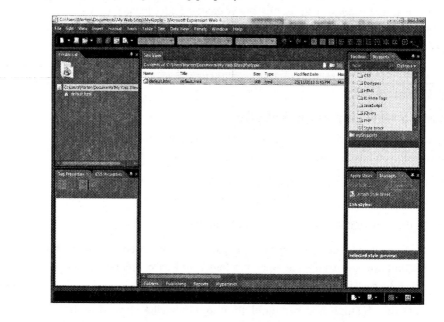

Creating Your First Web Page

Now that you have created a website, the Site view appears in place of the Split view you previously saw. You explored the different functions of this pane in Hour 2. For now, let's focus on creating your first web page.

As you can see, your new website contains one file called default.html. When a browser visits a domain or folder on the web, it always looks for the home page. By design, home page filenames are either: *index* and the less common *default* or *main*. All versions of Expression Web use default.html as the home page. A *home page* or *root page* is the page the browser looks for in a folder if the visitor does not specify a particular filename in the address bar.

Default.html is an HTML file that contains all the code a web browser needs to display the web page.

> HTML is the most prevalent markup or publishing language for creating websites. A markup language is a set of code snippets that define for a browser how it should lay out and format text. Used correctly, HTML is a powerful tool to organize and display large amounts of content in a simple and accessible way. For further information on HTML, visit http://en.wikipedia.org/wiki/HTML.

By the
Way

Double-click the filename and make sure you are in Split view (see Figure 3.3). As you can see, although it contains some code, it has no content. If you were to open the file in a browser at this point, all you would get is a white page. So, before going any further, you need to add some content.

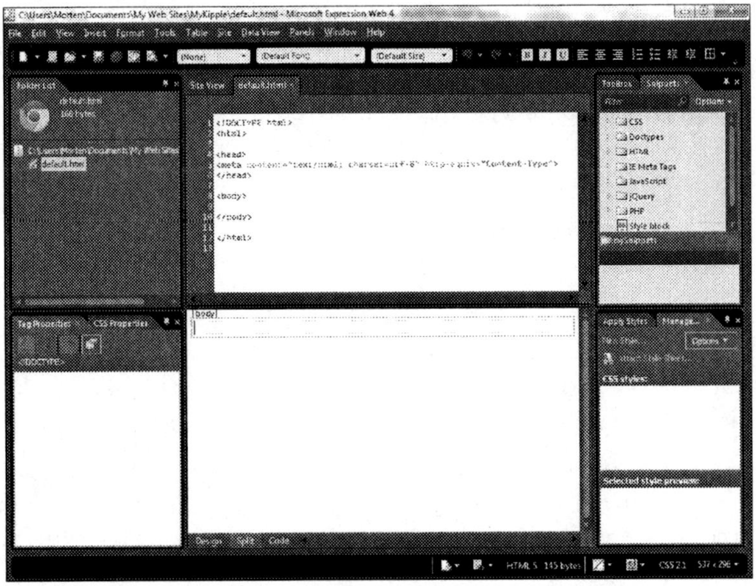

FIGURE 3.3
Even though Code view shows several lines of code, default.html is empty in Design view because there is no content yet.

To see how easy it is to create a simple web page, switch to Design view so that all you see is the blank page. When set to Design view, Expression Web 4 works in much the same way as a word-processing application such as Microsoft Word. This is great when you want to quickly edit content. Click anywhere inside Design view and start typing text. The text appears in a dotted box with a P hovering over it.

This box is a visual aid called Block Selection, and it gives a visual representation of what content a particular element applies to (in this instance, P or "paragraph"). If you click the dotted line itself, Expression Web 4 adds pink shading above and below it, providing a visual representation of the default margins the paragraph has. You can turn Block Selection and all other visual aids on and off from the Visual Aids menu under the View menu or from the Visual Aids button on the status bar (see Figure 3.4).

FIGURE 3.4
The Visual Aids button on the status bar lets you turn on and off visual aids as you work.

If you click somewhere else on the page, the Block Selection box disappears and you see the text as it appears in a browser. By moving the cursor to the end of this line, you can continue your current paragraph. If you press Enter, the cursor shifts down approximately two lines to start a new paragraph, and Expression Web 4 creates a new Block Selection box.

On the first line, enter your page title and select Heading 1 <h1> from the Style drop-down menu (see Figure 3.5) in the toolbar.

With the cursor at the end of the first line, press Enter to create a new paragraph, and a new P box will appear under your heading. Enter some more text—enough to fill at least three full lines. If you can't come up with anything to write, simply replicate some text out of this book or any other written material laying around.

Create a new paragraph by pressing Enter and typing a subheading. Use the Style drop-down menu in the toolbar to set the tag to Heading 2 <h2>. Directly underneath, type one more paragraph, this time using the *I* (italic) and **B** (bold) buttons in the toolbar to *emphasize* and **strongly emphasize** parts of the text.

FIGURE 3.5
The Style drop-
down menu
works much
the same as
the style menu
in a word-
processing
application
such as
Microsoft
Word.

You need two more elements: a bullet (unordered) list and a numbered (ordered) list. As in a word processor, press Enter to create a new line and click the Numbered List button (see Figure 3.6).

FIGURE 3.6
The Numbered
List and
Bulleted List
buttons work in
much the
same way as
they would in a
word-processing
application.

A number appears on the left, the Block Selection box shifts to the right, and its tag changes to LI (list item). Type a series of list items and separate them by pressing Enter. To end the list, simply press Enter to create a new list item and then either click the Numbered List button again to deactivate it or press the Backspace key on your keyboard. Doing so changes the new list item to a new paragraph.

Creating a bulleted list is done in the same way: Click the Bulleted List button and create a series of list items.

Finally, click the Save button or press Ctrl+S to save the file. Pat yourself on the back: You just created your first web page (see Figure 3.7).

FIGURE 3.7
The result as it appears in Design view in Expression Web 4.

Five Browsers You Should Have on Your Computer

A web designer or developer should always have the end user in mind. However, you don't know what browser or even what kind of computer the visitor will use when viewing your websites. Making an educated guess is the best you can do.

The majority of the computers connected to the Internet run some version of Microsoft Windows, and most of these computers have Internet Explorer as their default browser. Therefore, Internet Explorer should be at the top of the list. Because Expression Web 4 works only on Windows-based computers, you probably already have Internet Explorer installed by default. If not, you can get the latest version of Internet Explorer free from Microsoft by visiting www.microsoft.com/ie.

Mozilla's Firefox browser is the biggest competitor to Internet Explorer. In comparison with Internet Explorer 6, 7, and 8, Firefox has been a far more "reasonable" browser when it comes to code interpretation because it follows web standards pretty closely, although the release of Internet Explorer 9, which adheres to web standards, has narrowed the gap substantially. Nevertheless, many Internet users swear by Firefox and, for that reason, you should also have Firefox installed. You can get it free from Mozilla by visiting www.firefox.com.

Most Mac (Apple) users use the default Mac OS browser called Safari. Apple also has a Windows version of this browser. To ensure that Mac users get the same experience as Windows users, you should also test everything in Safari. You can get it free from Apple by visiting www.apple.com/safari/.

In 2008, Google released a new browser on the market called Chrome. This browser is entirely JavaScript based and is meant to run "lighter and faster" than any other browser available today. In the time since its release, it has managed to become one of the leading browsers in the world, and even though it is still in its infancy, it is now a staple browser that has to be considered. You can get it free from Google by visiting www.google.com/chrome.

Finally, there is the Opera browser. Although it doesn't have a large market share, Opera is a popular alternative to the mainstream browsers and has an extremely loyal following. It works on many cell phones and other portable devices. Opera is strict when it comes to web standards and can be an excellent tool for uncovering bad code that other browsers glance over. You can download Opera for free by visiting www.opera.com.

Testing Your Web Page in Multiple Browsers

When you design for the Web, it's important to continually test your pages in multiple web browsers to ensure that they work and appear the way you intend. A web browser is nothing more than a program that renders or interprets the code in your page and displays it accordingly. However, like human interpreters, there can be large discrepancies among browsers when it comes to interpretation. The WYSIWYG editor in Expression Web 4's Design view is a custom browser built to mimic standard browser behavior, but it is not perfect; some standard markup is not rendered accurately. Likewise, not all browsers are particular about web standards or they interpret web standards differently and, as a result, your page can look different depending on which browser you use.

To help with the testing process, Expression Web 4 can be set up to preview your page in all the different browsers installed on your computer, and in multiple different window sizes. This can be done from the File menu or from the Preview button on the Common toolbar.

To preview the current page in your default browser, click the Preview button on the Common toolbar. If you want to select a different browser or preview the page in multiple browsers, click the down arrow next to the Preview icon to get the Preview in the browser drop-down menu, as shown in Figure 3.8. By default, the list includes the currently installed version of Internet Explorer and your default browser, if different from Internet Explorer. If you have installed more browsers on your computer, you can add these to the list by selecting Edit Browser List from the bottom of the drop-down menu.

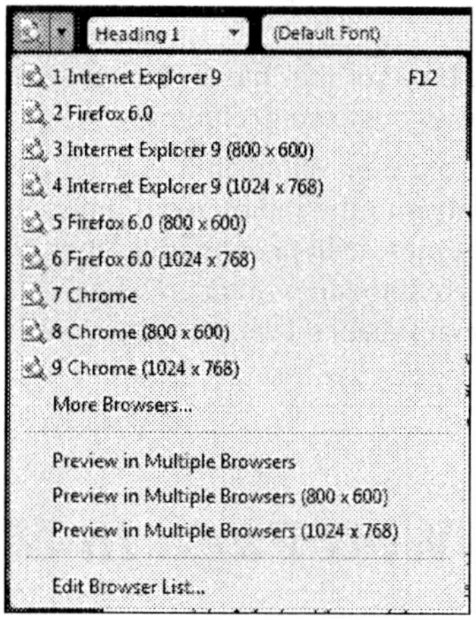

FIGURE 3.8
By clicking the down arrow next to the Preview icon, you can test your page in one or multiple different browsers (and windows sizes) installed on your computer.

Pressing F12 is the quickest way to test your current page against the last browser you tested in. By pressing F12, you cause the browser to open and you see the local instance of your page just as you would if it were stored somewhere on the Web. As you can see from Figure 3.9, the page looks the same as it did in Expression Web 4. Because you use only the standard styles h1, h2, p, and li, the text fills the entire width of the window. If you grab the edge of the window and resize it, the text reorganizes itself to fit the smaller or larger space.

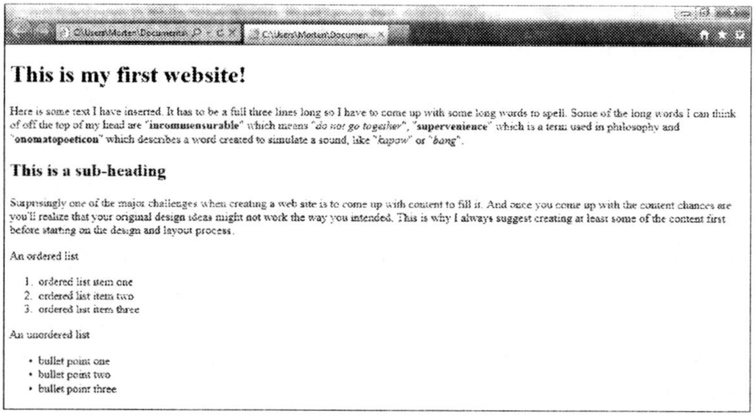

FIGURE 3.9
Your first web page as it appears in Internet Explorer 9.

When Browsers Go Bad: Internet Explorer

If you've worked with web design before or you've surfed the Web using different browsers, you've no doubt run into the infamous Internet Explorer problem, where pages that look fine in Internet Explorer are "broken" in other browsers, or vice versa. Internet Explorer 6 and 7 have a tendency to display pages, and especially those using CSS, differently from other browsers. This problem is often misconstrued as a problem with the other browsers, but in reality, it is the result of Internet Explorer interpreting web standards in a nonstandard way (no pun intended). This has lead to the rise in popularity of other browsers such as Firefox and Chrome, international campaigns to phase out Internet Explorer 6, and a phenomenon known as "IE Hacks," in which designers and developers have been forced to come up with special code hacks to circumvent these problems so that their sites appear identical across all browsers.

Fortunately, the Internet Explorer development team finally realized the error of its ways and, with the release of Internet Explorer 9 in March 2011, the browser is now fully standards compliant and pushing for even closer web standards integration on the Web. Microsoft has also launched a campaign to rid the world of Internet Explorer 6. You can check it out for yourself at www.ie6countdown.com.

Fortunately, the renewed push for web standards and the introduction of the new HTML5 standard has given the upgrade movement a big boost, and we can finally see a light at the end of the tunnel where IE 6 and 7 problems are concerned. Even so, many users run Internet Explorer 8, which is still not entirely up to standard, and it is estimated that a small minority of users will "hang on to" Internet Explorer 6 for years to come.

SuperPreview: A Sneak Preview

At this point, you are probably thinking two things: First of all, it seems awfully cumbersome to keep testing all of your pages in all these different browsers. Second, how are you supposed to test your pages against older browsers you don't have? After all, there is no simple way of installing Internet Explorer 6, 7, and 8 on your computer now that you have Internet Explorer 9 up and running!

To curb this problem, designers have turned to one of three strategies: virtual machines (where you set up virtual computers with older operating systems within your current operating system and run older browsers in them), multiple computers (where you have several different computers running at the same time, and you test the pages on all of them), or web-based "browser shot" applications (which produce screenshots of what the page looks like in multiple different browsers and configurations). The problem with all these is that they are cumbersome, time consuming, and not very effective.

Fortunately, now there is a fourth option, and it is built right in to Expression Web 4! When you installed Expression Web 4, you also installed an application called SuperPreview that makes cross-browser testing both simple and effective and gives you a series of tools previously unavailable to find, diagnose, and remedy browser inconsistencies and incompatibilities. Additionally (and this is revolutionary), SuperPreview comes with a full working model of Internet Explorer 6, 7, 8, and 9 in compatibility mode installed, giving you the ability to test your sites against this old-but-resilient browser without having to install it.

You learn how to use SuperPreview to its full potential in Hour 22, "Test Twice, Publish Once: Professional Cross-Browser Testing with SuperPreview," but if you want to, take a sneak peek at it right now by clicking the SuperPreview button on the Common toolbar. This opens SuperPreview as a separate application, and from here, you can pick what browsers you want to preview your page in and get a quick look at the differences, if any, in the way the browsers display the page. At this point, your page is too basic for SuperPreview to have any real value, but as you progress through this book, you can use this application instead of or in addition to regular browser testing to get a better idea of what browser compatibility testing is all about.

Summary

In this hour, you learned to create a one-page website from scratch and discovered how to edit an HTML file to make your first web page. You saw that editing simple text content in Design view is no different from editing text in a word processor. You also learned how to test your page in multiple browsers and why, in this case, quantity improves quality. Finally, you got a sneak preview of the new and revolutionary browser-testing application SuperPreview, which is discussed at length in Hour 22. I urge you to use SuperPreview to test your pages throughout this book to get used to the interface and make browser testing a part of your general routine.

From here until the end of this book, you work with this project to make the final site you saw in Hour 2. Starting from scratch is a great way to learn how to do things properly the first time around. In Hour 4, "Building a Home Page: A Look Behind the Curtain," you expand on the first page by introducing more text content and standard style elements. You see what goes on in the code and learn a bit about the HTML code language.

Q&A

Q. What is the difference between a website and a web page?

A. Simply put, a website is a group of web pages in a folder. A website is a dedicated space on the Web that contains a number of web pages that relate to each other. In practical terms, the combined content at www.pinkandyellow.com is a website, whereas a single page under the same domain, such as http://pinkandyellow.com/about.htm, is a web page.

Q. Can I build a website without knowing anything about HTML and other code?

A. Yes, you can. But as you see in the following hours, understanding the inner workings of a web page can save you a lot of time and energy and help you create better sites faster. That doesn't mean you have to become a code guru. You can get a lot done with a rudimentary understanding of HTML.

Q. Why does SuperPreview appear as a separate application in my program list?

A. SuperPreview was built to work both as an integrated part of Expression Web 4 and as a standalone unit. This is to give you, the designer, an easy way to test pages and sites from your computer, your network, or on the Web without having to import them into Expression Web 4 first. There is no qualitative difference between the SuperPreview you see inside Expression Web 4 and the SuperPreview you see when you use it as a standalone application.

Workshop

The workshop has quiz questions to help you put to use what you just learned. If you get stuck, the answers to the quiz questions are in the next section. But try to answer them first. Otherwise, you'll be cheating yourself.

Quiz

1. How do you preview a web page in a browser from within Expression Web 4?

2. Why is it important to test a page in multiple browsers?

Answers

1. From within Expression Web 4, you have many ways to preview a web page in a browser. The easiest way is to simply press F12; doing so opens the current page in the default browser. You can also open the page in a browser with a specific window size by selecting File, Preview in Browser and clicking the size you want to use. Finally, you can preview the page in multiple browsers simultaneously by clicking Preview in Multiple Browsers on the same menu.

2. No two browsers are created equally. As a result, your web pages might look different depending on the configuration of the visitor's computer. To put it into perspective, Internet Explorer versions 6, 7, 8, and 9 handle web pages in entirely different ways, so although a page looks great in Internet Explorer 9, it might be unreadable in Internet Explorer 6. The best way around this problem is to create standards-based websites, but even then you might run into browser incompatibilities. Continually testing your pages helps you catch problems early and figure out ways to fix them.

Building a Home Page: A Look Behind the Curtain

What You'll Learn in This Hour:

▶ How to read and edit basic HTML code in Code view

▶ How to import text from Microsoft Word and other documents

▶ How to clean up imported code using Code and Design views

In Hour 3, "A Website Is Really Just Text: Build One in 5 Minutes," you built a basic web page using functions similar to those in a word-processing program. But that is just half the story: In web design, what happens behind the curtain is what really matters. It's time to learn some basic HTML and see how the code affects the content. To do this, you build the basic structure of the home page of the MyKipple site.

Opening and Editing an Existing File Using Code View

If you haven't already done so, open the default.html file you worked on in Hour 3. The MyKipple site should open automatically when you open Expression Web 4. If not, you can find it by selecting Open Site from the Site menu or from the drop-down menu of the Open icon on the Common toolbar (see Figure 4.1).

FIGURE 4.1
The drop-down menu under the Open icon on the Common toolbar gives you quick access to open files and sites without having to go to the main menu.

The Open Site dialog lists all the sites created in Expression Web 4 (see Figure 4.2). When you create or manage a website with Expression Web 4, the program automatically generates a shortcut to facilitate easy access to the site from this list. If you can't find the project on this list, you can navigate to it as you normally would. If you followed the directions in Hour 3, the project is in the My Web Sites folder under Documents.

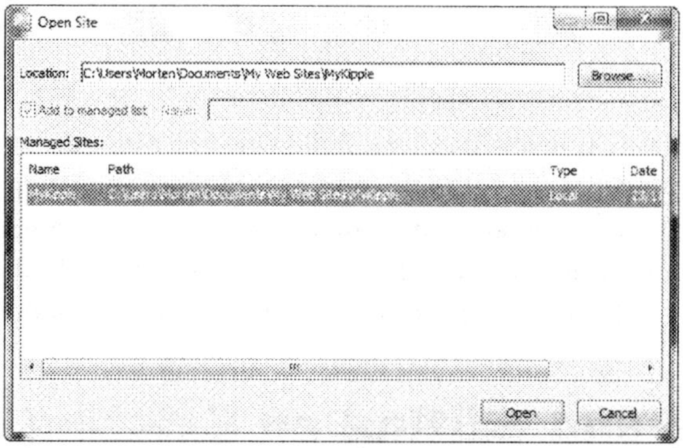

FIGURE 4.2
The Open Site dialog displays all the websites you created in Expression Web 4 (here seen with the My Kipple project).

> The Open Sites dialog isn't restricted to local sites. You can also use it to open **By the** and manage external websites both through Hypertext Markup Language (HTML) **Way** and File Transfer Protocol (FTP) if you have the necessary permissions to access the sites. If you use the Browse button or insert an address that Expression Web 4 does not already have on the list, the Add to Managed List box becomes active, and you can give the site a friendly name. In fact, you can use Expression Web 4 to make changes to live websites in real time.

Before going any further, let's look at what is happening in the page's code. Select Split view using the button at the bottom of the pane to reveal both Code view and Design view. Click anywhere on the heading and then click the h1 tag on the Block Selection box. This highlights the content affected by the h1 style in both Design view and Code view (see Figure 4.3). In Design view, you see a box with gray striped shading above and below. The gray areas are the default top and bottom margins for the h1 tag. In Code view, you see the text buffered or wrapped on both sides by code tags. These tags tell the browser to display the text in the h1 heading style.

FIGURE 4.3
When you click an element in either Code or Design view, that object is highlighted in both views for easy reference.

HTML is a basic markup language that can be summarized in one simple rule: Everything is wrapped between a beginning and an end tag. All beginning tags consist of a "less-than" bracket (<), the tag name and/or function, and a "greater-than" bracket (>). End tags look much the same, but with the addition of a forward slash (/) before the content. In this example, <h1> tags wrap the heading like this:

```
<h1>This is my first web page!</h1>
```

You now have two ways to change the appearance of your content. You can use the Style drop-down menu, as you learned in Hour 3, or you can go into Code view and manually change the style. Try changing the heading <h1> and </h1> tags to paragraph <p> and </p> to see what happens in Design view.

To use Design view to see changes you made in Code view, you need to click inside the Design view area or save the page. This is because as you change the code in Code view, you are temporarily breaking the code. Rather than trying to display broken code, Expression Web 4 waits for you to tell it when you finish editing before it refreshes the WYSIWYG (What You See Is What You Get) editor.

By the Way

Notice that when you change the beginning tag, Expression Web 4 highlights the end tag in yellow and red to tell you that your code is broken (see Figure 4.4). Likewise, the status bar at the bottom of the workspace puts up two warning signs: The first one tells you that it detects an HTML incompatibility; the second one tells you that it detects a code error. When you change the end tag to match the start tag, the errors go away.

FIGURE 4.4
When Expression Web 4 discovers a code error, it highlights the error with a yellow background and red text and shows a warning sign in the status bar.

Error in highlighted code

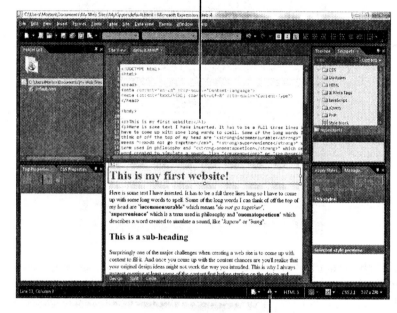

Code error warning

By studying the code, you see that all the different styles you applied in Hour 3 are actually just code tags:

▶ Heading 1 `<h1>`

▶ Heading 2 `<h2>`

▶ Paragraph `<p>`

▶ Emphasized (italicized) `<em>`

▶ Strongly emphasized (bold) `<strong>`

▶ Unordered (bullet) list `<ul>`

▶ Ordered (numbered) list `<ol>`

▶ List item for both lists `<li>`

Looking at the rest of the code, the <body> tag, which wraps all the content, tells the browser that this is the content to display. The <head> tag contains all the meta information that is available to the browser but that the browser does not display within the page. Meta information includes the page title displayed at the top of the window, info about the designer, and so on. Finally, the <html> tag, which tells the browser that the following content is written in the HTML language, wraps both the <head> and <body> sections. Scroll to the bottom of the Code view and you can see the </body> and </html> tags that close the page.

Importing Styled Text from a Document

What is a website if not a source of information? You need some real content to work with. Right now, the default.html file contains whatever text you inserted during Hour 3. The next step is to introduce some real content. In most cases, you will either be provided with or write your own content in some form of word-processing software. Your first instinct is probably to cut and paste this content straight into your page. The problem is that, depending on what word processor you use, a large amount of legacy formatting is likely to be attached to the document—code that becomes difficult to work with after it is imported into an HTML file. Newer versions of word processors, such as Microsoft Word 2010, have less of this code clutter, but simple copy-and-paste will still leave you with code that has no place in a website. To import the text correctly, you need to use a built-in tool in Expression Web 4.

In the lesson files for this hour downloaded from the book site is a Microsoft Word document called homepagetext.doc (see Figure 4.5). Open this document in Microsoft Word, and you see a standard document with headings, subheadings, and some text.

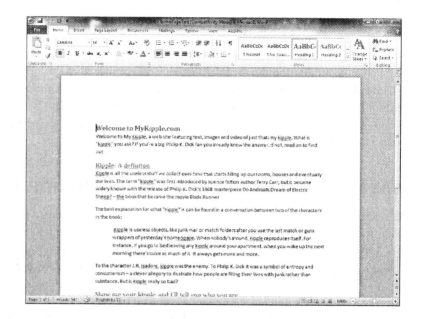

The next step is to move all this content over to the default.html file and translate the styling to standards-based markup.

With the default.html file open in Design view, select and delete all existing content. Then, go to the homepagetext.doc file in your word-processing software, select all the text, and press Ctrl+C (universal shortcut for Copy) to copy the content. Next, go back to the default.html file in Expression Web 4, place your cursor at the top of the page, click Edit on the main menu, and select Paste Text from the drop-down. This opens the Paste Text dialog (see Figure 4.6).

The Paste Text dialog provides you with five options:

▶ Plain text

▶ One <pre> formatted paragraph

▶ Many <pre> formatted paragraphs

▶ Normal paragraph with line breaks

▶ Normal paragraphs without line breaks

If you click each of them, you get a further description of each option in the Results section. For most purposes, including ours, the last option—Normal paragraph without line breaks—is the correct one. This Paste function inserts the text, wrapping each line or paragraph in its own <p> tag. This makes it easy to edit later.

Select the last option and click OK, and Expression Web 4 pastes in your content, wrapping each section in its own set of <p> tags.

> You don't need Microsoft Office or Microsoft Word to open Word (.doc) documents. If you don't have one of these applications installed, you can still access the lesson file by downloading and installing OpenOffice—an open source office suite that contains much the same kind of programs as Microsoft Office 100% free of charge. OpenOffice can be downloaded from www.openoffice.org.

By the Way

Advanced Tag Editing

With the text pasted into the document, you now have a page consisting entirely of paragraphs. But looking at the Word document, you see that the original text had headings, subheadings, and even an indented quote section. To finalize the conversion from document to web page, you need to apply the correct markup tags for each of these sections. You can do this either by using the Style drop-down on the Common toolbar or by using the Quick Tag Editor found at the top of the View panel.

To see how it works, click the first line of text in Design view. At the top of the View panel you will now see two tags in the Quick Tag Selector: <body> and <p> (see Figure 4.7). The Quick Tag Selector shows you what tags are applied to the selected element and also in which order they are applied, from the outermost on the left to the innermost on the right. If you hover your mouse over the <p> tag, you'll see a small down arrow appear on the right side. Clicking this arrow reveals the Quick Tag Editor drop-down menu (see Figure 4.8).

FIGURE 4.7
The Quick Tag Selector provides information about the currently applied tags and their order.

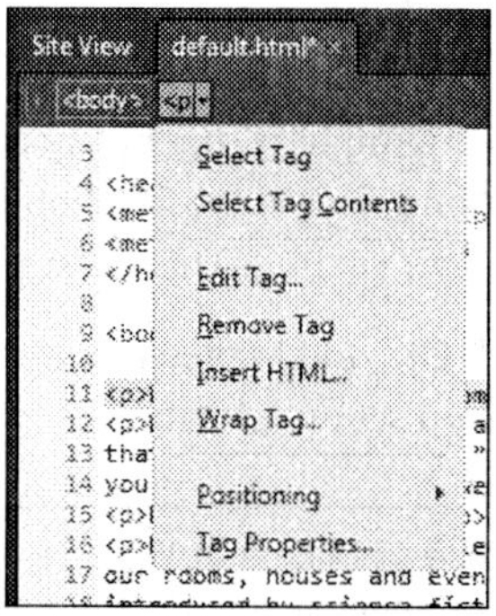

FIGURE 4.8
The Quick Tag Editor drop-down menu provides quick access to tag-editing and selection features.

From the drop-down menu, you can select the tag or the contents within the tag and edit, remove, or add additional tags directly. This tool is especially useful when you're changing or adding new tags because it changes both the beginning and end tags at the same time, thus ensuring you don't inadvertently break the code on the page.

To change the first paragraph to Heading 1, place your cursor on the first paragraph in Design view, activate the Quick Tag Editor for the <p> tag, and select Edit Tag. This opens the Quick Tag Editor dialog. In the dialog, change <p> to <h1> and click the green check mark on the far right (see Figure 4.9). This changes both the beginning and end tag to h1 and the first paragraph is now a heading. You can use the same technique to apply <h2> tags to the subheadings on the page.

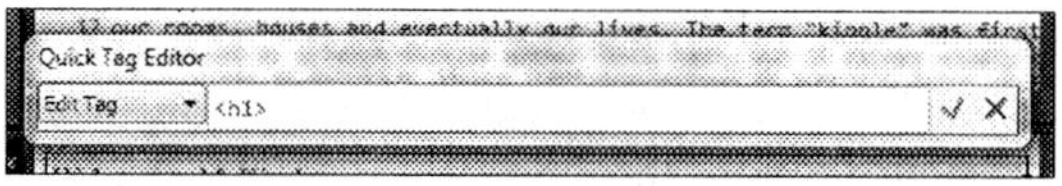

FIGURE 4.9
The Quick Tag Editor allows you to change the beginning and end tags of any tag on the page.

Looking at the Word document again, you'll notice the fourth paragraph is indented. In traditional publishing this is called a *pull quote* because it's a quote that is literally pulled out of the regular content and highlighted in a different way. HTML has a special tag for this type of content: <blockquote>. To match the Word document, use the Quick Tag Editor to change the paragraph tag surrounding the fourth paragraph to the <blockquote> tag.

With all the tags changed in your page, preview the page in your browser and note that the formatting now matches the Word document (see Figure 4.10).

FIGURE 4.10
With some simple formatting, the web page looks like the original Word document in Internet Explorer 9.

Summary

In this hour, you took a trip behind the scenes and learned a bit about how an HTML page works. You saw that the code boils down to wrapping the content in a beginning and an end tag and that changing these tags can be done from Code view and Design view. You got a preview of some of the code-editing tools available in Expression Web 4, the Quick Tag Selector, and the Quick Tag Editor, and you also learned how to import text content from external files and format the code so that it matches the original document. In Hour 5, "Getting Connected with (Hyper)Links: The Cornerstone of the World Wide Web," you create a second page and add hyperlinks to your pages to make them interactive.

Q&A

Q. *Why can't I simply cut and paste the content from a Word document straight into my web page?*

A. A word processor such as Microsoft Word inserts a large amount of hidden style code in documents. When you copy and paste text from these programs, all that code quite literally tags along. One example of this is pull quotes. When you press the Tab key in a word processor to visually distinguish a long quote by indenting it, you actually insert a block of style code defining how far in to indent the content. Therefore, when you copy and paste the content to Expression Web 4, that style code follows along and clutters up the code. This indentation code is unnecessary in HTML because there is already a dedicated tag for long quotes called <blockquote>. To avoid this problem, use the Paste Text command found under Edit on the main menu. This command strips the style code from copied text and inserts it as plain text with only the tags you request. Yes, using the Paste Text command forces you to apply the different heading and other tags manually, but it also ensures that all your code is up to standards, and that's what matters in the end.

Workshop

The Workshop has quiz questions and exercises to help you put to use what you just learned. If you get stuck, the answers to the quiz questions are in the next section. But try to answer them first. Otherwise, you'll be cheating yourself.

Quiz

1. In Code view, how do you tell the browser to treat one line of text differently from another?

Answer

1. To separate and group content, HTML uses tags. Any content placed between a beginning and an end tag is semantically defined by that tag so that browsers understand paragraphs as paragraphs, headings as headings, unordered lists as unordered lists, and so on. When you apply a particular style to content in Design view, you are actually telling the browser to find content wrapped by a certain tag and then apply the defined styles to this content.

Exercise

Find a Word document you already have on your computer or write a new one. Make sure it has several headings and subheadings along with bold and italicized content and a few lists. With the default.html file open in Expression Web 4, choose Save As under File, and select a new name (such as myTest.html) and save it. Delete all the content in your new file and import the content from the Word document. Clean up the code so the formatting matches the original document, and all bold and italicized content is strong and emphasized instead. Save the file and test it in your browser to verify that it works properly.

HOUR 5

Getting Connected with (Hyper)Links: The Cornerstone of the World Wide Web

What You'll Learn in This Hour:

- ▶ How to import a new page and link to it
- ▶ How to create links between pages on your website
- ▶ How to create links to other websites
- ▶ How to create links that open in new windows
- ▶ How to create bookmark links within your page

Hyperlinks (also known simply as *links*) are an integral part of any website. Hyperlinks work as both navigational tools within your website and pathways to further resources in your network or on the World Wide Web. They can also perform actions such as opening an email program and sending commands.

The hyperlink, in its basic form, appears on a web page as a colored and underlined segment of text with a web-page address attached. When you click the text, the browser goes to that new page. However, hyperlinks don't have to be only text. You can attach them to images and behaviors, and even empty areas within a web page. By knowing the capabilities and limitations of hyperlinks, you can build intuitive, functional, and visually compelling navigational tools and menus to make it easy for visitors to navigate and interact with your site.

For the most part, you use hyperlinks to navigate within your website or link to other websites. But, you can also use hyperlinks to give visitors access to other types of files, such as documents, compressed archives, and more. Although a web browser is limited in the file types it can display, it can be set up to interact with other programs on your computer to handle these file types. One such file type encountered often on the Web is the *Portable Document Format* (Adobe PDF). If you click a PDF file, your browser asks whether you want to save the file or open it (if you have Adobe Reader or a similar PDF-capable program on your computer). Then, the browser automatically calls for the program to open and display the file. The same goes for documents, spreadsheets, and numerous other types of files.

The two most commonly used links are internal links that point to other pages within a website and external links that point to other websites. To start this hour, you make an internal link. However, before you can do that, you need to have a new page to which you can link.

Import a New Page and Create an Internal Hyperlink

The lesson files include a file called myCameras.html. Follow these steps to import that file into your project:

1. From the menu bar, select File, Import, File (see Figure 5.1).

FIGURE 5.1
Importing a new page or other document can be done from the File option under Import in the File menu.

2. In the Import dialog, click Add File and browse to the location where you stored the downloaded lesson files on your computer.

3. Click Hour 5 and select the myCameras.html file. Click Open; myCameras.html is now visible in the Import dialog (see Figure 5.2). If you did not complete the default.html page in Hour 4, "Building a Home Page: A Look Behind the Curtain," or you want to ensure you are working with an identical version of the file to the one I used to write this book, I've also added the default.html file in the lesson file for you to use.

4. Click OK, and the myCameras.html file shows up in the Folder List panel.

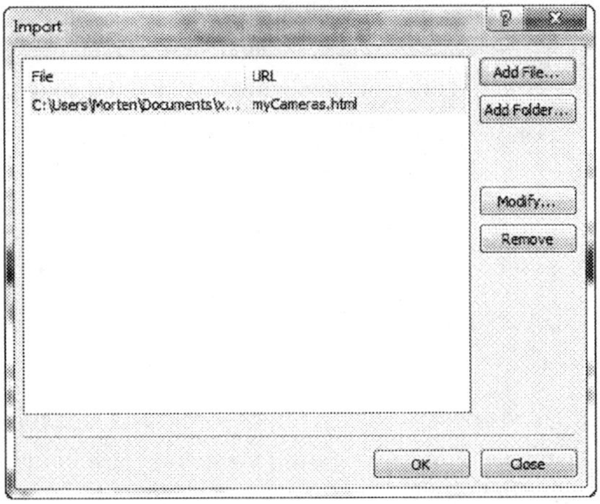

FIGURE 5.2
myCameras.html file selected in the Import dialog.

Now you have two files in the My Kipple website project: default.html and myCameras.html. The next step is to link the two pages to each other with hyperlinks. Open default.html by double-clicking the filename, and then select Design view from the buttons at the bottom of the page. The first hyperlink you make is an inline link—a segment of text that links to a further explanation of the topic.

Did you Know?

Inline links are prevalent throughout the Web and are just as useful as menu links because they mainly point directly to highly relevant information or further reading. For example, whereas a menu link might be generic and titled something such as "Norwegian Mythological Creatures" or "Scandinavian Christmas Traditions," an inline link would be titled "The Norwegian Nisse" with a link to a page exclusively about this mythical creature.

Scroll to the bottom of the page and find the last paragraph. On the second line, highlight the words "my collection of cameras." These four words will be the link to the new myCameras.html page. Right-click the highlighted text and select Hyperlink from the menu that appears. Doing so opens the Insert Hyperlink dialog (see Figure 5.3).

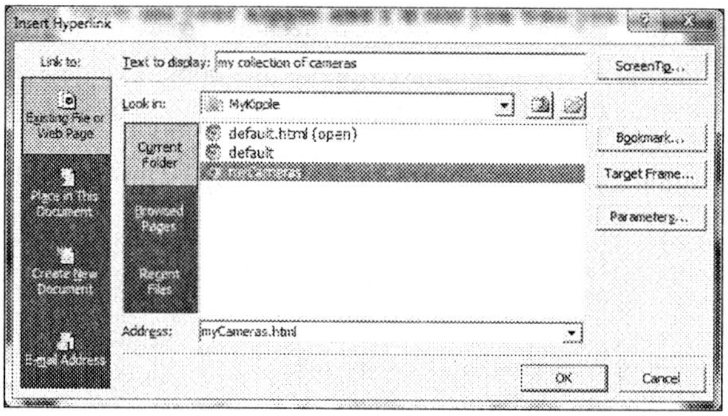

FIGURE 5.3
The Insert Hyperlink dialog can be opened by highlighting one or more words, clicking the right mouse button, and selecting Hyperlink from the pop-up menu.

From this dialog, you have complete control of your hyperlinks. On the left, you have four options that set where you are linking to:

▶ **Existing File or Web Page**—Lets you link to a file within your current site or enter a URL to an external web page.

▶ **Place in This Document**—Lets you link to bookmarks (also known as anchors) within the document. A *bookmark* is a destination within a document that can be targeted by a link. Longer documents, such as Frequently Asked Questions (FAQ) lists and registries, make heavy use of bookmarks.

▶ **Create New Document**—Lets you link to a new page you have not created yet. You define a name for the new file and have the option to edit it right away or simply link to the blank page now and edit it later. This is useful if you build a menu but haven't created the target pages. The reason for this option is obvious: You can't link to something that doesn't exist!

▶ **E-mail Address**—Creates the code necessary for the browser to open the default email program on the computer and insert a recipient address and even a default subject line if you so choose.

Did you Know?

URL stands for *uniform resource locator*. A URL is the web address that takes you to a web page, a file, or a specific server location. The URL to the site I built to accompany this book is http://expression.pinkandyellow.com and the URL to my blog is www.designisphilosophy.com.

In this case, you are linking to an existing file, so pick the first option. The Text to Display field shows the text you previously highlighted. This text becomes the link and is visible on the page. If you change the text here, the text in the page changes as well. Directly underneath is a standard file browser window where you can find and select the file you want to link to. As you can see, the main window lists both default.html and myCameras.html.

Expression Web 4 assumes that you intend to link to other files within your website, so these files are the first option you get. You can navigate away from this folder and link to other files, but any file you link to should always be either inside your website folder (or one of its subfolders) or a file that is already on the Web. Never link to a local file on your computer that is not in your website folder unless your website is only for use on your computer—the link will not work anywhere else.

Select myCameras.html. Its address shows up in the Address box. The last step is to add a ScreenTip or title to the link. This is not strictly necessary for the link to work but is required if you want your site to be accessible. A ScreenTip is the title attribute for a link (a short line of text that pops up next to the mouse pointer when you hover over a link). It gives the user more information about the link. In terms of accessibility, if the visitor uses a text-to-speech browser, the ScreenTip is read out loud to tell the user that there is a link and what the link points to. To add a ScreenTip, click the ScreenTip button in the upper-right corner of the Insert Hyperlink dialog. In the Set Hyperlink ScreenTip dialog that opens, type **Learn more about my camera collection and what I use them for** and click OK (see Figure 5.4). Click OK in the Insert Hyperlink dialog to finish the hyperlink.

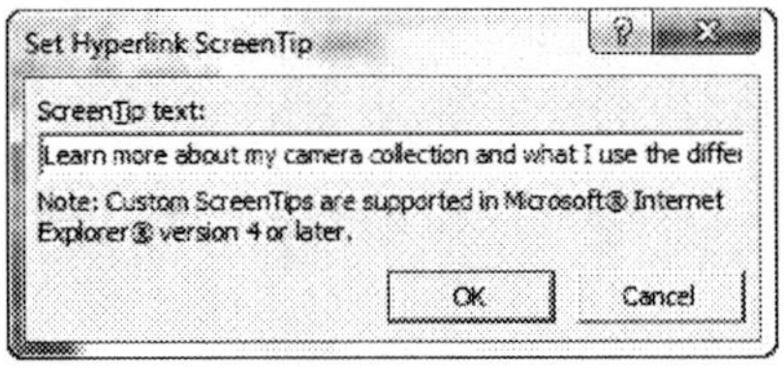

FIGURE 5.4
The Set Hyperlink ScreenTip dialog lets you add a detailed description to your hyperlinks and is necessary to make your links accessible.

The text you highlighted before is now blue and underlined, indicating to the visitor that it is a link. Save the file and test it in your browser (see Figure 5.5).

If you hover over the new link, a small box with the ScreenTip appears. If you click the link, the browser navigates to the linked file myCameras.html. However, there's a small problem: After you get to myCameras.html, you have no way to get back

unless you use the navigation buttons in the browser. To address this problem, you
need to create a Home link in the myCameras.html file to link back to default.html.

FIGURE 5.5
Firefox showing
default.html with
the new link and
its ScreenTip.

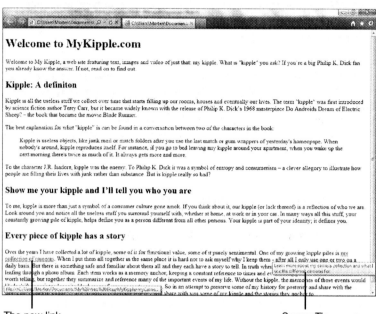

The new link　　　　　　　　　　　　　　ScreenTip

▼ Try It Yourself

Create a Home Link in myCameras.html

It's important to give the visitor an easy way to get back to the main page of any
website. The easiest way to do this is to create a Home link.

1. Open myCameras.html in Design view by double-clicking it in the Folder List
   task pane.

2. With the cursor at the beginning of the first line of the heading, press Enter
   once to shift the heading down one line, and then put your cursor up on the
   new first line. Use the Style menu to change the style of the new line to Paragraph.

3. Type the word **Home** and double-click the word to select it. Then, right-click
   the selected word and select Hyperlink from the menu that appears.

4. In the Insert Hyperlink dialog, select the default.html file and use the Set
   Hyperlink ScreenTip dialog to give it the ScreenTip text Go back to My Kipple.

5. Click OK. Save and test the file in your browser, making sure the ScreenTip works and that it links back to default.html.

▲

Hyperlink Syntax: Absolute, Relative, and Root-Relative

As you create hyperlinks in Expression Web 4, you will notice that the syntax of the link address in the Code view changes depending on what you link to. There are actually three different ways of writing a hyperlink address, all of which are used for different purposes:

Absolute hyperlinks are complete addresses that contain all the elements of a URL. They always start with some version of http:// followed by the domain name (for example, www.designisphilosophy.com) and optionally a page/folder. You use absolute hyperlinks when linking to pages outside of your current site that have a different domain name.

Relative hyperlinks are addresses that are relative to the current domain or location. They only contain the name of the target page prefixed with any necessary folder moves (for example, default.html). The browser sees that this is a relative hyperlink and adds the domain and folder location of the current page to the beginning of the link to complete it. If you use relative hyperlinks and you want to navigate from a page stored in one folder to a page stored in a different folder, you add the folder prefixes to the hyperlink. For instance, a relative link from a page in Folder 1 to a page in Folder 2 would be ../Folder 2/page.html, where the ../ tells the browser you want to go out of the current folder and into a new one. When you create hyperlinks between pages in Expression Web 4, they are always inserted as relative links so that the application can easily update them if you choose to move files around. However, if you move the files around on your computer outside of the Expression Web program, the hyperlinks break.

Root-relative hyperlinks are a subset of relative hyperlinks in which all the links are assumed to start from the root folder (domain name) of the site. They differ from the relative hyperlinks in that the address is prefixed by a forward slash (for example, /default.html). The browser applies only the domain to the beginning of this link. Root-relative hyperlinks are used in place of relative ones in large sites where there is a chance the files will be moved around without using an application such as Expression Web 4 to update them. Because they refer to the root of the site rather than the current location of the page they are placed in, they work regardless of where the file is placed as long as they remain under the right domain.

Creating External Links and New Windows

Now that you have created some internal links, it's time to link your website to other external websites. You do this in much the same way that you created your internal links, but instead of selecting a file from your computer, you go to the link's destination and find its URL to insert.

In the second paragraph of the home page (default.html) is a reference to the book *Do Androids Dream of Electric Sheep?* Some of the readers of this website might want to buy this book. Why not give them a link to the book's page on Amazon.com? To do this, you first need the address. In your browser, go to www.amazon.com and search for *Do Androids Dream of Electric Sheep?* Click one of the search results to get to the book's main page. Highlight the entire address in the address bar and copy it by using Ctrl+C (the universal copy shortcut). Alternatively, you can right-click the address and select Copy (see Figure 5.6).

FIGURE 5.6
Copying the Amazon.com URL for the book can be done by right-clicking and selecting Copy from the context menu.

Back in Expression Web 4, select the book title in the second paragraph, right-click the selection, and select Hyperlink as you did before. In the Insert Hyperlink dialog, select Existing File or Web Page and paste the Amazon.com URL into the Address field by clicking in the text box and either pressing Ctrl+V (universal paste shortcut) or right-clicking and selecting Paste (see Figure 5.7).

Open the ScreenTip dialog and type "**Do Androids Dream of Electric Sheep?**" is available from Amazon.com. Click OK twice and save the new file. Test it in your browser.

But, here is a new problem: After the visitor clicks the link, she goes to Amazon.com. How does she get back to your site? Unlike the myDesk.html file, you can't insert a home link in the Amazon.com page. How do you keep your visitor on your site and still let her visit other sites? One solution is to edit your link so that the external page opens in a new window.

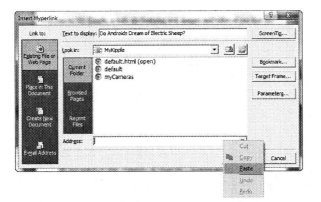

FIGURE 5.7
Pasting the Amazon.com URL for the book by right-clicking and selecting Paste from the menu.

Using the Browsed Pages Option to Obtain Hyperlinks

If you don't want to copy and paste the URL from the browser, there is an alternative built in to Expression Web 4: The application connects to the Internet Explorer browser history, which means you can get the URL from right inside the program itself. To use this option, go to the desired target location in Internet Explorer before creating the hyperlink. When inside the Insert/Edit Hyperlink dialog, click the Browsed Pages option (see Figure 5.8) in the main window to get the browsing history. From here, you can select any of the pages you have visited with Internet Explorer recently, and Expression Web automatically inserts the URL to that page for you.

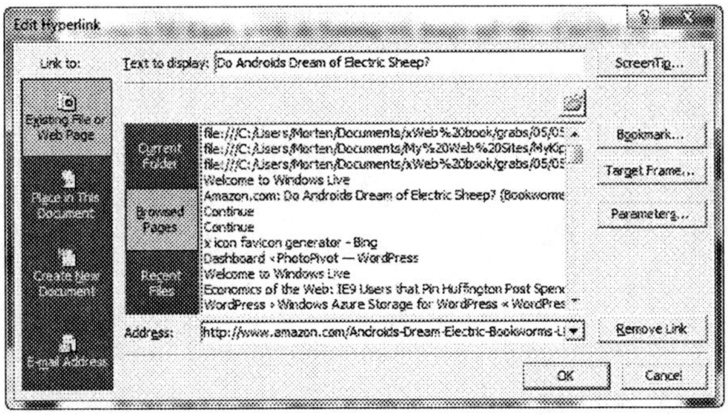

Did you Know?

FIGURE 5.8
The Browsed Pages option gives you access to the recent browser history from Internet Explorer.

1. Right-click the Do Androids Dream of Electric Sheep? link you just created and select Hyperlink Properties.

2. In the Edit Hyperlink dialog, click the Target Frame button on the right.

3. In the Target Frame dialog, select New Window under Common Targets. This tells the browser to open a new window (see Figure 5.9).

4. Click OK twice, save the file, and test it in your browser.

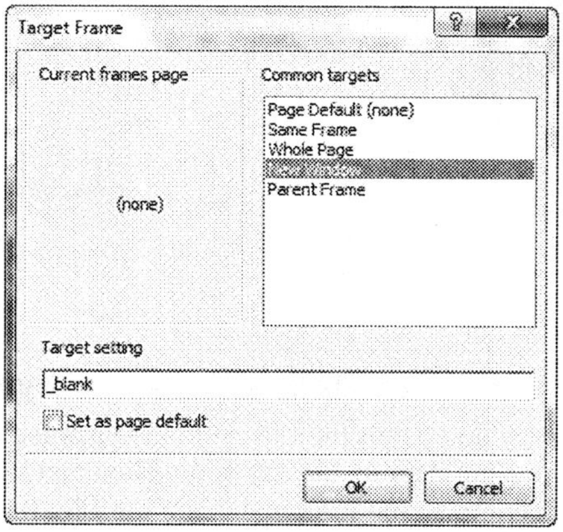

FIGURE 5.9
The Target Frame dialog within Hyperlink Properties lets you define where the linked page opens.

Now, when you click the link to the book, the page opens in a new window or tab in your browser. This is a basic way to make links open in new windows.

Creating Internal Links Within Documents Using Bookmarks

Another type of link you can create is a *bookmark* (also known as an anchor), which is a hyperlink that points to a specific position in the current page. Designers most often use this type of link to help people navigate longer web pages by providing a menu that leads to different sections. Bookmarks are also effective for linking directly to footnotes.

Before you make bookmark links, you have to insert the bookmarks in your document. In default.html, select the first subheading (Kipple: A Definition). Select Insert, Bookmark from the menu bar, or click Ctrl+G. This opens the Bookmark dialog. From here, you can set the bookmark's name. The name becomes the address of the bookmark and is included in the hyperlink. For that reason, underscores replace all spaces (see Figure 5.10).

> You can change the bookmark name to whatever you want, but it's a good idea to keep it consistent and meaningful, especially if your document has many bookmarks.

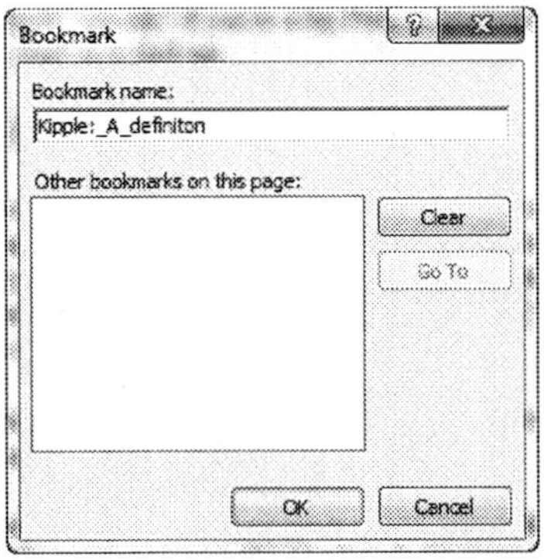

FIGURE 5.10
The Bookmark dialog lets you define a so-called "slug" for your bookmark anchor. Note the underscores between each word.

When you click OK, you see that the title now has a dotted underline in the Design view of the page. This is a visual reminder that the text has a bookmark attached and is visible only within Expression Web, not in the web browser. Follow the same process and attach bookmarks to the two other subheadings.

Now, all you have to do is make a menu with links to the bookmarks. This menu should go directly under the main heading. Make a new paragraph under the main heading by clicking the beginning of the first paragraph and pressing Enter. In the new first paragraph, create an unordered (bulleted) list. Each list item should be identical to the subheadings, like this:

- Kipple: A Definition
- Show me your kipple and I'll tell you who you are
- Every piece of kipple has a story

Highlight the first bullet point and right-click to open the Hyperlink dialog. By selecting Link to Place in This Document from the left-side menu, you open a list of the three bookmarks you created. Select the one that matches your title (see Figure 5.11). As before, attach a ScreenTip such as Jump to Kipple: A Definition to keep your page accessible. Finally, click OK and save your changes.

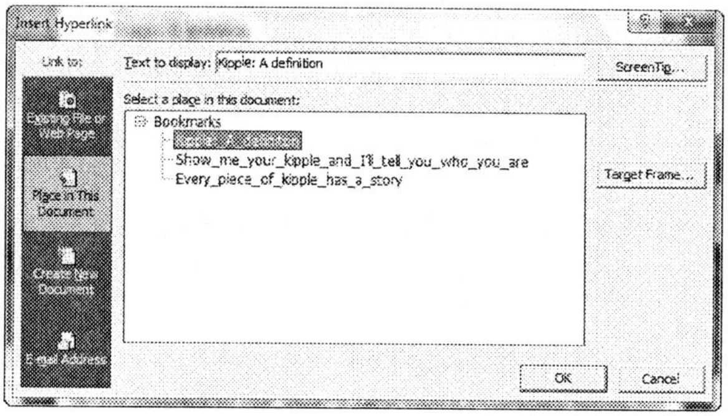

FIGURE 5.11
The Place in This Document option in the Insert Hyperlink dialog lets you link to a bookmark within the same page.

Do the same with the two other menu items. When you are done, save and test in your browser. You see that when you click the links, the browser jumps to the bookmarked section. Because the document is relatively short, it might not look like anything is happening when you click a link. However, if you reduce the width of your window to about half the size of your screen and then click the links, you should see the page jump.

Note that because a bookmark link is no different from any other link, the navigation buttons in your browser work on it as well. This makes more sense if you look in the address bar after clicking one of the bookmark links: When a bookmark link is clicked, the browser is directed to the page in question and the bookmark within that page, which is signified by a # symbol followed by the bookmark name like this:

"My Web Sites/MyKipple/default.html#Kipple:_A_definiton"

Creating an Email Hyperlink

The final option in the Hyperlink dialog is the E-mail Address link. With this option, you can create a link that opens the visitor's preferred email program and sets the To address and Subject line. This is the easiest way to provide contact information to your visitors because they don't have to copy and paste or type out the email address themselves.

To create an email hyperlink, you first need some text to work as a link. At the bottom of the home page, add a new paragraph and then type **If you want further information about my kipple, send me an e-mail.** Highlight the "send me an e-mail" portion of the text and open the Insert Hyperlink dialog. Select E-mail Address from the left-side menu to open the email options. In the E-mail Address line, enter the email address to which you want the message to go. When you start writing, the program automatically inserts a block of code, `mailto:`, directly in front of your address. This code tells the browser that this is not a regular link but an email link. In the Subject line, type the default subject line that you want emails generated from the website to have (see Figure 5.12). The Recently Used E-Mail Addresses option displays the most recent email addresses you linked to within Expression Web 4. Remember to set a ScreenTip for your email link and click OK.

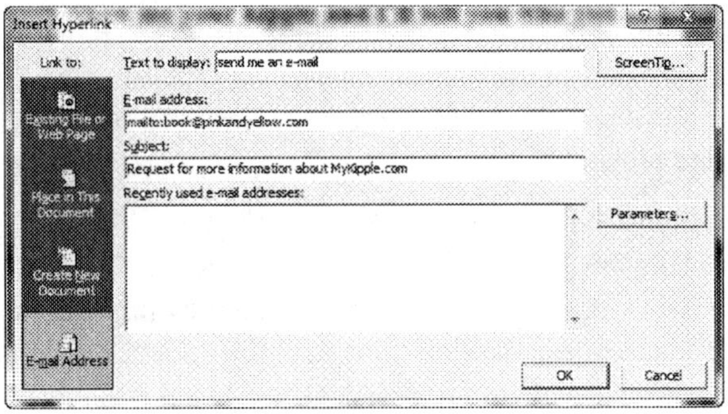

FIGURE 5.12
The E-Mail Address option under the Insert Hyperlink dialog lets you insert a receiving email address and a default subject line.

When you test the page in your browser and click the new link, your computer opens your default email program and starts an email with the address and subject line you chose.

Summary

Hyperlinks are what set the World Wide Web apart from other informational sources. By enabling the user to quickly navigate through large amounts of content and instantly move from one source to another, hyperlinks have revolutionized the way we find and use information. In this hour, you learned how to create hyperlinks within your own site, to the outside world, and even within one document. Hyperlinks are core components of any website and create navigation and links to the rest of the Web. You also learned how to create links that open in new windows. In Hour 16, "Using Code Snippets," you learn how to expand on this technique using Expression Web 4's built-in behaviors.

Q&A

Q. *When I copied and pasted the subheading into my unordered list, the text kept the dotted underline. Is this a problem?*

A. If you copy and paste content, such as text, in Design view, all the associated attributes come with it. In this case, you copied not only the text itself but also the bookmark. To get rid of the bookmark, highlight the text, right-click, and select Bookmark Properties. Simply click Clear and Expression Web 4 removes the bookmark.

Q. *Why are all my links blue and underlined? I don't like blue and I don't like the underline either. Can I change them?*

A. As with headings, paragraph, block quote, and other default styles, the link or anchor (<a>) tag has default properties in all browsers. That default is blue and underlined. Likewise, a previously visited link has a purplish color. In Hour 10, "Bringing Style to Substance with Cascading Style Sheets," you learn how to style your links by changing their color, font style, and size, and by adding underline and other effects.

Q. *What is the difference between a menu and a link?*

A. A menu is just a series of links styled to look a certain way. On a website, any item that takes you somewhere else when you click it is just a link created in the same way you created links in this hour. The reason menus look different is that they have heavy styling and usually use graphics instead of just text.

Workshop

The Workshop has quiz questions and exercises to help you put to use what you just learned. If you get stuck, the answers to the quiz questions are in the next section. But, try to answer them first. Otherwise, you'll be cheating yourself.

Quiz

1. What kind of content can a hyperlink be applied to?

2. What are the three different types of hyperlinks and when are they used?

3. How does a bookmark differ from a "regular" hyperlink?

Answers

1. Hyperlinks can be applied to any and all content in a page, although it is advisable to restrict them to smaller items such as short text segments or images.

2. The three types of hyperlinks are absolute, relative, and root-relative. Absolute links link to pages that are not inside your current site. Relative links link to pages that are within your site. Root-relative links link to pages that are within your site when there is a chance the pages will be moved around without using Expression Web 4.

3. Bookmarks make the browser navigate to a certain location within the current page, so instead of loading a new page, it jumps down or up in the current page to a different location.

Exercise

Throughout the default.html page are several items that you can link to sites with further information. For instance, you could link the name Philip K. Dick to the Wikipedia.org page about the author and the title *Blade Runner* to the imdb.com page about the movie. Use the Web to find further information on these items and make links that point to these sources. Make sure you attach a ScreenTip to each link and that each one opens in a new window.

HOUR 6

Getting Visual, Part 1: Adding Images and Graphics

What You'll Learn in This Hour:

- ▶ What the main image file types are and when to use them
- ▶ How to import an image into Expression Web 4
- ▶ How to insert an image into a page
- ▶ How to change the placement and appearance of an image in a page

Because the World Wide Web is a visual medium, making your website visually pleasing is important. The easiest way to do this is by adding images and graphics to the text. However, images can be so much more than just eye candy. As hinted at in Hour 5, "Getting Connected With (Hyper)Links: The Cornerstone of the World Wide Web," an image can also be used as a link or even as a navigational tool. If you dissect websites, you find images used as borders, backgrounds, buttons, underlines, and even text. The possibilities are endless.

In the past, heavy use of images in websites was frowned upon, mostly because people were on slow dial-up connections, and the images made the pages heavy and slow to load. But, now that broadband Internet is becoming more and more prevalent throughout the world and image-compression technology has evolved to a point where web-quality images take up little memory, web designers rely heavily on image elements to improve the look of their sites.

The bottom line is this: Used correctly, images can be a great tool to enhance the look and feel of your website.

Images on the Web: Three File Types for Three Uses

At first glance, it looks like all images on the Web have the same format. But, in reality, they are different. Web designers choose different file formats, with different attributes, depending on how they plan to use an image. That choice in turn affects how a page looks and works.

Most current browsers support three main image formats: GIF (Graphics Interchange Format), JPEG or JPG (Joint Photographic Experts Group), and PNG (Portable Network Graphics). Each format has advantages and limitations:

▶ The GIF format produces the smallest files for quick downloads. Unfortunately, the image quality of a GIF file is poor. When introduced, the GIF format was the only format that supported transparency. It gave designers the option to create graphics that could display on top of other graphics or display without an unsightly box around them. However, this transparency is coarse and effective only with images that have clean lines. In addition, the GIF format can display only up to 256 colors, severely limiting the kinds of images that designers can use it for. For these reasons, the GIF format is best suited for computer-generated content and line drawings. Today's designers use the GIF format mostly to display small icons and buttons (see Figure 6.1).

FIGURE 6.1
A GIF image with transparency on a white background and a transparent background. The file size is 3.82KB.

▶ JPEG or JPG is the most common image format on the Web. Its success stems from its high compression rate and low image noise. JPEG has become the standard format for images not only on the Web, but also in digital cameras and other devices. JPEG is a compression format that uses advanced algorithms to recalculate the image data and remove content that is not easily noticed by the human eye. Among the many different things a JPEG compressor does is evening the colors, duplicating similar looking areas, and compressing the actual image code to make it shorter. At high-quality (and low-compression) settings, JPEG compression can be excellent, but if you set the compression too high, the image can end up looking a bit like a paint-by-numbers painting (see Figure 6.2). The JPEG is "solid" and cannot be made transparent. Today it is recommended that you use the JPEG format for photos and other organic images. For computer-generated graphics, the PNG format is preferred.

FIGURE 6.2
A JPEG image with minimum compression to the left and maximum compression to the right. At minimum compression, the file size is 21KB; at maximum compression, it is 14.2KB.

▶ PNG is the newest of the three formats. PNGs fare bitmaps that carry with them an alpha layer that tells the browser what portions of the image are transparent. As a result, you can superimpose PNGs on top of other images with full transparency. Unlike the GIF format, PNG transparencies are clean (see Figure 6.3). The ability to create advanced transparencies makes the format ideal for logos and other superimposed and hovering graphics in websites. Some older browsers, in particular Internet Explorer 6, do not support PNG transparencies. The PNG format was designed to handle computer-generated graphics and does a far better job at it than the JPEG format.

FIGURE 6.3
A PNG image with transparency on a white background and a transparent background. Note that, unlike the GIF format, the transparency in the PNG is clean. The file size is 7.1KB.

Importing and Inserting an Image

Images are the most common *nontext* elements featured in web pages. And because images are so heavily used, there are many different ways to handle them depending on how the designer plans to use them.

The easiest use is simply inserting an image into a page. To do that, you need to import the image file into your project. But before you do, it's a good idea to start thinking about how your site is organized. Look at the Folder List panel, and you see that your site currently consists of two pages: default.html and myCameras.html. Now, you are adding image files to your site, which means they appear alongside your two HTML files. If you were adding just two or three images, this wouldn't be a problem. But as you saw in Hour 2, "Beginning at the End: A Walkthrough of the Finished Project," the final site has a large number of images and files. So, before things get too complicated, it's a good idea to start organizing everything in folders. In other words, you need to make a folder for your images.

Creating a New Folder and Importing a New Image

Folders serve as effective tools for keeping your site organized. Websites have a tendency to fill up with files fast, and it's important to think about file organization early. The Folder List panel gives you easy access to all the files and folders in your site, and you can use it to create new files and folders and organize them.

1. With the Folder List panel selected, click the arrow next to the New Document icon on the Common toolbar and select Folder (see Figure 6.4). Alternatively, you can right-click inside the panel and select New, Folder.

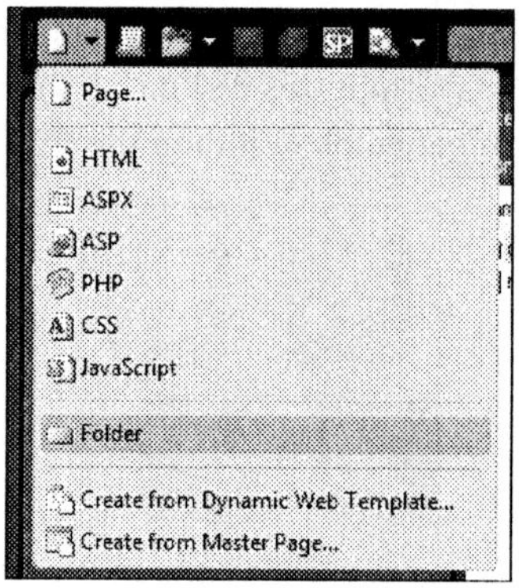

FIGURE 6.4
One of several ways to create a new folder is to select Folder from the New drop-down menu on the Common toolbar.

2. Name the new folder **Images** and double-click it.

3. Select File, Import, File as you did in Hour 5. In the Import dialog, click Add File and browse to the location where you stored the downloaded lesson files on your computer.

4. Click Hour 6 and select the file called camerasSmall.jpg. Click Open, and then click OK. Expression Web 4 copies the file and stores it in the Images folder. You can see it in the Folder List panel by clicking the + icon next to the Images folder (see Figure 6.5).

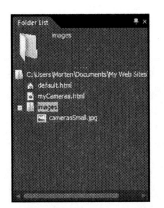

FIGURE 6.5
The imported image file as it appears under the Images folder in the Folder List panel when the + icon has been clicked. If you click the – icon, the folder is closed and the + icon reappears.

Watch Out!

Expression Web 4 is finicky when it comes to image files. If you add images into your website without importing them through Expression Web 4, they might not work properly in Design view, and you see a small square with a red X instead of the image. This doesn't mean that there is anything wrong with the image; in fact, if you preview the page in a browser, you see that the image is there. The problem has to do with how Expression Web 4 handles files internally. The best (and only) way to avoid this problem is to make it a habit to import all image files properly through the Import File dialog.

Now that Expression Web 4 has imported the image into your project, it's time to insert it into a page. You can do this in Design view by dragging and dropping the image into the text. To start, open the myCameras.html file. In the Folder List panel, click and hold the camerasSmall.jpg file and drag it to Design view. You see a gray dotted marker jump around inside the text indicating where the image insertion point will be. Place the image at the beginning of the first paragraph under the heading and let go. Doing so opens the Accessibility Properties dialog (see Figure 6.6).

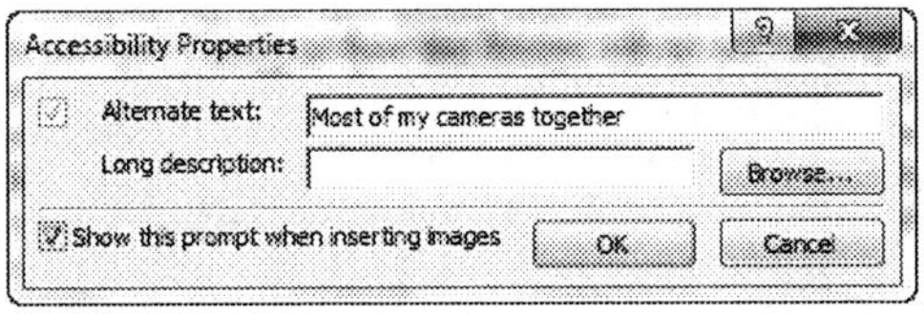

FIGURE 6.6
The Accessibility Properties dialog lets you customize the information attached to the image for those who can't view the image itself.

The Accessibility Properties dialog gives you the option to attach alternative text and a longer description to your images. Some visitors cannot see the images in your page because they are using a text-only browser, portable device, or text-to-speech browser. The alternative text displays in place of the image for these users and helps to explain what the image shows. It also appears if, for one reason or another, the image doesn't load properly when the page is opened by someone using a regular browser. The alternative text should be a description of what the image is. In this case, enter Most of my cameras together in the Alternate Text text box and then click OK. Expression Web 4 inserts the image in the text at the beginning of the first paragraph (see Figure 6.7).

FIGURE 6.7
The inserted image as it appears in Design view.

Save the file and preview the page in a browser. Something is a bit off; the image breaks the text and leaves a large empty area to the right (see Figure 6.8).

This big void appears because, by default, web browsers consider images to be "inline" elements, meaning they appear alongside the other elements on the line just like a letter or word. If you've ever placed images in a Word document, you are probably familiar with the concept of "text wrapping." The solution to the problem is similar when we work with websites: Tell the browser that the image should not be considered part of the text but rather an object around which the text should wrap. This can be done using the Picture Properties.

FIGURE 6.8
The page with
the inserted
image as it
appears in
Opera.

Using Picture Properties to Change the Appearance of an Image

After an image is part of a web page, you can use properties and functions to tell the browser how to display the image and how the image should relate to the surrounding content. In addition to simple HTML properties, Expression Web 4 gives you access to some basic image-editing options normally found only in dedicated imaging software. You can access some of these options by right-clicking the image in Design view and selecting Picture Properties from the context menu. Doing so opens the Picture Properties dialog (see Figure 6.9).

The General Tab

Under the General tab, the Picture field tells you the file with which you are currently working. You can change the file by using the Browse button or by typing a new filename in the Picture text box. The Edit button opens the source file in the default image editor on your computer.

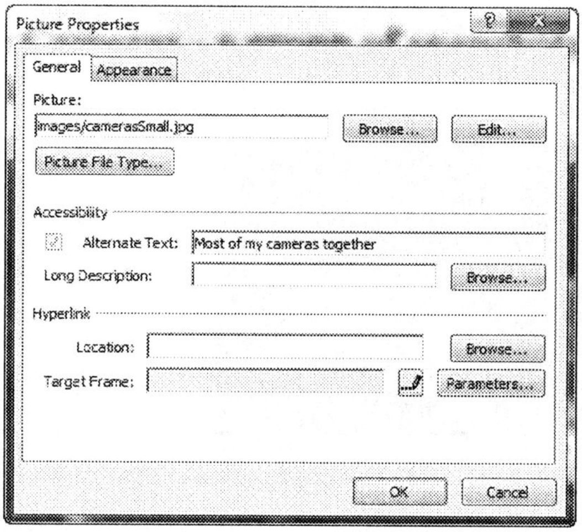

FIGURE 6.9
The General tab
of the Picture
Properties dialog.

FIGURE 6.9
The General tab
of the Picture
Properties dialog.

Watch Out!

Expression Web 4 Is Not an Image Editor!

Even though you are presented with the option of using Expression Web 4 to change the file formats for images, it is not something I suggest you do. Expression Web 4 is not an image-editing program, and the options you are given are both restrictive and potentially destructive. By changing the file formats of your images—from a transparent PNG to a low-resolution JPEG image, for example—you can inadvertently reduce the quality of your images to the point where they are unusable.

As much as possible, try to use a dedicated image editor to make changes to your images and then import the final product into Expression Web 4.

Directly underneath the Picture text box is the Picture File Type button. If you click this button, a new dialog opens (see Figure 6.10). From here, you can convert the file you are working with to any other main image format with a few mouse clicks. If you change the file type in this dialog, Expression Web 4 automatically replaces the image on your page. When you save the page, a dialog asks you where you want to store the new image file. My recommendation is to never use this function.

The next section of the General tab of the Picture Properties dialog is Accessibility. This displays the same options that appeared when you inserted the image.

The final section is Hyperlink. Here, you can make the entire image into a hyperlink pointing to a different page, a different site, or a file.

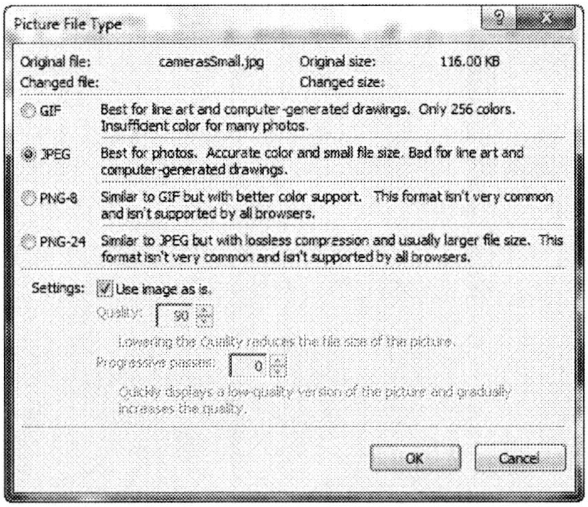

FIGURE 6.10
The Picture File Type dialog lets you change the file type of your images without having to open a separate image-editing application.

The Appearance Tab

The Appearance tab contains the most commonly used code controls for the image (see Figure 6.11). This is where you instruct the browser how to handle the image in relation to other content as well as specify border thickness, margins, and dimensions. The functions under the Appearance tab are styles that Expression Web 4 applies to the image. In later hours, you learn how to create styles that apply to all images in a site so that you don't have to set them for each individual image.

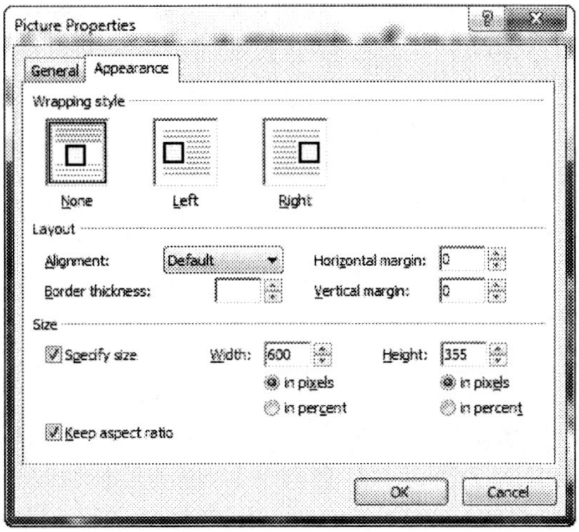

FIGURE 6.11
The Appearance tab of the Picture Properties dialog controls the image in relation to the other content on the page and sets the image dimensions, border, and margins/padding.

▶ The Wrapping Style options define how the surrounding text wraps around the image. The three buttons provide good illustrations of what the different options mean. None (the default) tells the browser to handle the image as if it were part of the text. This means that the image lines up with the rest of the text like a large letter and pushes the remaining text to the right to make room. Left means that the image lines up against the left side of the window and the text wraps on its right. Right works the same way as the Left option, except the image is now on the right with the text wrapping on the left.

▶ Alignment settings apply only if the wrapping style is set to None. In the Layout section, the Alignment option gives you control over where the image lies in relation to the remaining text on the line. For example, if you set the alignment to Top, the top of the image aligns with the top of the text line. If you set the alignment to Middle, the middle of the image aligns with the middle of the text line (see Figure 6.12). And if you set the alignment to Bottom, the bottom of the image aligns with the bottom of the text line. Expression Web 4 gives you eight different positions in addition to Default.

FIGURE 6.12
The Alignment attribute is set to Middle, centering the image vertically in relation to the line of text.

▶ The Layout section also contains the Border Thickness setting (which defines a border or outline that can be applied to the edges of the image) and the Horizontal Margin and Vertical Margin settings (which create empty space on the four sides of the image).

▶ The final section of the Appearance tab is Size, where you can manually set the dimensions of the image either in pixels or as a percentage of the original size. You can also toggle the Keep Aspect Ratio option on and off. As a rule of thumb, always keep the image size the same as the file itself and never change the aspect ratio. If you change the image size, you leave it up to the browser to resize the image, and its quality drops dramatically as a result. Changing the aspect ratio distorts the image by making it either too squished or too stretched out. In Hour 7, "Getting Visual, Part 2: Advanced Image Editing, Thumbnails, and Hotspots," you learn how to use one of Expression Web 4's built-in functions to create a thumbnail (small version of your image) that links to the larger version, thereby avoiding the need to manually resize your images.

Try It Yourself   ▼

Change the Properties of the Image

By default, an image inserted into a page appears directly next to the line of text where the designer placed it, and the image breaks the text. To make the page more appealing, it is necessary to separate the image from the text and give it some breathing room.

1. Right-click the image in Design view and select Picture Properties. Select the Appearance tab.

2. Click Left in the Wrapping Style section to align the image to the left and wrap the text to the right.

3. Set the border thickness to 3 pixels using the up and down buttons or by typing 3 in the box.

4. Set the horizontal and vertical margins to 15 pixels by using the up and down buttons or by typing 5 in the boxes, and then click OK. Save the file and preview the page in your browser.   ▲

The image now appears to the left with the text wrapped to the right. The image has a 3-pixel black border with a 5-pixel space between the image and the surrounding text (see Figure 6.13).

FIGURE 6.13
With styling
applied, the
image floats to
the left with the
text wrapping to
the right.

FIGURE 6.13
With styling
applied, the
image floats to
the left with the
text wrapping to
the right.

Summary

Images are an important part of any website. Not only do they increase the visual appeal of the site, but they can also help make the content more interesting and informative. In this hour, you learned that three main image formats are in use on the Web and that each has advantages and disadvantages. You also learned how to import images into your project and organize them in folders. At the end of the hour, you learned how to insert an image into a page using Design view and how to manipulate that image with the functions available in the Picture Properties dialog. You now have the basic building blocks to create a page with text and images.

Q&A

Q. *When I imported an image into Expression Web 4, it didn't end up in the Images folder but was stored alongside the files in the main folder. Why did this happen and how can I fix it?*

A. If the file you imported was stored in the main (or root) folder, you didn't select the subfolder before you started the import process. To avoid this problem, before you start the importing process, always double-click the folder you want to import files to. If a file ends up in the wrong folder, simply go to the Folder List panel or the Folders view in the Web Site pane and drag the file into the right folder. Expression Web 4 automatically updates all the files that link to the file and ensures that they still point to the right place.

Q. *When I inserted an image into my page, I accidentally grabbed one of the image sides and changed its size. Now it looks all weird and stretched. How do I fix it?*

A. If you make a mistake and notice it right away, the easiest way to fix the problem is by selecting Edit, Undo on the menu bar or by using the shortcut Ctrl+Z. You can also reset the image to its original size and dimension by opening Picture Properties and unchecking the Specify Size box. Doing so returns the image to its original size. Then, reselect the Specify Size option so that the image dimensions are specified in the markup. Even though your image still displays in a web browser even when you do not specify the image dimensions in the markup, it's good practice to specify the dimensions. Doing so helps the browser render the page layout correctly before the image downloads and appears on the page.

Q. *When I dragged and dropped an image into a page, it ended up in the wrong place. What do I do now?*

A. You can move the image anywhere on the page simply by grabbing it with the mouse and dragging it to a different location. Because an image acts like part of the text, you can place it anywhere within the text in the same way you move around words and paragraphs. When you grab an image and move the cursor outside its border and into the text, a small, fuzzy gray vertical line indicates where the image will land.

Workshop

The Workshop has quiz questions and exercises to help you put to use what you just learned. If you get stuck, the answers to the quiz questions are in the next section. But try to answer the questions first. Otherwise, you'll be cheating yourself.

Quiz

1. Why is it important to always provide alternative text when inserting an image into a web page?

2. What are the differences among GIF files, JPEG files, and PNG files? When would you use each format?

Answers

1. The alternative text displays whenever the image is not loaded because the connection is too slow, the image is not available, or the visitor is using a text-only or text-to-speech browser. The alternative text is both a courtesy to these users and a necessary substitute if your images do not load.

2. A GIF is a small file size, low-resolution image that can display coarse transparencies. GIFs mainly display smaller icons and simple line graphics. JPEG is the predominant image file format used to save photos and images with continuous tones, such as gradients. Most digital cameras and most other devices save images in this format. The JPEG format has good compression and relatively small file size. PNG is an image file format that has image quality the same as or better than the JPEG format, with the added bonus of clean transparencies. Some older browsers, most prominently Internet Explorer 6, do not support PNG transparencies. As a general rule of thumb, GIFs are used for icons, JPEGS for photos, and PNGs for computer-generated graphics.

Exercise

Insert a second copy of the camerasSmall.jpg image into the myCameras.html page anywhere you want. Give it alternative text of your choice. Use the Picture Properties dialog to position the image on the right side of the screen, to give the image a thin border, and to provide more margin space than you gave the other image.

Getting Visual, Part 2: Advanced Image Editing, Thumbnails, and Hotspots

What You'll Learn in This Hour:

▶ How to use the Pictures toolbar to insert and edit images
▶ How to create thumbnails using the Auto Thumbnail function
▶ How to create and edit hotspots

Now that you know how to import and insert an image, it's time to look at the image-editing tools featured in Expression Web 4. The program goes beyond the norm and gives you several quick-and-easy tools to make "quick and dirty" changes to your image files—changes that would normally require an image editor. One such feature is the ability to make thumbnails with a few mouse clicks. In this hour, you learn how to use these tools to make changes to image files you have already inserted into your page.

In addition to being visual elements, images in a web page can be functional elements if you turn them into links and buttons. You can even designate separate areas within an image to interact with the user either by highlighting when the user hovers over them or by linking to other images or pages. You do this by creating hotspots in your image.

Exploring the Pictures Toolbar

In Hour 6, "Getting Visual, Part 1: Adding Images and Graphics," you learned how to insert an image into a page and how to use the Picture Properties dialog to change the way the image relates to the other content on the page. But what if you want to change the appearance of the image itself? Maybe after you insert it into the page, you notice that it is too bright or that it needs cropping. Normally, this requires you to open the image file in an image editor such as Photoshop or Expression Design, make the necessary changes, reimport the image into Expression Web 4, and finally replace the image on your page with a new one. Well, those days are over. Expression Web 4 has a built-in set of tools to help you do simple image editing without leaving the program. The Pictures toolbar conveniently contains these tools (see Figure 7.1).

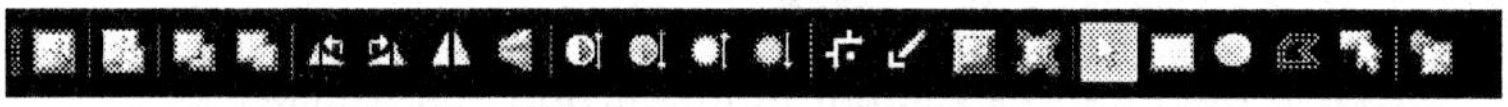

FIGURE 7.1
The Pictures toolbar gives you instant access to all the image editing features in Expression Web 4.

As you learned in Hour 1, "Getting to Know Microsoft Expression Web 4 Service Pack 2," all you have to do to open the Pictures toolbar is select View, Toolbars on the menu bar and click Pictures. The Pictures toolbar opens directly under the Common toolbar, and you can move it within the toolbar area to reposition it if you like.

If you haven't already done so, open the myCameras.html file. To activate the functions of the Pictures toolbar, click the image you inserted in Hour 6. Expression Web 4 always tells you which functions are available by fading out those that are unavailable. Place your cursor anywhere inside the page and notice that the icons in the toolbar fade out and become unavailable as is applicable.

With the image selected, hover over each button to view its ScreenTip and see what function the icon represents.

Insert Picture from File is the only button that remains active no matter where you are in the document. Clicking this button lets you insert a new image in the current cursor location or replace the selected image with a different image.

When you click **Auto Thumbnail**, Expression Web 4 creates a small version of the selected image and inserts it on the page in place of the larger one. The smaller image (the thumbnail) is fitted with a hyperlink that displays the larger image.

The **Bring Forward** and **Send Backward** buttons tell the browser to change the stacking order of your content. A good analogy is to think of the page as a deck of cards; when you click the Bring Forward or Send Backward button, you move the current card up or down in the stack. You use these functions when you start placing content on top of other content—for example, text on top of an image.

The orientation buttons change the orientation of the image. They are **Rotate Left 90°** (counter-clockwise), **Rotate Right 90°** (clockwise), **Flip Horizontal**, and **Flip Vertical**. These buttons are useful if you import an image from a digital camera in which the orientation is incorrect—for example, a photo taken with the camera in a vertical orientation but the image in a horizontal orientation.

The **More Contrast** and **Less Contrast** buttons bring the contrast levels of the image up or down. If you add more contrast to an image, the bright colors become brighter, and the dark colors become darker. If you reduce the contrast, the difference between bright and dark colors becomes more even. The **More Brightness** and **Less Brightness** buttons bring the overall brightness level up and down. If you bring up the brightness level, you usually also need to bring up the contrast level to prevent the image's colors from fading.

The **Crop** button lets you cut out an area of the image and discard the rest, much as if you used a ruler and a knife to cut out part of a photo.

The **Set Transparent Color** button lets you set a specific color to be transparent. This function works only with GIF images. If you apply the function to a non-GIF image, Expression Web 4 converts the image to the GIF format and reduces its color depth. Expression Web 4 warns you about this before performing any changes.

Bevel puts a beveled border on your image to make it look as if it's standing up from the page. Designers often use this function when creating buttons from images.

The **Resample** button becomes available only if you change the dimensions of the image in Design view or through the Picture Properties dialog. When you click this button, the image permanently changes to the new dimensions rather than simply resizing in the browser.

The next set of tools lets you insert and modify hotspots in the image. **Select** lets you select the whole image or the respective hotspots on it. The **Rectangular Hotspot, Circular Hotspot,** and **Polygonal Hotspot** tools set the hotspots within an image. The **Highlight Hotspots** button displays the image as an image map in which the hotspots are black and the rest of the image is white. This tool is a visual aid to help you find the hotspots and makes no actual changes to the image.

The most important button on the Pictures toolbar is the **Restore** button. It restores the image to its original state and undoes all the changes you made to the image since you last saved the page. Be aware that if you save the page you are working in, Expression Web 4 saves the new edited version of the image on top of the old version and the Restore button can no longer restore the older image.

All the editing functions on the Pictures toolbar (orientation, contrast, brightness, crop, color, and so on) are destructive image-editing tools. In this case, destructive means the function permanently changes the file it affects and you cannot reverse the change. For that reason, it is paramount that you always keep backup copies of your original image files in case you make changes you are not satisfied with. Likewise, if you use the same image several times throughout your site and you make a change to one of these instances of the image using the Pictures toolbar, the change affects all other instances of that image. If you intend to make a change to an image you are using in multiple locations, you must first make a copy of the image and then apply the change to only the copy.

Using the Pictures Toolbar to Add and Change an Image

Now that you know what the different tools on the Pictures toolbar do, it's time to put them to use. But first, you need a page to put some more images in. In the project files for this hour, you can find an HTML file called eos1.html. Create a new folder called Pages using the same technique you used in the last hour, and import the eos1.html file to that folder. In the lesson files, there is also an image straight from my digital camera called eos1.jpg. As you learned in Hour 6, the first step when dealing with an image file is to import it into Expression Web 4 by selecting File, Import File in the menu bar. Make sure the new image is stored in the Images folder in the Folder View task pane. If it isn't there, simply drag and drop the file into the Images folder.

After you import the image, open the eos1.html file. There are now three different methods to insert the image into the page. In Hour 6, you used the drag-and-drop option. You can also insert an image by putting the cursor where you want to place the image, opening the Insert, Picture submenu on the menu bar, and selecting From File (see Figure 7.2). Finally, you can use the Insert Picture from File button on the Pictures toolbar. The last two methods are the same function. Both approaches open a standard file browser window from which you select the file you want to insert.

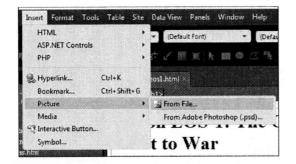

FIGURE 7.2
You can use the Insert Picture from File option on the menu bar to insert an image at the current cursor location.

In Design view, place the cursor at the beginning of the heading in the eos1.html page. Press Enter to create a new line over the heading and then change the new line to the Paragraph style using the Style menu on the Common toolbar. With the cursor in the new line, use one of the two options previously described to open the Insert Picture dialog. Navigate to the Images folder and select the eos1.jpg file you just imported.

Did you Know?

> From time to time, you might notice that recently imported images or files don't show up in the Insert Picture dialog or other file-browsing dialogs within Expression Web 4. To solve this problem, refresh the dialog by right-clicking in the file browser dialog and selecting Refresh or by pressing the F5 key.
>
> The same thing goes for the Folder List panel: After images have been imported properly, they don't always appear in the file list. To refresh the Folder List task pane, click inside it and press the F5 key.

When you click OK, the Accessibility Properties dialog opens, as it did when you inserted the camerasSmall.jpg image in Hour 6. Enter the alternative text **Canon EOS-1** and click OK. At this point, you might think you made a mistake because the Design View pane fills with an image that is a murky gray/brown color, much like Figure 7.3.

What you are seeing is the corner of a large image. This is a common problem: The image is not an appropriate size for the Web; therefore, it doesn't fit on a web page. In fact, the image you just inserted is more than three times as tall as a regular computer screen! If you click the image and look in the Tag Properties task pane at the bottom left, you can see that the image is 3744 pixels high and 5616 pixels wide. A good rule of thumb is that an image in a web page should never be more than 800 pixels at the longest side. Therefore, before you do anything else, you need to drastically reduce the size. To do so, right-click the image, open the Picture Properties dialog, and select the Appearance tab. In the Size section, enable the Keep Aspect Ratio check box and then change the Width setting (the longest side) to 600 pixels (see Figure 7.4). The height changes accordingly.

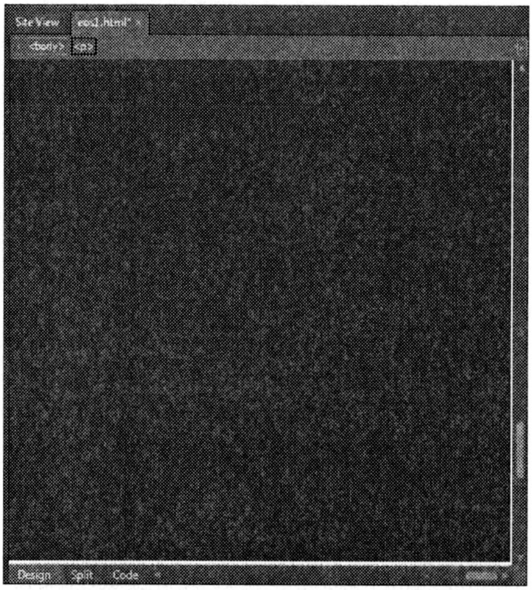

FIGURE 7.3
The page as it appears in Design view after you insert the eos1.jpg image.

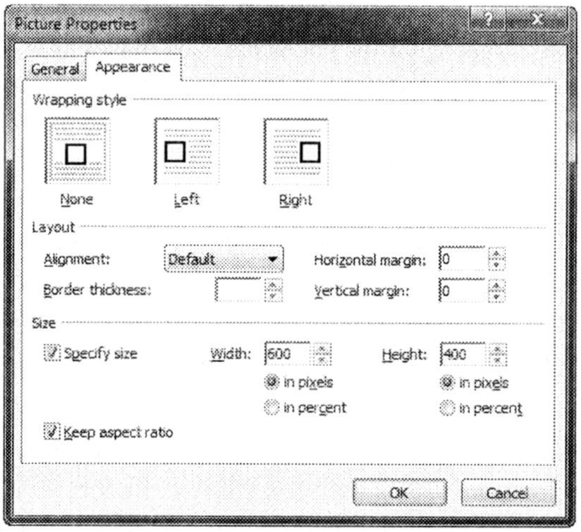

FIGURE 7.4
You can change the image to an exact size from Picture Properties.

When you click OK, Expression Web 4 reduces the image to a workable size. Now, you can alter the image to make it work better within the page. First, I took the image through a mirror so that it is reversed. To turn the image the right way, click the image to select it and then click the Flip Horizontal button on the Pictures toolbar.

The framing of the photo isn't very good and it could use some cropping. With the image still selected, click the Crop button on the Pictures toolbar. This produces a dashed rectangle that indicates the crop area within the image (see Figure 7.5).

Using your mouse, you can either draw a new crop area within the image by clicking and dragging the mouse to create a new rectangle, or simply resize the existing rectangle by grabbing the handles (marked by small squares) in the corners or at the middle of all four sides. Resize the rectangle so that you cut a bit off the top and the left and right sides. When you are satisfied with your crop area, press Enter. Expression Web 4 crops the image.

Now that the image is cropped, it is smaller than it was before. To bring it back to the 600-pixel-wide size, right-click the image, go to the Advanced tab under Picture Properties, and set the width to 600 pixels, just like you did before.

The photo is a little dark. To lighten the image, select it and click the More Brightness button one or two times and bring up the contrast one step by clicking the More Contrast button as well. This brings up the brightness of the image slightly.

If you are not satisfied with your alterations, this is the time to start over. If you want to undo any of your changes or just want some practice, click the Restore button to return the image to its original state. If you click the Restore button by mistake, simply go to the Edit menu and select Undo Edit Picture, or press Ctrl+Z on your keyboard.

One final step is left. You might remember from earlier in the hour that the Resample button becomes active only if you change the size of the image. You might also remember from Hour 6 that you should never make the browser resize your images for you. When you resized the eos1.jpg image earlier in this hour, you asked the browser to squish the large image down to make it fit certain dimensions. You now want to resample the image so that the picture in the image file is of the correct dimensions. You can do this in two ways: Either click the Resample button on the Pictures toolbar, or select Resample Picture to Match Size from the Picture Actions dropdown menu found under the small icon attached to the image (see Figure 7.6).

This function creates a new image file and replaces the old one. To make the changes permanent (also known as The Point of No Return), simply save the page. Expression Web 4 opens the Save Embedded Files dialog and asks you whether, where, and how you want to save the changed image file (see Figure 7.7). Now you can decide whether you want to save the image as a new file or overwrite the old one. If you are sure the image looks the way you want it to look, click OK, and the new image replaces the original one.

FIGURE 7.7
The Save Embedded Files dialog appears every time you make changes to other external files while modifying the page you are currently saving.

Creating a Thumbnail Using Auto Thumbnail

Because most web pages contain a lot of content and not all visitors are on high-speed connections, using smaller versions of images (commonly referred to as *thumb-nails*) that link to the larger versions is common. Using thumbnails helps the page load faster because the browser doesn't have to download large image files. In addition, thumbnails can help designers create manageable layouts because they can link to large images rather than inserting them in the page.

More than just eye candy, images can be used to supplement the text. In this page, a detailed image of some of the damage on the camera seems fitting and lends more reality to the story. A second image called eos1Detail.jpg is in the lesson files. Using the same method as before, import this image and place it in the Images folder. When the image is imported, place your cursor at the beginning of the third para-graph and insert the new image there using one of the three methods previously described in this hour. You now have a page with two images: one on top and one in the body of the text.

However, as you can see, even though the new image is a web-friendly size (600 by 600 pixels), it's much too big and makes the page difficult to read. What you want is a small thumbnail of the eos1Detail.jpg image that links to the bigger version. In Expression Web 4, you can do this with a single-click of your mouse: With the eos1Detail.jpg image selected, click the Auto Thumbnail button on the Pictures tool-bar or use the Ctrl+T shortcut.

This creates a 100-pixels-wide thumbnail with a blue outline that, when clicked, opens the original full-size image in the same window. Because the thumbnail inher-its whatever styling you applied to the original image (and you didn't apply any styling to the image), it appears at the top of the paragraph as part of the first line of text. You can quickly fix this by using the Picture Properties techniques you learned in Hour 6; on the Appearance tab, set the Wrapping Style to Left and Horizontal Margin to 10. When you click OK, the thumbnail places itself nicely to the left with the text wrapping around it, as shown in Figure 7.8.

To finalize this process, it is necessary to save the page. When you save the page, the Save Embedded Files dialog you saw in Figure 7.7 opens and asks you to save a new file called eos1Detail_small.jpg. This is the smaller thumbnail file that Expression Web 4 created and inserted in your page. By default, Expression Web 4 saves the thumbnail in the currently open folder, but you can pick a different folder by clicking the Change Folder button in the dialog. I recommend placing all images in the Images folder and maybe even separating the thumbnails by making a subfolder called Thumbs. Finally, click OK and preview the page in your browser.

▼

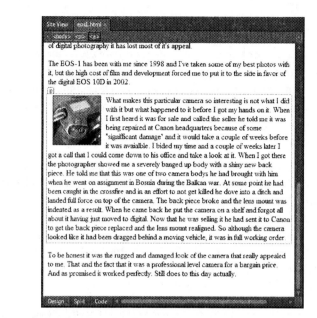

FIGURE 7.8
With the Wrapping Style and margins applied, the thumbnail appears as part of the paragraph.

If you don't want the thumbnail to have a blue border or you want it to be a different size, you can modify the Auto Thumbnail default settings from the Page Editor Options dialog. To do this, open the Page Editor Options dialog from the Tools button on the menu bar and select the Auto Thumbnail tab. From here, you can define the size of the thumbnail by setting the width, height, shortest side, or longest side to a specific pixel length, you can change the thickness of the border around the image (0 for no border), and you can even give the thumbnail a beveled edge.

Watch Out!

Note that changes to the Auto Thumbnail settings apply only to new thumbnails and not to ones that already exist.

Creating Hotspots

A *hotspot* is a defined area or region within an image that has a hyperlink attached to it. There is no limit to how many hotspots with different hyperlinks you can set in a given image. Hotspots are a great tool if you want to provide further information about a certain element within an image or use an image as a navigational tool.

By the Way

Just so there is no confusion: What Expression Web 4 calls a hotspot is more commonly called an *image map*.

Try It Yourself

Create a Hotspot and Link It to a File

In Expression Web 4, you can create and edit hotspots from the Pictures toolbar using the hotspot buttons:

1. In the myCameras.html file, click the camerasSmall.jpg image to activate the Pictures toolbar.

2. Click the Rectangular Hotspot button, and then click and drag the image to draw a rectangle around the top middle camera (see Figure 7.9). This opens the Insert Hyperlink dialog.

FIGURE 7.9
Creating a rectangular hotspot around the top middle camera.

3. In the Insert Hyperlink dialog, find and select the eos1.html page under the Pages folder. Set the ScreenTip to **Learn about the camera that went to war** and set the target frame to New Window. Click OK.

Save the page and preview it in your browser. Note that although the cameras Small.jpg image looks unchanged, if you hover your mouse over the top middle camera, the mouse pointer changes to a hand, indicating a hyperlink, and a Screen-Tip appears. If you click the hotspot, the browser navigates to the eos1.html page.

To edit the hyperlink or ScreenTip attached to the hotspot, simply right-click the hotspot in Design view and select Picture Hotspot Properties. If you want to resize the hotspot, you can do so by clicking it, grabbing the resizing handles on any side of the hotspot, and moving them. You can also reposition the hotspot by clicking and dragging it to a different location within the image.

Hotspots can also be circular or even polygonal. To create a circular hotspot, click the Circular Hotspot button and then draw the circle on the image in the same way you created the rectangle earlier. To create a polygonal hotspot, click the Polygonal Hotspot button and use the mouse to define each corner of the hotspot until you outline the desired area. To finalize a polygonal hotspot, you have to set the last corner point on top of the first one. Doing so opens the Insert Hyperlink dialog.

Because it can be hard to see exactly where all your hotspots are located, the Pictures toolbar features a Highlight Hotspots function. Clicking the Highlight Hotspots button replaces the image with an image map in which the hotspots have black outlines and the remaining image is gray. If you select one of the hotspots, it turns solid black (see Figure 7.10).

FIGURE 7.10
The cameras Small.jpg image with the Highlight Hotspots function.

This tool is only a visual aid and does not affect the image in any way. To close the image map and see the original image, simply click the Highlight Hotspots button again or click anywhere outside the image.

Summary

The ability to make quick alterations to images without having to leave the program is a feature that puts Expression Web 4 above the fold. Not to mention that it can be a real timesaver as long as you think things through and make backups of your image files before changing them. In this hour, you learned how to use the powerful tools in the Pictures toolbar to edit the appearance of images in your page. You saw that the Reset button on the toolbar gives you the ability to experiment with different effects without ruining your files, and that scaling down large photos to make them fit in your page is a relatively simple task.

You also learned how to use the Auto Thumbnail function to make linked thumbnails of your images with one click. Finally, you learned how to set and edit hotspots within an image to create a more interactive and immersive experience for your visitors.

You now have all the tools necessary to create and edit the content of your website. In the next hours, you learn how to style the content to make it more visually pleasing and easier to read.

Q&A

Q. *I imported the image as instructed, and I can see the image in the Folder List panel, but when I open the Insert Picture dialog, I can't find it anywhere.*

A. If you can see the image file in the Folder List panel but it doesn't appear when you browse for it, try right-clicking in the browser window and selecting Refresh. This works 95% of the time. The remaining 5% is usually caused by the image file being corrupt.

Q. *I placed the image in the page, but all I get in Design view is a box with a red X in it.*

A. There could be two reasons for this:

1. The image is not a supported image file or is not in a supported color mode. The most common cause for this problem is that the image is stored as CMYK (cyan, magenta, yellow, kelvin) instead of RGB (red, green, blue). CMYK is the color mode for professional printing and does not translate to screen graphics. To correct this, you need to open the image in an image editor and change the color mode.

2. Expression Web 4 didn't import the image properly. To test whether this is the problem, preview the page in your browser. If the image appears in your browser, it means Expression Web 4 messed up while importing the image and you need to reimport it.

Workshop

The Workshop has quiz questions and exercises to help you put to use what you just learned. If you get stuck, the answers to the quiz questions are in the next section. But try to answer the questions first. Otherwise, you'll be cheating yourself.

Quiz

1. There are three different methods to insert an image into your page. Name them and explain how they are used.

2. Why should you always use the Resample Picture function when resizing an image on a page?

3. How many hotspots can you insert into an image?

Answers

1. To insert an image into a page, you can drag and drop it directly from the Folder View task pane, use the Insert Picture from File function found under Insert on the menu bar, or use the Insert Picture button on the Pictures toolbar.

2. If you insert a large image on a page and resize it using the Picture Properties dialog, you force the browser to resize the image for you. That means that the browser downloads far more image information than it displays. As a rule of thumb, always reduce the amount of information downloaded by the browser to an absolute minimum. That means you need to resample all of your images so that the actual image dimensions match the displayed image dimensions.

3. In theory, there is no limit to how many hotspots an image can contain. In reality, however, the number of hotspots is limited to the number you can fit within the borders of the image. There is not much sense in inserting so many hotspots that the user can't find them or discern one from another.

Exercise

Use the Polygonal Hotspot tool to create hotspots around the different cameras in the photo. Set the hyperlinks to whatever you want; for instance, the camera manufacturer websites. (The cameras are all Canon, Nikon, or Polaroid, except for the huge one in the middle, which is a Hasselblad.) Give the hotspots descriptive ScreenTips and set the hyperlinks to open a new window.

HOUR 8

Cracking the Code: Working in Code View

What You'll Learn in This Hour:

- ▶ How to use IntelliSense to write quick and error-free code
- ▶ What specialized tools are available to you in Code view and how to use them
- ▶ How to use Code view as a learning tool
- ▶ How to dissect code in Split view

Until now, you have worked almost exclusively in Design view using the WYSIWYG (What You See Is What You Get) editor without paying much attention to what goes on behind the scenes. This isn't actually a problem because the code Expression Web 4 creates is clean and tidy enough that you don't need to worry too much about it. However, if you want to get a full understanding of how websites work and move beyond the basics, understanding at least the fundamentals of coding becomes vital. To this end, Expression Web 4 is a great learning tool because it generates standards-based code out of the box.

You might consider Code view the exclusive domain of web developers and code experts, but the tools Expression Web 4 provides make it easy even for a novice to work in Code view. Not only is it helpful to understand the code end of your site when something doesn't work properly, but you might also want to add custom elements into your site that require access to the backend.

HTML5, CSS3, and the Brave New World of Web Code

Since the release of Expression Web 4, the new coding standard HTML5 (including CSS3) has been rolled out and found full support on all major browsers. The HTML5 standard introduced a whole new range of semantic tags as well as new styling options through CSS3. In response to this development, Microsoft released Expression Web 4 SP1 with limited HTML5 support and, later, SP2 with full HTML5 support. In the process, they also changed the default document type from HTML 4 Strict to HTML5. This change has no direct impact on you in following this book. What it does mean is that as you move further into the subject matter and start looking at HTML5, CSS3, jQuery, and other advanced code topics, you will find full support in Expression Web 4 SP2 for these languages to help you in your learning and your web development process.

HTML5 and CSS3 largely fall outside the scope of this reissue, but I will touch on them briefly throughout. If you want to learn more about HTML5, I recommend getting the digital copy of Jeremy Keith's book *HTML5 for Web Designers*, published by A Book Apart:

http://www.abookapart.com/products/html5-for-web-designers

Tools in Code View

As with Design view, Expression Web 4 has an arsenal of tools available to help you work faster and more effectively in Code view. These tools can be found on the Code View toolbar, in the Toolbox panel, and inside Code view itself. We leave the last one—called IntelliSense—to the end of this hour.

Code view has a dedicated toolbar you can open from the Toolbar menu under View on the menu bar (see Figure 8.1). When opened, it docks under the Common toolbar on top of your workspace. If the Pictures toolbar is still open from the last hour, close it from the same menu.

FIGURE 8.1
The Code View toolbar appears directly under the Common toolbar when it is opened.

The Buttons of the Code View Toolbar and What They Do

The Code View toolbar has a set of useful tools that can help you write code or understand what is going on inside your code. In this and the following hours, you use most of them, so you might as well acquaint yourself with them right away.

The **List Members** button tells IntelliSense to provide a shortcut menu for the word or segment your cursor is on. Therefore, if you write <a and click the button, a drop-down menu with all the possible tags starting with the letter *a* appears. The **Parameter Info** button opens a list of the valid script parameters for the same segment. (This applies only to script languages such as JavaScript, ASP.NET, and PHP.) The **Complete Word** button completes the word you type based on an educated (and surprisingly accurate) guess.

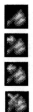

The **Follow Code Hyperlink** button lets you navigate to the destination of the selected hyperlink within Expression Web 4. The **Previous Code Hyperlink** and **Next Code Hyperlink** buttons work in much the same way as the Back and Forward buttons in a browser, taking you back and forth through hyperlinks you have already visited with the Follow Hyperlink button.

The **Function Lookup** box directs you to the function you select from the drop-down list of the available functions (such as JavaScript or PHP) in your document. This box works only if your document contains functions (small programs) that are present in the code. You create and use functions in Hour 16, "Using Code Snippets."

In Code view, Expression Web 4 lets you insert temporary bookmarks that you can use to quickly navigate between segments of your code. The bookmarks appear as small blue boxes on the far left side of the panel next to the line numbers (see Figure 8.2). The **Toggle Bookmark** button inserts a bookmark at the current line of code. The **Next Bookmark** and **Previous Bookmark** buttons navigate between the set bookmarks. The **Clear Bookmarks** button removes all bookmarks from the document.

FIGURE 8.2
A Code View bookmark is a small blue box beside the line numbers.

Code view bookmark

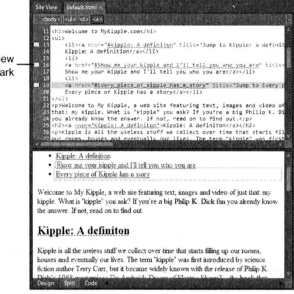

 Based on the current location of the cursor, the **Select Tag** button selects and highlights the active beginning and end tags and the content between them. This tool is helpful to see what content a certain tag affects. The **Find Matching Tag** button finds the beginning tag of the selected content when you first click it and the respective end tag when you click it again. This is an excellent tool if you are confused about where your tags begin or end, and you can use it to clean up code if beginning or end tags are missing.

 The **Select Block** button works the same way as the Select Tag button, except it finds and selects code blocks bracketed by braces rather than tags. The **Find Matching Brace** button works the same way as the Find Matching Tag button, except it looks for braces rather than tags.

The **Insert Start Tag** button inserts an empty start tag at the current location. The **Insert End Tag** button inserts an empty end tag at the current location. You must manually enter the names for these tags.

 New in SP2 are the **Comment** and **Uncomment** buttons. These were added to make it easier to comment out lines or selections. To use the Comment option, either place your cursor on the line of code you want to comment out or highlight the section you want to comment out and click the button or use the keyboard shortcut Ctrl+J. This adds the appropriate comment tags before and after the section. To use the Uncomment option, place your cursor anywhere inside a section that is commented and either click the Uncomment button or use the keyboard shortcut Ctrl+Shift+J. This seemingly simple addition to the Code View toolbar was frequently requested by power users such as myself and can be a huge timesaver, especially if you keep the keyboard shortcuts handy.

The **Insert HTML Comment** button inserts the beginning and end tags for nonfunctional HTML code comments. These comments can be inserted anywhere inside the HTML code. A code comment is text that is visible only in the code itself and has no function other than as a descriptive tool for the developer or anyone else looking at the code. Designers commonly use comments to keep track of changes or explain how or why certain parts of code work.

The **Insert CSS Comment** button inserts the beginning and end tags for nonfunctional CSS code comments. These comments can be inserted anywhere inside the CSS code, typically in a style sheet.

The **Options** button gives you direct access to the code-viewing options that define how code is displayed in Code view. You can also access these options by opening the Page Editor Options from the Tools menu and selecting the General tab. The options (see Figure 8.3) are Word Wrap, which wraps the lines of code to fit inside the window (removing the need to scroll sideways to read all the code); Line Numbers (self-explanatory); Selection Margin, which adds a space between the line numbers and the content so that you can click and drag in the margin with the mouse to select multiple lines of code; Auto Indent, which keeps the indentation from the current line when a new line is created by pressing Enter; Highlight Invalid HTML, which displays invalid HTML code as red font with a yellow background; and Highlight Incompatible HTML, which displays incompatible HTML with a wavy underline like the one commonly used to highlight typos.

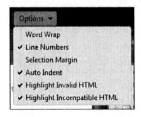

FIGURE 8.3
The Options button on the Code view toolbar gives you quick and direct access to the code-viewing options for controlling how code is displayed in the editor.

The temporary bookmarks in Code view are solely a visual and navigational aid to help in the coding process. They have no actual function in the document itself. These bookmarks should not be confused with HTML bookmarks, which were covered in Hour 5, "Getting Connected with (Hyper)Links: The Cornerstone of the World Wide Web."

Common HTML Tags in the Toolbox

To help in the coding process, Expression Web 4 provides a source of commonly used code through the Toolbox panel (see Figure 8.4). Under HTML, you find commonly used tags, form controls, and media-insertion tools. To use any of these, simply place your cursor where you want to insert the code in Code view and double-click the desired element. You can also drag and drop the elements directly into the code from the panel. If your Toolbox panel is closed, you can access the same commonly used code elements along with all other available elements under Insert on the menu bar.

FIGURE 8.4
The Toolbox task pane provides easy access to the most commonly used HTML tags.

Using Code View as a Learning Tool

More than just a design and development tool, Expression Web 4 is an excellent learning tool for designers and developers of all levels. It's a poorly kept secret that web designers and developers learn from what other people create. By using Design view and Code view, you can do the same no matter what level you are. Web pages are a bit unusual in that after they are published, the code (or blueprint) is available for all to see. That means if you find something you like on a website, you can look at the code to see what is going on and learn from it. In Expression Web 4, you can even open websites from the Internet without downloading them first. All you have to do is click Open from the File menu and insert the URL for the site you want to take a closer look at. When it is open in Split view, you have full access to all the code and other elements that make up the page, and you can see how everything fits together. Just remember that you should never copy code from someone else's page and pass it off as your own. If you use someone else's code, be sure to seek permission and credit them for it.

In the last four hours, you built a website with three pages containing a variety of content. Now you use Code view to answer that burning question: How do the pages really work? For a novice, opening a page in Code view can be intimidating. Fortunately, there is the option of using Split view, so you can see the code and the WYSI-WYG editor at the same time.

To start, open the default.html file in Split view. In Hour 4, "Building a Home Page: A Look Behind the Curtain," you learned that if you click an item in the WYSIWYG editor while in Split view, Expression Web 4 highlights the relevant section of code in Code view. You already know how basic styles such as headings and paragraphs appear in Code view, so let's concentrate on the new elements in the page.

Dissecting Hyperlinks in Code View

In Hour 5, you added several hyperlinks to the page. Now you can use Code view to see how they work. Click the hyperlink with the words "my collection of cameras." This highlights the same text in Code view. When you click the highlighted text in Code view and click the Select Tag button on the Code View toolbar, all the code within this particular tag is highlighted (see Figure 8.5). In this case, that is the hyperlink or <a> tag:

```
<a href="myCameras.html" title="Learn more about my camera collection
  and what I use them for">my collection of cameras</a>
```

FIGURE 8.5
Using the Select
Tag button on
the Code view
toolbar to high-
light the code
within the
selected tag.

Highlighted code

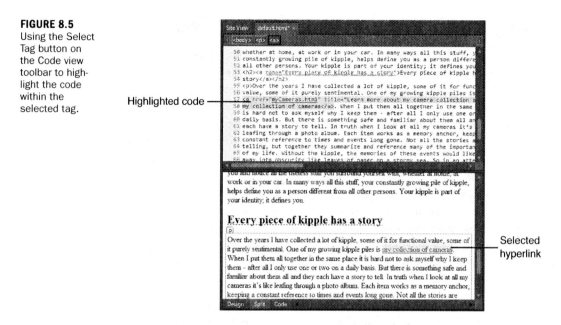

Selected
hyperlink

The highlighted code shows the basic elements of a hyperlink:

▶ The visible hyperlink text is contained between the <a> and </a> tags.

▶ The brackets of the first wrapper contain all the attributes relating to this specific link, separated by spaces. For example, <a attributeOne="attribute
value" attributeTwo="attribute value" attributeThree="attribute
value">.

▶ The destination address is set using the href attribute.

▶ The ScreenTip is set using the title attribute.

HTML, like most code languages, is littered with weird acronyms and abbreviations.
Many of them need to be placed in a historical perspective to make sense. Case in
point is the <a> tag and its href attribute. Although we commonly use the <a> tag to
create links, the original use—from which it gets its name—was actually to refer to
other places within the document through bookmarks that, back then, were referred
to as "anchors." It makes sense if you think about it: You place an anchor at a specific location and then link a chain to it so that you can get there. To this day, some
web-authoring tools still use the iconography of an anchor and a chain to signify
bookmarks and links. The href attribute name harkens back to the same era and
stands for "hypertext reference."

If you look at the code for the link to the book on Amazon.com you created earlier in
the page, you see that an added attribute, named target, is set to _blank:

```
<a href="http://www.amazon.com/Do-Androids-Dream-Electric-Sheep/(...)"
target="_blank" title="Do Androids Dream of Electric Sheep? is available
from Amazon.com">Do Androids Dream of Electric Sheep?</a>
```

This tells the browser that the target of the link (that is, what window it should open in) is a new, empty (blank) window. If no target is set, the link opens in the current window. You can also force the target to be the current window by setting it to _self.

At the bottom of the page, you inserted a hyperlink to open the default email program on the computer:

```
<a href="mailto:kippleinfo@pinkandyellow.com?subject=Email generated from
the MyKipple website"
title="Send all your questions about this site here">send me an email</a>
```

The href attribute in this hyperlink contains a code rather than an address. This code has two sections:

▶ mailto: tells the browser that the following is a recipient email address for insertion into the default email program.

▶ ?subject= tells the browser that the following text is the subject line to insert into the email.

You also created several bookmarks within default.html. They are the headings with the dotted underlines in Design view. If you click one of these headings and look at them in Code view, you see that the <a> tag wraps them, too. However, unlike the hyperlinks, they don't have an href attribute. Instead, they have a name attribute that matches the bookmark name you set in the Bookmark Properties dialog:

```
<h2><a name="Kipple:_A_definition">Kipple: A definition</a></h2>
```

Inspecting the code for the menu items you created at the top of the page, you can see that the name attribute preceded by a # works as the hyperlink address to the bookmarks within the document:

```
<a href="#Kipple:_A_definition" title="Jump to Kipple: A definition">
Kipple: A Definition</a>
```

Hyperlink code can wrap around many elements, not just text. In the eos1.html file, you created a hyperlink attached to an image. To see an example of this, open eos1.html in Split view and click the thumbnail of the detail photo you created using Auto Thumbnail. By highlighting the relevant code using the Select Tag function in Code view, you can see that the only difference between this hyperlink and the previous examples is that an image has replaced the content between the <a> and </a> tags:

```
<a href="../Images/eos1Detail.jpg">
<img alt="Canon EOS-1 detail" class="style1" height="100"
src="../Images/eos1Detail_small.jpg" style="float: left" width="100" />
<!-- MSComment="autothumbnail" xthumbnail-orig-image=
"file:///C:/Users/Morten/Documents/My Web Sites/MyKipple/Images/eos1Detail.jpg"
   -->
</a>
```

Note the commented section, which is shown in gray in Code view. Expression Web 4 inserted this nonfunctional code to explain the origins of the thumbnail. The comment is wrapped inside a special tag that starts with `<!--` and ends with `-->`.

Images in Code View

In Hour 3, "A Website Is Really Just Text: Build One in 5 Minutes," you learned that all web pages are text documents filled with code. But how does that work when it comes to images? When you inserted images into the page, you didn't convert them into code first. And when you click them and inspect them in Code view, all you get is what looks like a hyperlink. So how do images appear in web pages?

The answer is simple: Images in web pages belong to a group of elements known as *replaced elements*. A replaced element is a segment of code that has no content in it, but instead points to external content that the browser displays in its place. So when you insert an image into your web page in Design view, you are inserting a small piece of code that tells the browser to find a specific image file, insert it in place of the code, and apply a set of attributes to it.

Select the camera detail thumbnail in Design view and look at the section of code highlighted in Code view:

```
<img alt="Canon EOS-1 detail" class="style1" height="100"
 src="../Images/eos1Detail_small.jpg" style="float: left" width="100" />
```

Unlike the tags you saw earlier, the `<img>` tag doesn't have a corresponding `</img>` tag but rather ends with `/>`, telling the browser that it is closed. This makes sense because, as you previously saw, any text content between a beginning and an end tag is visible in the browser, but there is no such content in the case of an image. Within the tag, you find all the information you inserted using the Picture Properties dialog: The `alt` attribute defines the alternative text; the `height` and `width` attributes define the height and width; and the `src` attribute defines the location of the external image file. The remaining attributes, `class` and `style`, are explained in future hours.

When the page opens in a browser, the browser reads the information in the image tag and performs the necessary replacements: In this place, insert the eos1Detail_small.jpg image, located under the Images folder, with the alternative text **Canon EOS-1 detail** and a height of 100 pixels. The image belongs to style class style1 and should float to the left with the adjoining text flowing around it to the right.

Other replaced elements include, among other things, Silverlight applications and Adobe Flash movies (.swf files), both covered in Hour 20, "Working with Flash and Other Embeddable Content."

Unordered and Ordered Lists in Code View

Working with lists in Design view can get complicated, especially if you have lists within lists. Fortunately, lists have an organized code structure that makes Code view ideal for advanced list editing.

As you learned in Hour 4, there are two types of lists. Unordered lists, signified by the <ul> tag, are what we usually refer to as bullet lists. When the browser finds a <ul> tag, it assumes that each list item should have a bullet in front of it unless otherwise specified. Ordered lists, signified by the <ol> tag, are what we usually refer to as numbered lists. When the browser finds an <ol> tag, it assumes that each list item should have a consecutively higher number in front of it than the previous one.

The items in ordered and unordered lists are usually prefixed by either a number or a bullet, but in many cases, these elements don't work well with your design. In Hour 13, "Getting Visual, Part 3: Images as Design Elements with CSS," you learn how to turn the numbers and bullets on and off or swap them for image files using CSS.

The HTML list structure, regardless of whether it is an unordered or an ordered list, is simple. It starts with the <ul> or <ol> tag, telling the browser what kind of list it is, and then wraps each list item between <li> and </li> tags. The end of the list is indicated by the closing </ul> or </ol> tag. The structure looks like this:

```
<ul>
    <li>First List Item</li>
    <li>Second List Item</li>
    <li>Third List Item</li>
</ul>
```

To change this list from an unordered list to an ordered list, all you need to do is change the <ul> and </ul> tags to <ol> and </ol>.

You can build lists within lists just as easily. The following is an unordered list with three list items in which the second one is an ordered list with three subitems:

```
<ul>
        <li>First List Item</li>
        <li>
            <ol>
                <li>First Sub List Item</li>
                <li>Second Sub List Item</li>
                <li>Third Sub List Item</li>
            </ol>
        </li>
        <li>Third List Item</li>
</ul>
```

▼   **Try It Yourself**

Introducing IntelliSense—Your New Best Friend

Joining the Code view toolbar and the Toolbox panel on the list of tools to help you navigate and write code in Expression Web 4 is IntelliSense. In my view, IntelliSense is one of the most powerful and helpful tools in the application, and I am certain that when you see how it works, you will agree with me. And with the addition of HTML5, CSS3, JavaScript, and even jQuery script support, it is now, in my opinion, the most powerful IntelliSense offering available. In short, IntelliSense is a tool that helps you write proper code faster. The best way to understand exactly what it does is to see it in action. In this example, you insert an image in Code view with the help of IntelliSense:

1. With the myCameras.html file open in Split view, find the second paragraph wrapped by <p> tags. Place the cursor next to the <p> tag before the text.

2. Still in Code view, type a "less-than" bracket: <. A drop-down menu appears below the bracket—this is IntelliSense presenting you with all the available code snippets that start with a less-than bracket. You are inserting an image, so you want the img tag. To find this, enter an i and IntelliSense brings up all the available tags that start with <i (see Figure 8.6). Use the arrow keys to skip down to <img and press Enter to insert the <img tag.

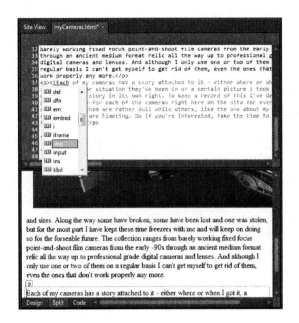

FIGURE 8.6
IntelliSense pops up in Code view to suggest possible code segments you could insert.

3. You need a source for your image. Press the spacebar and IntelliSense pops up with new options. This time, it gives you only available attributes for the img tag. As you previously learned, the image location is set with the src attribute, so type s to narrow the search. IntelliSense takes you straight to src, and all you need to do is press the Enter key.

4. Because the src attribute requires a URL (uniform resource locator), IntelliSense inserts the necessary code and asks you for the location of the image. Click the Pick URL button, shown in Figure 8.7, and navigate to the desired file (in this case, eos1Detail_small.jpg, located under the Images folder).

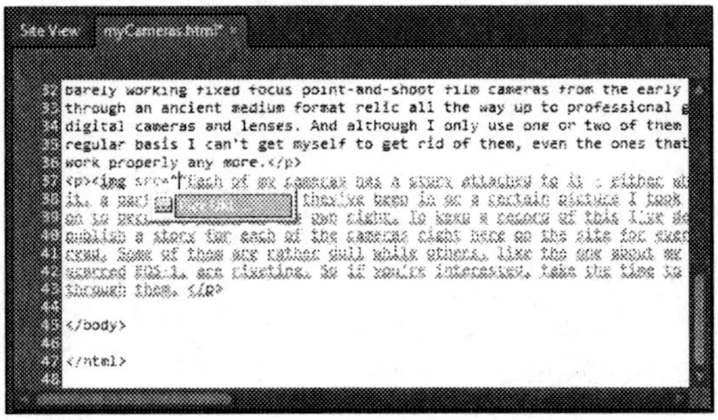

FIGURE 8.7
IntelliSense finishes the code and provides a button to open a browser to select a URL for the image.

5. Before you close the tag, remember to add the alternative text using the `alt` attribute. This is done by following the same steps you used previously, but starting with the letter **a**. If you want to, you can add more attributes to your image using IntelliSense.

6. To close the img tag, simply type `/>`. The final code looks like this:

```
<img src="Images/eos1Detail_small.jpg" alt="Another thumbnail" />
```

If you click outside the active text or accidentally press Backspace, IntelliSense closes. To open it again, use the Ctrl+L shortcut.

IntelliSense helps you write a number of different code languages, including HTML, CSS, PHP, JavaScript, ASP.NET, and even Visual Basic. More important, it keeps tabs on your code to prevent you from making errors. For instance, if you insert a beginning tag, IntelliSense automatically inserts a matching end tag. The same goes for braces and quotes. The code output of IntelliSense matches the code settings for the current document. The status bar at the bottom of the work area tells you what code language and version you are working in. If you want to change the IntelliSense settings, open the Page Editor Options under Tools on the menu bar and select the IntelliSense tab.

You will be introduced to CSS in Hour 10, "Bringing Style to Substance with Cascading Style Sheets," and PHP in Hour 21, "Beyond the Basics, Part 1: PHP in Expression Web 4."

Summary

Understanding the code that makes up a web page can greatly enhance your ability to create professional-looking and functional sites for yourself and your clients. Expression Web 4's Code view is an excellent tool not only to write flawless and standards-compliant code but also to understand and learn how this code works. With its arsenal of tools, such as IntelliSense, the program keeps tabs on what you are doing and makes sure your code remains valid by inserting all the necessary little extra pieces. It's like having an assistant that looks over your shoulder and makes subtle changes and additions as you work.

In this hour, you learned how to use Code view and Split view to get a better understanding of how the code works. You got an introduction to the many tools for use in Code view, such as the Code View toolbar, IntelliSense, and the Toolbox task pane. You learned how to use those tools and their functions to make quick and error-free changes and additions to your page.

You used Split view to learn a great deal about HTML semantics; that is, how the HTML language is put together. Using the Code view tools, you inspected and altered hyperlinks and images, and by doing so you learned how these code elements work to produce the desired output.

In the upcoming hours, you use both Code view and Design view to continue building the MyKipple website. That way, you learn not only how the code works but also why it's better to handle some tasks in the backend rather than in the frontend.

Q&A

Q. *Why doesn't the* `<img>` *tag close with a separate* `</img>` *tag like the other tags I have used?*

A. Unlike the other tags you have learned about, the `<img>` tag does not affect any visible text but works instead as a replaced element. Any text contained between two tags is visible in the browser. The way you closed the `<img>` tag by simply ending it with `/>` is a shorthand version of the tag code. Ending the tag by closing the beginning tag and following it directly with an end tag produces the same results:

```
<img src="Images/eos1Detail_small.jpg" alt="Another thumbnail"></img>
```

Q. *When I insert new code into Code view, other segments of code turn red or are highlighted in yellow. Why is that?*

A. While you are inserting new code in Code view, you often temporarily break the code. When this happens, Expression Web 4 immediately highlights the incorrect code to tell you something is wrong. You'll note that when you break the code, only small segments of code are actually highlighted. Usually these are beginning or end tags. This is because Expression Web 4 tracks the source of the error rather than highlighting the affected area. This makes it easier to clear out any mistakes quickly. On a side note, this function is excellent for debugging websites other developers and designers have created because any errors pop out immediately upon opening them in Code view and can be easily remedied.

Q. *There are all these strange code snippets in my text in Code view, such as* `&quot;` *and* `&#39;`*. What do they mean?*

A. If you look closely at the code, you see that it is full of symbols you would often use in text—symbols such as quotation marks, ampersands, apostrophes, and so forth. These symbols are functional code elements, and if they appear as themselves in the code, the browser interprets them as code rather than text elements. To avoid this, all special characters displayed in the text are assigned HTML entities; that is, alternative snippets of code that tell the browser which symbol to insert. The most common entities are " (for a quotation mark), & (for an ampersand), ' (for an apostrophe), © (for the copyright symbol), and   (for a nonbreaking space; used in the same way you would normally press the spacebar if you want to insert an empty paragraph or an empty space). If you don't know the HTML entry for a particular symbol, the easiest way to find it is to simply type in the symbol in Design view to see what it produces in Code view. You can find complete lists of all available HTML entries by searching for HTML entries on the W3C (World Wide Web Consortium) website at www.w3.org.

Workshop

The Workshop has quiz questions and exercises to help you put to use what you just learned. If you get stuck, the answers to the quiz questions are in the next section. But try to answer them first. Otherwise, you'll be cheating yourself.

Quiz

1. How do you find out what tag is affecting a particular portion of the content of your page?

2. In this hour, you were introduced to two tools that help you write code. What are they and how do you use them?

Answers

1. To find the relevant tags for your content, place the cursor anywhere within the content in question in Code view and click the Select Tag button on the Code view toolbar. Doing so highlights the current tags and all content within them.

2. Two code-writing tools were introduced in this hour: IntelliSense and the Toolbox task pane. IntelliSense helps you write proper code by constantly suggesting the closest matching code snippets when you write them and giving you ScreenTips about what elements this code needs to include to work properly. The Toolbox task pane provides you with drag-and-drop HTML elements for easy insertion into your document.

Exercise

With the help of IntelliSense, use only Code view (not Split view) to insert the eos1Detail_small.jpg file in the default.html page. Locate the reference to the movie *Blade Runner* in the same page, and use Code view to link the text to the IMDB.com entry for the movie. Remember that the active visual link text must be between the <a> and the </a> tags. If you are uncertain about the syntax, look at the code for the other links on the page.

Getting Boxed In, Part 1: Using Tables for Tabular Content

What You'll Learn in This Hour:

- ▶ How to create a table from scratch
- ▶ How to change the appearance of a table
- ▶ How to use the Tables toolbar to work with tables
- ▶ How to use table and cell properties to change the appearance of tables
- ▶ How to use AutoFormat to quickly change the appearance of your tables

So far, you have learned about simple text elements, such as the headings, paragraphs, blockquotes, lists, and links. But these let you display your content in only a linear manner. What do you do if you want to introduce more structured content into your web page or control the position or relation between certain content? In many cases, the answer is tables. Just like in a word-processing application, Hypertext Markup Language (HTML) tables can display content in a well-organized and structured way. And they work in much the same way as the other text elements, too.

Tables are composed of cells organized in rows (horizontal lines) and columns (vertical lines) just like a spreadsheet. You can style each element inside the table to achieve the desired look and feel. You can control the color, size, and appearance of the borders, cells, rows, and columns. Thus, when used correctly, tables can greatly enhance the experience for the visitor by making your content more visually appealing and meaningful.

One-Minute History of Tables in Web Pages

When HTML originated in the 1980s, it was as a simple standardized markup language for use by physicists to share research data and results on the Web in an easy and manageable way. Much of the data was contained in tables, so tables became an important addition to HTML. However, as designers, developers, and the public started to see the potential in HTML and the World Wide Web, the content made available quickly moved beyond simple text documents with a few images and some tables to more advanced designs with background graphics, menus, and advanced interactivity. As the demands of the new users expanded, so did the capabilities of the markup language. As a result, what began as a simple way to communicate text content grew into a hugely complicated code set with heavy focus on the visual aspects of presentation rather than on the content.

One of the big elements of this development was the use of tables as a layout tool. If you have ever tried to make content look nice in a word-processing application, you know you can use tables to make backgrounds, separate text, and insert other eye candy. This quickly became the standard for web design at the cost of legibility: Nonessential information, such as layout and design code, cluttered the simple HTML markup.

To solve this problem, a new language, called Cascading Style Sheets (CSS), developed. The idea behind CSS was to separate the HTML code from all the styling and layout code and return it to its intended use as a markup language. As CSS became more prevalent, the standard-setting body of the Internet weeded out or deprecated the styling elements that had made their way into HTML.

The idea behind standards-based code, which is what you make by using Expression Web 4, is to return HTML to its intended use as a markup language and separate it from the styling. In other words, tables are to display tabular data and nothing else. For example, rather than making a menu consisting of a series of table cells with graphic buttons inside, you make a menu using an unordered list styled using CSS. (You learn how to make such a menu in Hour 17, "Building a Functional Menu.")

There is an ongoing battle within the design and development community over the use of tables as design elements. I stand firmly on the side of standards-based code and CSS, and only briefly touch on how to use tables as a layout tool. That's not to say doing so is wrong—you are free to design using tables if you choose. However, you will not learn how to do so here. With that said, it's time to make tables!

Creating a Table from Scratch

The most common use of tables is to display some form of statistical data in which each item has several variables. Good examples of tables are address lists with name, address, phone number, and email address as variables; archives of your books, music, or movies; or purely statistical data, such as temperature variances and financial data. In truth, a table can display any type of information that needs some form of structure.

In this lesson, you create a table based on the photo of all the cameras. In that table, you list their variables. The following steps show you how to create a table in Design view:

1. Open the myCameras.html file in Design view. Scroll to the bottom and make a new h2 subheading with the text **Camera Inventory**.

2. Make a new paragraph under the heading and click the Insert Table button on the Common toolbar. This opens a drop-down panel consisting of empty boxes (see Figure 9.1). By sliding your mouse over the boxes, you can highlight the number of rows and columns you want. In this example, you want 12 rows and 5 columns. Because the drop-down panel allows only for tables up to 6 rows and 7 columns, you need to click the More Options button to open the Insert Table dialog and set the rows and columns manually. We cover this dialog in more detail later. For now, just set Rows to 12 and Columns to 5, and click OK.

FIGURE 9.1
Use the Insert Table button on the Common toolbar to easily create tables with different row and column configurations.

You now have a 12-by-5 table in your page. By default, HTML tables are invisible, meaning they have no color and no borders. They simply separate the content within them, as indicated by the dotted lines.

You can control how tables appear in your page by using the functions found under Table on the menu bar or by right-clicking the table and accessing the options from there. However, the easiest way to edit your tables is by using the Tables toolbar found under View, Toolbars. If you haven't already done so, close the Code View toolbar from Hour 8, "Cracking the Code: Working in Code View," and open the Tables toolbar (see Figure 9.2). It docks underneath the Common toolbar.

FIGURE 9.2
The Tables tool-
bar contains
most of the tools
you need to edit
your table.

Before going any further, the table needs some content. The five columns represent the five values Camera Name, Camera Type, Recording Medium, Lens Type, and Year of Purchase. To insert the table headings for these titles into the first row, select the upper-left corner cell by clicking inside it and start typing. As you write, the cells expand to the right. This is because the cell width and height in a default table is set to auto so that it conforms to whatever content you insert. To move to the next cell, press the Tab key on your keyboard, click the next cell with the mouse, or use the arrow keys. Fill in the next two headlines.

To save you the time of filling in the rest of the table, I created a version of the lesson file completed to this point that you can install directly from the lesson files for this hour. Simply close the myCameras.html file, import the new myCameras.html file from the lesson files, overwrite the old one, and open the new file.

Changing the Appearance of a Table

When you create a table from scratch, it is set to default. That means all the text in the cells aligns to the left and centers in the vertical space and that all the text looks the same. With the tools built into Expression Web 4, you can easily change these settings to change the look of your tables.

Creating Table Headings

The first row of your table contains the headings that explain the content below. The markup should reflect this by using the <th> (table heading) tags for the cells instead of the regular <td> (table data) tags. You can do this either manually in Code View or by using the Quick Tag Editor. When the table heading tag is applied, the text appears centered in the cell and the font is bold.

If you don't like this appearance and want to change the heading row, you first need to select all the cells in the row. You can do this in two ways: Click and hold inside the first cell and drag your mouse over the four others. When the mouse pointer is out of the first cell, it changes to a + sign indicating that you are selecting more than one cell. You can use this technique to select groups of cells from rows, columns, or both. Alternatively, you can right-click any of the cells in the row and click Select, Row (see Figure 9.3).

With the row selected, you can change the appearance of the entire row of table headings. For example, you can change the background color of the cells by clicking the Fill Color button on the Tables toolbar and selecting a new color (see Figure 9.4).

FIGURE 9.4
The Fill Color button on the Tables Toolbar lets you pick the background color for the cells selected from a selection of pre-defined colors or with a color picker.

Changing the Vertical Alignment of Cell Content

By default, all the content in a table centers vertically in the cells. This looks strange when some cells have one line of text and others have several. To change the vertical alignment of the cells, select the remaining cells using the click-and-hold technique and click the **Align Top** button on the Tables toolbar. You can choose to align text to the top, center, or bottom of the cells.

Adding Rows and Columns to the Table

 When you create a table, you often find that you need to add more rows or columns. If you want to add one or two, the quickest way is to use the Tables toolbar. To add a new row below the last row of your table, select any of the bottom cells and click the **Row Below** button on the Tables toolbar. You can also add a row above the selected row by clicking the **Row Above** button. To add a column, you click either the **Column to the Left** or **Column to the Right** button.

If you want to add several rows or columns, select the cell in which you want to create new rows or columns next to and choose Table, Insert, Rows and Columns from the menu bar, or right-click and select Insert, Rows and Columns from the context menu. This opens the Insert Rows or Columns dialog, where you can set how many rows or columns you want and whether to insert them above, below, to the left, or to the right of your selection (see Figure 9.5).

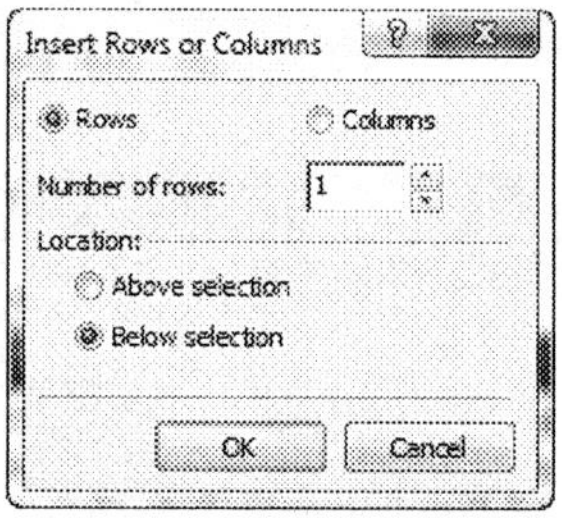

FIGURE 9.5
The Insert Rows or Columns dialog lets you insert multiple rows or columns in your table.

Merging and Splitting Cells

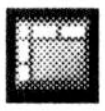

Sometimes it is necessary to merge cells to display certain types of content within the table. Let's say you want to insert a subheading in the table to go underneath the heading and across the whole table. If you simply insert a new row underneath the heading, you still have five columns to work with when you need only one. To insert a subheading in your table, first insert a new row underneath the heading using the Row Below button. Note that if you chose a fill color for the heading row, the styling (color) is automatically copied down to the new row. After inserting the new row, select all the cells in that row and click the **Merge Cells** button on the Tables toolbar. Doing so merges the five cells into one. Now, you can insert a subheading that goes across the entire table.

Likewise, you can split a cell into several new rows or columns using the **Split Cell** button. After you select a cell and click the button, Expression Web 4 asks how many rows or columns you want to create within that cell.

Did you Know?

You can also merge and split cells by highlighting them, right-clicking, and selecting Modify and Merge Cells or Split Cells from the pop-up menu.

Deleting Cells, Rows, and Columns from the Table

Now that you know how to add rows and columns to a table, you need to know how to remove them. To delete a cell, right-click the cell and select Delete, Cell from the context menu or click the **Delete Cells** button on the Tables toolbar. Both actions delete the cell in question, and the remaining cells shift to the left to accommodate the deletion. Deleting a cell leaves an empty space filled with the background color.

To delete a row or column, right-click inside a cell on the row or column you want to delete and then select Delete, Row or Column or select all the cells in the row or column you want to delete and click the Delete Cells button on the Tables toolbar. Expression Web 4 deletes the row or column, and the remaining rows or columns realign themselves to fill the void.

Watch Out!

If you delete a cell, row, or column, you also delete all the content within it.

To delete an entire table, you can right-click anywhere inside the table and select Delete Table; Expression Web 4 deletes the table.

Changing Row and Column Sizes

When you first entered text into the cells in your table, you noticed that the width of the columns changed accordingly. The same thing happened with the height of the rows when you entered several lines of text in one of the cells. This is because both row height and column width are set to AutoFit by default. In most cases, you want to manually control the height and width of your rows and columns to achieve a certain look. You can do this in several ways.

The first method uses the **Distribute Rows Evenly** and **Distribute Columns Evenly** buttons on the Tables toolbar to make changes to the whole table. To use one of these buttons, simply place your cursor anywhere inside the table and click the button. The program gives the rows or columns an even distribution based on their content and gives them a fixed height or width. To revert to AutoFit, simply click the **AutoFit to Contents** button.

The second method is a more direct approach in which you manually set the width and height of each row or column by grabbing the margins of the table cells by clicking and holding them with the mouse and pulling them up, down, left, or right. When you let go, the width and height are permanent just like in the first method, but they are now set to your specifications rather than evenly distributed.

You can also use the second method to resize the entire table. By default, the table width setting is 100% so that the table fills whatever area it is in (no area is yet defined, so the table fills the entire width of the screen), but you can change this by grabbing the sides of the table and resizing it.

By the Way

> The table's content defines the minimum size of a table and its cells. In other words, a cell cannot be smaller than the size of what is inside it. For example, a cell with three lines of text cannot be the height of a cell with two lines of text. Even if you set the height in pixels to be smaller, the cell remains tall enough to fit its contents. And because rows are the height of the largest cell, the content of the largest cell, not the pixel value, decides how tall each row will be. The same goes for the table as a whole. You cannot make the table smaller than the size of its contents no matter how hard you try. This is one reason why tables are not ideal as layout tools.

Using Table Properties to Change the Appearance of Your Table

If you want to make changes to the size or appearance of the entire table, you need to open Table Properties by right-clicking anywhere inside the table and selecting Table Properties or selecting Table, Table Properties on the menu bar. From here, you can change all the main aspects of your table (see Figure 9.6).

The Size setting lets you define how many rows and columns the table should have. The Layout setting sets the `alignment` and `float` of the entire table in relation to the page, the width and height of the table in pixels or percentages, and the cell padding and cell spacing.

Cell padding is the space between the walls of the cell and the content within it (see Figure 9.7). Cell padding of 0 pixels means that the content of the cell is touching the four walls, whereas cell padding of 5 pixels leaves an empty 5-pixel "buffer zone" between the walls and the content. Cell spacing, as shown in Figure 9.8, is the space between the cells that separate them from each other. Cell spacing of 0 pixels means that the cells touch each other, whereas cell spacing of 5 pixels means there is a 5-pixel gap between each cell. Cell spacing is especially useful if you want to create a table with clearly defined borders between the cells because the cell spacing area is transparent and shows the background color of the table.

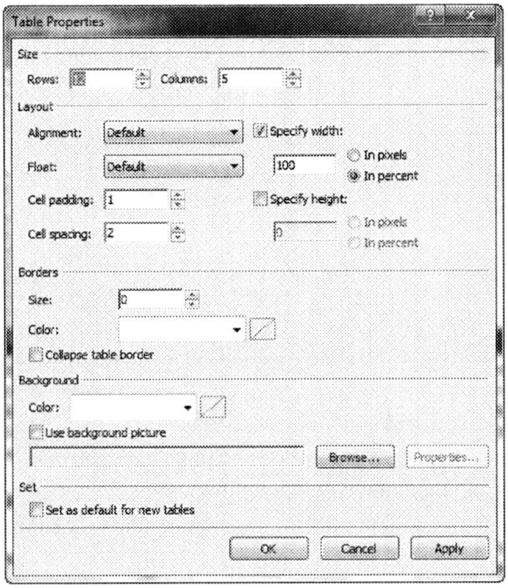

FIGURE 9.6
From the Table Properties dialog, you can make changes to the table as a whole.

The alignment and float attributes serve the same purpose: to place the table on the left or right side of the page. The alignment (or align) attribute is deprecated and is replaced by the CSS float attribute. Therefore, I recommended that you use float to align your table.

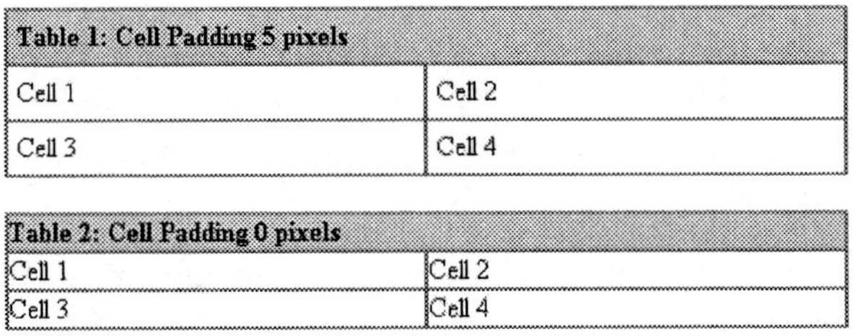

Watch Out!

FIGURE 9.7
Other than the use of cell padding, these two tables are the same. The cells have a white background color, and the tables have a gray background color.

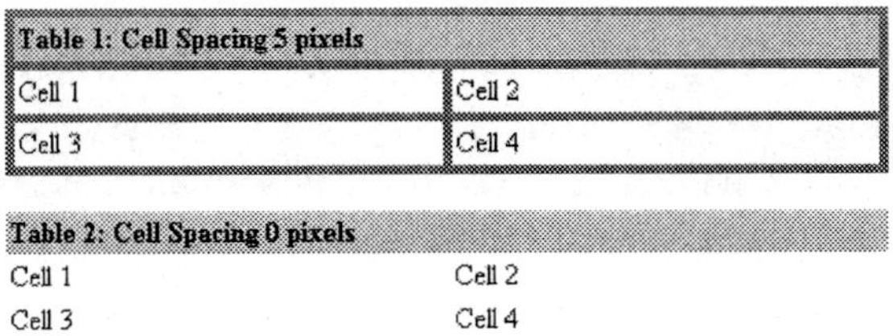

FIGURE 9.8
The cells in these two tables use different values for cell spacing. The cells have a white background color and the tables have a gray background color.

The Borders setting values define the thickness and color of the border of the table. The border is a box that surrounds the entire table (see Figure 9.9). By default, the border is invisible (0 pixels). Depending on the settings, the border can be unique in that it has a 3D look to it: The top and left sides are slightly lighter in color than the bottom and right sides. The Collapse Table Border check box changes the relationship between the table border and the outer cell spacing.

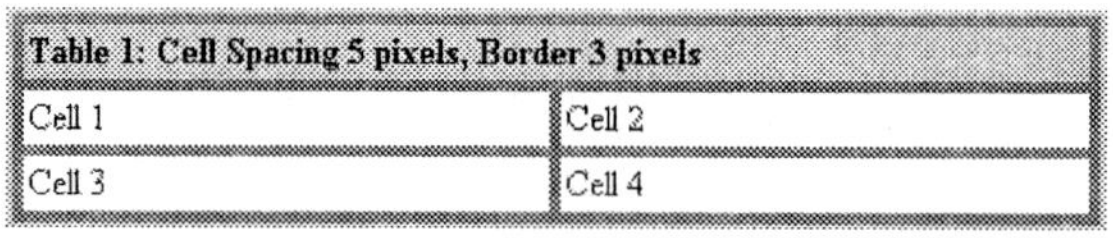

FIGURE 9.9
Borders in real life: Table 1 as it appears in Figure 9.8 but with the addition of a 3-pixel border that wraps around the outside of the table.

Table 1: Cell Spacing 5 pixels, Border 3 pixels	
Cell 1	Cell 2
Cell 3	Cell 4

The Background setting indicates the background color or background image of the table. By default, tables are transparent, and the background color or image shines through. If you define the color of a cell or group of cells, they will no longer be transparent. To make a table with white cells and blue lines around each cell, set the table background color to blue and the cell background color to white. The cell spacing remains transparent and lets the blue color shine through, and the white cells block the background color.

The Set value lets you define the current table layout as the default layout for future inserted tables.

Using Cell Properties to Change the Appearance of Your Cells

You can also change the appearance of a single cell, or group of cells, in a table by highlighting the cell and selecting Cell Properties from the context menu or choosing Table, Cell Properties on the menu bar. This opens the Cell Properties dialog, as shown in Figure 9.10.

From here, you can change the layout, borders, and background of each cell or a group of cells. The Borders and Background settings work in much the same way as in the Table Properties dialog, but there is some new functionality in Layout.

The Horizontal and Vertical Alignment settings define where the content appears within the cell. Horizontal Alignment works just like alignment in a word processor (left, right, center, justified), and Vertical Alignment defines whether the content within the cell should be positioned on the top, middle, or bottom of the cell.

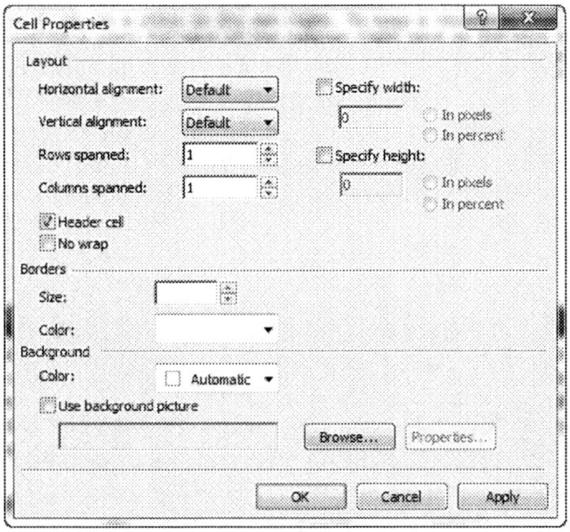

FIGURE 9.10
The Cell Properties dialog lets you control the appearance of individual cells or groups of cells independently of the other cells in the table.

The Rows Spanned and Columns Spanned settings change the layout of the table by letting the cells span more than one row or column. If you let one cell span two rows, the displaced cells in the row below shift to the right to make room. As a result, the rightmost cell protrudes from the right side of the table. If you let one cell span two columns, the remaining cells in the row shift to the right, and the leftmost cell protrudes from the right side of the table. These functions can easily make your table very confusing, so use them with care.

The Specify Width and Specify Height settings give you the ability to specify the width or height of the selected row or column in pixels or percentages. The effect is the same as when you used the mouse to drag the width and height of the rows and columns but is more precise because you set the values manually.

The Header Cell setting changes the content of the cells to center-aligned and bold, as is normal in table headers. The name Header Cell is a bit misleading because you can apply the effect to any cell in a table, not just the header. The true purpose of a Header Cell is that in the markup the tag changes from <td> to <th>, which identifies it as a header for styling and accessibility purposes.

The No Wrap attribute tells the cell not to split lines even if they don't fit within the cell. If No Wrap is checked, lines of text that are too long to fit on one line do not continue on the next line but instead hide behind the next cell.

When you insert content in a HTML page, the order of the elements applied to that content matters; the closer an element is to the actual content, the more important it is. In practical terms, this means that the *cell properties* are more important and take priority over the *table properties* because they are closer to the *cell content*. You will meet this principle, referred to as the *cascade*, again when you are introduced to CSS in Hour 10, "Bringing Style to Substance with Cascading Style Sheets."

Using AutoFormat to Quickly Change the Look of Your Tables

Making tables more interesting to look at can be an arduous task. To help ease the workload, Expression Web 4 has a long list of prepackaged table layouts at your disposal through the AutoFormat option. To apply one of these layouts, all you have to do is select the table you want to change and click the **Table AutoFormat** button or the **AutoFormat Combo** drop-down menu on the Tables toolbar. Clicking the AutoFormat button opens the Table Auto-Format dialog, as shown in Figure 9.11.

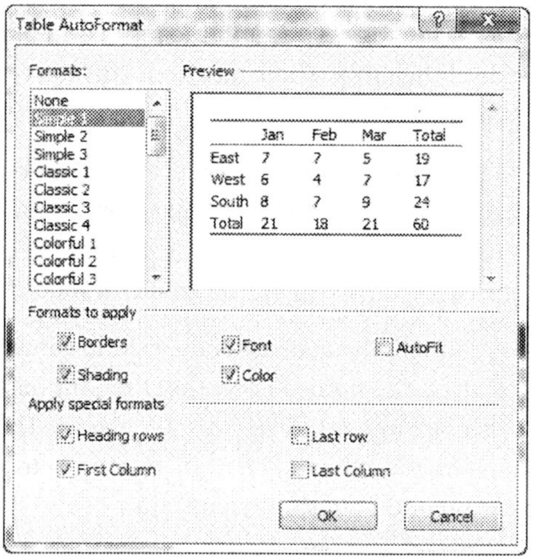

FIGURE 9.11
Use the Table AutoFormat dialog to make your tables look great with a few mouse clicks.

From here, you can preview the various layouts available and make changes to them using the check boxes. All these table layouts are different, and the check boxes affect them in different ways depending on the layout, so it's a good idea to experiment to get that perfect look. When you are satisfied with what you see in the preview, click OK, and Expression Web 4 applies the AutoFormat. If it is not what you want, simply press Ctrl+Z or select Edit, Undo from the menu bar and try again.

If you already know what Table AutoFormat you want, you can select it from the Table AutoFormat Combo drop-down menu on the Tables toolbar. This bypasses the Table AutoFormat dialog and applies the AutoFormat directly.

Table AutoFormat creates a series of different CSS styles and applies them to the table. To change the final look of your table, you need to change these styles. In upcoming hours, you learn how to modify existing styles and create new ones from scratch.

Summary

Tables are an integral part of web design, both as a tool to display data and as a means to create layouts. In recent years, designers and developers have moved away from using tables as a design tool and started using them exclusively for their intended purpose: to display tabular data.

In this hour, you learned how to create tables and how to modify their appearance using the many tools available in Expression Web 4. You learned how to change the sizes of tables and cells, how to add and remove cells, and how to change the background color of both the table as a whole and individual or groups of cells.

In upcoming hours, you learn how to create page layouts without using tables, and how to use CSS to style your tables to create layouts like the ones you applied with AutoFormat.

Q&A

Q. It seems cumbersome to first insert a table and then set all the properties. Is there a way to perform both actions at once?

A. Yes, there is. If you place your cursor where you want the table to appear and select Table, Insert Table from the menu bar, an Insert Table dialog opens with the same options as the Table Properties dialog. Using this function lets you set the table properties before inserting the table.

Q. You said that the `align` attribute is deprecated and that I should use the `float` attribute instead. But `float` has only an option for left and right and no center. What do I do if I want to center my table on the page?

A. In the coming hours, you dive headfirst into the world of Cascading Style Sheets. The idea behind CSS is to move all styling elements out of the main body of the page and into their own section. This applies as much to tables as anything else. In fact, most of the styling you did in this hour was CSS, although you didn't know it. In the next hours, you learn how to control the styling of your document, and an important part of this is to learn how to position and align content on the page. If you are in a hurry and want to get your table centered right away, go to Hour 11, "Getting Boxed In, Part 2: Knee Deep in CSS," and read about centering an image using CSS.

Q. *Even though I grabbed the edge of my table and made it smaller, it still appears larger when I preview the page in my browser. What am I doing wrong?*

A. By default, the table width setting is 100%. When you change the width by dragging it in Design view, you are not changing it to a pixel width but changing the percentage width. If you want your table to be a set or fixed width, you need to go to the Table Properties dialog and change the width from percent to pixels. Keep in mind that 100 or fewer pixels is a very small size, so you need to change the pixel size to something larger. After you change the size of pixels in the Table Properties dialog, you can resize the table in Design view, and the size stays the same when you preview the page in your browser.

Workshop

The Workshop has quiz questions and exercises to help you put to use what you just learned. If you get stuck, the answers to the quiz questions are in the next section. But try to answer them first. Otherwise, you'll be cheating yourself.

Quiz

1. There are three different methods for changing the height and width of rows and columns. Name them.

2. What is the difference between cell padding and cell spacing?

Answers

1. To change the height and width of rows and columns, you can use the Distribute Rows and Columns buttons on the Tables toolbar; resize the rows and columns manually by clicking and dragging the dividing lines; or use cell properties to change the height or width of individual cells by entering the desired value in pixels or percentages.

2. Cell padding is the space between the cell walls and the content within the cell. Cell spacing is the space between the cells.

Exercise

Add more rows and columns to the table and insert new content. Change the background color of the table and set the color of the cells to white. Make the table 600 pixels wide, and change the column widths so that the first and last columns are smaller than the middle one. Use the Table AutoFormat function to restyle the table so that the rows have alternating colors.

Bringing Style to Substance with Cascading Style Sheets

What You'll Learn in This Hour:

▶ What Cascading Style Sheets are

▶ How to create new styles from scratch

▶ How to modify existing styles using the style tools

▶ How to use styles to change the appearance of words, sections, or even whole page

Although it might be informational, a website with no style is plain boring and probably won't get many visitors. Now that you have a firm grasp on how to create content for your website, it's time to make it look good. Enter Cascading Style Sheets (CSS), a code language that lets you change the appearance of your pages and sites without messing up the Hypertext Markup Language (HTML) code. This is where Expression Web 4 really excels. With Expression Web 4's built-in CSS capabilities, creating standards-based and cross-browser-compatible styles is easier than ever before, even if you don't understand exactly what's going on.

Expression Web 4 gives you a multitude of ways to create and apply styles, many of which don't require you to write a single line of code. In fact, you can make highly advanced and elaborate styles and layouts using these tools without even glancing at the actual code!

By the Way

CSS—The Driving Force Behind the New Web

Whenever I start talking about CSS and how powerful a tool it is, I see people's eyes glazing over. And no wonder—almost every designer and developer I know (me included) did the same thing when we first started. Why? Because CSS is so cryptic and foreign. With HTML, at least you have some form of logical structure and meaning. When it comes to CSS, it is just endless lines of seemingly similar code repeated over and over with no rhyme or reason. And deciphering style sheets—especially ones you have not been involved in writing—can be a real headache. I'm really selling it, aren't I? Well, there's a point to all this, and what I'm about to tell you is the honest truth: Before I started using Expression Web, CSS was a bit of a mystery to me! I could use it; I could hack it; but it never really made any sense.

I'm telling you this because I think it's important you understand that CSS is not as complicated as it looks. It's all about perspective. I will try my best to introduce you to this phenomenal coding language in a way that helps you understand it.

Why do I think it's so important that you get a firm handle on CSS? Because, right now, CSS is the most powerful tool on the Web. I dare say it is what is driving the new Web. And if you understand CSS—and I do mean really understand it—you are well equipped to build a career in web design.

CSS, and with it the separation of style and content, is one of the central building blocks of what is known as Web 2.0 or the social web. CSS lies in the foundation of pretty much every new web invention you can think of. From blogs like my own (www.DesignIsPhilosophy.com was built from the ground up in Expression Web 4 and is entirely CSS based) to the new WhiteHouse.gov website to Facebook and CNN.com, style and content have been successfully separated. As a result, visitors can ingest the content in any way they want—from RSS feed readers, on their cell phones, via email updates, or by visiting the sites. And for every method available, the content conforms to fit the display medium, providing a more user-friendly experience and better communication.

It might sound a little pompous, but I'm telling you: CSS is the wave of the future. And it's here right now. So jump on and enjoy the ride!

Styles can apply to individual objects, sections of a page, or even an entire site. It all depends on what you, the designer and/or developer, want to do. Styles can do simple things such as change the font or color of a heading, or advanced things such as position content and set behaviors and multiple styles at the same time. Right now, CSS is probably the most powerful tool in a web designer's arsenal, and it is the basis of most modern websites and blogs. Designers and developers with strong CSS skills are in high demand, and because Microsoft built Expression Web 4 specifically to handle and generate proper standards-based code and CSS, you already have a leg up just by using the program.

CSS3: The New Style of the Web

Earlier in the book I mentioned the introduction of HTML5 as the new standard for web code. Within the HTML5 standard lies the third version of the CSS standard, unsurprisingly called CSS3. And with this new standard come new possibilities and new challenges. Expression Web 4 SP2 ships with full support for most new CSS3 features, both in the Manage Styles panel and in IntelliSense, which makes it easy for you to start using these new techniques in your websites.

There are a few caveats though: Some of the CSS3 standard has yet to be implemented across all new browsers, and most older browsers have no support for these functions. That means when you use new CSS3 features such as corner-radius (rounded corners), box-shadow, and media queries, you have to be aware that they may not work for every person who visits your site.

That's not to say you shouldn't use these new features—far from it. What it means is that you have to design your sites in such a way that if a visitor does not have access to these new features, his experience will not suffer from it. Thinking recursively about this is known as *graceful degradation*, but I like to use the forward-thinking moniker *progressive enhancement* instead. Rather than thinking about what happens when people don't have the new features, I design my sites so that the ones who do get an extra bonus in the form of a more attractive or more functional user interface.

When implementing HTML5 or CSS3 features in a site, it's always a good idea to know how broad the support is for those features. Luckily there's a website for just that: www.caniuse.com keeps track of every new feature under the HTML5 umbrella and what browsers support it.

CSS Sans Code

Because of Expression Web 4's setup, you don't need to know anything about CSS code to create styles in your document. In fact, creating and applying styles to documents can be as easy as a couple mouse clicks.

Creating Styles with a Click of Your Mouse

In this example, you change the style or look of the subheadings in the default.html document. The idea of this exercise is to show you that changing one style can affect multiple sections within the page. If you haven't already done so, open the default.html page in Design view.

1. With the default.html page open, click New Style in the Apply Styles panel (see Figure 10.1). This opens the New Style dialog.

2. In the New Style dialog, shown in Figure 10.2, open the Selector drop-down menu and scroll down to h2. Select h2 or, alternatively, type **h2** in the Selector bar. Doing so means the style you are creating applies to all the text that has Heading 2 as its style.

3. With the Font category selected, change the font-family setting to Arial, Helvetica, sans-serif using the drop-down menu. Set font-size to 1.2 and change the units to em. Set font-weight to bold and text-transform to uppercase. Finally, change the color to gray using the drop-down menu (see Figure 10.3).

As you make these changes, you see them in real time in the Preview box and you see the code being generated in the Description box. Click OK to apply the changes.

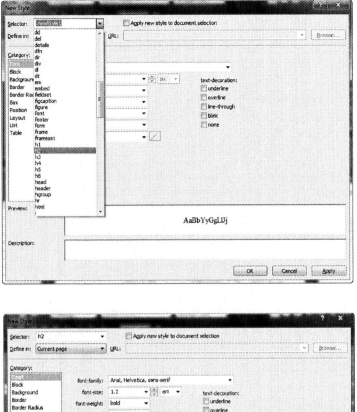

FIGURE 10.2
The New Style dialog showing the Selector drop-down menu with h2 chosen.

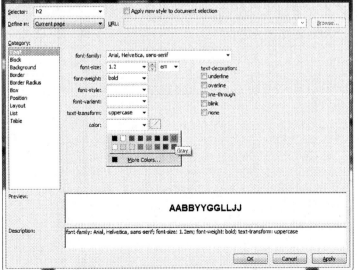

FIGURE 10.3
The New Style dialog provides point-and-click access to most style variables and an instant preview of the style and the style code.

By looking through the page in Design view, you can see that the subheadings you styled with Heading 2 have changed. They are now a different font, all uppercase, and gray in color. Now that you've changed the subheadings, you probably want to change the main heading as well. To do so, simply click the New Style button again and follow the same procedure you used to change the subheadings, but change the Selector setting to h1 instead of h2. Because h1 is the primary heading, it should be slightly larger than h2, so a size of 1.4em is appropriate.

Font Sizes and How to Use Them

When you changed the font size of the styles, you probably noticed that you had many different units from which to choose: px, pt, in, cm, mm, pc, em, ex, and %. You are probably familiar with px (pixel), in (inch), cm (centimeter), mm (millimeter), but pt (point), em (em space; historically the width of the letter *m* but now the height of the letter *m*), and ex (x height; the height of the lowercase letter *x*) are new to most people. To be honest, it is confusing that there are so many options. When you work in a word-processing application, you just set the font size, so why do you have to decide what kind of measurement to use when it comes to websites? The answer is both simple and complicated: The content of a website, although most often viewed on a computer monitor, can be displayed on a multitude of different media—from cell phones to text readers and even paper printouts. CSS gives you the ability to define different styles depending on what type of media the viewer is using. So, although it makes sense to size content displayed on a computer monitor using pixels, it might make more sense to size content intended for printouts in centimeters or inches.

There is also the issue of absolute and relative sizes. Inches, centimeters, and millimeters are absolute sizes, meaning that they should always be the same size no matter what medium is displaying them. Pixels, em spaces, and ex heights are relative sizes, meaning they will vary in size depending on the medium displaying them and the settings in the program used to display them. (Pixel measurement is a bit different because it is relative based on the pixel size and resolution of the display unit; that is, better resolution means smaller pixels.)

So, how do you decide which unit to use? There is no definite answer to this question, but you are relatively safe if you go by these two rules:

▶ Use px for content that must have a set size (images, fancy headings, menus, and so on).

▶ Use em for content that the user can resize to facilitate readability.

Many users have browsers that enable them to increase the size of the font on the page; em facilitates this sizing. In contrast, older browsers do not allow resizing of text sized with px.

The downside to using em as the sizing unit is that it is not consistent throughout different fonts, so a size of 1.2em in one font might be small but in another font might be large. The em size is also a relative one, meaning that if you have set an em size in one container and then set another em size for content within that container, the second em size is relative to the first, not to the overall document.

For further reading on the em size and why you should use it, I recommend the article "The amazing em unit and other best practices" found at http://www.w3.org/WAI/GL/css2em.htm.

Creating Inline Styles

The previous example demonstrates how to make styles that affect all the content to which they apply, including new content you add later. If you want to make a style change to just one section of the page and do not use the style elsewhere, you create what is called an *inline style*.

1. In Design view, place the cursor anywhere inside the first paragraph to select it. Click the New Style button in the Apply Styles panel as before.

2. In the Selector drop-down menu, select (Inline Style).

3. In the Font category, set font-size to 1.1em and font-weight to bold. In the Border category, uncheck the Same for All boxes and set the Border-bottom-style to solid, the Bottom border-width to 2px, and the Border-bottom-color to gray (see Figure 10.4). Click OK.

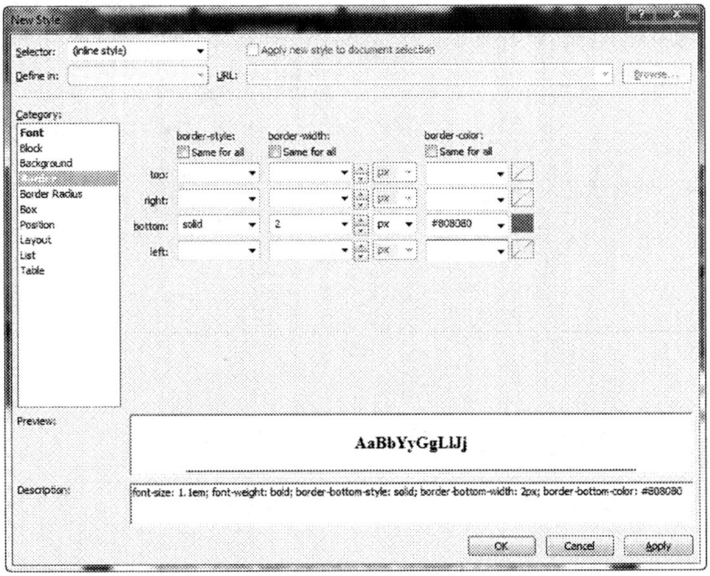

FIGURE 10.4
Under Border in the New Style dialog, you can set the style, width, and color of each of the four border sides.

As you can see in Design view, the font in the first paragraph is now bold and a 2-pixel-thick line separates it from the rest of the text. This style is inline because it affects only one tag or segment of content rather than the whole page.

Styling Small Selections

In the extreme, you can even set the style of just a small selection of words or even one word or one letter within a word by creating spans within the text and applying styles to them. You can do this in two ways. Here's the first method:

1. In Design view, select the word *kipple* in the second sentence of the second paragraph.

2. Using the tools available from the Common toolbar, change the font to Courier New, give the word an outside border using the Outside Borders button, and change the font color to green using the Font Color button.

And here's the alternative method:

1. In Design view, select another word in the second paragraph.

2. Click New Style in the Apply Styles panel to open the New Style dialog. Check the Apply New Style to Document Selection box to ensure that the style applies only to the word you selected (see Figure 10.5).

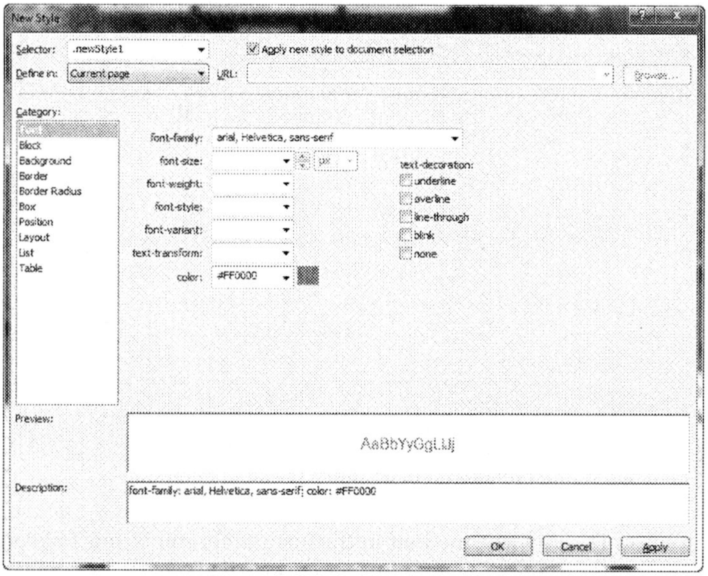

FIGURE 10.5
The Apply New Style to Document Selection check box ensures that the style only applies to the content you highlighted in Design view.

3. Under the Font category, change font-family to Arial, Helvetica, sans-serif and then change font-color to Red.

4. Under the Border category, set border-style to solid, border-width to 1px, and border-color to Black.

These two methods produce two new style classes—`.style1` and `.newStyle1`—that change the appearance of the two words you highlighted. The first method is quick and easy if you are making rudimentary changes; it produces a class called `.style1`.

The second method is more cumbersome but gives you far more flexibility in terms of the final product; it produces a class called `.newStyle1`. One illustration of the difference between the two is that when you use the first method, the color of the box is the same as the color of the font. In the second method, you can set the color of the box to whatever you want and even set each side of the box to a different color. Save the file and test it in your browser to see the result of your style applications so far (see Figure 10.6).

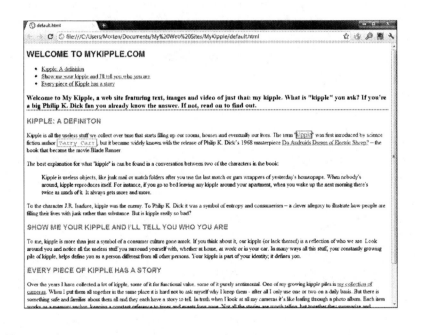

FIGURE 10.6
Default.html as it appears in Chrome with the inline style and the span styles applied.

Setting the Font Family for the Entire Document

Now you know how to make changes to preset styles, sections, and individual selections of a document. But what if you want to define certain attributes for the entire page, such as setting all text to one particular font family unless otherwise specified? By default, unstyled HTML text displays in Times New Roman. You can override the default by applying styles to any tag within the HTML code of the page—even the `<body>` tag that wraps all the content. By creating a body style, you can affect all the content within the `<body>` tag (that is, all the visible content on the page).

Here is how to change all the text in the document to Arial, Helvetica using the <body> tag:

1. Click New Style in the Apply Styles panel to open the New Style dialog. You do not need to select or highlight any portion of the document to create the body style.

2. In the Selector drop-down menu, select body or type body.

3. Under the Font category, change the font-family to Arial, Helvetica, sans-serif. Click OK.

By setting the font-family of the <body> tag, you changed to the new font any text that has not had its font-family defined by a custom style. In this example, because you created a special style for the word *kipple*, it retains the Courier font. The same is true for the headings, although you can't see it because the body font and the heading fonts are the same.

How Exactly Does CSS Work?

This last example begs the question, "Why does the word *kipple* retain its special font-family even when the font-family for the entire document changes?" The short answer is that this is where CSS gets its name: CSS works based on a cascade, meaning that the last style or rule in the sequence has the highest priority and is the one applied. This is, of course, a simplified version of events, and it doesn't always apply, but for now, it is sufficient. For an in-depth look at CSS, pick up Eric A. Meyer's book *CSS: The Definitive Guide, Third Edition*.

Styling Links (Also Known as Getting Rid of the Blue Underline)

You probably noticed that even though you changed the font-family for the entire document, the links retain that garish blue color and underline. The first things new web designers want to know are how to get rid of the underline and change the color of links. As you might have guessed, the answer is by using styles.

In Hour 5, "Getting Connected with (Hyper)Links: The Cornerstone of the World Wide Web," you learned that all links are defined using the <a> tag. Therefore, it follows that if you create an a style, you change the links.

1. Click New Style in the Apply Styles panel to open the New Style dialog. You do not need to select or highlight any portion of the document to change the link style.

2. In the Selector drop-down menu, select *a* or type *a*.

3. Under the Font category, check the none option under text-decoration. (Even though it is not checked, the default setting for links is underline, so you have to explicitly tell the browser to not apply this option.) Click OK.

Now, the underline is gone but the links are still blue. Most designers want their links to be a different color; to change the color, you need to modify the style you just created. You can do this using the Modify Style function.

1. To access the styles you have already created, click the Manage Styles tab in the Apply Styles panel (see Figure 10.7). The Manage Styles panel gives you a list of all the styles relating to the current document and uses visual aids to tell you what styles are active and what styles are applied to the current selection. If you place the cursor on a link, you see that the a style is highlighted, telling you that this is the last style in the cascade applied to your selection.

FIGURE 10.7
The Manage Styles panel gives you information about available styles, active styles, and what style is applied to the current selection.

2. To edit the existing style, right-click a and select Modify Style from the context menu. This opens the Modify Style dialog, which is the same as the New Style dialog.

3. Under the Font category, change font-color to a calmer blue using the More Colors option (see Figure 10.8). Click OK.

Now all the links are a nicer shade of blue. However, so are the subheadings!

FIGURE 10.8
The More
Colors option
is always avail-
able whenever
you set a color.
From here, you
can pick a
color from the
expanded
palette or use
the eyedropper
tool to pick a
color from any-
where on your
screen (even
outside
Expression
Web 4).

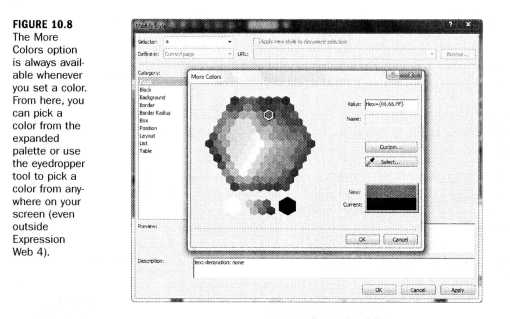

Try It Yourself

Using the Cascade to Override Styles

In Hour 5, you set the subheadings as bookmarks using the <a> tag, and now the color of the a style is overriding the color of the h2 style. This is where the cascade shows its true strength: By using CSS, you can define multiple attributes to the same content, and the browser picks the one that is most relevant based on a set of rules. In this case, you want to create a style that applies only to text that is both a subheading and a link.

1. Click the New Style button in the Manage Styles panel to open the New Style dialog.

2. In the Selector bar, type **h2 a**. This literally means Heading 2 links. In the Font category, change font-color to gray and click OK.

Now the subheadings return to their gray color because the browser picks the most specific style in the cascade. (h2 a is more specific than either h2 or a.)

By the Way

Caveat: Not Everyone Has Your Fonts!

You might have noticed when you select a font style that off the top Expression Web 4 offers you font families rather than particular fonts, and the remaining single fonts appear underneath. This is because Expression Web 4 knows that not every computer has every font, so it gives the browser a variety of similar-looking fonts to choose from. The three main font families are based on the most common fonts that almost all computers have installed by default:

- ▶ Arial, Helvetica, sans-serif
- ▶ Georgia, Times New Roman, Times, serif
- ▶ Courier New, Courier, monospace

All these families work the same way. The browser looks for the first font to see whether the computer has it installed. If not, the browser goes to the second font. If the computer has neither of the two fonts installed, the browser looks for the first font that falls under the category (sans-serif, serif, or monospace).

You can set your text to any font you want, but if you go outside the three main font families, you increase the chance that the computers used to view your page don't have the necessary fonts, and the page will not display properly. If the browser cannot find the defined font, it picks one of the default fonts—in certain cases, this can lead to strange results.

To be certain your page appears the same across all computers and browsers, I strongly advise you to stick to the three main font families for HTML text.

One other option is worth mentioning: CSS3 allows you to use the `@font-face` function to embed custom fonts from the Web in your site (a.k.a. web fonts). This is an advanced technique, but it's fairly simple to implement. If you want to experiment with web fonts, check out the Google Web Fonts Library at www.google.com/webfonts and the many free fonts available from services such as FontSquirrel (www.fontsquirrel.com).

CSS Tools in Expression Web 4

Expression Web 4 has a variety of built-in tools to help you create CSS correctly and efficiently. You already used some of them in earlier examples, and now it's time to take a closer look and familiarize yourself with each of them individually.

The Quick Tag Tools

Working with HTML documents, it can be hard to remember, or even figure out, exactly what is going on because most of the content is in tags within tags within tags. Trying to navigate through this mishmash of code can be a daunting task for even an experienced developer. To fully understand why a certain element or segment of text looks and behaves the way it does, you need to know exactly what tags are applied and in what order. Doing this manually is a lot of work. But with the Quick Tag tools, it is so easy it borders on the absurd. To get a complete ordered list of all the tags applied to an element in Design, Split, or Code view, simply place the cursor on that element and look at the top of the view pane. There, the Quick Tag tools list the entire sequence of tags and give you the option to edit each of them individually (see Figure 10.9).

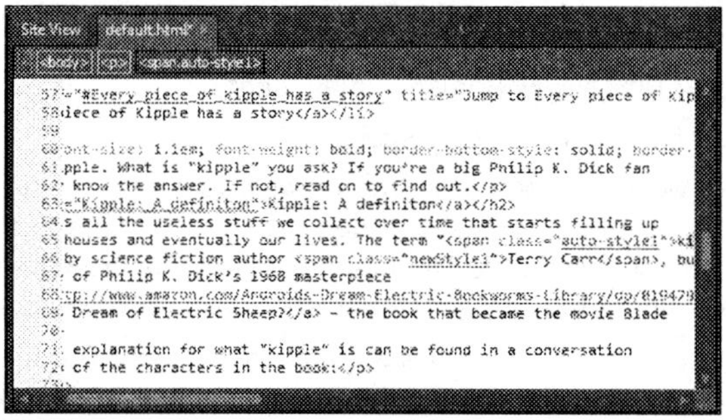

FIGURE 10.9
The Quick Tag tools list all the tags applied to the selected content in order.

The Quick Tag tools also interact with other tools, such as the Tag and CSS Properties panels and the Apply and Manage Styles panels, to give you a complete picture of what Expression Web 4 is doing to the content.

The Quick Tag Selector is the bar itself. After you click something in the page, the Quick Tag Selector displays all the applied tags. By hovering over each of the tags displayed on the bar, you cause a box in Design view to highlight the affected area of that tag. From here, you can click any tag in the Selector to display its tag or CSS properties or to show what style is applied. You can open the Quick Tag Tools drop-down menu by clicking the arrow button next to the tag and make changes to the tag without navigating through all the code (see Figure 10.10).

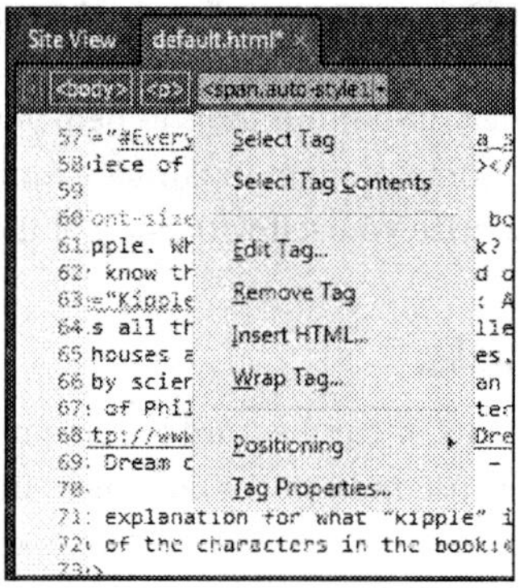

FIGURE 10.10
You trigger the Quick Tag tools drop-down menu by clicking the down arrow next to each tag.

From here, you can open the Quick Tag Editor, which lets you edit the tag by clicking Edit Tag, insert new HTML, and even wrap the existing tag in a new tag. You can also remove the tag altogether, change the positioning of the content, or select just the content or the whole tag in Code view.

By the Way

Not only are the Quick Tag tools excellent for helping you keep track of your own work, but they also make short process out of dissecting complicated websites designed by others. I regularly use the Quick Tag tools in combination with the Code View toolbar to quickly track down and fix errors in large web pages because they give me instant access to only the elements I care about.

The Quick Tag tools are an important part of the CSS creation and editing process because most tags have attached styles, and you need to know what tags are at the end of the cascade to see what styles apply to a tag and what, if anything, needs to be changed.

By the Way

If you can't find the CSS Properties panel, go to Panels on the main menu and select CSS Properties. It appears in the bottom-left corner.

The CSS Properties Panel

The CSS Properties panel gives you a more detailed breakdown of what styles are applied to the selected elements and exactly what they do.

The top half of the panel provides a list of all the applied rules or styles (the cascade), and the bottom part lists the attributes applied to the selected rule. You can select individual rules by clicking them in the top half of the panel or by clicking the tags in the Quick Tag Selector. By default, the bottom half of the CSS Properties panel displays a list of all the available attributes for the selected style. If you want to see only those attributes that have a value, click the Summary button.

As you have learned, CSS allows the same attribute to have many different values, and the browser picks the one furthest down the cascade. The CSS Properties panel shows you which attribute values are applied and which are ignored by using a red line to strike out the ones not in use. To see this in action, place the cursor on one of the subheadings (see Figure 10.11). This way, you can easily see how the cascade is flowing and track errors in value attribution.

The CSS Properties panel lets you make direct changes to the selected CSS style by entering new values for all the attributes. This is a quick way to make the same kind of changes you made in the Modify Style dialog, but it doesn't give you the same kind of trial-and-error environment because all the changes are immediate. The

CSS Properties panel works in direct conjunction with the Apply and Manage Styles panels.

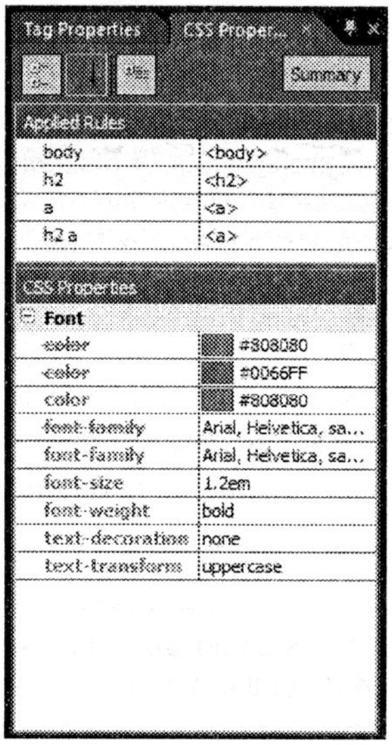

FIGURE 10.11 The red lines show that Expression Web 4 is ignoring the original colors and applying the third defined color.

The Apply Styles Panel

The Apply Styles panel, as shown in Figure 10.12, provides a visual representation of the applied and available styles by previewing them in a list. The primary function of this panel is to provide an easy way to apply styles to the selected content. To do so, simply select the content in Code or Design view and click the desired style. You can also use the Apply Styles panel to remove styles from the content and select all the content to which the style is applied on the page.

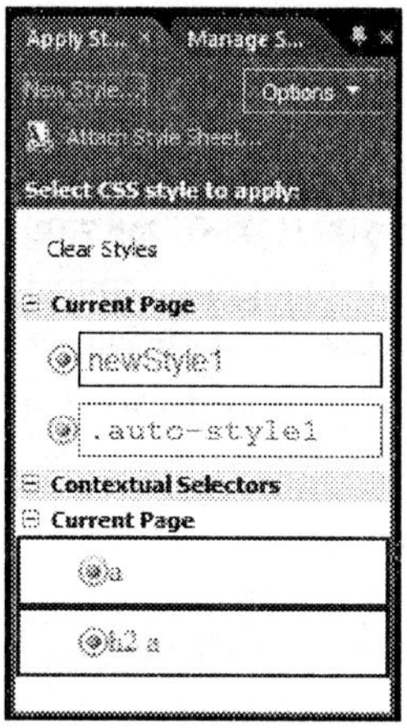

FIGURE 10.12 The Apply Styles panel displays all the applied and available styles and provides an easy way to apply new styles to the selected content.

The Manage Styles Panel

The Manage Styles panel, as shown in Figure 10.13, works in much the same way as the Apply Styles panel, with the one major difference that you can't simply click a style to apply it to a page. (You need to right-click it and select Apply Style from the context menu.) The Manage Styles panel provides a complete list of all the styles available in the page and a preview of the selected style. As the name suggests, the Manage Styles panel is an excellent tool for managing styles both when you want to edit a particular style and also when you start dealing with styles stored in different locations, such as multiple external style sheets. The combination of these functionalities makes Expression Web 4 an incredibly powerful tool when it comes to creating, editing, and troubleshooting CSS code. By familiarizing yourself with them, you can work not only quicker and more effectively, but also learn how to use CSS in a fun and hands-on way.

FIGURE 10.13
The Manage Styles panel displays a complete list of all styles related to the open page and is an excellent tool for managing these styles.

Color Coding in the Apply and Manage Styles Panels

By the Way

A colored dot that sometimes has a gray ring around it prefixes the styles in both the Apply and Manage Styles panels. The dot's color indicates the category to which each style belongs:

- ▶ Blue means the style affects regular tags, such as p, h1, a, and block-quote.
- ▶ Yellow means the style is an inline style.
- ▶ Red means the style is a CSS ID (prefixed by #).
- ▶ Green means the style is a CSS class (prefixed by a period [.]).
- ▶ A gray circle surrounds the colored dot if the style is in use in the current page.

You learn what CSS IDs and classes are in Hour 11, "Getting Boxed In, Part 2: Knee Deep in CSS."

Using Various CSS Tools to Apply and Change Styles

Now that you know all the different CSS tools available, it's time to put them to use. In this example, you use the various panels to apply styles to content and then change the styles without using the Modify Style dialog.

1. In Design view, find and highlight the word *homeopape* in the blockquote.

2. With the Apply Styles tab selected in the panel, click .newStyle1 to apply it to the selected text.

3. Click <span.newStyle1> in the Quick Tag Selector to select the correct tag. If Summary is active in the CSS Properties panel, click the button to deactivate it so that you get a list of all available attributes.

4. Pin the Folder List panel to the side to get full access to the CSS Properties panel. Use the CSS Properties panel to change font-color to Maroon by clicking the drop-down menu under Font and Color. Scroll down to font-variant and set it to small-caps.

5. To change the border, scroll up until you find the border attribute and click the + sign to see all the available attributes. Delete the current attributes by clicking the border attribute value and pressing the Delete key or the Backspace key on your keyboard. Scroll down to border-bottom (you might have to change the layout of your workspace to see the whole name) and set the Border-bottom-color to Maroon, the Border-bottom-style to dotted, and the Border-bottom-width to 1px.

The changes you just made to the .newStyle1 style are instant and affect both words that Expression Web 4 applied the style to. This technique is effective for making smaller adjustments or changes to your styles, but be careful: Unlike in the Modify Style dialog, you cannot reset multiple changes with a simple click. If you make many changes to your style, it can be hard to retrace your steps even with the Undo button.

Summary

Using Cascading Style Sheets (CSS) gives you precise and easy control over how your content appears to the visitor. And with Expression Web 4's many integrated CSS tools, even a novice can create advanced and standards-based styles without writing a single line of code. In this hour, you learned how to use these tools to edit existing styles and create new ones as well as how to apply styles to the whole page, sections of a page, and individual words. You saw how easy it is to modify existing styles using the Modify Style dialog and the CSS Properties panel, and how the Quick Tag tools can help you find the relevant tags and styles quickly and decipher complicated code to see how and why elements in the page look the way they do.

Cascading Style Sheets apply to the page in a cascade. In this hour, you got a basic understanding of what this means and how to use this knowledge to style your content and solve problems. But so far, you have scratched only the surface of what CSS is capable of. In the next hours, you learn how to use CSS as a layout tool and unlock its true potential and how to move beyond simple point-and-click page styling to full-fledged CSS authoring and the creation of separate style sheets.

Q&A

Q. *I changed my text size from 12px to 12em, but now the text is incredibly large! What is the correct equivalent of 12px in ems?*

A. One em is the width of the letter *m* that is defined as standard in the browser the user uses. Therefore, 12em is the width of 12 *m*'s next to one another, thus the huge size. Because em is a relative size measurement, there is no correct answer to this question. Depending on what font you use, a 12px equivalent is usually between 0.8em and 1em. To get the perfect size, you need to do a bit of trial and error. Just remember that when dealing with ems, always use decimals rather than full integers.

Q. *I followed the tutorial and applied a class to some text but nothing happened!*

A. If you created a class and nothing happened, one of two things went wrong: Either you didn't actually create the style (by accidentally pressing Cancel perhaps?) or the style wasn't applied to the content. First, check whether the style is listed in the Manage Styles panel. If it is, click the element you wanted to style and then check the Quick Tag Selector to see if the correct selector or class is applied. If you created a new class and the selector says only <p> or <h1>, you need to apply the class manually by selecting the selector and clicking the class in the Apply Styles panel.

Q. *When I select the different colors from the drop-down color options, they are replaced by a weird code starting with # and followed by six letters and numbers. What is this?*

A. When working with colors in the digital realm, every shade has a distinct hexadecimal code preceded by #. That way, the color is interpreted the same way by all applications whether it is an image editor, web browser, or word processor. In CSS, you set colors by using their hexadecimal codes.

Workshop

The Workshop has quiz questions and exercises to help you put to use what you have just learned. If you get stuck, the answers to the quiz questions are in the next section. But try to answer them first. Otherwise, you'll be cheating yourself.

Quiz

1. What part of the document does a CSS style apply to?

2. What happens if several styles with different values for the same attributes are applied to the content?

Answers

1. CSS styles are applied to the content within their respective tags; that is to say, a p style will be applied to any content within the <p> tags, an a style will be applied to any content within an <a> tag, and so on. You can also create spans around content and apply styles to them as well.

2. If several different attribute values are applied to the same content from different styles, the browser goes through the cascade and selects the attribute that is furthest down the line or is most specific. In most cases, this means the style that is attached to the closest tag.

Exercise

Two other selectors in the default.html page were not styled in the earlier examples: the paragraph and the blockquote. Use the techniques you learned in this hour to create a p style and a blockquote style, and apply some different attributes to them. Remember that because the font-family has already been set in the body style, you don't need to change it. Try experimenting with background colors, borders, and text decorations and explore the many different options available under the Font category.

Getting Boxed In, Part 2: Knee Deep in CSS

What You'll Learn in This Hour:

▶ How to create and apply classes to individual tags

▶ How to use divs to define sections of content

▶ How to apply classes and IDs to divs to style sections of content

▶ How to use pseudoclasses to give visual cues to the visitor

▶ How the box model works and how to use it to create layouts

In the previous hour, you learned how to use Cascading Style Sheets (CSS) to style text content. But that's just one small part of what CSS can do. You realize the true strength of the CSS styling language when you use it not only to style individual elements but also to define different sections within a page that have different styles, and to create and manage layouts and position content.

CSS lets you build a hierarchy of the styles applied to different portions of your page so that a paragraph in one part of the page can have a completely different style from a paragraph in another part of the page. Likewise, CSS can organize content within the page so that certain content appears to the left or right of other content, even though it is not in a table.

To understand how CSS operates as a layout tool, you first need to understand the box model. In this hour, you explore the box model to see how it interacts with your content. Through this knowledge, you get a firm understanding of how CSS puts everything in boxes and how you can use these boxes to create advanced and visually stunning layouts without destroying the markup.

CSS Classes—Because Not All Content Should Be Treated Equally

In Hour 10, "Bringing Style to Substance with Cascading Style Sheets," you learned how to apply styles to a page using the standard tag selectors such as p, h1, h2, and a. However, these styles applied to the entire page, so you had to make an inline style to change the style of just one section of the page. This is an acceptable solution if the change happens only once, but if you plan to use this special style again somewhere else in the page, this approach quickly becomes cumbersome. You need a way to group the content into separate classes so that each section can get its own style, even though the same selectors define them all. Enter CSS classes.

Create a Class and Apply It to the Content

A CSS class defines a subsection of the content that has its own set of styles. An example illustrates this best: Right now, there is no clear separation between the beginning part of the default.html page and the rest of the content. To remedy this, you can make a class to style this portion of the page:

1. With the default.html page open in Design view, place the cursor inside the first paragraph to select it. In the Apply Styles task pane, right-click the inline style you created in Hour 10 and select Remove Inline Style from the context menu. This returns the paragraph to its original appearance.

2. Click the New Style button and change the Selector name to .abstract. The punctuation mark in front of the name defines this style as a class.

3. In the Font category, set font-family to Georgia, Times New Roman, Times, serif; font-size to 1.2em; font-weight to bold; and font-style to italic. In the Block category, set text-align to justify.

4. In the Border category, uncheck all the Same for All boxes and change the bottom values to solid, 2px, and #000000 (black). Click OK to create the new style class.

5. To apply the new class to an existing element within the page, place the selector on the element (in this case, the first paragraph) and click the .abstract class in the Apply Styles task pane.

When you click the first paragraph after applying the new class, you can see that the p tag in the Quick Tag Selector has changed to include the new class. It now reads <p.abstract>, as shown in Figure 11.1.

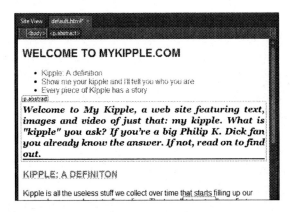

FIGURE 11.1
The .abstract style applied to the first paragraph in default.html.

Using the method described here to apply a new class results in the class being applied to the last tag in the chain of the selected items. This means that when you have grouped objects such as lists, you need to pick which tags you want to apply the class to. If you click one of the list objects at the top of the page and apply the class, it affects only the selected list item. If you highlight the entire list or select the <ul> tag from the Quick Tag Selector, Expression Web 4 applies the class to the list as a whole.

Using CSS Classes to Center an Image

This way of using classes is often preferred when positioning content such as images in pages. You might recall from Hour 6, "Getting Visual, Part 1: Adding Images and Graphics," and Hour 7, "Getting Visual, Part 2: Advanced Image Editing, Thumbnails, and Hotspots," that the align attribute is deprecated. Although you can position elements left and right using the float attribute, there is no option to position items in the center of the page. To properly center nontext content with standards-based code, you need to use CSS. However, although you want the *option* to center your images and other content, you don't want to center every image. Making a class to center content is the perfect solution to this problem.

Before you start, replace the current myCameras.html file with the fresh one from the lesson files for this hour. You should do this because, when you inserted and changed the properties for the images in Hours 6 and 7, you created a series of styles. This new file has no styles and gives you a fresh start.

1. With the myCameras.html page open in Design view, click the New Style button and change the Selector name to .alignCenter.

2. In the Box category, uncheck the Margin: Same for All box and set right and left to auto. (Leave top and bottom empty.)

3. In the Layout category, set `display` to `block`. This tells the browser that whatever content this class is applied to is to appear as a separate block or box independent of the rest of the content (that is, on its own line). Click OK to create the new class.

4. Click the image of the cameras and click the new `.alignCenter` class to apply it.

Save the page and test it in your browser, and you see that with the new `.alignCenter` class applied, the image centers itself on its own line in the page, as shown in Figure 11.2.

FIGURE 11.2
The photo of the cameras is centered on the page using the `.alignCenter` class.

The clever thing about using the method to set the left and right margins to auto is that you leave it to the browser to decide where the center of the page is by telling it that the two side margins are to be identical.

You can create similar classes for `.alignLeft` and `.alignRight` by setting the `display` attribute under the Layout category to `inline` (to keep the image on the same line as the text) and setting the `float` attribute to `left` for `.alignLeft` and `right` for `.alignRight`. That way, you don't have to use the Picture Properties dialog to position your images, but you can apply classes to them individually instead.

Using Boxes to Separate Content

Using CSS classes in the ways described in the previous section is an excellent way to apply changes to multiple individual objects throughout a page. But sometimes you want a whole section of a page to have a different look from the rest. You can use classes for this purpose, too, but rather than applying them to selectors, such as p, h1, a, and img, you now apply them to a new tag called <div>.

<table>
<tr>
<td>I am not entirely sure what <div> actually means. In my research, I have found many suggestions, and the one that sounds the most reasonable to me is that "div" is short for "divider." However, it has recently been suggested to me that it stands for "division," so I guess the search for the actual meaning continues.</td>
<td>**By the** Way</td>
</tr>
</table>

To understand what the <div> tag does, you need to delve a little deeper into the inner workings of tags and CSS. When Expression Web 4 applies a tag to content, it draws an invisible box around the content. You can see a visual representation of this phenomenon when you hover your mouse over the tags on the Quick Tag Selector bar and the corresponding boxes are outlined in Design view. When you create a style using CSS, you are, in reality, telling the browser to apply a set of variables to this box and what's inside it. This is why when you open the New or Modify Style dialog, you always have the option to create top, bottom, left, and right borders around the content, even if it is a single word in a sentence. The <div> and <span> tags create such boxes that wrap around the content and their tags so that attributes such as size, background color, and positioning can be applied to the content as a whole. In short, creating a div and putting content into it is like drawing a box around content on a page.

Creating a Div and Placing It Around Content

To understand when and how you would use divs to wrap content, you apply the .abstract class to all the content before the first subheading in default.html. As you saw in the previous example, adding the .abstract class to individual sections of the page causes Expression Web 4 to treat each section as a separate entity (refer to Figure 11.1). Now, you want to create a box that contains both the first paragraph and the list above it and treat them as a single entity. You use the Toolbox panel to assist you in the next task. The Toolbox should be visible on the top-right side of the workspace. If it is not, you can activate it by clicking Panels from the main menu and selecting Toolbox.

1. With the default.html page open in Design view, drag and drop a `<div>` instance (found under HTML, Tags in the Toolbox task pane) into the page and place it in the empty space between the first heading and the list. This should create a new empty horizontal box directly under the heading (see Figure 11.3).

FIGURE 11.3
An empty div can be dragged from the Toolbox panel directly into Design view and placed anywhere within the text.

2. To move the content into the div, simply highlight the first paragraph and drag and drop it into the div. For layout purposes, which will make sense later, you want the list to appear underneath the first paragraph, so select it and drag and drop it inside the div underneath the text.

Now, the first paragraph and the list are both contained within the new div (see Figure 11.4), and when you place your cursor on either, the Quick Tag Selector shows that the div comes before any of the other tags in the cascade.

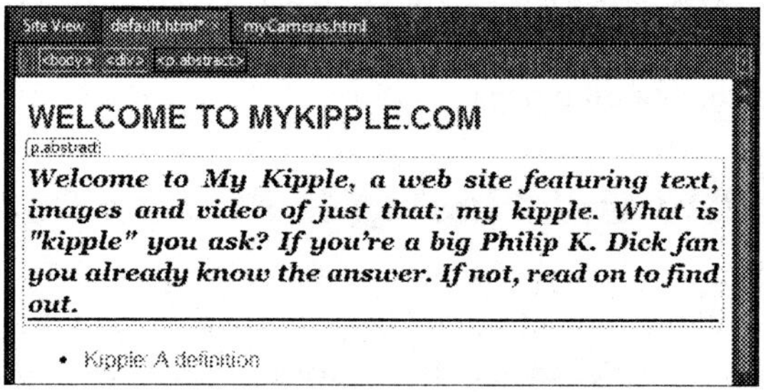

FIGURE 11.4
The first paragraph and the list are now both contained within the div selector.

Now that we have separated some of the content from the rest of the page, it is time to make that content appear separated visually and in the code. To do this you use a different kind of style element called an *ID*. In addition to style classes, you also have style IDs. The ID differs little from the class—so little, in fact, that many wonder why it exists at all.

Introducing ID—Class's Almost Identical Twin

The ID works in the same way as the class: You can apply attributes to it, apply it to any tag, and create custom styles that appear only within divs that belong to this ID. The only difference between the class and the ID is that whereas you can use the class many times throughout a page, you can use the ID only once. (Or rather, if you want your page to remain compliant with web standards, you can use an ID only once per page—most browsers allow the repeated usage of the same ID in a page even though it's technically a breach of the standards.)

So what is the point of using IDs or having them at all? From a designer and developer standpoint, the ID is a great tool for separating content and making the code more readable. As an example, a common practice when designing blogs is to use IDs to define the main sections of the page and classes to define components that repeat several times within these sections. For example, the front page of a blog may have an ID called content that holds all the articles, and each article is kept in a class called post. For someone looking at the code, it is far easier to understand what is going on in large pages if the developer lays out the code this way.

Creating a Sidebar Using an ID

To make the page layout more interesting, let's make the new div you just created into a sidebar that appears on the left side of the screen. To do this, you assign it an ID called #sidebar and then style that ID to make it float to the left.

1. Click the New Style button in the Apply Styles panel to open the New Style dialog. Set the Selector to #sidebar. (The # symbol prefix tells the browser that this is an ID.)

2. Under Background, set the background-color to #CCCCCC (a light gray) using the More Colors swatch or by inserting the hex value manually.

3. Under Border, leave the Same for All boxes checked and set the borders to solid, px, and #808080 (a darker gray).

4. Under Position, set the width to 250px. By default, the width of a div box is 100%. This sets it manually to a fixed size.

5. Under Layout, set float to left. This pushes the box to the far left, letting the remaining text float around it, as you saw with the images earlier. Click OK to create the new ID.

To apply the new ID, select the div by clicking the <div> box in the Quick Tag Selector and then click the new #sidebar ID in the Apply Styles panel. When the #sidebar ID is applied to the div, the browser creates a gray box around the content and shifts it to the left, as shown in Figure 11.5.

FIGURE 11.5
With the #sidebar ID applied, the div floats to the left and is styled with a gray background and a border.

Using an ID to Center the Page

A common question from new web designers is how to center the contents of a page using CSS. There is a lot of confusion about how to do this, and most of it stems from the fact that people think of web design tools as word-processing applications on steroids. However, as you have seen, this couldn't be further from the truth. In the past, a common way to center the content on a page was to put it in a one-cell table and center the table using text-align. This is not an ideal solution because by putting the content inside a table, you are inadvertently restricting the options for future layout changes and fancy styling. In addition, you learned in Hour 9, "Getting Boxed In, Part 1: Using Tables for Tabular Content," that tables should be used only for tabular content, and it would be quite a stretch to argue that all the content of an entire page is tabular data that should be displayed in one cell!

Even so, the table idea is a good one; it's just using the wrong type of box. If you paid close attention to the earlier sections of this hour, you might already have figured out how to do this using only CSS.

1. Go to Code view and drag and drop a `<div>` instance found under Tags in the Toolbox task pane into the page directly before the line that reads `<h1>Welcome to MyKipple.com</h1>`. Go back to Design view and a new box appears at the top of the page.

2. Create a new style and give it the Selector name **#wrapper**.

3. In the Box category, uncheck the Margin: Same for All box and set `left` and `right` to auto. Leave `top` and `bottom` blank (see Figure 11.6).

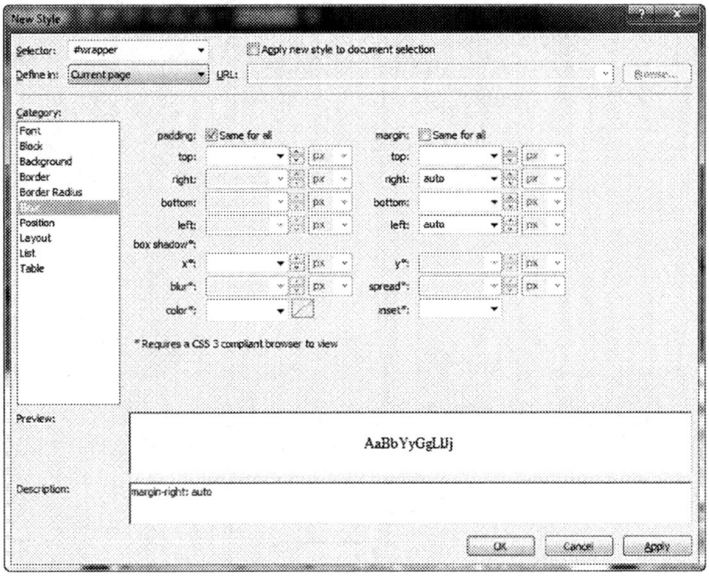

FIGURE 11.6
Setting the left and right margins of the #wrapper ID to auto.

4. In the Position category, set `width` to `800px`. This will be the total width of the content on the page. Click OK to create the new ID.

5. In Design view, highlight all the content underneath the new div, including the sidebar, and then drag and drop it into the div you just created at the top of the page.

6. Select the div tag belonging to the new div from the Quick Tag Selector bar and click the new #wrapper ID in the Apply Styles task pane to apply the ID. The tag changes to `<div#wrapper>`. Save and then press F12 to preview the page in your browser. The content of the page should now be restricted to the center of the page and remain so even if you resize your browser window (see Figure 11.7).

FIGURE 11.7
The #wrapper
ID applied to
the outermost
div reduces the
width of the
box to 800
pixels and
centers the
content in the
browser
window.

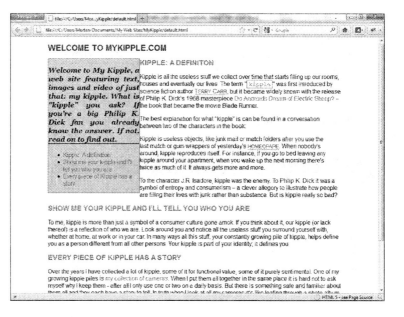

When you apply this ID to your div, Expression Web 4 reduces the width of the div to 800px and tells the browser to place the div within two equally wide margins: one on the left and one on the right. Naturally, this results in the div box appearing in the middle of the screen. To position the content to the left or right of the screen, simply remove the two margin attributes and set `float` to `left` or `right` instead.

This is the pure CSS method for centering content in the browser. In extremely rare cases, it doesn't work properly because some older browsers don't follow or understand proper CSS code and become confused by the margins set to `auto`. Nevertheless, this is the correct way to perform the task.

Creating Custom Styles Within IDs and Classes

When you have content that is contained within a div that has an ID or class, you can create custom styles that affect only the tags within that class. You do so by making the tags a subelement of the class. To do so, create a new style but give the tag a prefix in the form of the class name. For example, you can make a custom version of the `.abstract` class that applies only to content within the `#sidebar` div. To do so, create a new style and give it the selector name **#sidebar .abstract**. In the Font category, set font-size to 1em and font-weight to normal. When you click OK to create the new style, you see that attributes from both of the `.abstract` classes are applied to the content but that the attributes from the `#sidebar  .abstract` class have preference. That is because the more specific style is further down the cascade and closer to the content.

You can apply this technique to any standard tag, whether it is a heading, paragraph, link, blockquote, or something else. If you ever wondered how you can create several different paragraph styles within one document, now you have the answer!

Classes Within Classes: Micromanaging the Content

In the earlier example, you saw that you can create special styles for content within IDs and classes. There is no limit to how far you can take this technique by applying multiple IDs, classes, and tags within each other. See the layout in Figure 11.8 as an example.

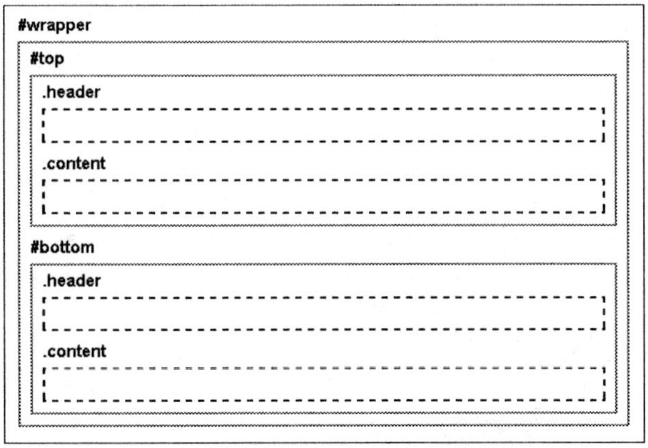

FIGURE 11.8
A layout using multiple IDs and classes to separate the content. IDs are outlined with a solid line, and classes are outlined with a dashed line.

In this figure, multiple IDs and classes divide different parts of the content. By understanding how to properly name your style selectors, you can micromanage the content within these IDs and classes for a highly customized look. You do so by creating selector names that have the relevant IDs, classes, and tags listed with spaces between them. Here are some examples of different selector names:

▶ p styles all paragraphs on the page, both inside and outside the IDs and classes.

▶ #wrapper p styles all paragraphs within the wrapper ID.

▶ #wrapper #top p and #top p style paragraphs within the top ID only.

▶ .header p styles all paragraphs within the header class regardless of ID.

▶ #wrapper #top .header p and #top .header p style paragraphs within the header class inside the top ID only.

Using Classes to Control IDs

To see just how flexible the tag, class, and ID structure is, consider this trick used by professional designers for quick-and-easy prototyping: Right now, the sidebar floats to the right because the ID contains a `float` variable. However, you can also use a class and apply it to the ID to do this! Earlier in this hour, you created two alignment classes called `.alignLeft` and `.alignRight` in the myCameras.html page. Now, create the two classes in default.html and give them the following attributes:

- ▶ For .alignLeft, set `margin-right` to 10px and `float` to `left`.

- ▶ For .alignRight, set `margin-left` to 10px and `float` to `right`.

Next, open the Modify Style dialog for the #sidebar ID by right-clicking the style in the Apply Styles panel and selecting Modify style from the pop-up menu. In the dialog, go to the Layout category and remove the `float:left` attribute. Click OK to save the change, and the text should no longer wrap around the sidebar.

Now comes the fun part: Place your cursor anywhere inside the sidebar box and select the <div#sidebar> box in the Quick Tag Selector to select the whole div. Then, go to the Apply Styles panel and click the `.alignLeft` style to apply it. With the application, the sidebar floats to the left with a nice 10px margin as a buffer against the other content. Without making any changes, click the `.alignRight` style instead and, as if by magic, the sidebar jumps to the right with the text floating to the left. This is because Expression Web 4 won't let you apply two styles to the same div, so it overwrites the last one you applied. This way, you can quickly see which layout you like better. And this trick doesn't just apply to the sidebar—you can do the exact same thing with images and other elements on the page.

Pseudoclasses

In addition to tags, classes, and IDs, HTML supports something called *pseudoclasses*. These specialized versions of selectors come into play when the user interacts with the page; that is, when the user hovers over or clicks content or a link. There are five such pseudoclasses, all of which are normally used in conjunction with the <a> tag:

- ▶ `:active` refers to an element that is currently active. For example, a link during the time the user is holding the mouse button down and clicking it.

▶ :focus refers to an element that currently has the input focus, meaning that it can receive keyboard or mouse input. To understand focus, think of an input table with the current cell highlighted—that cell has the focus. When you press the Tab button, the focus changes to the next cell.

▶ :hover refers to an element being hovered over by the mouse pointer.

▶ :link refers specifically to an element that is an unvisited hyperlink. Unlike the preceding pseudoclasses, :link applies to the a tag only.

▶ :visited refers to a link that has already been visited. Like the :link pseudoclass, :visited only applies to the a tag.

Use Pseudoclasses to Style Links

If you do not define an a style, browsers will style hyperlink so that :link is set to blue, :active is set to red, and :visited is set to purple. If you define only an a style, it overrides all the default settings and the link appears the same regardless of what the user does. To give the visitor a visual guide to what she is doing, it is a good idea to style the main pseudoclasses for links within your page. To use pseudoclasses, all you need to do is attach them directly after the tags in the selector name.

1. With default.html open in Design view, create a new style. In the Selector area, use the drop-down menu to find a:active or type **a:active**.

2. In the Font category, set the color to red (#FF0000). Click OK to finalize the new style.

3. Create a new style and give it the selector name **a:hover**. In the Font category, check the underline box under text-decoration. Click OK to finalize the new style.

4. Create a new style and give it the selector name **a:visited**. In the Font category, set the color to gray (#808080). Click OK to finalize the new style.

You will not see any changes in Design view, but when you save and preview the page in your browser, you will see that the links on the page are blue when they have not been visited and are not being hovered over. They have an underline when they are being hovered over, turn red when you press and hold them, and turn gray if they have already been visited. Note that because you attached the pseudoclasses to the general a style, they are applied to all the instances of the <a> tag in the page, including the subheadings that work as bookmarks. And because the pseudoclasses are more specific, they override the h2 a link as well. If you want the h2 links to have separate pseudoclasses from the other links on the page, all you have to do is create a new style with a selector name, such as h2 a:hover.

> You can apply the pseudoclasses :active, :focus, and :hover to many tags, not just links. For example, the :hover pseudoclass is sometimes used to highlight sections of lists, tables, and paragraphs to help with readability. When you are doing this, it is important to make the nonlink components visually different from the links to avoid confusing the visitor. The :hover style applied to nonlink content commonly changes the background color of the content rather than the font color.

For even more advanced control, you can combine several pseudoclasses by stacking them. As an example, right now when you hover over a link, it retains the current color and displays an underline regardless of whether you visited it before. By creating a separate style with the selector name a:visited:hover, you can display hovered-over visited links in a different color. Just as with tags, classes, and IDs, you can attach any styling attribute to pseudoclasses.

Understanding the Box Model

Previously in this hour, you learned that when you attach tags to your content, Expression Web 4 creates an invisible box around the content. To understand how the content behaves and how you can style it, you need a firm understanding of the box model. To assist you in this understanding, I've created a box model reference for you in Figure 11.9.

To get a better understanding of what the box model is and how you use it, let's take a closer look at the #sidebar ID you created in default.html. To do so, right-click the #sidebar ID in the Apply or Manage Styles task pane and then select Modify Style to open the Modify Style task pane. All content wrapped inside tags has four main areas. In the center is the content itself, and surrounding the content, is the padding. The padding is the "breathing space" that separates the content from the next area, the border. The padding retains the same background color or image as the content. The border is the outer edge of the box. It can be given any color, be solid, or have a number of different textures. Outside the border is the margin. The margin works as the buffer area between the outer edges of the box (the border) and the other content on the page. The margin is transparent and you cannot give it a distinct color.

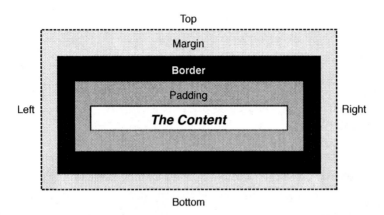

FIGURE 11.9
This box model
reference
shows all the
different ele-
ments of the
box model.

You can set the values of each of the four sides of the padding, border, and margin independently or in groups from the New and Modify Style panels. To set all four sides of the padding, border, or margin, check the corresponding Same for All box and enter the desired value in the first box. To set the values for each side independently, uncheck the Same for All box and set each value. If you leave any values empty, the default value applies. The default value is usually 0px.

The tricky part about the box model is the calculation of width and height. Generally, the width and height of any boxed element are equal to the distance from side to side or top to bottom of the content area before the padding is applied. The thickness of the padding, borders, and margins add to the total width and height of the box. This means that if you create a div with a width of 800px, as you did earlier, and give it a border of 2px on each side and a padding of 10px on each side, the total width of your div becomes 824px. As a result, if you want to keep the total width of your div at 800px, you need to subtract both your border width and your padding width and set the width of your div to 776px. It's not rocket science, but if you forget this little piece of information, you could easily end up with content that doesn't fit and not understand why.

Try It Yourself ▼

Using the Box Model to Style Content

Now that you know how the box model works, you can use it to create layout elements that are far more functional than tables. In this example, you change the appearance of the sidebar default.html page by changing the #sidebar ID style.

1. With default.html open in Design view, right-click the #sidebar ID and select Modify Style to open the Modify Style dialog.

▼

2. Right now, there is no space between the edge of the div box and the text, so the text appears attached to the left wall. To solve this problem, change the padding of the div: Under the Box category, check the Padding: Same for All box and set padding on all four sides to 10px. This creates some breathing space between the inner edge of the box (the content) and the borders. You can use the Preview box to make sure the space is created correctly. Click OK to apply the changes to the style.

When you save and preview the page in your browser, you can see that the breathing space inside and around the sidebar (previously added with the alignment class) gives the entire page a much nicer layout (see Figure 11.10). Because the outer #sidebar ID has a specific width defined and you have now added padding, you have to reduce the width attribute if you want to keep it at 250px width.

FIGURE 11.10
By utilizing your knowledge of the box model, you can create visually pleasing layouts without using graphics or tables.

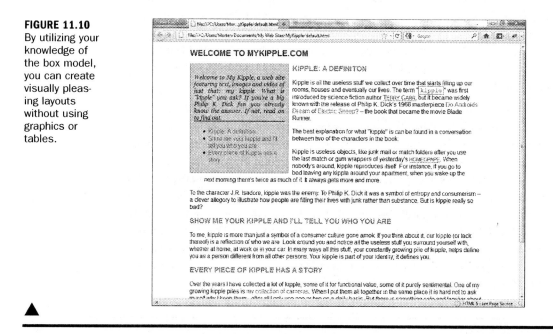

CSS3 Rounded Corners with Border Radius

Rounded corners have always been a desired design attribute that was hard to maintain in web design. With the introduction of CSS3, this is no longer the case. CSS3 allows us to create advanced rounded corners using only code, and it works quite well in newer browsers. As an added bonus, if the browser does not support CSS3 rounded corners, the corners will just be regular squares without any fuss.

With Service Pack 2 for Expression Web 4, a new Border Radius category option was added to the Add and Manage Style panels specifically to create rounded corners. You can see how it works by applying rounded corners to the #sidebar ID.

Open the Manage Style panel for the #sidebar ID and select Border Radius from the Category list. This opens the new Border Radius dialog. From here you can set a consistent border radius for all four corners or for each individual corner and you can also use the Oval option to set the height and width of each corner. The value you input in the fields defines the radius of the corner circle, so the higher the number, the rounder the corner gets. Set the radius to 5px, as in Figure 11.11, and click OK to apply the change.

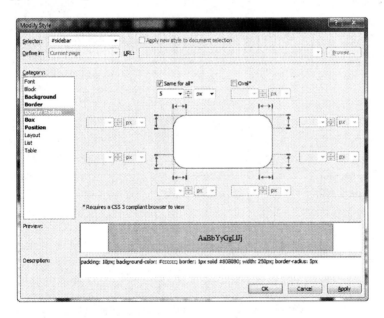

FIGURE 11.11
You can create rounded corners from the Border Radius option under Add and Manage styles in Expression Web 4 SP2.

Note that in Design view, nothing changed. This is because Expression Web 4's Design view does not support advanced CSS3 features such as Border Radius. That doesn't mean your change didn't take effect—it just means you can't preview it in the application. To see your rounded corners, you have to preview the page in a modern browser.

Summary

As you can see, CSS is a powerful tool that goes far beyond merely changing the color and size of fonts. In this hour, you got a glimpse of how you can use CSS to create highly complex and visually compelling layouts and how easy it is to make dramatic changes to the look of the page without destroying the content in the process. The examples in this hour merely scratch the surface of what is possible when you use CSS as a layout tool, but they give you a good idea of what you can do. Finishing this hour, you have better ideas of why having strong CSS skills gives you an advantage in the web design market and why Expression Web 4 is an excellent tool not only to create but also to learn CSS.

In this hour, you learned how to move beyond simple text styling to create classes that change the appearance of specific elements within a page. You also learned how to group sections of the page using divs and how to assign IDs and classes to these divs to get detailed control of your content. You learned how to set selector names so that certain styles apply to only certain elements within an ID, class, or subclass, and how to apply and modify those styles to change the overall look of your page. In addition, you got an introduction to pseudoclasses and learned how to use them to style active content within a page to give the visitor a more interactive experience. Finally, you learned how the box model works and how you can use it to create layouts and style content. In the next hour, you look at the CSS code and learn how to manipulate the code to achieve the same results you saw in this hour. You also learn how to completely separate the style from the content by creating standalone style sheets and how to apply the styles you have already created to other pages you build.

Q&A

Q. *I can't find this Quick Tag Selector bar you keep talking about! Where is it?*

A. By default, the Quick Tag Selector is on, but you might have accidentally turned it off. If it is not visible directly under the tabs at the top of the View pane, open the View menu from the menu bar and click Quick Tag Selector to activate it. The Quick Tag Selector has an orange box with a check mark to its left when it is active.

Q. I changed the name of a style/class/ID I created and now it isn't applied to the content. Why is that?

A. If you change the name of a style, class, or ID, you also need to change the name in the tags that the style, class, or ID is applied to. You can do this by selecting the tag using the Quick Tag Selector and opening the Tag Editor.

Q. I followed the tutorial and created pseudoclasses for my links, but I still can't see them in Design view. Am I doing something wrong?

A. Design view displays only the plain link style, not the pseudoclasses. To test the pseudoclasses you created, you have to preview your page in a browser.

Workshop

The Workshop has quiz questions and exercises to help you put to use what you just learned. If you get stuck, the answers to the quiz questions are in the next section. But try to answer them first. Otherwise, you'll be cheating yourself.

Quiz

1. What is the difference between styles, classes, and IDs?

2. Can you apply multiple styles, classes, or IDs to the same item?

3. What is the difference between padding, border, and margin in the Box model?

Answers

1. A style is a set of styling parameters applied to a specific selector, such as p, h1, ul, li, or td. A class is an independent set of styling parameters that can be applied to any selector and divs and spans. An ID is similar to a class, except each ID can be used only once per page.

2. Yes, you can apply multiple styles, classes, and IDs to an item, but not all at the same time. To do this, you need to place the different styles, classes, and IDs in concentric circles around the item. For instance, if you want a block of text to be affected by an ID, a class, and a specific style, you need to place the content inside a div with the class applied that is surrounded by a div with the ID applied.

3. The padding is the space between the content and the inner sides of the box. The border is the demarcating line that separates the inside and the outside of the box. The margin is the space between the outer sides of the margin and the surrounding content.

Exercise

Create a new div and place all the content except the main heading and the sidebar inside it. Create a new class called .content and apply it to the div. Use your knowledge of the box model to position the text so that the space below the sidebar box is empty.

Styling with Code: Fully Immersed in CSS

What You'll Learn in This Hour:

▶ How to read CSS code

▶ How inline styles differ from other styles

▶ How to apply styles, classes, and IDs to tags in Code view

▶ How to create external style sheets and apply them to multiple pages

In Hour 10, "Bringing Style to Substance with Cascading Style Sheets," and Hour 11, "Getting Boxed In, Part 2: Knee Deep in CSS," you learned how to create styles and apply them to content in Design view. But that's just half the story. To fully grasp what Cascading Style Sheets (CSS) is all about, you need to go to the source and learn how to read the code.

Fortunately, CSS code is simple to learn, especially when you have Expression Web 4's many CSS tools available whenever you get confused. Just as in Design view, you have full access to the CSS panels when you work in Code view, and all the tools you used in the past two hours are available for use in the same way.

This hour goes beyond the basics, and you learn how styling actually works and how to create, apply, and modify styles without using the tools every time. Because the tools Expression Web 4 provides are excellent, they are sometimes cumbersome to use, especially if you make quick, minor changes and already know what to do. Other benefits to using Code view are that you have more control when it comes to the placement and attribution of tags, and you can get a better overview of what is happening to your code. Also, you get a much clearer picture of the meaning of the phrase "separating the style from the content."

In addition to how to read, write, and dissect CSS code, this hour covers how to create separate style sheets and apply them to multiple files. You also see how easy it is to move styles from one file to another and to apply a style created in one file to other files without having to re-create it. By the end of this hour, you will have the necessary tools and understanding to use CSS not only as a styling tool, but also as a platform to create visually stunning websites with clean and concise code that looks the same across most, if not all, browsers and platforms.

Introducing CSS: The Code Version

In the previous two hours, you created a series of styles, classes, and IDs. In this hour, you inspect and expand on these, so if you didn't do all the tasks in earlier hours, you should replace the default.html file and the myCameras.html file with the ones supplied in the lesson files for this hour.

To work, CSS requires two sets of code: the styles and the tags to which the styles are attached. Let's take a closer look at the styles as they appear in code form. Expression Web 4 gives you multiple ways to view the CSS code. By far, the easiest way of doing so is simply to hover over the style in question in the Manage Styles panel. When you do so, a ScreenTip opens to display the entire style code in a pop-up window (see Figure 12.1).

FIGURE 12.1
Hovering the mouse pointer over a style in the Manage Styles panel brings up a ScreenTip that displays the CSS code for that style.

With the default.html file open, hovering over the #sidebar style gives you the following output:

```
#sidebar {
    padding: 10px;
    border-radius: 5px;
```

```
    background-color: #CCCCCC;

    border: 1px solid #808080;

    width: 250px;

}
```

This is a typical style. It consists of the style name followed by a set of curly braces. The braces contain all the actual styling code: Each attribute followed by its respective values after a colon. A semicolon separates the attributes.

As you can see, the CSS code Expression Web 4 generates is easy to read. The only reason why each attribute is on a separate line is for readability. If you want to, you could remove all the line breaks and write the entire style on one line, but, as you can see, it would be much harder to read:

```
#sidebar { padding: 10px; border-radius: 5px; background-color: #cccccc;

border: 1px solid #808080; width: 250px;}
```

> Because of the limited physical width of this book, the entire line doesn't fit on one single line when printed. Normally, if you look at the line in Expression Web 4, it would appear on one line. Just like in this book, there are times when CSS confined to a single line is arbitrarily divided into multiple lines by the application you use to look at the code. Even so, the style works the exact same way. The information you should walk away with here is that it is the semicolons that define when a line of code ends, not the line breaks.

By the Way

Now that you know what the CSS code looks like, the next logical question is, "Where is it located?" If you paid close attention when you created the styles in the previous two hours, you might already have a good idea. Directly under the Selector box in the New and Modify Style dialog was the Define In box, which was set to Current page. That means all the styles you created so far are stored in the same page as the content—more specifically, at the top of the page inside the <head> tag. The <head> tag contains functional but nonvisual content and information about the current page.

To see where the styles are stored, switch to Code view and scroll to the top of the page. Directly under the <meta> tags is a tag that says <style type="text/css">. You can find all the styles within this tag (see Figure 12.2).

In Hour 8, "Cracking the Code: Working in Code View," you were introduced to the Code View toolbar. Now is a good time to use it. To get an idea of how much code Expression Web 4 created for you when you created the styles, place your cursor on any of the lines with CSS code and then click the Select Tag button on the toolbar. This highlights all the CSS code. Likewise, to highlight the code within one style, you can use the Select Block button. However, reading this code can still be daunting. Currently, you have 13 styles defined, and many style sheets have hundreds or even thousands of styles.

FIGURE 12.2
You can find the CSS code at the top of the default.html page inside the <head> tag in Code view.

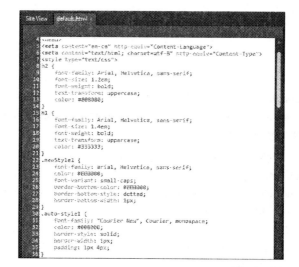

To find a particular style in Code view, all you need to do is click the style in question in the Manage Styles panel, and Expression Web 4 highlights the style for you. While in the Manage Styles panel, you can even use the arrow keys to navigate between styles for quick-and-easy access to the particular style, class, or ID on which you want to work.

The Value of Separation

Throughout this book, there have been several mentions of the styles being separate from the content. Now, for the first time, you see what this means in real life: The style code is literally separate from the rest of the content in the page. There are several reasons for this. First, keeping the styles separate means that style code does not clutter the content portion of the page. Second, it's easier to make changes to both the styles and the content because they are easily distinguishable. Last, it means you don't have to insert styling code in the page whenever you add new content.

When you add CSS code to the head of an HTML page, the browser reads it and applies it to whatever content it finds below. In practical terms, it works kind of like a coin sorter. If you just dump various coins in a bucket, they have no order. However, a coin sorter sorts, separates, and puts each different coin size in its own collector. In HTML, the CSS code becomes the different coin slots, and as the content flows through the filter, the different kinds of content fall into their appropriate slots. Therefore, rather than sorting each piece of content individually by applying styles directly to it, CSS works as a template from which all the content sorts simultaneously.

Understanding Inline Styles

But what is a rule without an exception? In Hour 10, you created an inline style that applied to just one section of the page. You removed that inline style and replaced it with a class in Hour 11, so you need to make a new one. But this time, you see what goes on in the code and, through that, learn how the inline style gets its name.

1. With the default.html page open in Split view, scroll to the bottom of the page and place the cursor anywhere inside the last paragraph. Click the New Style button to create a new style and then use the drop-down menu to set the selector name to (Inline Style).

2. In the Font category, set font-size to 0.8em and font-variant to small-caps. In the Block category, set text-align to center. Click OK to apply the new inline style, the result of which you can see in Figure 12.3.

FIGURE 12.3
You can use inline styles to create specialized styles for small segments of content that should appear different from the regular content.

The last paragraph of the page changes appearance after you apply the inline style. But what matters is what happened in Code view. Look at the tag for this particular paragraph:

```
<p style="font-size: 0.8em; font-variant: small-caps; text-align: center">
```

Rather than creating a new style and adding it to the list at the top of the page, Expression Web 4 added this style inside the tag of the affected paragraph. The style is in the same line as the content—hence the name inline style. This explains not only why the style you just created affects only this particular paragraph, but also serves as a good example of why you should always try to keep your styles separate from your content. Just imagine what your HTML code would look like if every tag had to contain the necessary style attributes! With that said, inline styles are useful if you need to apply a special style featured only once in the entire page or site.

▼ **Try It Yourself**

Create a New Style in Code View Using IntelliSense

In Code view, you can make direct changes to the CSS code or create new styles with the help of IntelliSense. In this example, you create a new img style from scratch to give the image the appearance of having a white background with a gray border.

1. With the myCameras.html page open in Code view, find the `<style type="text/css">` tag and create a new line directly below it.

2. To create the new style, type **im** and IntelliSense suggests img. Press the Enter key to accept img, press the spacebar, and type a beginning curly bracket ({). In response, IntelliSense automatically moves you to the next line, inserts the end curly bracket on the line below, and brings up a list of all available attributes that apply to the img tag (see Figure 12.4).

FIGURE 12.4
IntelliSense automatically closes any bracket you start and gives you a list of the available attributes.

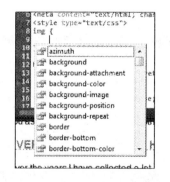

3. To create 5-pixel padding around the image, type **pa**. IntelliSense suggests padding. Press Enter to complete the word.

4. IntelliSense now opens a ScreenTip to tell you what kind of information the padding attribute requires. Because you want 5-pixel padding on all four sides, you can type **5px** and be done with it. If you want different values for each side, follow the ScreenTip and type, for example, **5px 4px 4px 10px** (top, right, bottom, left). Complete the line by entering a semicolon and pressing Enter to create a new line.

▼

To create a border, you need to set three attributes: `border-style`, `border-width`, and `border-color`. To help you remember this, IntelliSense reminds you and helps you set all three variables on one line: On the new line, type **border:**. This opens the Screen-Tip for the `border` attribute. IntelliSense now asks you for the values it needs. First up is `border-width`. Type **1px** and press the spacebar. The ScreenTip automatically jumps to the next variable, `border-color`, and opens a drop-down menu of colors for you (see Figure 12.5). Pick the gray color and press the spacebar. IntelliSense now asks you for the `border-style`. Select `solid` from the drop-down menu and finish the line with a semicolon. The two new lines should read `padding:5px;` and `border: 1px gray solid;`.

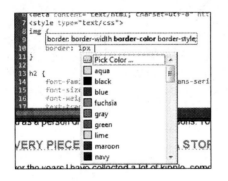

FIGURE 12.5
Depending on which variable is required, Intelli-Sense provides a drop-down menu of options for you to choose from. In this case, it provides a list of colors for the `border-color` variable.

To see the effects of your changes, click anywhere inside Design view to apply the changes. The image now has a 1-pixel solid gray border and 5 pixels of white padding. This example shows you how easy it is to write and make changes to CSS code in Code view and how IntelliSense works with you to simplify the code-writing process.

Applying Classes to Tags in Code View

In Hour 11, you learned to apply special styles to certain content with the use of classes. In one example, you used classes to change the position of the image in the myCameras.html page. This example provides a good basis for learning how Expression Web 4 applies classes to tags in Code view. If you open myCameras.html in Split view and click the image, the relevant code highlights in Code view (see Figure 12.6).

```
<img alt="Most of my cameras together" height="355"
src="Images/camerasSmall.jpg"
width="600" class="alignCenter" usemap="#FPMap0" />
```

FIGURE 12.6
The img tag for
the image high-
lights in Code
view when you
click the image
in Design view.

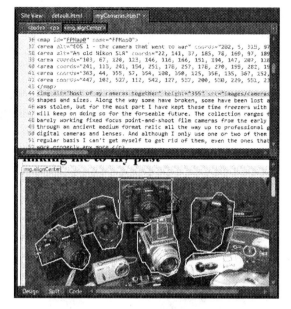

Inspecting the tag code, you see a new attribute toward the end:
class="alignCenter". This is how Expression Web 4 applies classes to tags, whether
they are selectors, spans, or divs. To change the class, all you need to do is edit the
class name in Code view. In Hour 11, you learned how to create two more alignment
classes. To apply one of these instead, simply change the class name to either
alignLeft or alignRight and you'll immediately see the changes in Design view.
Adding a class to an existing tag is just as easy: Simply type the word **class** before the
end bracket of the beginning tag, and IntelliSense gives you a drop-down list of all
available classes.

To see the CSS code for the class in Code view, right-click the class in the Manage
Styles panel and select Go to Code, or simply double-click the class to go right to it.
No matter where you are in the program, these functions take you straight to the rel-
evant CSS code in Code view.

Using Divs and Spans to Separate Content

We touched on both the <span> tag and the <div> tag earlier, and now it's time to take
a closer look at these separators. The main difference between the two is that span is
an inline separator, whereas div is a block separator. In other words, span's display
attribute is inline by default, whereas div's display attribute is block. You saw the difference between the two when you used the .alignCenter class to center the thumbnail
earlier: The inline value means that the content, although separated from the surrounding content, is still on the same line as the rest. In contrast, the block value creates a block or box on its own line that holds only the content inside the tag.

The default.html page contains two instances of the <span> tag that you created to highlight the word kipple and the random word you chose in the first paragraph. If you find the words in the Design portion of Split view and click them, you can see the corresponding <span> tags and how they are applied in Code view:

```
<span class="auto-style1"> kipple</span>
```

As you can see, the class application is no different in the span tag than in any other tag. However, because you were just starting to learn how to create styles, you didn't give the class a proper name, so it has the nondescript name auto-style1. It's important to give all your styles, classes, and IDs proper descriptive names so that you know what they do. But how do you do so without afterward going into the code and manually changing all the references to the style?

Renaming Styles and Applying the Change to All Tags in a Page

When you work with large pages or sites, you often run into situations in which you need to rename a style, class, or ID. The problem is that Expression Web 4 already applied these elements to many tags within your pages, and if you change the name of the style, class, or ID, all the references have to change as well. To help simplify this process and save you from the trouble of tracking down every reference to your now changed style, class, or ID, Expression Web 4 can make all the substitutions for you.

1. With the default.html page open in Split view, navigate both the Code and Design views so that you can see both span instances you created earlier by clicking one of them.

2. In the Manage Styles panel, right-click the .auto-style1 class and select Rename Class "auto-style1" from the context menu. This opens the Rename Class dialog.

3. In the Rename Class dialog (see Figure 12.7), give the class the new name highlight. Be sure to enable the Rename Class References in This Page box and click OK.

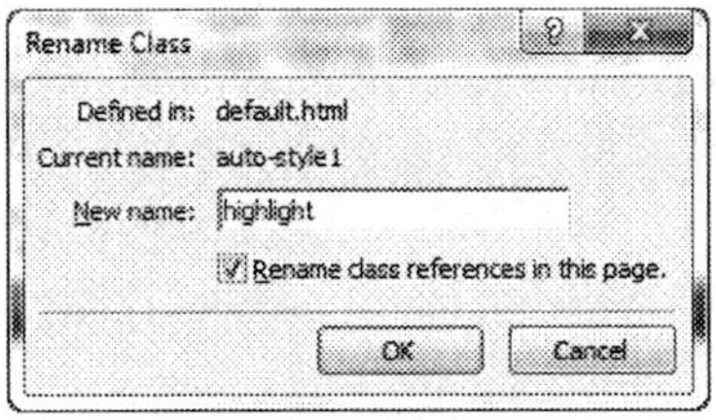

Rename Class

Defined in: default.html
Current name: auto-style1
New name: highlight
☑ Rename class references in this page.

OK   Cancel

FIGURE 12.7
The Rename Style, Class, and ID dialogs give you the option of renaming all references to the renamed element in the current page or in all pages affected by it.

When you click OK, not only does Expression Web 4 rename the class, but it also changes the references to the class in the page, as you can see in Code view. Changing all the references to a style, class, or ID to correspond with a name change extends to external style sheets, meaning that when you learn how to create an external style sheet and apply it to multiple pages, Expression Web 4 changes all references to the changed name throughout all these pages for you, even if they are not open!

In Hour 11, you used divs to create blocks that separated and sectioned the contents of the page. default.html now has two divs: one outer box with the ID wrapper and an inner box with the ID sidebar. To see how Expression Web 4 applies those divs, click the sidebar in Design view to see all the tags applied to it. When you click the <div#wrapper> tag in the Quick Tag Selector, all the content affected by the tag highlights both in Code and Design view. To find only the beginning tag, click the Find Matching Tag button on the Code View toolbar. As you can see, the application of an ID is similar to that of a class: <div id="wrapper">.

Because divs box in larger sections of content, it can be hard to see exactly where they apply and how much content they contain. You already saw how to use the Quick Tag Selector to highlight all the content affected by a tag. Another way is to use the Select Tab button on the Code View toolbar. If you need to see where the end </div> tag is located, click the Find Matching Tag button again, and Code view jumps to the end tag.

Creating Divs in Code View

As you may have experienced in Hour 11, dragging and dropping divs into Design view can be a bit tricky. A much easier and more effective way of applying divs is to use Code or Split view because in Code view, you can see exactly what content you are wrapping and place the beginning and end tags in the precise location you want them. You already inserted two divs in the default.html page, and now you are going to insert the same divs in the myCameras.html page.

1. With the myCameras.html page open in Split view, click the Home text button you created earlier to navigate both views to the top of the page.

2. From the Toolbox panel, drag an instance of the <div> tag into Code view and place it directly under the <body> tag. This creates a beginning and an end div tag: <div></div>.

3. Highlight and cut out the </div> end tag by pressing Ctrl+X. In Code view, navigate to the bottom of the page. There, you can see that the </body> tag is now red with a yellow background, indicating that the code is broken. Paste

the `</div>` tag you just cut out into the line directly above the `</body>` tag. If you click an element within the page, you can see that the `<div>` tag is now present in the Quick Tag Selector.

4. Add the sidebar to the page. Just like in the default.html page, the sidebar should appear alongside the content off the top, so in the markup it should appear right after the `<div>` you just created. Find the beginning `div` tag and add a new line directly underneath it. Drag and drop a new `<div>` tag into the new line or enter **`<div>`** manually. IntelliSense creates the end tag for you to keep the code from breaking. Again, highlight and cut out the end tag. Because this page doesn't have a descriptive section, the sidebar should contain only the Home link, so place your cursor at the end of the line containing the Home link and press Enter to create a new line. Paste the `</div>` end tag you cut out into this new line or enter **`</div>`**.

The myCameras.html page now has two divs, just as the default.html page does. However, the classes and IDs you used to style the divs are still in the default.html file. To apply them to myCameras.html as well, you need to create an external style sheet.

Creating External Style Sheets

By far the most powerful feature of CSS is that it gives you the ability to create styles, classes, and IDs stored in one central location and applied to many different pages or entire sites. This is where the Sheets part of the name Cascading Style Sheets (CSS) comes from.

An external style sheet is a dedicated file with the extension .css that contains only style code. Until now, Expression Web 4 has inserted all the style code you created into the head of your HTML pages, but doing so limits their application to that particular page. Now you need to move the styles from the HTML page to a new style sheet so that you can apply the same styles to multiple pages.

To create an external style sheet, you first have to create a .css file. The easiest way to create a .css file is to click the down arrow next to the New icon on the Common Toolbar and select CSS in the context menu. This creates a new file named Untitled_1.css. In most cases, the style sheet name is simply styles.css, but it is often a good idea to be more specific in naming to ensure that you know which site each sheet belongs to. After creating the new file, go to File, select Save As, and give it the name **kippleStyles.css**. When saved, it appears in the Folder panel, as shown in Figure 12.8.

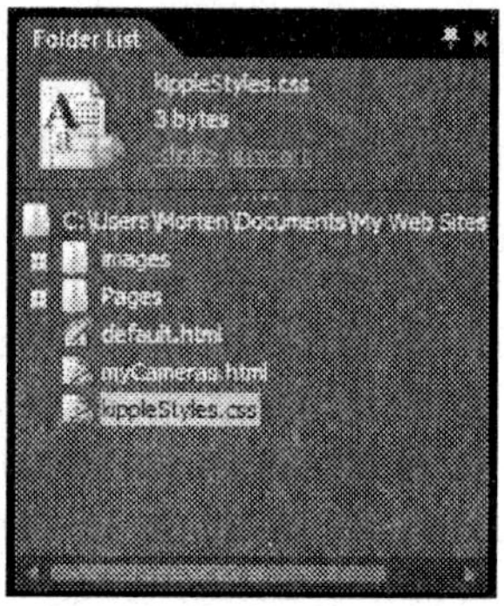

FIGURE 12.8
It's usually a good idea to give your .css files site-specific names to make sure you know where they belong.

Opening the new CSS file, you can see that it is completely empty. That is because unlike HTML and other markup files, a CSS file doesn't need any code other than the actual styles to function. Because it's a new file, there are no style definitions yet.

The next step is to attach the style sheet to your pages by using the Attach Style Sheet button in the Apply and Manage Styles panel. With the default.html page open, click the Attach Style Sheet button to open the Attach Style Sheet dialog (see Figure 12.9).

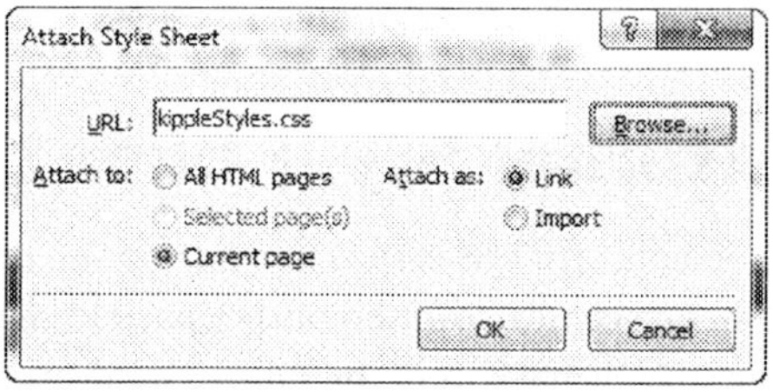

FIGURE 12.9
The Attach Style Sheet dialog lets you attach an external style sheet to the current page or all pages in the site using either the link or import method.

From here, you can browse to the style sheet you want to attach and choose whether you want to attach it to all the pages in your site or just the current page. (The Selected pages option becomes available if you highlight a series of pages in the Folders panel before opening the Attach Style Sheet dialog.) You also have the choice of whether to attach the style sheet using the link method or the import method. They produce nearly the same results, but the Link option provides the most consistent results.

Browse and select the kippleStyles.css file you just created. Select the otion Attach to All HTML Pages and then select Attach as Link. This attaches the new style sheet to all the HTML pages within your site by inserting the following line of code in the <head> tag:

```
<link href="kippleStyles.css" rel="stylesheet" type="text/css" />
```

The attached style sheet now appears in the Manage Styles panel under the styles embedded in the current page (see Figure 12.10).

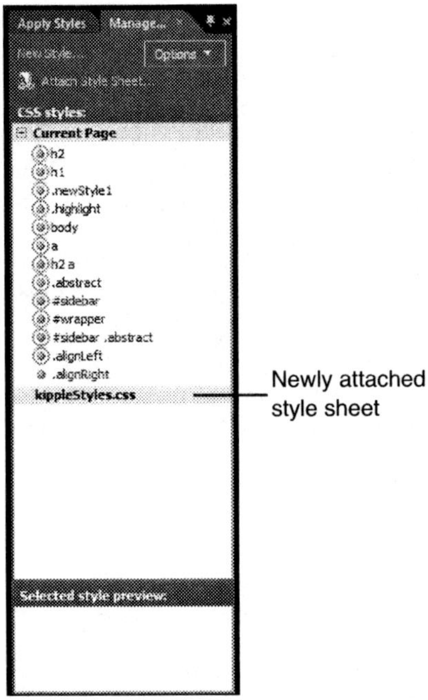

FIGURE 12.10
The newly attached style sheet appears in the Manage Styles panel underneath the locally embedded styles.

Newly attached style sheet

By the Way

The Difference Between Linking and Importing

The two methods for attaching a style sheet to an HTML file are linking and importing. The difference between the two is subtle and comes into play only in special cases.

The linking method simply tells the browser that styles are stored in the linked file for application to the content below. If you want to attach another style sheet to the page, you add a new link and so on. The linking method works across all browsers, no matter how old.

The importing method is somewhat different. First, you can use it within a style sheet to import another style sheet so that instead of calling two style sheets from the HTML file, you call one, and then the first style sheet calls the second one. But more important, the importing method does not work with some older browsers, and this can be used to prevent older browsers from trying to read style code they can't understand. However, this applies only to very old browsers and should not be a deciding factor in picking one method over the other. For all intents and purposes, both methods work the same way.

Moving Styles to and from the External Style Sheet

After the external style sheet is attached to all the pages in your site, the styles set in the kippleStyles.css file affect all the pages instead of just one. You have already created many styles in different pages, but they are stored in the head of each page and not in the style sheet. The obvious way to solve this is to cut and paste the code out of the pages and into the style sheet, but this method is both cumbersome and prone to error. Expression Web 4 provides a better solution in the form of the Manage Styles panel.

1. With the default.html file open, click and drag the body style from the Current Page area down the kippleStyles.css area. When you let go, the style appears below the kippleStyles.css heading.

> For this exercise, it is a good idea to pin the Toolbar panel to the side and let the Manage Styles panel cover the entire height of your screen. You can always unpin the panel later.

2. Using the same method, move the rest of the styles, classes, and IDs from the Current Page area to the kippleStyles.css area (see Figure 12.11).

3. When you finish moving all the styles, classes, and IDs to the kippleStyles.css area, scroll to the top of default.html in Code view. Note that all the style code is gone. All that is left is the `<style>` tag. In the Manage Styles panel, right-click any of the styles and select Go to Code. The new kippleStyles.css style sheet opens, and you can see that all the code previously housed in the head of the HTML file is now in the style sheet.

4. Open myCameras.html. Note that the styles you just moved from default.html now appear under kippleStyles.css in the Manage Styles panel for this page. Using the same technique, move the styles from myCameras.html to kippleStyles.css.

5. Press Ctrl+S to save the changes. This opens the Save Embedded Files dialog, which asks whether you want to save the changes to the kippleStyles.css file (see Figure 12.12). Click OK.

The kippleStyles.css file now contains all the styles from both default.html and myCameras.html. Expression Web 4 still applies the styles to the content of those pages, and they appear the same in Design view and in any browser you preview them in.

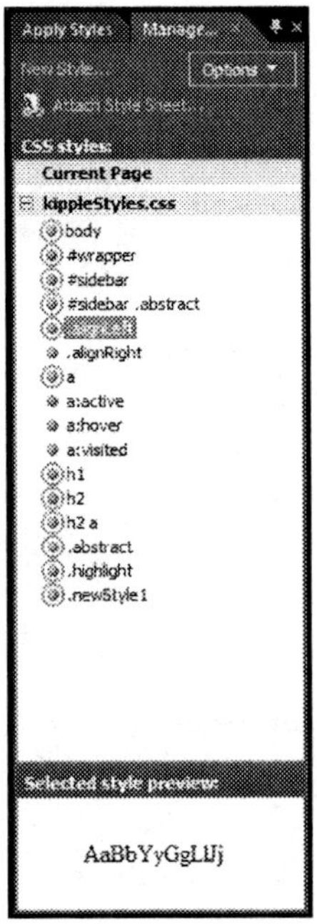

FIGURE 12.11
You can move styles, classes, and IDs from the current HTML file to the new .css file by dragging and dropping them into the new file area in the Manage Styles panel.

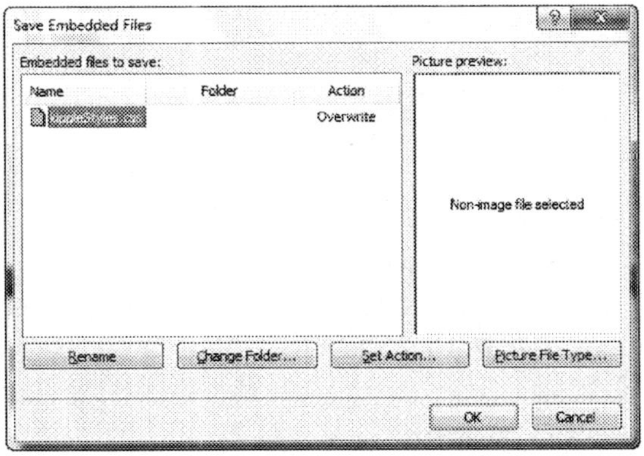

FIGURE 12.12
When you're saving an HTML file after making changes to styles contained in an external style sheet, Expression Web 4 always opens the Save Embedded Files dialog to ask whether you want to save the changes made in the style sheet as well.

Inspecting the code in kippleStyles.css, you can see that the order of the styles corresponds with the list of styles in the Manage Styles panel. If you change the order of the styles in the panel, the code reorganizes in the same manner. This is because the order of styles in the style sheet is relevant to the cascade: The lower in the sheet the style is, the more weight it has in deciding what the content should look like.

Did you Know?

> If you want to keep a style, class, or ID in both style sheets, you can use the same drag-and-drop technique to copy them. To do so, simply press and hold the Ctrl key on your keyboard while dragging and dropping the element. Just keep in mind when you do so that you will now have two styles with the same name, and the one in the style sheet that is listed furthest down in the cascade has precedence.

In some cases a style, class, or ID applies to only one page. In that case, it is a good idea to keep the element in the relevant page rather than in the style sheet. For example, in default.html, you created a class called `highlight` that applied to two words as an inline style. Now, the style sheet contains this class, but because only the default.html page uses it, the class should be only in that file. To return this particular class to its original location, simply open default.html and drag and drop the `.highlight` class back to Current Page (see Figure 12.13).

FIGURE 12.13
The final style structure of the styles for default.html.

Applying External Styles to a Page

Styles nested in an external style sheet act in the same way as styles nested in the current document. Therefore, Expression Web 4 applies them in the same way. Earlier in this hour, you created two divs to section out the content in the myCameras.html page. Now that you have attached the external style sheet, you can apply the same IDs and classes you used to change the layout of default.html to change the layout of myCameras.html.

1. With the myCameras.html file open in Split view, click anywhere inside the page in Design view and then click the first `<div>` tag in the Quick Tag Selector to select the div that wraps all the content. This highlights all the content in both Code view and Design view.

2. In the Manage Styles panel, right-click the #wrapper ID and select Apply Style from the context menu (see Figure 12.14). The tag in the Quick Tag Selector and in Code view changes to `<div#wrapper>` and the wrapper ID is applied.

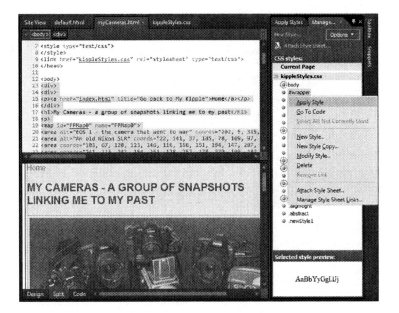

FIGURE 12.14
Applying a style from an external style sheet is no different from applying a style nested within the file itself.

3. In Code view, move the cursor one line down to select the next `<div>` tag, right-click the `#sidebar` ID in the Manage Styles panel, and select Apply Style. The tag changes to `<div#sidebar>` and the `#sidebar` ID is applied.

4. Because the position of the sidebar is no longer defined by the `#sidebar` ID, you also need to apply a class to the div. This action can also be done from the Apply Styles panel by selecting the relevant div (now `<div#sidebar>`) and clicking the appropriate alignment class (`.alignLeft` or `.alignRight`) in the Apply Styles panel. The tag changes to `<div#sidebar.alignRight>` and the alignment class is applied. Save the file and preview it in your browser (see Figure 12.15).

By previewing the page in a browser, you can see the styles you created for default.html applied to myCameras.html.

FIGURE 12.15
The layout IDs and classes created for default.html applied to myCameras.html. By navigating between the two files, you see they now look consistent when previewed in Internet Explorer.

Summary

Even though Expression Web 4 creates proper standards-based CSS code out of the box, understanding the CSS code can make your life as a designer a lot easier. In fact, in many cases, it makes more sense to work directly with the code rather than to use the point-and-click tools in the application. Fortunately, you can choose either way and customize your work process depending on the task.

In this hour, you learned how to build a CSS style using code and how to edit it in Code view with the help of IntelliSense. You also learned how to insert spans and divs in your page from Code view, and why doing so is often easier than doing it in Design view. In addition, you saw how inline styles differ from other styles and where the name inline stems from. You also learned how to rename both inline and other styles without going through all the code and renaming each instance afterward.

Most important, you learned how to completely separate the styles from the content by creating an external style sheet and how this makes styling groups of pages or an entire website much easier. Understanding this process is fundamental; it dramatically reduces your workload and makes changing and upgrading the look and feel of large websites an easy and straightforward process.

At this point, you should begin to realize the true power of standards-based web design and the use of HTML and CSS. In upcoming hours, you use this knowledge to turn up the "wow" factor of the myKipple site by creating advanced layouts and menus.

Q&A

Q. *When I try to apply an inline style to a single word, it is applied to the entire text block instead. What am I doing wrong?*

A. When you create an inline style, the new style is applied to the closest tag. That means that, unless you have separated the single word from the rest of the block using the <span> tags, the inline style will be applied to the block tag. To apply the inline style to a single word, you have to wrap it in <span> tags first and then create the new inline style.

Q. *I followed the tutorial to create divs in code view, but everything looks the same as it did before!*

A. When there is a problem with content being wrapped with <div> or <span> tags and nothing looking any different, the answer is usually answered by the following three questions: Does the <div> or <span> actually wrap anything? A common mistake when inserting these elements is to forget to place the end tag at the end of the content. This is because both IntelliSense and other tools automatically place the end tag right after the beginning tag before the content. The second question is, do the tags close properly? You might have forgotten to paste the end tag in after cutting it out, or you might have placed it in the wrong spot. If so, the code will be broken, and you should see the little warning sign in the status bar and find highlighted code further down in the document. Finally, did you actually apply the class or ID to the tag? If you click the content that should be styled by the class or ID, and the Quick Tag Selector reads <div> or <span> without the class or style attached, you need to apply the style or ID to make everything work properly.

Workshop

The Workshop has quiz questions and exercises to help you put to use what you just learned. If you get stuck, the answers to the quiz questions are in the next section. But try to answer them first. Otherwise, you'll be cheating yourself.

Quiz

1. What is the difference between a <span> tag and a <div> tag?

2. What are the two main methods used to make new styles, classes, and IDs you have been introduced to?

3. What is the benefit of moving styles to an external style sheet?

Answers

1. The `<span>` tag is an inline tag, meaning that if it's applied to content in a line, the content stays on the same line. The `<div>` tag, on the other hand, is a block tag, meaning it creates a new block or line that the content it wraps is placed on. For this reason, `<span>` is used to highlight words or elements, whereas `<div>` is used to group sections.

2. You now have two methods to create styles: You can use the New Style button on the Apply and Manage Styles panel and create a new style through the dialog, and you can create a new style from scratch in Code view with the help of IntelliSense.

3. By placing your styles in an external style sheet, you can now use the same styles to control the look of several pages. It also means you can make changes to one style and see those changes applied to all the pages it is attached to without ever opening them.

Exercise

Using the techniques you learned, change the layout of the eos1.html page by adding divs and styling them with IDs and classes to match the default.html and myCameras.html pages.

Getting Visual, Part 3: Images as Design Elements with CSS

What You'll Learn in This Hour:

▶ How to apply images as backgrounds

▶ How to use repeating background images to achieve a consistent look

▶ How to use background images as style elements

▶ How to replace list bullets with images

▶ How to import and change .psd files directly inside Expression Web 4

In Hour 6, "Getting Visual, Part 1: Adding Images and Graphics," and Hour 7, "Getting Visual, Part 2: Advanced Image Editing, Thumbnails, and Hotspots," you learned how to insert images as objects in a web page. However, if you have spent any length of time on the Web, you know that images are used for so much more and most prominently as design elements. In fact, most of the nontext content you find on a website is an image in some form or another. This is because the basic building blocks of a web page (HTML and CSS) can only go so far in creating graphic elements. And even though with the introduction of HTML5 we can now make rounded corners and box shadows and even use advanced graphics, using regular image elements is often easier and more backward compatible. Fortunately, HTML and CSS give you a huge variety of ways in which you can introduce images as design elements by adding them as backgrounds, replaced items, and even buttons, without thereby displacing the actual content on the page. Understanding how to achieve this means you can take your site from a plain-looking boxes-and-borders layout to a graphics-heavy visual masterpiece.

When creating graphics-heavy websites, you move out of the realm of strict web authoring and into that of a designer. This is because, for all its virtues, no web-authoring software yet includes full-fledged design capabilities; it can't make graphics from scratch. Microsoft Expression Studio includes a powerful design application in Expression Design, but most designers are already using Adobe Photoshop as their base of operations. For this reason, Expression Web 4 includes a powerful Photoshop import feature that lets you import .psd files and slice them into workable pieces right in the web-authoring application. This feature is a huge timesaver if you know its capabilities and limitations. The lessons of this hour show you how to use graphics and CSS to create visual design elements for your site and then how to use the Photoshop import feature to generate workable graphics.

Images as Backgrounds: A Crash Course

In Hours 6 and 7, you learned how to insert images into the content of your page. But as you saw, these images were content elements. What you want now are design elements, and that requires a somewhat different approach.

As you have already learned, when you insert an image into a web page, you are actually inserting a replaced item, a link that is replaced with an external file. This same technique can be used to replace items such as CSS backgrounds, meaning that rather than giving your box a flat-color (or no-color) background, you can use the image of your choice as the background.

Furthermore, you can control the way in which this image displays to achieve different effects. As with the content images, any image used as a background must be RGB and in one of the three main formats: GIF, JPEG, or PNG.

Using an Image as a Background with CSS

In the lesson files for this hour is a series of image files. Before going any further, you need to create a new folder called Graphics and import these files into it using the technique you learned in Hour 6.

In this first lesson, you apply an image as a background to see how you can easily change the look of an entire page, even with a small image file.

1. With the default.html page open in Design view, open the Modify Style dialog for the body style you created previously.

2. In the Background category, use the Browse button next to the background-image attribute to navigate to the Graphics folder you just created. Select the file called demoTile.gif and click OK. In the Preview box, you see a red-and-black texture appear behind the text (see Figure 13.1). Click OK.

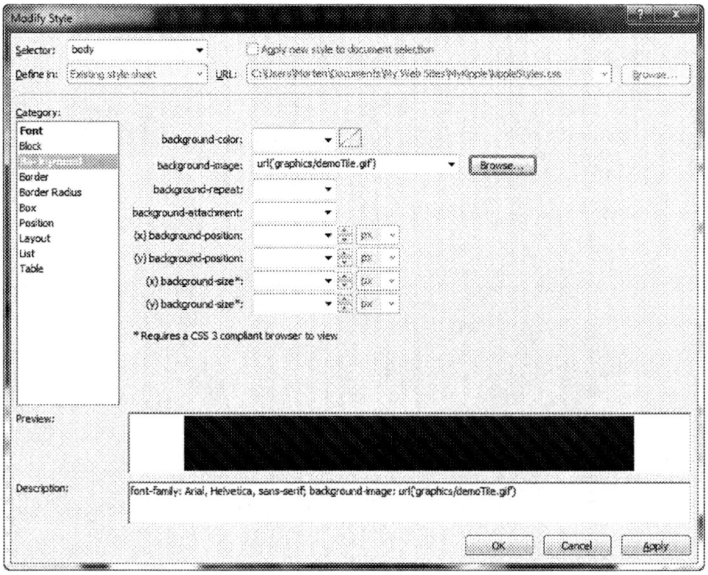

FIGURE 13.1
When the demoTile.gif file is defined as the background image for the body style, you can preview it in the dialog.

In Design view, you now see that the entire background of the page has been over-taken by a red-and-black texture. However, if you open the demoTile.gif file you just inserted as a background in your regular file explorer outside of Expression Web 4, you see that it is, in fact, just a 20-pixel-by-20-pixel image. So, how is it covering the entire background? By default, if you set an image as a background for any style, the image automatically repeats or tiles both horizontally and vertically from the uppermost-left corner down to the end of the page. This gives the designer the ability to use a tiny image to cover a large area. Otherwise, the background image would need to be as wide as the display on the largest monitor imaginable and as tall as the longest page you could come up with, and that would be a very large image indeed.

The Background Attributes

To see how this tiling works in real life, you can turn it off. To do so, go back to the Background category of the body style and set the background-repeat attribute to no-repeat. Now, only one instance of the background appears in the upper-left corner (see Figure 13.2).

The background-repeat attribute can be set to one of four values that give you a variety of options in terms of how to display your background image. You've already seen what no-repeat does; repeat is the default setting by which the image is tiled both horizontally and vertically; repeat-x tiles the image only along the x-axis, meaning there will be one line of tiles along the top going from left to right;

and repeat-y tiles the image only along the y-axis, meaning there will be one line of tiles along the left side going from top to bottom.

FIGURE 13.2
With the background-repeat attribute set to no-repeat, the background image appears only once in the upper-left corner of the area.

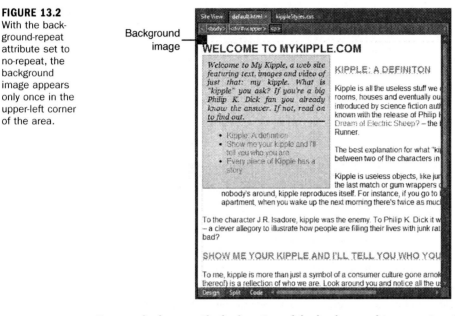

You can further specify the location of the background image using the (x) background-position and (y) background-position attributes, in which you can give the background image an absolute position with a numeric value or you can set it to left, center, or right for the x value and top, center, or bottom for the y value. For example, by setting both the (x) background-position and (y) background-position attributes to center, the image will be located in the middle of the area relative to the total width and height of the area within the tags (see Figure 13.3).

The Background category also lets you set the background-attachment attribute for the image. The default value of this attribute is scroll, meaning that the background is affected if you scroll up, down, left, or right in the page, just like the rest of the content. If you set this attribute to fixed, the background image is fixed in the same location relative to the browser window, so the image stays even if you scroll through the content.

New in SP2 is the addition of the X and Y background-size attributes that let you resize the background image to a specific size or a percentage. This is a CSS3 feature and only works in some browsers. To see what browsers support background-size, go to www.caniuse.com.

FIGURE 13.3
With the (x)
background-
position and
(y) background-
position attrib-
utes set to
center, the
background
image is cen-
tered on the
page relative to
the total width
and height.

The background-color attribute comes into play whenever you use a background-repeat value other than default or repeat and when the image does not display for whatever reason. All the area not covered by the background image has the color defined by the background-color attribute.

As a rule of thumb, always set the background-color of the body because you never know if visitors have images turned off or have set their browsers to apply a color other than white to pages with no background color defined. To drive this point home, some designers have started posting screen grabs of sites with their "underwear showing" (that is, no background color defined) in a Flickr group by the same name. To see the growing list of such sites and what happens when you forget to give your site underwear, visit www.flickr.com/groups/underwearshowing/.

Did you Know?

How Backgrounds Relate to the Content and the Page

Background images work exactly the same way that background colors work in styles, meaning they cover the area within the confines of the box that contains the content within the beginning and end tags. In the preceding example, you gave the style that governs the body tag a background image, meaning that the image is applied to the background of the entire page. If you define a background image for any other style you have created, the attributes act in the same way, but they will be applied in relation to each individual object to which they are applied.

Applying a Background Image to an ID

To fully understand how background images in CSS work, you need to see how they relate to the content and to each other. In this example, you apply two background images: one to the body style and one to a new ID you are going to create to contain the individual page content.

1. Open the Modify Style dialog for the body style and change the background image to the file tile.jpg.

2. Remove all the other styling to ensure that the image tiles throughout the entire page. The new image is a gray-and-white texture on which the page will be built (see Figure 13.4). At the same time, set the background-color to #FFFFFF (white) to ensure that the page looks great even if images are disabled.

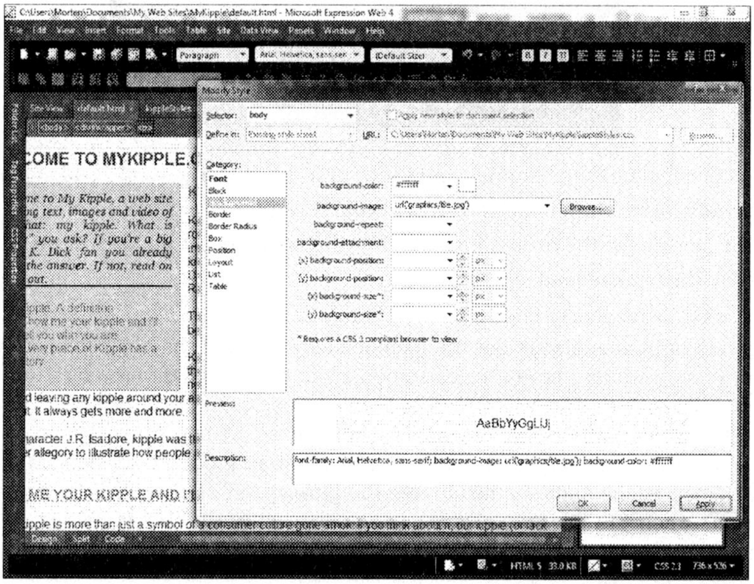

FIGURE 13.4
Clicking Apply rather than OK in the Modify Style dialog gives you the ability to see the style applied without closing the dialog.

3. In Hour 14, "Harnessing the Power of CSS Layouts," you learn how to use CSS to section off different parts of the page to create flexible layouts. Here's a little sneak peek: To separate the header area of the page (where the title and menu will go) from the rest of the content, you need to wrap the main content in a new ID. In Split view, find the line wrapped in <h1> tags and create a new line directly below. Type <div id="mainContent"> and IntelliSense creates the end </div> tag for you (see Figure 13.5). Select and cut out the end </div> tag, scroll to the bottom of the page, and paste it in just before the end </body> tag. Now, the content of the page is wrapped separately and can be styled separately.

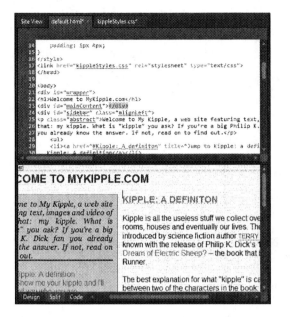

FIGURE 13.5
Inserting new
<div> tags is
usually easier in
Code view.

Did you Know?

As you can see from the bottom of the code page, after a while, you start to get a lot of end tags that are hard to distinguish because they are identical. An easy way to keep track of what end tag belongs to what beginning tag is to use code comments to name them. What I do is select an end tag, such as </div>, and click the Find Matching Tag button on the Code view toolbar to find the beginning tag. I note the name, click the Find Matching Tag button again to go back to the end tag, and place a comment directly after it to keep track. In HTML, comments are wrapped in special tags starting with <!-- and ending with -->. You can use the Insert HTML Comment button on the Code View Toolbar or press Ctrl+/ to insert a comment tag. For example, in my page, the two div end tags look like this:

```
</div> <!-- END #mainContent -->
</div> <!-- END #wrapper -->
```

4. Create a new style with the ID #mainContent to match the <div> you just created. Make sure it is defined in the kippleStyles.css style sheet.

5. In the Background category, use the Browse button to set background-image to paperTile.png. Set the background-repeat attribute to repeat-y so that the image tiles only vertically.

6. When you click Apply, you see that the background image has an edge to it and that the text is currently overflowing it. To realign the text so it fits on the inside of the graphic, go to Box and set padding-right and padding-left to 15px. Click OK to apply the changes; then save and preview the page in your browser (see Figure 13.6).

FIGURE 13.6
With the new background images applied to the page, it looks dramatically different.

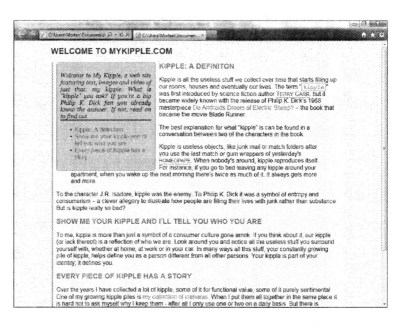

As you can see, the backgrounds are relative to the tag to which they are applied; the body background covers the entire page regardless of how wide or tall the window is, whereas the `#mainContent` background is constrained inside the div.

Background Images and the Box Model

To see how the background images relate to the box model, open the Modify Styles dialog for the h2 style, set `background-image` to `underline.png` and `background-repeat` to `no-repeat`. Click OK to apply the style change. By looking at the headings in Design view, you see that they now have a gray line behind them toward the top. However, there are two problems: First, the image is called "underline," so it is obviously meant to be an underline, and second, the image is missing from the top h2 title.

Let's tackle the last one first. If you click the top title and look at the tag selector box, it is obvious why you can't see the underline graphic behind the text: Even though the sidebar box pushes the text to the side, the h2 box still stretches to the far-left side of the page and the background with it (see Figure 13.7). To solve this problem, you need to change the `display` attribute for the h2 style. By default, all headings have the `display` attribute set to block, meaning they appear on their own line and span the width of the box in which they are placed (in this case, the `#mainContent` div). To make the box shift to the side to accommodate the sidebar, open the Modify Style dialog for the h2 style, go to Layout, and set `display` to inline-block.

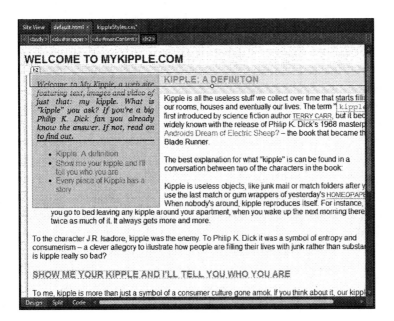

The first problem is less cryptic and can be solved with some common-sense thinking: To move the line to the bottom of the box, simply set the (y) background-position to bottom and the (x) background-position to left. However, even so, the line still appears behind the text, not under it. This is where the box model comes into play.

As you learned in Hour 12, "Styling with Code: Fully Immersed in CSS," the background spans the entire area inside the box drawn by the tags. The same thing goes for the background image. You also learned that the padding defines the space between the content and the inner edges of the box. This means that if you want an image to appear above, below, to the left, or to the right of your content, you need to increase the padding to leave room for it in whatever direction you want the image to appear.

In this case, you want the background image to appear below the text content of the h2 headings. You set the (y) background-position attribute to bottom, which means the image hugs the bottom of the box. Therefore, if you increase the bottom padding, the image shifts down relative to the text. To do so, open the Modify Style dialog for the h2 style and go to the Box category. The next step is a bit of trial and error: Uncheck the Same for All box for Padding and then set bottom-padding to 5px. Click Apply and move the Modify Style dialog to the side to see whether this produced the result you were looking for. In this case, the image didn't move far enough down, so use the up and down buttons to increase the bottom-padding value to 10px and click Apply again. If you are satisfied with what you see, click OK to finalize the change.

Stacking Order Means You Can Pile Your Images

Because background images are style elements contained within the box model, they act just like any other feature in the box. The most obvious advantage of this is that it gives you the ability to stack multiple images on top of each other, just like a pile of photos, by setting them as backgrounds for different elements. This method also preserves any transparencies (if the browser supports them), meaning you can place one transparent image on top of another one and thus see one through the other. In fact, using this method, there is no limit to how deep your stack of images can be, except the capabilities of the computer that displays them.

As with all other style elements, the cascade decides the stacking order of images used as backgrounds: The tag closest to the content has top position, followed by the second closest, and so on. This way, the background of the most relevant object ends up on top. While you were following the lessons earlier in this hour, what you were actually doing was stacking one image on top of another. When you test the current page in your browser and look at the h2 headings, you see the underline.png image stacked on top of the paperTile.png image, which in turn is stacked on top of the tile.jpg image. And as you can see from Figure 13.8, the transparencies of the two topmost images stay intact throughout the page.

FIGURE 13.8
Default.html now has three background images stacked on top of one another: tile.jpg, paperTile.png, and underline.png. Each appears on top of the other because of their order in the page hierarchy.

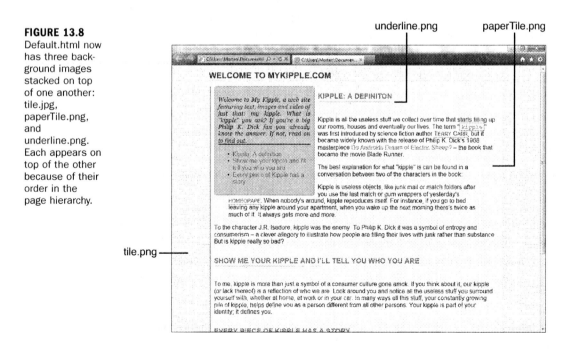

Using Images as List Bullets

In addition to images being used as backgrounds, they have another extremely use-ful application: They can be used to replace list item bullets.

When you change the style of lists, keep in mind that depending on what you want to achieve, there are three different tags to which you can attach styles. An ol style affects all the list items in ordered lists as a group. A ul style affects all the list items in unordered lists as a group. An li style affects all list items individually regardless of whether they are in an ordered or unordered list. You can target only list items in ordered lists by creating an ol li style and an unordered list with an ul li style. Of course, you can also make these styles subsidiary to any class, ID, or group of classes or IDs.

By default, a bullet precedes all unordered list items. However, this is but one of many different options. Figure 13.9 shows how the eight main list styles appear in a browser when no additional styling has been applied. But for all their convenience and functionality, these items are basic and exchanging them for images is a quick-and-easy way to bring your design to that next level.

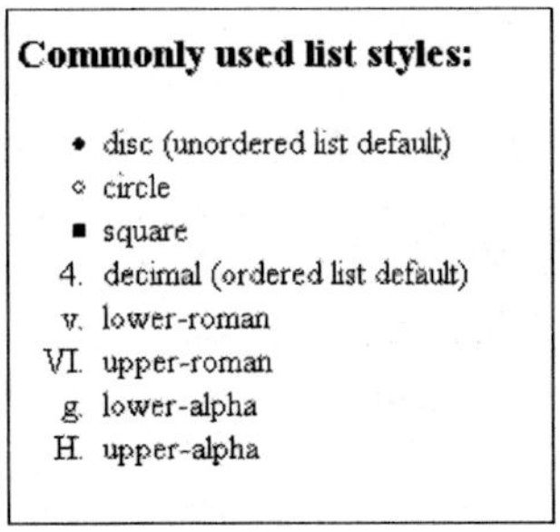

Commonly used list styles:

- disc (unordered list default)
- ○ circle
- ■ square
- 4. decimal (ordered list default)
- v. lower-roman
- VI. upper-roman
- g. lower-alpha
- H. upper-alpha

FIGURE 13.9
The eight main list styles as they appear in a browser with no additional styling.

Switching out the bullet for an image is similar to changing the bullet style. Because list items are a special type of content in HTML, there is a separate section for them in the New and Modify Style dialogs.

1. With the default.html page open in Design view, create a new style with the selector name ul. This style affects all list items in unordered lists. Make sure Define In is set to Existing Style Sheet and kippleStyles.css is the URL.

2. In the List category, use the Browse button to select the arrow.gif file (see Figure 13.10). Click OK to create the new style.

The new style you made replaces the bullets in front of the list items with small arrows. As with the backgrounds, any image file can be used as a list bullet. (Although, for obvious reasons, I advise you to use small ones.) However, unlike the backgrounds, the bullet image is not directly related to the box but rather to the first line of text in each item. In practical terms, this means that if you add left padding, the distance between the bullet image and the text increases, but if you add bottom padding, the bullet stays on the line. This situation can produce some strange results if you use a large font size because the bullet image stays in its original position in relation to the first line of text rather than grow with the font size. Figure 13.11 demonstrates how both regular bullets and bullet images react to different styling of the li tag. Note that standard HTML bullets size according to the font size.

Watch Out!

The height of the image itself decides the vertical positioning of a bullet image, not the font size or any other style element. If you want a bullet image to appear higher in relation to the text, you need to make it physically taller in your image-editing program by adding more space at the bottom of the image.

The List category in the New and Modify Style dialogs also includes the list-style-position attribute. It can be set to either inside or outside. (outside is default.) This attribute describes the position of the bullet in relation to the box. If it is set to outside, the bullet or bullet image appears outside of the box. If it is set to inside, the bullet or bullet image appears inside the box. This value does not change the actual distance between the bullet and the text, however. As you can see in Figure 13.11, the distance remains the same and is changed with the padding-left attribute. The difference between the two becomes apparent when the list item has more than one line of text: If list-style-position is set to inside, the bullet is treated as if it is part of the text, and the second line of text lines up with the edge of the box underneath the bullet.

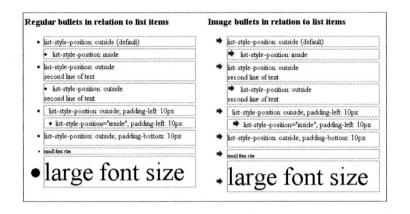

FIGURE 13.11
Two identical lists show how the standard HTML bullet and a list-style-image behave in relation to the list item text when different style attribute values are applied. To show the bullet in relation to the box, each list item has a 1-pixel gray border on all four sides.

Did you Know?

Because of the somewhat odd behavior of list-style-images, many designers set the list-style-type for the list to none and create an li style using a regular no-repeat background image with the (x) background-position set to left and the (y) background-position set to center instead. Unlike the list-style-image, this background image centers vertically with the box for each line. Keep in mind that if you do this, you have to apply the background to the li style. If you apply it to the ul or ol style, the background image is applied to the list as a whole and not the individual list items.

Importing Adobe Photoshop Files

The term *web design* is a somewhat confusing one, especially when talking about the tools used. You can question whether the actual design of a page or site takes place in web-authoring software, such as Expression Web 4, or in other applications, with Expression Web 4 and similar programs merely used to build the framework to display the design. Regardless of where you stand in this debate, you cannot dismiss one fact: Pure design applications, such as Expression Design and Adobe Photoshop, play an integral part in creating visually stunning websites.

More than just a tool for photographers to manipulate and clean up their photos, Adobe Photoshop has grown into a design platform from which you can create everything from artwork to broadcast graphics and websites. However, creating graphics for a website using Photoshop has always involved cropping and exporting images that you then imported into the web-authoring application. And because the two applications were not connected, any change required in the image required a new round of exporting and importing the altered image. With Photoshop Import, the Expression Web development team has done away with this cumbersome process, at least partially.

In addition to regular file imports, Expression Web 4 has a dedicated function for importing Adobe Photoshop (.psd) files. And because .psd files usually contain several layers, you are given the ability to select which layers to include in the import so that you can produce several different images out of one file.

1. With the default.html page open in Design view, click File on the menu bar and select Adobe Photoshop (.psd) under Import. This opens a browser dialog where you select the .psd file you want to import. Select the file named myKipple sticker art.psd from the lesson files and click Open. This opens the Import Adobe Photoshop (.psd) File dialog (see Figure 13.12).

FIGURE 13.12
The Import Adobe Photoshop (.psd) File dialog gives you a series of options for importing and converting Adobe Photoshop files to web-ready images.

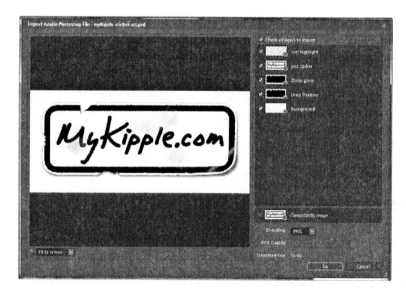

2. By default, the Check All Layers to Import option is checked, meaning the output will be the image as it appears with all the layers activated. By unchecking individual layers, you can select which layers to include in the final export. Although you can't see it, the total area covered by the exported image

changes with the content you choose to export, so if you uncheck the Background layer, the image size shrinks to contain only the remaining content.

3. When you are satisfied with your layer selection, you can choose whether to export the image as a GIF, JPEG, or PNG from the Encoding drop-down menu. If you choose JPEG, you have the further option of deciding how much compression to apply (lower quality means higher compression). Sliding the bar back and forth gives you a real-time preview of what the different compression settings do to the image. Choose the lowest possible quality that doesn't produce artifacts that ruin the image, as is the case in Figure 13.13. For this particular image, you can go as low as 33% without losing much in terms of quality.

FIGURE 13.13
Setting the JPEG quality too low can lead to unsightly image artifacts. Use the slider to find a good middle ground between compression and quality.

4. With the Background layer unchecked, set the encoding to PNG and click OK. This opens a standard Save As dialog. Give the compressed image file the name MyKippleSticker.png and place it in the Images folder. The image is added to your file tree in the Folder List task pane.

5. In the default.html file, delete the heading and then drag and drop the new image into the h1 box instead. Give it the alternative text **MyKipple.com sticker**. Save the file and preview the page in your browser (see Figure 13.14).

FIGURE 13.14
The imported Photoshop image is inserted in place of the original heading.

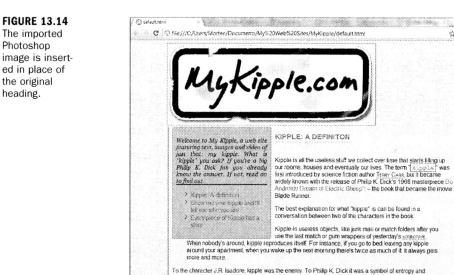

After placing the image on your page, you might find that it doesn't quite work with the rest of the elements, or maybe you need to omit more layers or even change another element within the image. Because you created the image using the Photoshop import option, Expression Web 4 retains a link to the original .psd file, so if you want to make changes to the image, you can do so directly from Design view.

When you right-click an image imported from a .psd file, a new item called Adobe Photoshop (.psd) appears in the drop-down menu. From this submenu, you can choose Edit Source to open the original .psd file in whatever software is set as your default .psd editor (probably Photoshop), or you can choose Update from Source to reopen the Import Adobe Photoshop (.psd) File dialog. From here, you can perform all the same functions as when you first imported the image, and those changes will be applied to the imported file. If you have made changes to the .psd file outside of Expression Web 4 and want to update the image in the page to reflect these changes, click Import again.

Watch Out!

> Although it is a great tool for easy management of imported images from .psd files, the Photoshop Import function is far from perfect. It does not support some of Photoshop's more advanced features, such as blending options and certain effects. To get the most out of this function, it is necessary to flatten blending and adjustment layers and blending options in Photoshop before importing the file into Expression Web 4. Otherwise, you might end up with some strange results. Fortunately, the Preview window is accurate; if an effect is not supported, you see it immediately.

Summary

For your websites to go to the next level, they need to have some visual elements included in the design. That means including images as noncontent elements. You can do this by adding images as backgrounds in your styles, classes, and IDs.

In this hour, you learned how to use images in different ways to make backgrounds work for different purposes. You saw that, through the use of tiling, a small image can be used to cover a large area. Depending on how you choose to repeat these background images, you can achieve many different looks with the same image. Using a set of simple background images, you gave the entire page a new look, you gave the main content a new background, and you even added an image-based underline to the h2 style. These diverse applications of background images should give you an idea of how far you can take your designs using more than just colored backgrounds.

Images can also style list items, and in this hour, you learned how to use the List category in the New and Modify Style dialogs to change the overall appearance of lists to include list-style-images as bullets. Moreover, you learned how lists function differently from the other elements of a page and how to use this knowledge to your advantage.

Finally, you got an in-depth look at the Adobe Photoshop import function, which lets you import and edit already imported .psd files right inside Expression Web 4 to significantly simplify the process of going from designing to authoring. With a firm understanding of this feature and its limitations, you can make your use of these two different programs far more effective.

Q&A

Q. *I added one of my own images as a repeating background, but I can see where each image ends and the next image begins like if I put tiles on a wall. How do I get that seamless floating feel to my backgrounds?*

A. The tricky part about using tiled images as backgrounds is that the left side has to match the right side, and the top has to match the bottom. Otherwise, you can see the "seams" between each of them. There is no magical snap-of-the-fingers way to make these images; it requires a lot of trial and error. It is often easier to find free tiling images by searching for "seamless background" on the Web and use them.

Q. *I imported a transparent Photoshop file, but when it is placed in the page, it is no longer transparent. How do I preserve the transparency?*

A. As you learned previously to preserve transparency, you have to use either the GIF or PNG file format. By default, imported Photoshop files are saved as JPEG files with no transparency. To make your image transparent, open the Photoshop Importer dialog again and resave the file as a PNG.

Workshop

The Workshop has quiz questions and exercises to help you put to use what you just learned. If you get stuck, the answers to the quiz questions are in the next section. But try to answer them first. Otherwise, you'll be cheating yourself.

Quiz

1. Given an image that has a 10-pixel-wide solid box on the left, how do you use it as a background for a heading without the text appearing on top of the black box?

2. What is the maximum number of images you can pile on top of one another in a web page?

Answers

1. To avoid having the text appear on top of the box, move the text to the right compared to the background image: Set the (x) `background-position` to `left`, and set the `left-padding` to 15px. That way, the text appears 15 pixels to the right of the left edge and 5 pixels to the right of the box.

2. In theory, there is no limit to how many images you can pile on top of one another. However, in reality, you are limited by the connection speed and processing power of the visiting computer: If you start stacking a lot of images, the page will be slow to load, and the browser might not display the page properly. That doesn't mean you shouldn't do it; just think about how many images are actually necessary. In most cases, you can get away with flattening most of the images into one and only using one or two images in the final design.

Exercise

The arrows with which you replaced the bullets in the list are too close to the text. Change the distance between the arrows and the text to give them some more breathing space.

Change the myKipple.com sticker image to a low-resolution JPG to see what this does to the background transparency using the Photoshop import functionality.

Harnessing the Power of CSS Layouts

What You'll Learn in This Hour:

- ▶ How to design the layout of your page using pen and paper
- ▶ How to separate the elements of the layout using boxes
- ▶ How to understand and use CSS positioning
- ▶ How to create CSS layouts using the prepackaged layouts featured in Expression Web 4
- ▶ How to apply a separate layout style sheet to existing pages

Designing a web page or website is more than just adding content and applying styles. Layout is also an important consideration. A good layout means better readability and, for that, better communication between the author and the reader. Likewise, a bad layout can easily lead to the message getting lost and the reader ending up with a poor understanding of what the author meant to communicate.

So far, you have focused mainly on content and learned how to style it. Now that you have a firm grasp on how to do that, it's time to start thinking about how to position the content on the page to make it more accessible, more pleasant, and easier to read. And you want to do this without adding any unnecessary content into your markup. You can do this in several different ways, but in this book, the focus is on using groups of divs to contain and separate the content into a cohesive and intuitive layout.

In past hours, you have made some small layout changes to pages using Cascading Style Sheets (CSS). But in this hour, you fully immerse yourself in CSS layouts and learn how to apply them to existing content. You are also introduced to the CSS reset and see how it works to make your layouts cross-browser compatible.

Starting with Pen and Paper

This might come as a bit of a surprise, but it is often a good idea to start designing a website by sketching it out on a piece of paper (see Figure 14.1). Not only is a sketch faster and easier to change than any other design method, it also gives you a blueprint of sorts to go by when you start building the framework to display the content of your site.

FIGURE 14.1
Drawing a sketch of your site layout on paper is a good starting point that gives you an idea of how to section out the page.

The benefit of starting with a sketch is that you can see almost right away whether the overall layout works and, if it does, what sections you need to define to make it work. As you learned previously in this book, creating layouts using CSS means creating boxes within boxes within boxes, and you need to know and understand the relationship between these boxes before you build them.

Figure 14.1 shows a rough sketch of the layout of the main page of myKipple.com. The layout has several different elements that need to be treated separately: the corkboard background that hovers in the center behind the content, the header (containing the page title and main menu), the pageContent (containing all the text and images of the respective page including the sidebar), and the footer. All the page content is centered and should, therefore, be placed in a separate container. From this information, you can draw a set of boxes to indicate how to separate the content (see Figure 14.2).

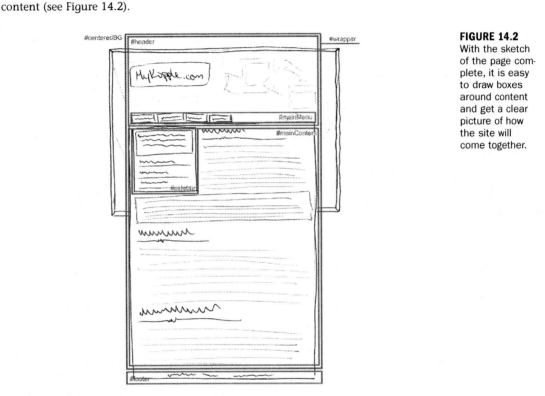

FIGURE 14.2
With the sketch of the page complete, it is easy to draw boxes around content and get a clear picture of how the site will come together.

Building the Framework from Boxed Parts

Now that you know how you want to section the page, it's time to build the actual framework. In Hour 13, "Getting Visual, Part 3: Images as Design Elements with CSS," you already started the process of boxing in the content, but to get a firm idea of how this process comes together, let's start again from scratch.

There are many ways of doing this, and none of them is wrong. Many designers prefer to build the framework by hand, but it can be nice to get some help if you are new at design. Expression Web 4 has a series of ready-to-use, prepackaged CSS layouts that give you a bit of a head start.

1. Click New, Page from the File option on the menu bar. This opens the New dialog with the Page tab selected.

2. Click CSS Layouts in the first list to open the prepackaged CSS layouts in Expression Web 4. By clicking each of the options in the second list, you get a short description of the layout along with a preview (see Figure 14.3).

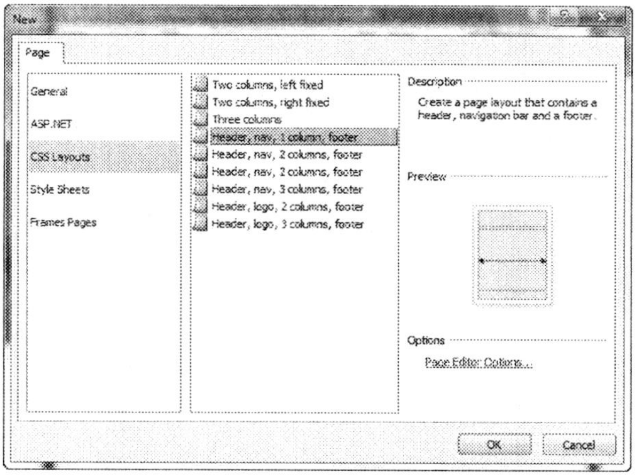

FIGURE 14.3
From the New dialog, you can select a series of different prepackaged layouts for different applications, including CSS.

3. Select the layout closest to the framework you drew in your sketch. In this case, it is the Header, Nav, 1 Column, Footer design. Select this option and click OK.

After you click OK, Expression Web 4 opens two new files: Untitled_1.css and Untitled_1.html. Both are empty except for the layout styles. This gives you the ability to work with the layout boxes without content and to match the overlay drawings you previously created. Because you already have a series of styles defined for your pages, what you do is create a separate style sheet that contains only the layout portions of the pages (so that you end up with two style sheets: one for content styles, one for layout styles). That way, you can make quick changes to the layout without touching all the other styles.

Employing CSS Reset

Before you make any changes on your own, it is a good idea to insert a CSS reset into your style sheet. A *CSS reset* is a block of CSS code that removes all the preconceived notions that a browser might have about your page by setting everything to zero. Eric A. Meyer created the most comprehensive CSS reset around, and you can find it at http://meyerweb.com/eric/tools/css/reset/.

To apply the CSS reset, simply copy the code in its entirety from the web page and paste it into the top of the Untitled_1.css file you just created. Save the CSS file as layout.css. Because the Untitled_1.html file already links to the CSS file, the link updates automatically. Save the Untitled_1.html file as **layoutTest.html**.

Updating the ID Names

The next step is to change the ID names to match your drawing. You can do so directly in the CSS file or using the Modify Style option from the Manage Styles task pane. Change the name of #masthead to #header, #top-nav to #mainMenu, and #page-content to #pageContent. Leave #footer as it is. In layoutTest.html, go to Split view and make the same changes to the div IDs.

According to Figure 14.2, the mainMenu ID should reside within the header ID. Go to Code view and move the </div> end tag for the header ID below the one for the mainMenu ID—now the header div wraps the mainMenu div.

The drawing also calls for two new IDs: #centeredBG and #wrapper. To wrap all the existing IDs, create a new <div> on the line before the first div and give it the ID wrapper. Then, create another box to contain the #wrapper ID and give it the #centeredBG ID. With all the changes made, the page's code inside the <body> tags should look like this (comments added to make it easier to read):

```
<body>

<div id="centeredBG">
<div id="wrapper">
<div id="header">
<div id="mainMenu">
</div> <!-- #end mainMenu -->
</div> <!-- #end header -->
<div id="pageContent">
</div> <!-- #end pageContent -->
<div id="footer">
</div> <!-- end #footer -->
</div> <!-- end #wrapper -->
</div> <!-- end #centeredBG -->

</body>
```

Now that you have inserted calls to the #centeredBG and #wrapper IDs, you need to add these styles in the layout.css file. You can do this manually in Code view with the help of IntelliSense or by using the New Style button in the Manage Styles pane. For now, just create the styles without any style code.

Styling the Layout Boxes

With the layout boxes created, it is time to style them to make the page match the sketch. This requires the use of all the techniques you learned in earlier hours and some new ones. The goal here is to remove all the layout styling from the kippleStyles.css file and store it in the new layout.css file. You can choose to make the following style modifications using the Modify Style dialog, directly in the layout.css file using IntelliSense, or both.

1. You already did this step in Hour 13, but there is no harm in repeating it: The layout drawing calls for a tiled graphic background that covers the entire page. In the new page layoutTest.html, create a new style with the selector body, set background-image to the tile.jpg file found in the Graphics folder, and set background-color to #FFFFFF (see Figure 14.4). Note that you want to create a new body style even though the CSS reset already has one. Always leave the CSS reset code alone.

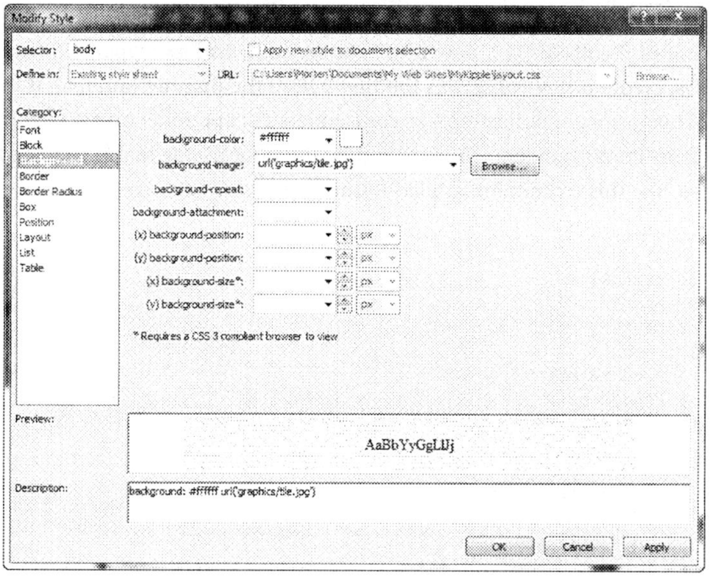

FIGURE 14.4
Change the body style to add a tiled background that repeats throughout the page.

2. The content of the page hovers in the middle of the page with a specific width. Center the content by setting the #wrapper ID margin-left and margin-right attributes to auto. Set the width attribute to 810px (see Figure 14.5).

The design calls for a background image that spills outside of the edges of the wrapper. This is a popular effect that is heavily used in blog design. The premise is that you have a background graphic that spills beyond the outer-left and outer-right edges of the content yet moves with the content when the window is resized. This is achieved using the CSS attribute min-width, which is not available in the New and Modify Style dialogs.

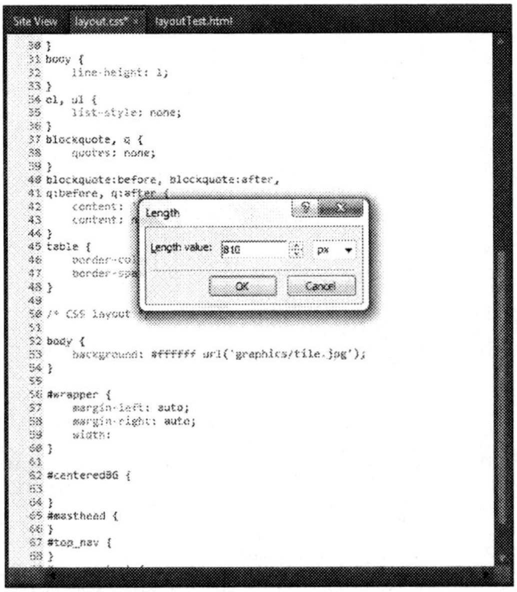

FIGURE 14.5
It's often just as easy to make quick changes to the styles in a CSS page by editing the code directly. Here, the width attribute in the #wrapper style is set using IntelliSense. Note the somewhat confusing wording as IntelliSense asks for the "length" of the width.

3. To achieve the hovering centered background image effect, first import the corkboard.png file from the lesson files for this hour and place it in the Graphics folder. In Code view of the layout.css file, find the #centeredBG style and set the background-image attribute to the corkboard.png file with the help of IntelliSense. Set background-repeat to no-repeat and background-position to center and top. Now the corkboard image hovers in the center of the screen behind the content, even when the window is resized. Unfortunately, it insists on hovering in the center also when the window is smaller than the width of the image, which will ruin the effect. To prevent this, set min-width to the exact width of the image, which in this case is 1000px (see Figure 14.6). This tells the browser that the #centeredBG box should not be reduced to a width less than 1,000 pixels.

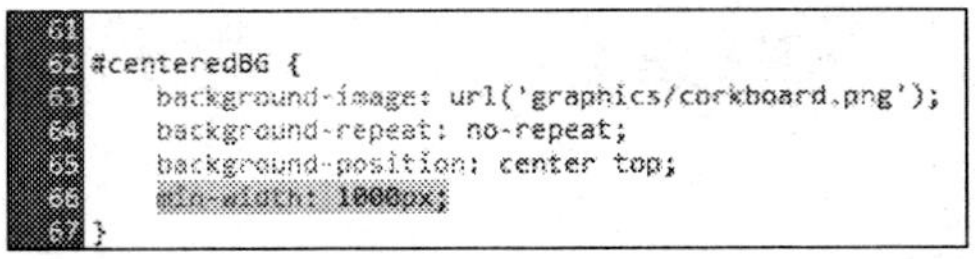

FIGURE 14.6
Although the New and Modify Style dialogs are extensive, they do not cover every CSS attribute available. To curb this problem, those attributes not covered by the dialogs are still covered by IntelliSense.

4. The header of the page has to be set to a fixed height to ensure that the relationship between the header and the main content remains the same regardless of the size of the main content. To do this, set the #header style height to 285px.

5. On the drawing, the #mainMenu ID is along the bottom and aligned to the left of the #header box. To make this happen, you need to make some changes to the position attributes of both #header and #mainMenu. First, change the position of the #header ID to relative. Then, set the position attribute for the #mainMenu ID to absolute and set the bottom and left attributes (under the Position category in the Modify Style dialog) to 0px.

As you can see from Figure 14.7, you now have the basic framework for the page as it appears in the drawing. And all this was done using only CSS, which means the HTML markup has not changed.

FIGURE 14.7
When everything is set correctly, the #mainMenu ID should hover to the lower-right side of the #header box, independent of the remaining content.

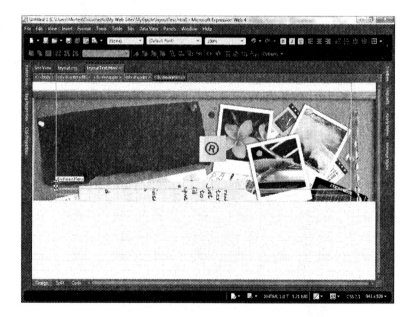

In step 4, you used the position attribute to force the mainMenu div down into the left corner of the header. This gives you a first glimpse of the powerful and often misunderstood CSS tool called positioning. Understanding positioning means you have the power to control your content in ways you could never do before.

Understanding Positioning

In the last part of the preceding example, you used the `position` attribute to place a div in the lower-left corner of another div. This is a nice segue into the confusing and often misunderstood issue of positioning in CSS.

If you open the Modify Style dialog for any of the current styles, classes, or IDs, you see that the `position` attribute (found under the Position category) has five options: `absolute`, `fixed`, `relative`, `static`, and `inherit` (see Figure 14.8). The physical position of any object in a page depends on what this attribute is set to in the current style and whatever style that wraps it.

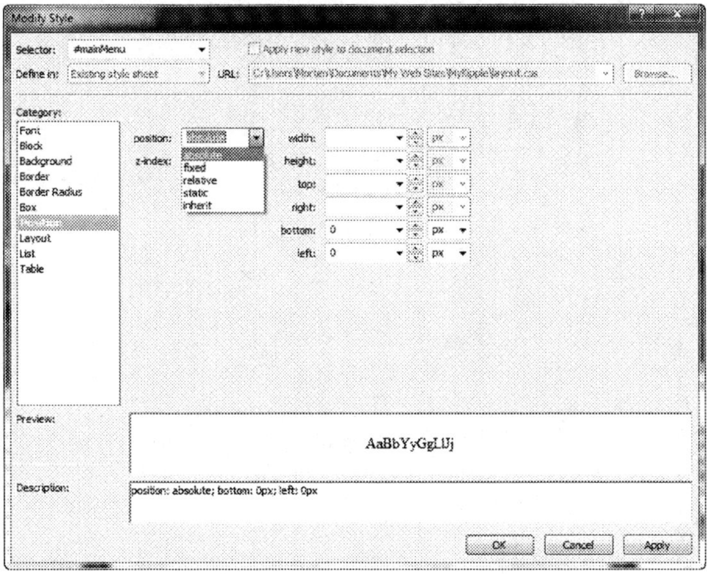

FIGURE 14.8
You can set the position attribute found under the Position category in the New and Modify Style dialog to absolute, fixed, relative, static, or inherit.

position: absolute;

The easiest way to explain an element with an absolute position is to think of it as an image (or any other object) pasted onto a page and ignore the rest of the content. The physical placement of an element with an absolute position is decided by setting the pixel value of its distance from the nearest positioned container with the `top`, `right`, `bottom`, and `left` attributes. In other words, an object with absolute position that has a `top` value of `20px` and a `left` value of `30px` appears exactly 20 pixels from the top and 30 pixels to the left of the edge of the page or the closest container box that has a `position` value other than `static`. Setting an object's `position` attribute to absolute removes it from the flow of the page. That means unless you pay close attention, you might accidentally place objects with absolute positions directly on top of other content.

In the layoutTest.html page, the #menu div has an absolute position of 0 pixels from the bottom and 0 pixels from the right side of the #header div because the #header position is set to relative. If you change the position attribute of #header to static, the #menu div is positioned absolutely in relation to the nearest parent with a position other than static (in this case, the body), which means it aligns itself with the edge of the page and ends up in the lower-right portion of the window.

If you set the position attribute of a style, class, or ID to absolute without setting values for top, right, bottom, and left, the object appears in the default upper-left corner position (see Figure 14.9).

FIGURE 14.9
In this example, the image style has its position attribute set to absolute. Because the containing div has its position attribute set to relative, the position of the image is relative to this div rather than to the page as a whole.

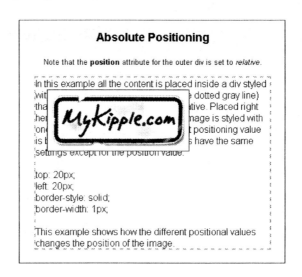

position attribute for the outer div is set to *relative*.

In this example all the content is placed inside a div styled with ... dotted gray line ... that ... tive. Placed right here ... nage is styled with one ... positioning value is ... have the same settings except for the position value.

top: 20px;
left: 20px;
border-style: solid;
border-width: 1px;

This example shows how the different positional values changes the position of the image.

position: fixed;

Fixed positioning works similarly to absolute positioning except that whereas the physical position of an object with an absolute position can relate to other positioned objects, the physical position of a fixed object is always based solely on the outer edges of the page as a whole (see Figure 14.10).

Watch Out!

The first version of Microsoft Internet Explorer to support the fixed value for the position attribute was Internet Explorer 7. Older versions of Internet Explorer do not understand the value, and your layout will not work properly in them.

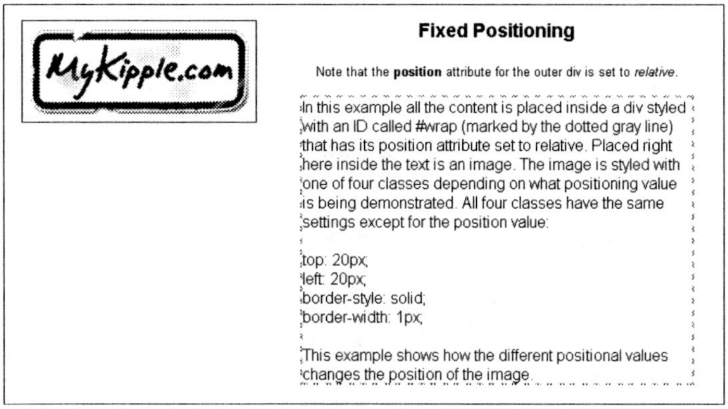

Fixed Positioning

Note that the **position** attribute for the outer div is set to *relative*.

In this example all the content is placed inside a div styled with an ID called #wrap (marked by the dotted gray line) that has its position attribute set to relative. Placed right here inside the text is an image. The image is styled with one of four classes depending on what positioning value is being demonstrated. All four classes have the same settings except for the position value:

top: 20px;
left: 20px;
border-style: solid;
border-width: 1px;

This example shows how the different positional values changes the position of the image.

FIGURE 14.10
In this example, the image style has the position attribute set to fixed. Unlike in Figure 14.9, the positioning of the image in this page is relative to the page as a whole.

position: relative;

The easiest way to explain relative positioning is to imagine that you have cut an image out of a printed page and repositioned it somewhere else on the page. Because you cut out the image from the page, there is a hole where it was, and the image covers content wherever you glue it.

Placement of an object with a relative position is in relation to its original location in the flow of the page. As an example, that means an image with its position attribute set to relative and its bottom attribute set to 20px appears 20 pixels above its normal location where it was originally inserted, and the space it would have occupied remains empty (see Figure 14.11).

Relative Positioning

Note that the **position** attribute for the outer div is set to *relative*.

In this example all the content is placed inside a div styled with an ID called #wrap (marked by the dotted gray line) that has its position attribute set to relative. Placed right

here   side the text is
an imag   ur classes
depending on what positioning value is being
demonstrated. All four classes have the same settings
except for the position value:

top: 20px;
left: 20px;
border-style: solid;
border-width: 1px;

This example shows how the different positional values changes the position of the image.

FIGURE 14.11
In this example, the image style has its position attribute set to relative. The space the image would normally occupy is left empty, but the image is shifted to the right and down because of the top and left values.

position: static;

Static is the default setting for any style. Setting an object's position attribute to static places the object in the flow as normal. The object is unaffected by the top, right, bottom, and left attributes (see Figure 14.12).

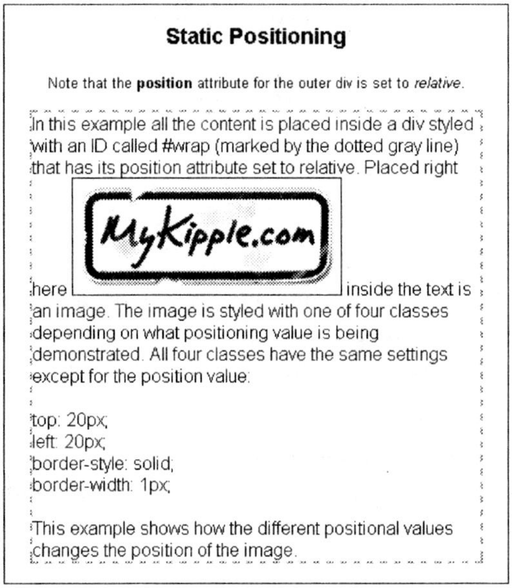

FIGURE 14.12
In this example, the image style has its position attribute set to static. The image lines up with the rest of the text and is not displaced despite the top and left attribute values being the same as in Figures 14.9, 14.10, and 14.11.

position: inherit

If you look closely, you'll see that the value inherit appears in almost every drop-down menu when you create CSS. It literally means that the current element "inherits" this style from whatever elements are directly above it in the cascade.

Applying the Framework to Existing Pages

Now that you have created the framework for the myKipple site in a different style sheet from the one you were working on before, you need to alter the existing markup files and style sheet. Because default.html is the home page, it is a good place to start. Before you go any further, remove the big sticker graphic in the header and replace it with the text **Welcome to MyKipple.com**.

The first step is to remove some of the styles you created in Hour 13 to avoid the new styles clashing with the old ones. Editing style sheets in Expression Web 4 is easy. You can delete these styles directly from the Manage Styles panel by highlighting them and pressing the Delete button on your keyboard or by right-clicking and selecting Delete from the context menu. Delete the body style and the #wrapper style.

With the old styles removed, it is time to apply the new ones. To do this, you need to attach the new layout.css style sheet to the page. As you previously learned, you do this by clicking the Attach Style Sheet button in the Apply and Manage Styles task panes. Select the layout.css file with the Browse button and be sure to enable the Attach to All HTML Pages option.

With the new style sheet attached, you see a dramatic change in how the page appears in Design view. That is because the new style sheet contains the CSS reset that removes all default styling from the content (see Figure 14.13). Furthermore, when you attach a second style sheet, you insert it below the first one in the HTML code, and this means it gets more weight or importance in the style cascade. The CSS reset affects all default selectors, but in the kippleStyles.css file, you have already styled several of these, so you want your old styles to have more weight. To give kippleStyles.css more weight than layout.css, simply change the order of the two styles as they appear in the HTML code so that layout.css is first and kippleStyles.css is second. After the change, the two lines of code directly before the </head> end tag should read as follows:

```
<link href="layout.css" rel="stylesheet" type="text/css" />
<link href="kippleStyles.css" rel="stylesheet" type="text/css" />
```

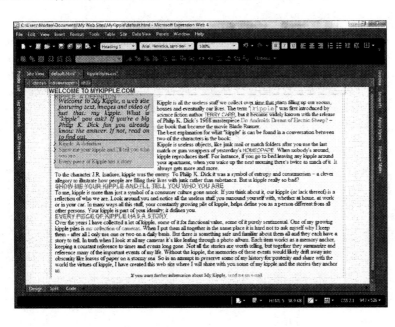

FIGURE 14.13
After applying the CSS reset to your page, all the content that has not been styled will be crammed together. It might look weird, but this is actually what you want because it means you now have a clean slate to work with.

If you preview the page in your browser at this point, you notice three things: First, the header graphic you spent so much time aligning earlier is nowhere to be seen. Second, all the text is bunched together; that is, there is no breathing room between the paragraphs, headings, and blockquotes, except for the h2 headings. This might look like a big problem, but it is exactly what you want: If the different selector boxes are stacked directly on top of one another (meaning there is no breathing room between the paragraphs, headings, and so on), the browser is not making any assumptions about your styles if you do not provide a style. In other words, your page looks the same in all browsers. Third, the text has reverted to the Times New Roman font. This is because you deleted the old body styles that contained the font-family definition for the entire page. This last one is the easiest one to fix, so let's do it before you get into the meat of things: Find the second body style in the layout.css style sheet (the one that has the background tile image defined), open the Modify Style dialog, and set font-family to Arial, Helvetica, sans-serif. Click OK to apply the change, and the font switches back to Arial.

Applying the New Framework to the Page

Now that you have attached the new style sheet, you can apply the new framework to the page. Most of it is already there because you added it in Hour 13, but some elements are still missing:

1. With default.html open in Split view, find the <body> tag in the Code area, and create a new line directly below it before the #wrapper div. On the new line, insert a new div with the ID #centeredBG. When you close the tag, IntelliSense automatically inserts an end </div> tag. Cut it out as before, scroll to the bottom of the code page where the #mainContent and #wrapper divs are being closed, create a new line directly over the </body> end tag, and paste in the </div> end tag, giving it the comment <!-- END #centeredBG -->.

2. Find the <h1> tag that contains the heading you previously inserted. Create a new line directly above it, and insert a new div with the ID #header. Place the closing </div> tag on a new line directly after the <h1> tag.

Save and preview the page in your browser, and you see that the page now has the corkboard background off the top and the header has plenty of space before the page content begins (see Figure 14.14).

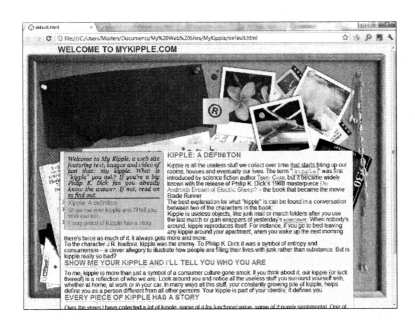

FIGURE 14.14
With the framework applied, the page has started to look like the drawing in Figure 14.1.

Looking back on the drawing in Figure 14.1, you can see that one element still has not been added to the page: the footer. Adding this element is done in the exact same way as before: Scroll to the bottom of the page and find the paragraph that starts with "If you want further information...." Place your cursor anywhere on the line and look at it in Code view. You see that the `<p>` tag is littered with style code. Remove all the style code, leaving only the clean `<p>` tag. Create a new line directly over it and insert a new div with the ID `#footer`. Place the closing `</div>` tag directly after the closing `<p>` tag before the closing tag for the `#mainContent` ID. Find the `#footer` style in the layout.css file and set `font-variant` to `small-caps` and `font-size` to `0.8em`. To align the text to the center, go to Block and set `text-align` to `center`. Click OK to save the new style, and the footer text should look exactly as it did before; however, this time it is styled from the layout.css style sheet rather than an inline style.

Now, you have a decision to make. Although the drawing in Figure 14.1 calls for the header of the page to have plain text, you can choose to replace the plain text with the sticker image you imported earlier. I give you this option because although it is becoming more popular to use plain text for headings, the vast majority of sites designed these days use fancy images and graphics for the site name and headings. The site works the same either way, so I leave it up to you to decide what kind of heading you want. That said, you should still learn how to insert and use images as headers, so even if you want to keep the site name as plain text, do the following exercise anyway, and then you can revert later.

▼ **Try It Yourself**

Adding a Header Image and a Menu

In the sketch of the page layout (refer to Figure 14.1), the header features a large MyKipple.com sticker and a menu. These are important elements of any website—the header image (or site name) provides an intuitive link back to the home page and the main menu. In effect, the header functions as a primary navigational tool for the visitor.

1. Remove the <h1> tag along with the heading inside it. Because the header contains the sticker, there is no need to have the text there as well. The Images folder contains the image file MyKippleSticker.png that you created earlier. Click and drag the image into the header in Design view, and give it the alternative text Welcome to MyKipple.com.

2. When inserted, the image has both padding and a 1-pixel gray border (see Figure 14.15). This is because it is being styled by the img style you created in a previous hour. To ensure that the img style applies only to images within the #mainContent area, use the Manage Styles task pane to change the Selector Name of the img style to #mainContent img. When you change the style name, the kippleSticker.png file changes position to hug the upper-left corner of the #header box.

FIGURE 14.15
When inserted, the kippleSticker.png image has both a border and padding applied by the img style created in an earlier hour.

3. To line up the sticker image with the background, you have to create a new style. Click the New Style button in the Manage Styles task pane, and set the Selector Name to #header img. This style applies only to images within the #header ID. Change the Define In field to Existing Style Sheet, and select kippleStyles.css from the drop-down menu. Under the Box category, set padding-top to 90px. Click OK to apply the style. The top of the header image now lines up with the background image (see Figure 14.16).

FIGURE 14.16
With the new #header img style applied, the image lines up with the background image.

4. Right now, the sticker is too big. To change it, right-click the picture and select Picture Properties from the pop-up menu or double-click the picture to open the same dialog. In the Picture Properties dialog, go to the Appearance tab and change the Height to 130px, making sure that the Keep aspect ratio box is checked. Click OK to apply the change, and use the Picture Actions button that appears at the bottom of the picture to Resample the picture to match size.

5. To make the image link back to the home page, right-click it again, select Hyperlink from the pop-up menu, and set the hyperlink to the default.html page and set the ScreenTip to Home.

With the new image heading inserted and formatted, save and preview the page. Expression Web 4 asks you if you want to save the attached files because you changed both the style sheets and the kipple sticker file. When previewed in a browser, the page should now look like Figure 14.17.

FIGURE 14.17
With the new #header img style applied, the image lines up with the background image.

Summary

When it comes to communicating a message with visual media, whether printed or on screen, design and layout are paramount. If the content doesn't look inviting, no one will give it a second look. Nowhere is this truer than when it comes to the Web. With the millions upon millions of websites out there, your site has to stand out if it is to generate an audience. To do that, it needs to have a solid and easy-to-understand layout, and it has to look the same no matter who is viewing it.

In this hour, you learned to use CSS to create layouts. By using CSS, you are separating the layout information from the content information, thereby making it easier for everyone to access the information you are communicating through your site. You learned how to use the prepackaged CSS layouts as a starting point to create a proper framework to house all your content, and you learned how to apply this framework to existing pages using a variety of methods in Code view and Design view.

To ensure that your page looks the same across all browsers, it is necessary to remove all assumptions that a browser might make about the styling of your content. You can achieve this by inserting a CSS reset in your style sheet. This code resets all the styles on the page so that you have a clean slate to start with. And because of the cascade, applying a CSS reset in the top of your CSS file means you can restyle all the content further down in the cascade to get the results you want.

CSS positioning is a topic that can be confusing even to seasoned professionals. This hour presented a thorough walkthrough of what the four different positioning values (absolute, fixed, relative, and static) mean and how they work. Understanding these values, and how to use them, means you can easily create advanced layouts that go outside the norm.

In the next hour, you learn about buttons and how to use Expression Web 4's built-in functions to create advanced buttons.

Q&A

Q. *When I create a new CSS layout, all I get is a series of empty boxes. Why is that?*

A. The prepackaged CSS layouts in Expression Web 4 are little more than empty divs with some basic positioning in them. The intention is to give the user a clean slate to work with, but in reality there is little difference between using the prepackaged layouts and creating the layouts from scratch. The one advantage of using the layouts is that all the divs have proper names and positions, so you don't have to keep tabs on absolutely everything.

Q. *When I added the new layout.css style sheet, I noticed that there are now many different versions of the styles, such as* body *and* p. *Isn't that a problem?*

A. The new style sheet includes the CSS reset, which has all the available selectors listed and set to 0. Further down in the style sheet and in the kippleStyles.css style sheet, the same selectors are styled a second and sometimes even a third time. This isn't a problem as much as a deliberate exploitation of the cascade: You reset the styles to 0 at the start and then create new styles that apply fresh styles further down the line. This piling of styles is a good illustration of how the cascade works and is something you should take note of for future reference: The farther down in the style sheet a style is, the more weight or importance it has.

Workshop

The Workshop has quiz questions and exercises to help you put to use what you have just learned. If you get stuck, the answers to the quiz questions are in the next section. But try to answer them first. Otherwise, you'll be cheating yourself.

Quiz

1. What is the benefit of using CSS to create page layouts?

2. What is a CSS reset and why should you always use it?

3. Given an image placed in the middle of a block of text, briefly describe what happens to the image when its position is set to `absolute`, `fixed`, `relative`, and `static`.

Answers

1. CSS layouts have many benefits, but the most important one is that they enable you to completely change the layout of multiple pages without actually changing the pages themselves. You can also create multiple layouts that visitors can choose from to suit their preference without cluttering the markup. Finally, you can "port" a good layout to a new page easily by attaching the existing style sheet to the new page and just adding some classes and IDs to the divs in the new page.

2. A CSS reset is a block of CSS code that sets all the different styles that browsers usually make assumptions about to zero. By applying it to your designs, you ensure that different browsers don't start changing your designs or layouts on a whim just because the browser designer thinks all paragraphs should have a 15px top padding, for instance.

3. With absolute positioning, the image is taken out of the flow of the page and appears in the top-left corner of the page or whatever containing element has a positioning other than `static`. With fixed positioning, the image is taken out of the flow of the page and appears in the top-left corner of the page no matter what. With relative positioning, the area the image takes up remains in the flow of the page, and the image itself appears in a set position relative to its original location. With no other values attached, it appears where it was placed. Static positioning is the default position, and the image appears in the flow of the text where it was placed.

Exercise

The new layout.css style sheet includes a CSS reset that removes all the regular styling from the content within your page. As a result, most of (if not all) the text is crammed together. Create and modify styles to space out the text and make it more approachable by using what you learned in this and previous hours. In particular, create or modify the styles for `#content p`, `#content ul`, and `#content blockquote`.

Using what you learned about positioning, try to change the location of different content in the page. For example, see whether you can move the menu in the header to the upper-right corner of the page.

Buttons, Buttons, Buttons

What You'll Learn in This Hour:

▶ How to create simple box buttons using CSS

▶ How to create a rounded-corner button with CSS3

▶ How to make the simple box buttons more advanced by using background images

▶ How to use the sliding doors technique to use one background image for multiple button stages

▶ How to combine the box button with an image to create a Web 2.0 button

What makes a website different from all other visual media is the ability to navigate through content with the use of hyperlinks. However, plain text hyperlinks are not always the best option. If you want to showcase a particular link or if you create a menu, you need to turn those links into buttons.

There are many ways to create buttons—some easy and some more complicated. This hour explains how to use some button-making techniques and describes their advantages and disadvantages.

As before, accessibility is a primary focus of this hour. In other words, if you strip away all the styles, graphics, and scripting, there should still be an understandable hyperlink left in the markup. Designers often ignore this aspect and that can, in some cases, prevent the visitor from navigating through a site when the images, Flash movies, or other elements don't load properly. But because making buttons accessible is easy, there is no good reason not to do it.

Buttons: A Brief Definition

What is a button in web terms? In the absolute basic form, a button is a clearly defined and contained visual object on a web page that functions as a hyperlink. This object can be plain text with a background, text with an image background, just a static image, or an interactive or animated graphic element that changes with the mouse behaviors. A button differs from a hyperlink in that it is not merely a string of text but is some form of graphic element with a clearly defined active area.

Of course, as with all definitions, experts can question and dispute this one. For this book, however, this definition suffices.

Watch Out!

> ### Don't Use Interactive Buttons!
>
> If you go to Insert on the main menu, you will see an option called Interactive Button. This option allows you to create an interactive button on your page, but it is one I strongly urge you never to use. The Interactive Button option is a legacy option that, in my opinion, should have been removed a long time ago. It uses a button technique long since expired and does not produce well-functioning or attractive buttons. For this reason, the section on how to use the Interactive Button feature has been removed from this book and replaced by the rounded-corner button examples, which are more attractive, more accessible, and more modern.

Creating Buttons from Scratch Using CSS

Designers often need to create their own buttons from scratch to achieve a particular look in their sites. Using the techniques you learned in previous hours, you can use Cascading Style Sheets (CSS) to make advanced buttons that leave you in control of every element, from font to color to how the button behaves.

Creating a Classic Box Button

When designers first started to focus on buttons as a navigational tool, they could rely on only basic functionality. The most basic button of all is a string of text with a colored box around it (see Figure 15.1). The Classic Box Button was heavily used on the Web in years past and it utilized the border attribute to mimic a crude 3D effect. To understand how to build and use buttons with CSS, the Classic Box Button is a good starting point.

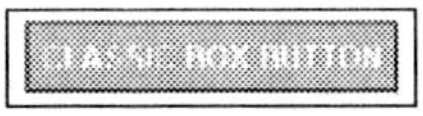

FIGURE 15.1
The basic box button was the staple of web design for many years.

1. Create a new page with the name buttons.html. Create a new paragraph with the text **Classic Box Button**.

2. Highlight the button text and make it a hyperlink pointing back to the current buttons.html page.

3. Click the New Style button and create a new class called `.basicBox`. In the Font category, set `font-family` to `Arial, Helvetica, sans-serif`; `font-size` to `0.8em`; `font-weight` to `bold`; `text-transform` to `uppercase`; `font-color` to white (`#FFFFFF`). Check the None box under `text-decoration` to get rid of the line under the text.

4. Under Background, set `background-color` to a light blue (`#99CCFF`). Under Border, set `border-style` to `solid` for all, `border-width` to `2px` for all, the `border-top` and `border-left` colors to a medium blue (`#0F87FF`), and the `border-bottom` and `border-right` colors to a dark blue (`#004F9D`), as shown in Figure 15.2. This gives the button the appearance of popping out from the screen.

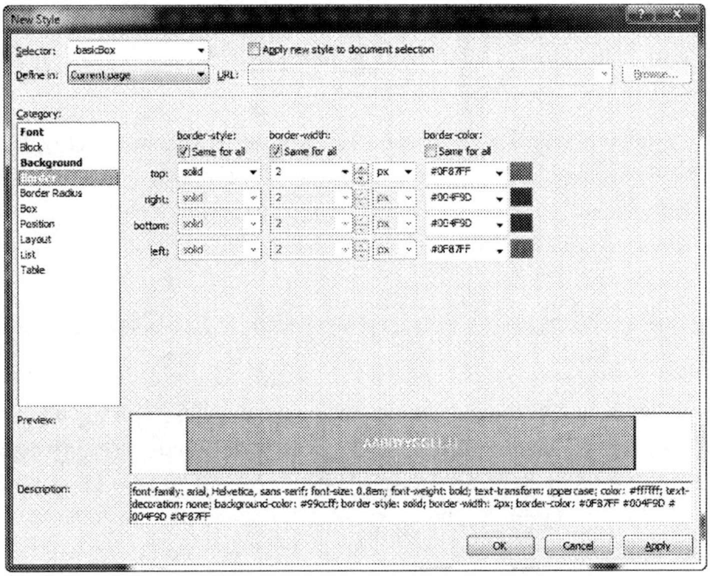

FIGURE 15.2
Setting different colors for the top and left borders and bottom and right borders can create the illusion of the button hovering or being pushed into the page.

5. In the Box category, set padding to 5px for all four sides. Click OK to create the new class.

6. Select the button text you created, use the tag selector to select the <a> tag, and use the Apply Styles task pane to apply the new class.

7. To make the button react when the user hovers the mouse over it, you also have to make a :hover pseudoclass with different styles. This is where CSS shows its power: Because you are only changing some of the attributes with the :hover state, you don't need to redefine all the ones that don't change. By creating a new style with the selector .basicBox:hover and changing only those attributes that are different between the two states, you are making less code clutter and using the cascade wisely.

8. With .basicBox:hover open in the Modify Style dialog, set font-color to black (#000000) and invert the border colors so that the lighter blue is on the right and bottom sides while the darker blue is on the top and left sides. This gives the appearance of the button being pressed down when it is hovered over. Click OK to apply the changes, and then save and test in your browser (see Figure 15.3).

FIGURE 15.3
The two button states as they appear next to one another.

As with all other styles, you can create separate styles for each pseudoclass for more advanced visual interaction with the button.

In this example, the actual styling of the button came from applying a class to the <a> tag. But this is not the only way to create box buttons. You can easily group one or several buttons within a <div> or <span> class or ID, and create a style instead. The result would be the same.

Creating a Modern Rounded-Corner Button with CSS3

The Classic Box Button is called "Classic" for a reason—although the functionality is still current, the appearance is not. To get the CSS button up to modern standards, we need to add some more breathing space, better colors, and the all-important rounded corners. By combining the Classic Box Button with some CSS3, you can easily make modern buttons that are indistinguishable from those seen on famous websites—because they are made the exact same way!

Let's see how we can make the old and outdated Classic Box Button look more modern:

1. Below the Classic Box Button, create a new paragraph with the text **Click me** and make it a hyperlink pointing back to the buttons.html page.

2. Make a new class called .modernBox by using the New Style dialog.

3. Set the font-family to Arial, Helvetica, sans-serif; font-weight to bold; color to #ffffff. Check None under text-decoration.

4. Under Background, set background-color to #57D5FF.

5. Set all four borders to solid, 2px, and #CCCCCC.

6. Here come the rounded corners: Under Border Radius, set radius to 10px.

7. To give the text plenty of whitespace (breathing space), go to Box and set padding top and bottom to 10px and left and right to 2em.

8. Finally, to give the button itself some breathing space, go to Layout and set display to inline-block. This is done to pull the button out of the regular text flow of the site and make the browser treat it as its own entity.

When you save and preview the page in your browser, you'll see a modern-looking rounded-corner button. To make a hover state, repeat the process from the earlier example by creating a new style with the selector .modernBox:hover that has the background-color value set to #FF9933 and border-color set to #333333. This produces a button with a modern hover state, as seen in Figure 15.4.

FIGURE 15.4
The modern box button has rounded corners, and the color changes for the hover state.

When creating a rounded-corner button like this, you have to keep in mind that visitors with older browsers will not see the rounded corners. However, like I've said before, these browsers are being phased out and before long everyone will be able to see beautiful rounded CSS3 corners when they visit your site.

Creating an Advanced Box Button with Images

The modern box button might be easy to create, but in some cases you want a button with more flare. That's where the Advanced Box Button with Images comes in. The key is to replace the background color with a background image, as shown in Figure 15.5.

In this example, you use a different styling technique to apply the same style to multiple buttons:

1. Below the modern box button, create an unordered list with three buttons: Button 1, Button 2, and Button 3. Make each list item into a hyperlink back to the current page.

2. Make Create a new class called .advancedBox by using the New Style dialog. Under the List category, set the list-style-type to none. Click OK to create the class and apply it to the <ul> tag using the Quick Tag Selector (see Figure 15.6).

3. Import the images named blueButtonUp.gif and blueButtonOver.gif from the lesson files and save them in a new folder called buttonGraphics.

4. Make a new style and give it the selector name `.advancedBox a`. In the Font category, set `font-family` to `Arial, Helvetica, sans-serif;` `font-size` to `0.8em;` `font-weight` to bold; `text-transform` to uppercase; and `font-color` to white (#FFFFFF). Check the None box under `text-decoration` to get rid of the line under the text.

5. In the Background category, set `background-image` to the blueButtonUp.gif image you just imported, and set `background-repeat` to `no-repeat`. Because the image is larger than the text and you want it to surround the text, go to the Box category and set `padding` to 13px on all sides. Click OK to apply the style.

6. In Design view, you can see that the new button background is applied, but the buttons are covering each other (see Figure 15.7). This is because the list items have not yet been styled, and the browser assumes that the list items are the height of the text without the padding.

7. To fix this problem, create a new style with the selector name `.advancedBox li` and set the `padding-top` and `padding-bottom` attributes to 13px to match the link style you just created. Click OK to apply the new style, and the buttons no longer overlap.

8. To create a hover-over effect, create a new style with the selector name `.advancedBox a:hover`. Because the `:hover` pseudoclass inherits all the styling from the main a class, all you need to do is change `background-image` to blueButtonOver.gif. Click OK, and then save and preview in your browser.

Now instead of the background color changing when the mouse hovers over the button, the background image swaps out. Because the background image is part of the a style, the entire image is clickable, not just the text itself.

FIGURE 15.7
The .advanced-
Box a style is
applied to the
new buttons,
but they cover
each other
because the list
item style has
not been modi-
fied yet.

The problem with this technique is that it requires two images to work. This might not seem like a big deal, but if the user is on a slow connection, the page is on a slow server, or if there is something else that slows the system down, the user might experience noticeable lag between hovering over the button and the new background image being loaded. One way around this problem is to preload the images using behaviors, but this requires JavaScript to work properly.

Creating Text-Free Buttons with Sliding Doors

The problem of preloading content has become more prevalent with the emergence of blogs because many blogs have a lot of scripts running at the same time, and it is important to reduce the load on both the network and the computer as much as possible to make things work smoothly. A technique often referred to as *sliding doors* was developed to enable the designer to use one image file as two different backgrounds. This is done by creating a file that has two versions of the background, either on top of or to the side of one another. The name *sliding doors* refers to the action of literally sliding the background from one side to the other to display only half of the image at a time (see Figure 15.8).

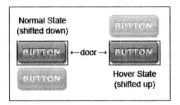

FIGURE 15.8
The name *slid-ing doors* refers to the action of sliding the background image so that only half of it is visible, depending on how the mouse interacts with the button.

You can use a similar technique to hide text content. As you have seen, the regular method of creating buttons requires there to be text superimposed on the background. If you don't want the text to appear, the quick answer is to simply swap out the text for an image and use it as a button. However, if you do this, the link is not visible if the image doesn't load or the visitor uses a text-only browser. The way to solve this is to push the text out of the way so that only the background image appears. Another reason to use this technique is that designers often want to use custom fonts or font effects in their buttons. To do this and retain full accessibility, they need to hide the regular HTML text first. In this example, you create a button that uses the sliding doors technique and hides the text at the same time.

1. Import the file named slidingButtons.gif into the buttonGraphics folder from the lesson files. Under the three buttons you just created, add a new subheading and call it Sliding Doors Button with Hidden Text. Below it, add a paragraph with the text **Button** and make it into a hyperlink pointing back to the current page.

2. Make a new class called .slider. Create a span around the new button text using the Toolbox panel (make sure the <span> tags go on the outside of the <a> tags), and apply the .slider class to it using the Quick Tag Selector (see Figure 15.9).

3. Make a new style and give it the selector name .slider a. Because you are going to hide the text, you don't need change any of the Font attributes. In the Background category, set background-image to slidingButtons.gif and background-repeat to no-repeat.

4. To create the sliding effect, you need to change the position of the background image and define the visible area within the page. The image has two buttons on it: The top one is for the regular state, and the bottom one is for the :hover state. Set the (x) background-position to left and the (y) background-position to top. This locks the image in place.

5. To define the visible area of the button, you need to first set the `display` attribute under the Layout category to Block to create an independent box in which to display the content and then change the size of the box under the Position category. The height of the image is 88px, and because you will be displaying half of it at one time, the `height` attribute should therefore be 44px. To contain the active area of the button to the area of the image, set the `width` attribute to 92px, which is the width of the image. Click OK to apply the style, and the button appears in Design view, as shown in Figure 15.10.

FIGURE 15.9
The new button text is wrapped in a <span> tag and the .slider class is applied.

FIGURE 15.10
After styling, the button appears as it should, but the text is still visible.

6. As you can see, the button looks the way it should, but the text is still visible. To hide the text, open the Modify Style dialog for the style, go to the Block category, and set the `text-indent` attribute to -9999px (see Figure 15.11). Click OK to save the change.

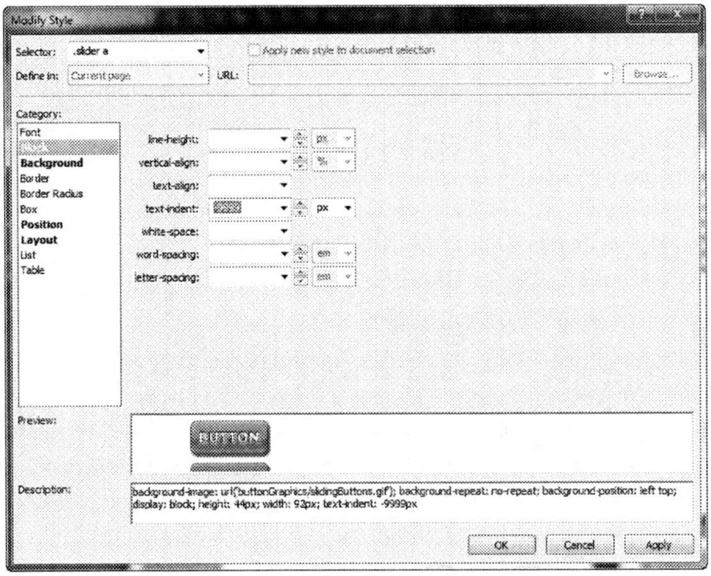

FIGURE 15.11
Setting the `text-indent` attribute to `-9999px` places the text of the button 9,999 pixels to the left of the screen, making it invisible to the visitor.

7. Finally, create a new style with the selector name `.slider a:hover`. Because of the cascade, any pseudoclass inherits all the styling from its parent unless the style is changed. Therefore, you need to make changes to only the `background-position` attributes, and the rest of the attributes will stay the same. Set `(x) background-position` to `0px` and `(y) background-position` to `-44px bottom`. This shifts the background image up so the bottom of the image aligns with the bottom of the box 44 pixels, and the bottom half is shown in place of the top half. Click OK and then save and preview in your browser.

Designers frequently use the sliding doors technique to create eye-catching rollovers without load times getting in the way. In this example, the background image only had two versions, but you could have an image with more instances. Likewise, you can place the images next to one another instead of on top of each other and change the `(x) background-position` value instead.

You can find more information and tutorials on how to use the sliding doors technique at the A List Apart website (www.alistapart.com).

By the Way

Summary

Buttons are an integral part of a website, both as navigational tools and as design elements. Knowing how to make and when to use different styles of buttons makes your life easier as a designer and your sites easier to navigate for the visitors.

Buttons can be anything from simple colored boxes with text inside them to advanced image-based elements with different graphics for each state. The layout and design of the page, and what the designer wants out of it, drive the choice of what kind of button to use.

In this hour, we've covered how to create several different types of CSS-based buttons. The advantages of CSS buttons are that they are text based and standards compliant, and a visitor who uses a text-only browser can still see the hyperlinks within the buttons. In this hour, you learned how to create simple box-type buttons with interactive features using CSS. You also learned how to take these buttons to the next level by replacing the solid color backgrounds with images. Finally, you learned how to use the sliding doors technique to use one image as the base for multiple different button states. You do this by sliding it in the background to show different versions of the same button image.

Q&A

Q. *I created a second copy of the sliding doors button, but it shows up underneath the first one no matter what I do. Why can't I make these buttons show up next to each other?*

A. Although sliding doors buttons can easily be lined up next to one another, the one you made in this example cannot do so without each of the buttons being put in a separate table cell. The reason for this has to do with the hiding of the button text, not the sliding doors function.

Workshop

The Workshop has quiz questions and exercises to help you put to use what you just learned. If you get stuck, the answers to the quiz questions are in the next section. But try to answer them first. Otherwise, you'll be cheating yourself.

Quiz

1. What happens to a CSS-based button if the CSS style sheet is not loaded or doesn't work?

2. When creating the basic and advanced box buttons, do you need to create separate styles for each of the buttons?

Answers

1. If the CSS style sheet is not loaded or doesn't work, the CSS-based button returns to its native state as a standard text link. This means even in suboptimal conditions, where things don't work the way they are supposed to, your button links will still work—they'll just look less attractive.

2. No, not unless you want to. The idea behind using CSS to create box buttons is that you can apply the same styling and background (either color or image) to multiple buttons with one set of styles. That way, you can make quick changes to multiple buttons throughout your site by changing only a few styles rather than having to change each individual button separately. You can, however, make individualized buttons with individual backgrounds or styles by wrapping each button instance in a <span> tag.

Exercise

To give the visitor a visual cue that the button has been pressed before, make styles for the :active and :visited pseudoclasses for all the different CSS buttons you created. The :active style usually has a bold appearance (bright colors and dark font), whereas the :visited pseudoclass is usually more muted than the other styles.

HOUR 16

Using Code Snippets

What You'll Learn in This Hour:

▶ What code snippets are
▶ How to use the new Snippets panel
▶ How to use the different code snippets that ship with Expression Web SP2
▶ How to create and edit your own code snippets

One of the many challenges of building websites is the code languages themselves. Or more specifically remembering the many complicated syntaxes, formulas, and code configurations used to make certain things happen or create certain effects. After years of writing web code, the code languages become second nature, but even then it's often hard to remember large and complicated blocks of code from project to project. To help with this process, Expression Web ships with a built-in code snippets function.

Up until the release of Expression Web 4 SP2, this code snippets function was a bit crude and rudimentary. Activating the code snippets function would give you a list of available snippets that would be pasted into your code. This worked well enough, but there was a lot of room for improvement.

Simultaneously, and seemingly unrelated, the earlier versions of Expression Web also shipped with a panel called Behaviors. This panel carried with it a long list of legacy functions relying on old and outdated coding practices and complex and unfriendly code.

Based on input from the Expression Web community and Expression Web MVPs like myself, the development team decided to make some drastic changes to the snippets functionality of the application and also include some up-to-date functions and functionalities in the process to replace the outdated Behaviors panel. The result of this work is the new Snippets panel, which in my opinion is the most important and most exciting feature of Service Pack 2.

Snippets: An Introduction

The code snippets function in Expression Web 4 SP2 is a powerful but easily over-looked feature that can and will save you a lot of time and effort once you start using it. Out of the box, it comes with a long list of useful snippets for HTML, CSS, JavaScript, jQuery, PHP, and more, and you can create new snippets yourself to serve your specific coding requirements.

By default, the Snippets panel appears in the top-right pane area behind the Toolbox tab. To see the Snippets panel, simply click the Snippets tab (see Figure 16.1).

FIGURE 16.1
The Snippets panel docks to the top-right panel when it is opened.

The Snippets panel contains a list of folders, some of which contain snippets and some of which contain further folders. The default snippets are stored in folders that correspond with the code language, so CSS snippets live in the CSS folder, HTML snippets in the HTML folder, and so on.

The snippets are code snippets, so they are used in Code view. To use a code snippet, you first place your cursor where you want the snippet to appear in Code view and then use one of two methods to insert the snippet: Either double-click the snippet directly in the Snippets panel or press Ctrl+Enter to jump to the Snippet search function and then start typing in the name of the snippet you want to use. The search function will narrow down your options and display only snippets with names that match what you have written, as in Figure 16.2.

FIGURE 16.2
The search function shows only snippets that match your search.

To insert a snippet from a text search, use the arrow keys to highlight the correct snippet and press Enter. Alternatively, you can simply double-click the highlighted snippet. You can also reset your search by clicking the X at the right side of the search area.

When you select a snippet—either by clicking it once with your mouse or by navigating to it with search and the arrow keys—you will see the name, description, and code output for the selected widget in the preview area at the bottom of the Snippets panel. This gives you the ability to check whether the snippet is the correct one before you insert it.

▼ **Try It Yourself**

Use a Snippet to Create a Custom Tooltip

To see how to use the snippets and understand how to make them work, let's start by creating a custom tooltip function using a CSS snippet:

1. Create and open a new HTML page called snippetsDemo.html in Split view.

2. At the top of the page, create a paragraph and write **MyKipple.com is a great place to find information about kipple**.

3. In Code view, scroll to the top and place your cursor right before the end </head> tag. Press Enter to create a few new empty lines.

4. In the Snippets panel, find the Style Block snippet and double-click it to insert it in the <head> tag. This inserts the standard code block that contains CSS code in HTML pages.

5. With your cursor on the empty line between the beginning and end <style> tags, press Ctrl+Enter to make a snippet search. Type **Tooltip**, and one snippet is revealed called Tooltip with CSS (see Figure 16.3). Press Enter or double-click Tooltip with CSS to insert the code snippet.

FIGURE 16.3
After searching for "Tooltip," only one snippet appears. The instructions on how to use the snippet can be seen in the preview area at the bottom of the Snippets panel.

▼

It would be logical to assume that once we've added the snippet, everything should work automatically. However, that's not the case. Apart from the jQuery UI Widgets snippets, which we'll cover later on in this hour, most of the snippets are just starting points for more work. Case in point, the tooltip snippet does nothing unless we add the `.tooltip` class to some content and create a span to contain the tooltip itself. If you select the Tooltip with CSS snippet again in the Snippets panel and look at the description in the bottom of the panel, you see the following instructions: "If you want to display a tooltip, just add the class 'tooltip' to an element and write your Tooltip Text in a span tag within the element." So let's do just that:

1. In Code view, find the beginning `<p>` tag and attach the `.tooltip` class.

2. Still in code view, place your cursor after the word MyKipple.com, insert a new `<span>` tag, and write **The home of my kipple**. Then end with the `</span>` tag.

If you click inside Design view to refresh the page, you'll see that the new tooltip does not appear. But if you save the page and preview it in your browser, the tooltip will appear when you hover over any of the text in the paragraph. This is a very basic demo of the Tooltip with CSS snippet, and the tooltip itself is not particularly attractive, but it provides you with the building blocks to create advanced tooltips of your own simply by adding a class and a span tag to an element (think image).

The Default Snippets

The default snippets shipped with Expression Web 4 SP2 provide a wide range of effects, functions, and options. Depending on the type of snippet, the usage and application differs. Here, I'll walk you through the bulk of them and provide you with the correct method for using them in your own projects.

CSS Snippets

The CSS snippets are divided into three main folders: Action, Effect, and Text. All the snippets in these folders provide standard CSS markup that can be inserted either in the head of the HTML page itself (contained within a standard `<style>` block provided by the Style Block snippet) or in a CSS file or external style sheet. To apply a CSS snippet to an element on the page, you attach the snippet class to that element. Keep in mind that a lot of these functions are CSS3, meaning they will not work in all browsers.

CSS – Action

▶ **Replace text with image**—The `.replace` class replaces text with a defined image when text is hovered over.

▶ **Tooltip with CSS**—The `.tooltip` class displays a tooltip wrapped in a `<span>` tag when the containing element is hovered over.

CSS – Effect

▶ **Box Shadow**—The `.boxShadow` class adds a box shadow to the containing box. The size and color can be changed by changing the values.

▶ **Circle**—The `.circle` class draws a circle with CSS. The size and color can be changed by changing the values.

▶ **Horizontal-Vertical align**—The `.align` class aligns the element to the horizontal and vertical center of the browser window.

▶ **Image Button**—The `.imageButton` class attached to the input button element replaces the default button with a custom image of your choice.

▶ **Opacity**—The `.opacity` class sets the opacity (transparency) of the element. 0.0 or 0 is fully transparent; 1 or 100 is fully opaque.

▶ **Rotate Box**—The `.rotate` class rotates the element box by degrees.

▶ **Rounded Corners**—The `.round_border` class adds rounded corners to the element box.

CSS – Text

▶ **Change Color of Selected Text**—Globally changes the color of text across the entire page when highlighted with a mouse.

▶ **Disable Select Text**—The `.unselect` class prevents the visitor from selecting text in the element for copying and such.

▶ **First letter in color and uppercase**—Globally sets the first letter of each element red and uppercase. Can be specified by changing style element from `:first-letter` to `p:first-lettedsdf`, for example.

▶ **Text Ellipsis**—The `.ellipsis` style adds an ellipsis (...) to the end of text when not all text is displayed due to overflow (the box is too small to display all text).

▶ **Text Shadow**—The `.text-shadow` class adds text shadow. Limited browser support at this time.

▶ **Text Outline**—The `.outline` class uses the `text-shadow` attribute and white text to create the appearance of outlined text.

Doctypes Snippets

The Doctypes snippets provide the default doctype calls for the standard doctypes used on the Web today. They are as follows:

▶ HTML 4.01 Strict

▶ HTML 4.01 Transitional

▶ HTML 5 (default in Expression Web 4 SP2)

▶ XHTML 1.0 Strict

▶ XHTML 1.0 Transitional

▶ XHTML 1.1

The doctype is inserted as the first line of code on a page. A page should never have more than one doctype.

HTML Snippets

The HTML snippets are a mixed bag of `<head>` and `<body>` snippets:

▶ **Definition List**—Add in `<body>`. Inserts a standard definition list in the body of the page. The `<dt>` tag wraps the definition keyword while the `<dd>` tag wraps the definition itself.

HTML – Hyperlink

To be added in the `<body>` of the page:

▶ **Add to favorites**—Creates an "Add to favorites" (that is, bookmark this page) link to your page.

▶ **Mail to link**—Creates a click-to-email link. Replace "@@email@@" with the target email address.

▶ **Open in new window**—Creates a link that opens the target in a new page using JavaScript.

HTML – Meta

To be added in the `<head>` of the page:

▶ **HTML 5 UTF-8 Meta**—Sets the character set of the page to UTF-8.

▶ **Meta keywords**—Adds meta keywords to the page. The cursor is automatically placed where keywords are to be added.

▶ **Meta refresh**—Tells the browser to auto-refresh the page and go to a different URL after a set time. Can also be used to refresh the page. Commonly used on newspaper sites to ensure new content is always displayed.

HTML – IE Meta Tags

IE meta tags are used to force various versions of Internet Explorer to interpret the content of the page in accordance with different standards. These are highly specialized functions most often used when deploying old code or when targeting old browsers. They are added at the very top of the `<head>` tag before any files such as style sheets are called. For a more in-depth explanation, go to the IE Blog and read the following article:

http://blogs.msdn.com/b/ie/archive/2008/06/10/introducing-
ie-emulateie7.aspx

JavaScript Snippets

The JavaScript snippets contain most normal functions, elements, and control structures used when writing JavaScript, in addition to a few handy conversion functions that are fully built out. Combined with the JavaScript IntelliSense support in Expression Web 4 SP2, you have a fully stocked and powerful JavaScript coding application right at your fingertips.

JavaScript falls outside the scope of this book, so I will not cover this component in more detail.

jQuery Snippets

jQuery is a popular JavaScript library that makes it easy to perform complicated actions and add cool effects and functionality to your site. jQuery is open source, and a large community of jQuery enthusiasts on the Web publishes tutorials, plug-ins, and information about the library and how to use it. The inclusion of jQuery both in the Snippets panel and in IntelliSense makes it easier than ever to start using these powerful functions in your own sites right away. For more information on jQuery, visit www.jquery.com. For practical purposes, which will become apparent later, I am presenting the jQuery snippets out of order and the UI Widgets will be explained later on.

jQuery – General

To run jQuery scripts, you must first call the jQuery library itself from within the page. The location of the library can be your own site or a Content Delivery Network. Microsoft hosts several versions of jQuery you can reference, and so does Google. For more information on URLs to the Google hosted jQuery and other libraries, visit http://code.google.com/apis/libraries/devguide.html. The General jQuery snippets call the jQuery or jQuery UI libraries from different locations:

▶ **jQuery script reference – MS CDN**—Calls the jQuery library from Microsoft's Content Delivery Network.

▶ **jQuery UI script reference – Local**—Calls the jQuery UI library from a location on your domain or one of your choosing.

▶ **jQuery UI script reference – MS CDN**—Calls the jQuery UI library from Microsoft's Content Delivery Network.

▶ **Document Ready**—Inserts a generic document-ready block. The document-ready block will wrap (contain) all the jQuery code and ensure that it is running when the rest of the content on the page is loaded.

jQuery – Forms

The Forms snippets under jQuery allow you to add automated functionality to your forms. Once you've added a jQuery library, you can insert any or all of these Forms snippets in the Document Ready snippet for enhanced functionality. Each snippet has a description explaining the functionality. Most of them are designed to target form elements with specific IDs that are inserted in the snippet.

jQuery – Styling

jQuery is often used to change styling attributes on elements either by adding, changing, or removing classes or by performing other actions on the elements that can't be applied with static CSS or HTML.

▶ **Add-Remove class on hover**—Adds a class named .hover to the element with the defined ID when it is hovered over. The .hover class is removed when the item is no longer being hovered over.

▶ **Highlight input label**—For use in forms. Highlights the form label of the defined element when the form field is in focus.

▶ **Zebra stripes**—Adds a class named .oddClass to every odd element in lists and tables. Combined with CSS, this can produce a nice zebra stripe look to the list or table for easier reading.

PHP Snippets

As with the JavaScript snippets, the PHP snippets offer up a long list of standard elements, functions, and control structures for writing PHP. Combined with the PHP support in IntelliSense, this makes Expression Web 4 SP2 an ideal platform for both learning and writing PHP. I myself work almost exclusively with PHP and the Snippets panel, and IntelliSense is a huge help in that regard.

Stray Snippets

In addition to all the snippets just listed, there are two stray snippets that are not added to a folder. You have already used one of them—the Style Block—but the other one is so unusual it requires special mention:

▶ **Web slice**—The web slice is a technology introduced with Internet Explorer 8 that allows the website owner to create a mini version of the page that a visitor can pin to her Favorites bar in the browser and check later. The snippet will introduce into the page the necessary code to make such a web slice work. This is a highly specialized function that only works with IE8 and IE9, and I have only seen a few good implementations of it, most notably a tracker for eBay auctions. For more info on web slices, visit the IE Blog at http://blogs.msdn.com/b/ie/archive/2008/03/06/activities-and-web-slices-in-internet-explorer-8.aspx.

Using the jQuery UI Widgets Snippets

In the preceding list of all the snippets, I intentionally skipped the UI Widgets snippets, and with good reason. Of all the snippets that ship with Expression Web 4 SP2, the UI Widgets are the most effective and elaborate, and they deserve special attention.

jQuery UI is a variant of the standard jQuery library that allows you to do some pretty nifty things with minimal effort. The jQuery UI library has a series of widgets built in that you can hook into and create some very advanced effects on your site with only a small amount of code. And SP2 ships with three of these widgets all built out and ready to use. They are an accordion, a tabbed box, and an interactive calendar. All these three widgets can be dropped in anywhere on your site and used out of the box or with only minor configurations.

But before you can use these widgets, you have to add the jQuery UI head to your page:

1. In Code view, scroll to the top of the page and create a new line right before the end </head> tag.

2. In the Snippets panel under jQuery, UI Widgets, find and click the jQuery UI head widget. This inserts 30 lines of code, most of which is commented out (see Figure 16.4).

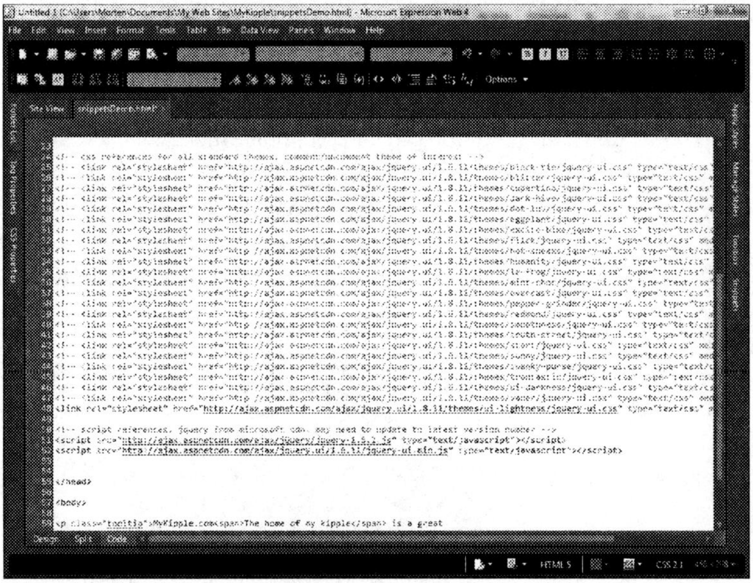

FIGURE 16.4
The jQuery UI head widget inserts commented-out calls to all the standard jQuery UI theme style sheets as well as calls to the jQuery and jQuery UI libraries as hosted by Microsoft CDN.

The snippets consist of three elements: Calls to all the standard theme style sheets for jQuery UI (all the commented out lines + the one active style sheet reference), a call to the jQuery library as hosted by Microsoft CDN, and a call to the jQuery UI library also hosted by Microsoft CDN.

When you add a jQuery UI Widget, the jQuery and jQuery UI libraries will kick in and the widget will use the theme style sheet for the presentation elements.

Create a Dynamic Accordion Effect with the jQuery UI Widgets Snippet

Now that you have the jQuery UI head installed in your page, you can use the jQuery UI Widget snippets to add some cool functions to it:

1. In Code view, scroll down and place your cursor directly underneath the paragraph you created earlier.

2. Press Ctrl+Enter to go to Snippet search and type **Accordion**. This highlights the Accordion jQuery UI Widget snippet.

3. Press Enter to insert the code snippet into your page.

4. Save the page and preview it in your browser.

When previewing the page in your browser, you should see an accordion matching the one in Figure 16.5. The accordion works by revealing the text and other content within each panel and collapsing the other open panel when you click the corresponding tab. Going back to Expression Web and looking at the source code, you'll see that the accordion is in fact nothing more than a series of nested divs and headings marked up with standard HTML. That means you can change the content of the accordion in any way you want using the normal techniques you have learned (and will learn more of in this book) and that content will automatically display in the accordion.

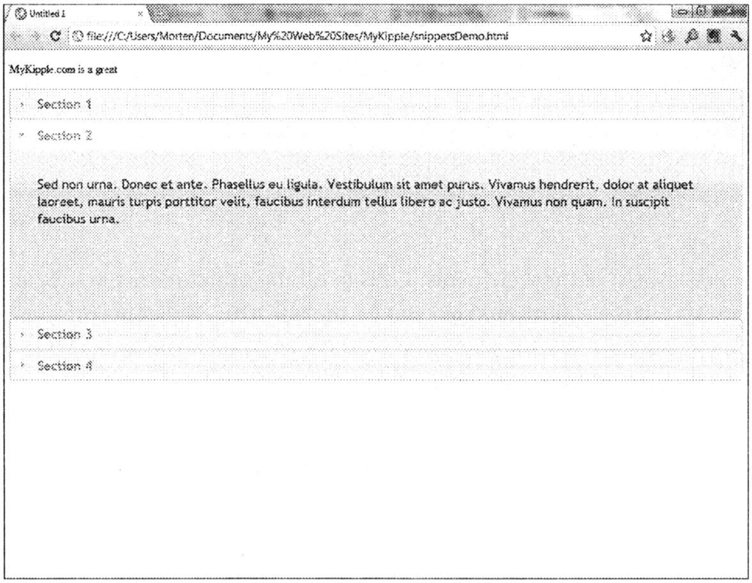

FIGURE 16.5
The Accordion jQuery UI Widget snippet creates an advanced accordion function in your page with just a few clicks.

▼

If you want to change the appearance of the accordion itself, you can do so either by commenting out the active stylesheet link in the jQuery UI head and uncommenting one of the many other default style sheets or by writing your own stylesheet based on the default ones. If you want to learn more about the Accordion widget, how it works, and how you can configure it, visit http://jqueryui.com/demos/accordion/.

Calendar and Tabs Widgets

The Calendar and Tabs jQuery UI Widgets snippets work much the same way as the Accordion snippet: You add them to the page the same way and they are controlled by the same style sheet and the same jQuery and jQuery UI reference. Therefore, even if you have an accordion, a calendar, and a tab on the same page, you only need one jQuery UI head. Also, if you change the style sheet, all three widgets will change appearance at the same time.

The Calendar widget adds an interactive calendar to a date form field or date field on the page. When the user clicks the field, the calendar opens up so that the user can select a date without punching in any numbers, as shown in Figure 16.6.

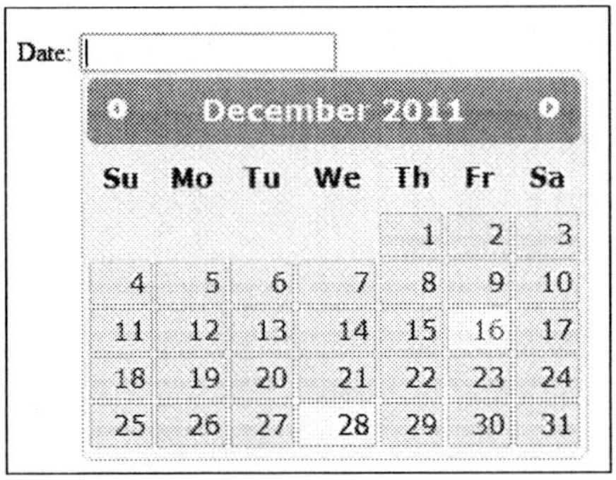

FIGURE 16.6
The Calendar snippet adds an interactive calendar to a form field for easy date selection.

The Tabs widget can be seen as a horizontal version of the accordion widget. When added in the page, it creates a tabbed box where the contents of each tab are displayed when the tab is clicked, as shown in Figure 16.7. Like with the accordion, the HTML code is straightforward and easy to edit and configure.

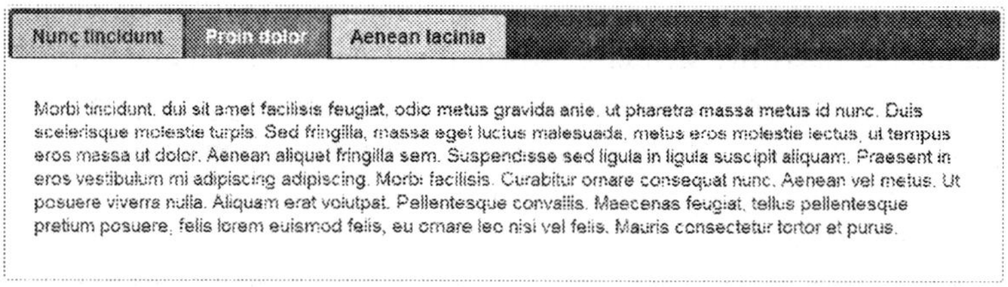

FIGURE 16.7
The Tabs snippet adds an interactive tabbed box where content is displayed when different tabs are clicked. The look and feel of the tabbed box can be changed by altering the style sheet.

Creating and Editing Snippets

In addition to using the default snippets that ship with Expression Web 4 SP2, you have the ability to create your own custom snippets to add to your preconfigured coding arsenal. That way, as you encounter code snippets you use a lot, you can add them to the panel for easy access later. I've created about 50 custom snippets in different folders I use when I create and configure WordPress sites, and this ability to store and recall useful pieces of code has made my work far more effective.

Adding folders and snippets is done from the Snippets panel.

▼ **Try It Yourself**

Add a New Snippet

In Hour 17, "Building a Functional Menu," you learn how to build a functional menu using unordered lists and CSS. This is a common process that is repeated pretty much every time you create a new website, and that makes it a perfect candidate for a custom code snippet. So even though technically you don't learn this until the next hour, let me give you a head start:

1. Go to the Snippets panel and make sure every folder is collapsed and that no folder is selected.

2. Click the Options button and select New Folder from the drop-down menu. This creates a new folder called Snippet.

3. Right-click the new folder, select Rename, and rename it **Custom Snippets**.

4. With the new folder selected, click Options again and select New Snippet. This opens the New/Modify Code Snippet panel (see Figure 16.8).

FIGURE 16.8
The New/Modify
Code Snippet
panel enables
you to create
new or modify
existing code
snippets.

5. Give the new snippet the name **Standard Menu Markup** and the description **Standard unordered list markup for HTML list-based menu**.

6. Under Type, leave Insert/Replace checked.

7. In the text area, write out the code for a standard unordered list with one list item with a link inside, as follows (the ## segments indicate areas that must be edited once the list is inserted):

```
<ul>
    <li><a href="##link##" title="##title##>##Menu Item##</a></li>
</ul>
```

8. To tell Expression Web where to put the cursor, you can insert a pipe character (|) anywhere in the snippet. If you want Expression Web to highlight a portion of the snippet for immediate replacement, you can wrap it in pipe characters. In this case, we want Expression Web to immediately highlight the ##Menu Item## section so that when you start typing, you are typing in the menu item name. Therefore, place a pipe character on either side or both sides, like this: |##Menu Item##| (see Figure 16.9).

9. Click OK to create the new snippet.

FIGURE 16.9
The new snippet
is fully config-
ured with an
immediately
editable area
defined by the
pipe characters.

Now that the snippet is made, you can insert it anywhere in your code by double-clicking it from the Snippets panel. When you insert the snippet, the ##Menu Item## text is immediately highlighted. If you start typing, it is replaced with the new text.

Editing an existing snippet is done using the same dialog. To edit an existing snippet, either right-click the snippet and select Edit Snippet from the menu or select the snippet and click the Edit button at the top of the preview area in the Snippets panel.

Moving Snippets

If you create custom snippets on one computer and want to move them to another computer, share them with your friends or co-workers, or want a backup in case something happens to your computer, you can access the snippets directly from your file browser outside Expression Web. Depending on your operating system, the snippets can be found in the AppData folder for Expression Web 4. On Windows 7 that would be \Users\YourName\AppData\Roaming\Microsoft\ Expression\Web 4\mySnippets. From here, you can copy any and all snippets and snippet folders and move them to other computers.

Summary

Snippets may be the most exciting addition to be introduced with Expression Web 4 SP2, and it is a feature power users such as myself have been asking for for a long time. In this hour, you learned how to use the Snippets panel and the code snippets functionality to quickly and easily add blocks of code to your pages, style sheets, and other elements. You got a walkthrough of the different snippets and their functions and uses, and you got a demo of how to use the advanced jQuery UI Widget snippets to add some fancy interactive features into your pages with pretty much zero effort. Finally, and most importantly, you learned how to create your own custom widgets. This is a feature I urge you to start using immediately and build on. Using custom snippets will save you a lot of time and effort in the future, especially if you work on multiple computers and you move or sync the snippets folders between them. With what you have learned in this hour, you are now fully equipped to use the Snippets panel like a pro.

Q&A

Q. *I added the jQuery UI head and jQuery UI Widget snippet X, but my page just shows a block of text/a form field without any of the fancy stuff you talked about. What's going on?*

A. Do you have an Internet connection? If not, the widgets will not work, and here's why: The standard jQuery UI head code assumes you have an Internet connection and tries to call the stylesheet as well as both the jQuery library and the jQuery UI library from a server on the Web. If you don't have an Internet connection, those files are unavailable and the function won't work. If you still want it to work, you have to download the jQuery and jQuery UI libraries (available for free at www.jquery.com and www.jqueryui.com), place them in your site, and change the URLs in the header code to point to your local instances instead.

Workshop

The Workshop has quiz questions and exercises to help you put to use what you just learned. If you get stuck, the answers to the quiz questions are in the next section. But try to answer them first. Otherwise, you'll be cheating yourself.

Quiz

1. What is the quickest way to access the Code Snippets panel?

2. What is the one type of code you can't put in a code snippet?

Answers

1. Whether the Code Snippets panel is open or not, the quickest way to access it is to place your cursor in Code view and pressing Ctrl+Enter. This will take you straight to the search box in the Code Snippets panel.

2. Trick question: You can put any type of code in a code snippet. That's the whole point.

Exercise

Use the jQuery UI Widget code snippets to create an accordion with three types of content: a block of text, an image, and a list of links. Test it in your browser and make sure it works. For extra credit, create your own code snippet with standard text content from lipsum.com or another Lorem Ipsum generator. You can create several snippets, one with one paragraph, one with two, and so on.

Building a Functional Menu

What You'll Learn in This Hour:

- ▶ How to build a vertical menu using CSS
- ▶ How to build a horizontal menu using CSS
- ▶ How to convert the horizontal menu to a standards-based drop-down menu using only unordered lists and CSS

Menus are a great tool for simplifying navigation in a website. They enable you to group several different pages or links together visually and give the user an intuitive and interactive experience when surfing your site. There are many types of menus—from the standard vertical list menu to horizontal menus to drop-down menus of all shapes and sizes. And all of them can be built using standards-based code and CSS. You just have to know how.

Participating in web design forums and answering comments on my blog and emails, I've realized that creating menus, especially drop-down menus that work properly, is a common challenge for new designers and developers. Much of the confusion seems to stem from the myriad of different techniques available and a lack of understanding of the processes behind them and the problems created by browser inconsistencies. This is unfortunate because the principles behind creating functional drop-down menus are simple.

This hour shows you how to make proper, functional, and lightweight CSS-based menus of the vertical, horizontal, and drop-down variety that you can implement into any site. You see how, using some simple CSS tricks, you can make seemingly boring text-based menus to look both inviting and interactive.

Making the Basic Vertical Menu Exciting

The most basic standards-based menu available is the vertical unordered list. Not only is it easy to build (all you need to do is create an unordered list in which each list item is a link), but it is also easy to maintain, and it works no matter what browser the visitor uses. That said, there is no good reason why it should look bland and boring. Using the CSS techniques you have picked up by reading the preceding hours of this book, you are well equipped to make the good-old vertical menu look modern and stylish.

Throughout this hour, you learn to make three different kinds of menus. To keep everything in one central location so that you can go back at any time to look at what you did (and copy the code into future pages), create a new folder called **menus** with a page called **menus.html** to work from.

1. If you haven't already done so, create and open the menus.html page in Design view.

2. Create a standard unordered list with five menu items named Menu Item One, Menu Item Two, and so on.

3. Directly above the unordered list, insert a new paragraph, type **Basic Vertical Menu**, and change the style to H1.

4. Press Enter to create a new paragraph and then insert a couple of lines of text explaining that this is a basic vertical menu based on an unordered list. You should now have a page that looks like Figure 17.1.

5. The whole idea of a menu is to create navigation. To do so, make each of the menu items a hyperlink back to the menus.html page.

6. Switch to Split view and create a div to wrap the heading, paragraph, and list. Give the div the ID vertMenuBox.

7. Now it's time for the styling. First, create a new ID style for #vertMenuBox and set font-family to Arial, Helvetica, sans-serif; color to #333333; background-color to #EBEADF; and all four borders to solid, 1px, and #C4C2AB. To give the content some breathing space, set top and bottom padding to 5px, and right and left padding to 10px. Finally, to constrain the size of the menu, set width (found under Position) to 250px. Click OK, and you see that the menu is now contained in a nice box with a beige color (see Figure 17.2).

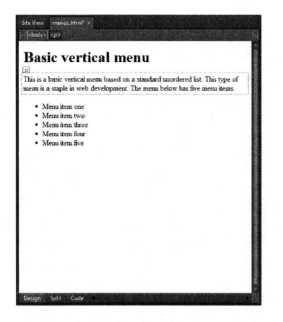

FIGURE 17.1
To start, the menus.html page should have an H2 heading, a paragraph, and an unordered list with five items.

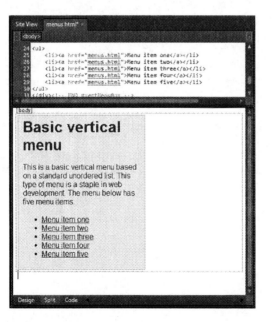

FIGURE 17.2
By styling the #vertMenuBox ID alone, the menu already looks much better.

8. Now, for the menu itself. To remove the list bullets and align the menu items with the left side of the box, create a new style with the selector #vertMenuBox ul and set the padding and margin values to 0px and the list-style-type under List to none. Click OK to apply the new style.

9. Next up are the links. Create a new style with the selector #vertMenuBox ul li a and set font-size to 0.8em, text-transform to uppercase, color to #666666, and check None under text-decoration. To style each of the links so they are farther apart, set the top and bottom padding to 5px and create a further visual separation by setting border-bottom to dotted, 1px, and #333333. Finally, set display to block to make the links into block-level elements. Click OK to apply the new style.

10. Create a new style with the selector #vertMenuBox ul li a:hover and set color to #333333. Click OK, save the page, and test it in your browser.

Now, you have a basic vertical menu with some styling that makes it look less boring. But it's still pretty basic. To make it stand out, add a couple of extra style tricks to the menu:

1. Open the Modify Style dialog for the #vertMenuBox ul li a style and set padding-left to 5px. Click OK to apply the change.

2. Open the style with the selector #vertMenuBox ul li a:hover and set background-color to #FAFAF5. Click OK to apply the new style, save, and test the page in your browser.

By setting the list item links to block-level elements and giving them a lighter background color on the hover state, you are both making the menu buttons easier to click because they are larger and making them more visually attractive (see Figure 17.3).

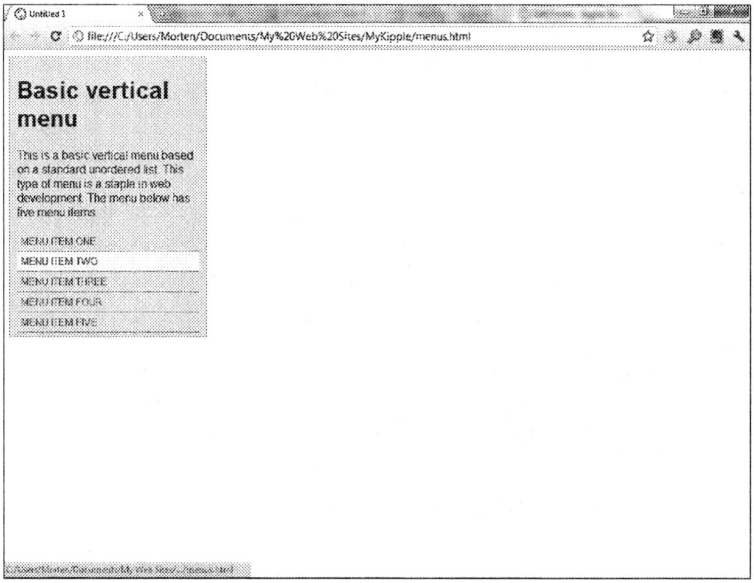

FIGURE 17.3
The block-level list item anchors combined with the background color change in the :hover pseudoclass adds a sophisticated interactive experience to the menu with only minor effort.

The Horizontal Menu—Laying a List on Its Side

As you saw in the preceding exercise, making a vertical menu based on an unordered list look interesting with CSS isn't all that hard. However, you don't always want your menus to be vertical. In many cases, a horizontal menu looks better and is more functional. But how do you create a horizontal menu from an unordered list when the unordered list by its very nature is a list, and therefore vertical? The answer is simple. Lay it on its side:

1. Below the Basic Vertical List box you just created (and outside the box), create a new unordered list with the same five list items as before, and make each a link back to the current page.

2. In Split view, wrap the new list in a div with the ID #horizontalMenuBox. Create a new style with the selector #horizontalMenuBox and set font-family to Arial, Helvetica, sans-serif; background-color to #EBEADF; border to solid, 1px, #C4C2AB; and margin-top to 1em to create some space between the Basic Vertical Menu and the new one you are about to create.

3. Create a new style with the selector #horizontalMenuBox ul and set padding and margin to 0px for all sides.

4. To get the menu items to appear on one line instead of as a list, create a new style with the selector #horizontalMenuBox ul li and set display to inline under the Layout category. Click Apply, and you see that the list items are now on one line (see Figure 17.4).

5. To give the menu some more weight, you want to create some vertical space above and below the links. However, if you go to Box and set padding-top and padding-bottom to 10px and click Apply, you see that nothing changes. To change the line height and thereby the vertical space above and below the list items, go to the Block category and set line-height to 25px. Click OK to apply the style.

6. Right now, the menu items are stacked almost directly against one another. To give them some breathing room, create a new style with the selector #horizontalMenuBox ul li a and set padding-right and padding-left to 1em. To match the vertical space created earlier, set padding-top and padding-bottom to 5px. At the same time, set the font-size to 0.8em, text-transform to uppercase, color to #666666, and text-decoration to none. Click Apply to see the changes take effect.

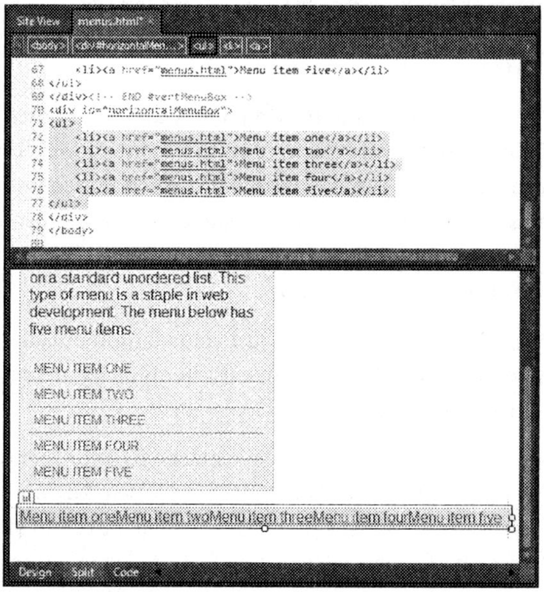

FIGURE 17.4
To make the items of an unordered list appear next to one another, simply set the li style to display:inline.

7. Finally, to make the menu items react when the visitor hovers her mouse over them, create a new style with the selector #horizontalMenuBox ul li a:hover and set color to #333333 and background-color to #C4C2AB. Click OK to apply the new style, save, and test the page in your browser.

As you can see in Figure 17.5, the items in the horizontal menu react in much the same way as in the vertical one, with one major difference: The entire hover area is a link. This is because you used the padding in step 6 to expand the link area to cover an area larger than the text itself. You can use the same technique to make the entire area of the vertical menu into a link.

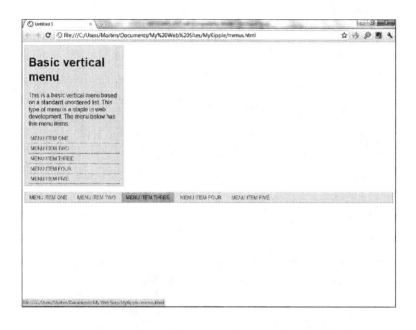

FIGURE 17.5
With some basic styling, the unordered list is turned into a functional horizontal menu.

Pure CSS Drop-Down Menus: A Clean Alternative

Now that you've created a vertical and a horizontal menu, it is time to merge the two into a more advanced drop-down menu in which the main menu is horizontal and the submenus are vertical. As you have learned, if you want your page to be as accessible as possible and standards-compliant and cross-browser compatible, you must base all of your menus on ordered or unordered lists. That way, the menu is still meaningful if the visitor is on an old computer or uses a text-only or text-to-speech browser. The ideal solution for making drop-down menus should be to create an unordered list with sublists styled using CSS. And, in an ideal world, this wouldn't be that much of a problem. Unfortunately, the idiosyncratic nature of the most prolific browsers (especially Internet Explorer 6) has made it all but impossible to make a CSS drop-down menu without using some form of custom coding for these browsers or adding JavaScript or behaviors to make everything work properly.

As new versions of the many different browsers emerge, these problems with inconsistencies become less and less prevalent. Sometime in the foreseeable future, they will likely disappear completely or at least diminish to the point where they are no longer a concern. In the meantime, designers have to live with one of two options: Create pure CSS drop-down menus that might have problems in older browsers, or make menus that have JavaScript built in to fix the browser problems.

Here, we focus on merging the preceding two menus to create a drop-down menu using only CSS and no special browser-specific code. As a result, it might not work properly in Internet Explorer 6.

Step 1: Make a Menu List

To start things off, we need to mark up the actual links we are going to convert to menu buttons. This is done using an unordered list.

1. In the menus.html page, insert a new div underneath the code for the horizontal menu and give it the ID #dropDownMenu. Inside the new div, create another copy of the unordered list menu from above by copying and pasting everything within the <ul> tags (see Figure 17.6).

FIGURE 17.6
You can duplicate the basic unordered lists by copying and pasting them within Code view.

2. Create sublists for three of the new menu items. In Split view, select the Menu Item Two list item. In Code view, place the cursor right before the closing `</li>` tag and then press Enter to create a new line. Type **<ul>** to create a new unordered list (IntelliSense closes the tag for you), press Enter again to create a new line, and create a sublist item by typing **<li>**. Create three sublist items named Sub List Item One, Sub List Item Two, and so on (see Figure 17.7).

FIGURE 17.7
To create a list within a list, you need to edit the code in Code view. Although doing so is not necessary, splitting up the tags and spacing them as shown in this screenshot helps with readability.

3. Now that you have a sublist, go back to Design view and make all the new items into links that point back to the current page.

4. Repeat steps 2 and 3 for two of the other main menu items (see Figure 17.8).

Step 2: Style the Main Menu

Now you have a working set of hyperlinks, but it looks nothing like a menu. The next step is to turn the menu into a horizontal one like you did in the menu previously in this hour.

1. Create a new style with the ID #dropDownMenu. Set font-family to Arial, Helvetica, sans-serif; background-color to #EBEADF; border to solid, 1px, #C4C2AB; and margin-top to 1em to create some space.

2. Create a new style with the selector #dropDownMenu ul and set padding and margin to 0px for all sides. Note that, in Design view, all the list items line up to the left side of the box regardless of what level they are at. To ensure that the menu retains its height, go to Position and set height to 25px.

3. Create a new style with the selector #dropDownMenu ul li and set display to inline under the Layout category. In the preceding menu, this was enough to align the menu items left to right rather than top to bottom, but if you click Apply, you see that the list items still stack vertically. This is because the sublists are too wide to fit on one line and are considered one item (see Figure 17.9).

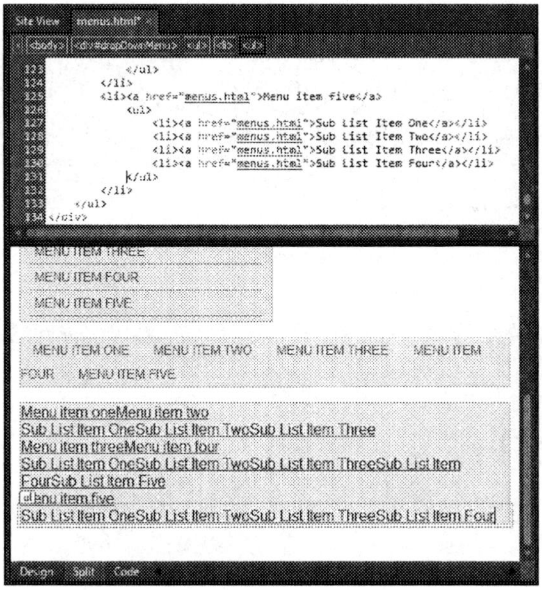

FIGURE 17.9
Even with the li
style set to dis-
play:inline, the
list still stacks
vertically.

4. To get the new menu to stack properly, you need to do two things: Define a specific width for each list item and make them float to the left. Still in the #dropDownMenu ul li style, set width under Position to 150px. You can set it wider if you want, but any narrower and the text in the submenu items won't fit. Then, go to the Layout category and set float to left. Click Apply again, and you see that now the main menu items line up from left to right, and the submenu items appear as vertical lists under their respective parent item (see Figure 17.10).

5. Because we are operating with two layers of list items, the basic font styling should be done in the li style: Still in the #dropDownMenu ul li style, set font-size to 0.8em and text-transform to uppercase. To give the buttons some breathing space, set height under Position to 25px. Click OK to apply the changes.

6. You now need to style the links like you did earlier. Create a new style with the selector #dropDownMenu ul li a. Under Font, set color to #666666 and set text-decoration to none. Go to Background and set background-color to #EBEADF manually, or you can use the Eyedropper tool and pick the background color from one of the other menus. Click Apply, and you see that the links now have the right font and background color, but that the background is visible only directly behind the links, as shown in Figure 17.11.

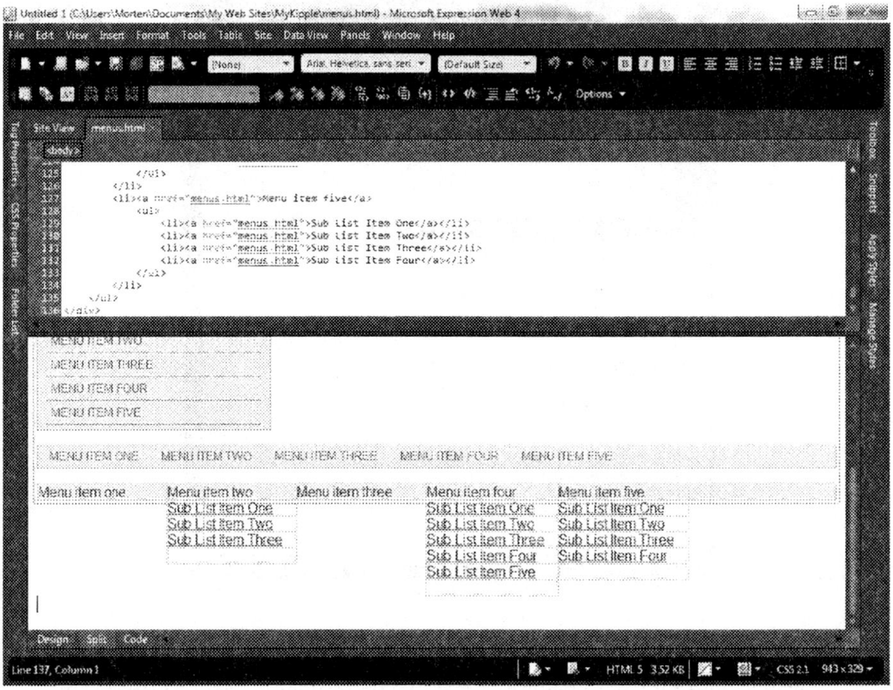

FIGURE 17.10
With the width and float attributes set, the list starts to look like a drop-down menu.

FIGURE 17.11
Unless otherwise defined, the background color only appears directly behind the link text.

7. For the menu to look and function properly, the link area needs to extend beyond the text to cover the allotted area in the boxes the li style has created. In the earlier horizontal menu, you used the padding attribute to do this, but this time, you use the line-height and display attributes: Still in the #dropDownMenu ul li a style, go to Block and set the line-height attribute to 25px to match the height you set in the #dropDownMenu ul li style earlier. Next, go to Layout and set display to block. Finally, set padding-left to 8px to create some space between the left edge and the text. Click OK, and the backgrounds now fill out the correct areas, as shown in Figure 17.12.

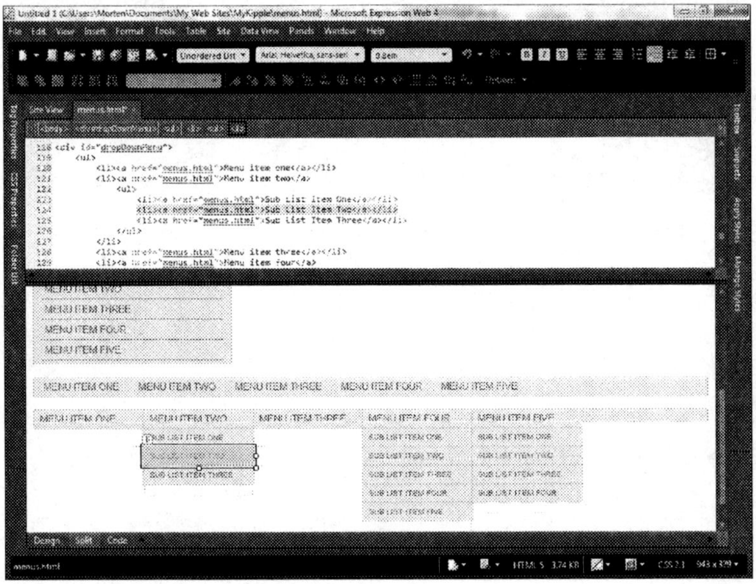

FIGURE 17.12
With the line-height and display properties set properly, the link backgrounds extend to "fill out" the menu boxes.

8. Now that the buttons extend to fill the required area, create a new pseudoclass with the selector #dropDownMenu ul li a:hover and set color to #333333 and background-color to #C4C2AB. Click OK, save the page, and test it in your browser.

Previously in this book, you learned that the block attribute caused the element to which it was applied to appear on its own line and fill out that line. The same thing happens when the attribute is applied to the style in step 7, but because the list item style (li) has already been set to inline with a fixed width, the block is constrained by the li box and fills out only the area within it.

Did you Know?

Step 3: Make the Drop-Down Menus Drop Down

As you can see in Figure 17.13, the main menu and submenus line up correctly, but the submenus are all visible all the time. However, the whole point of drop-down menus is that they drop down only when the visitor hovers over them. To achieve this, use the :hover pseudoclass with the visibility attribute to hide the submenus.

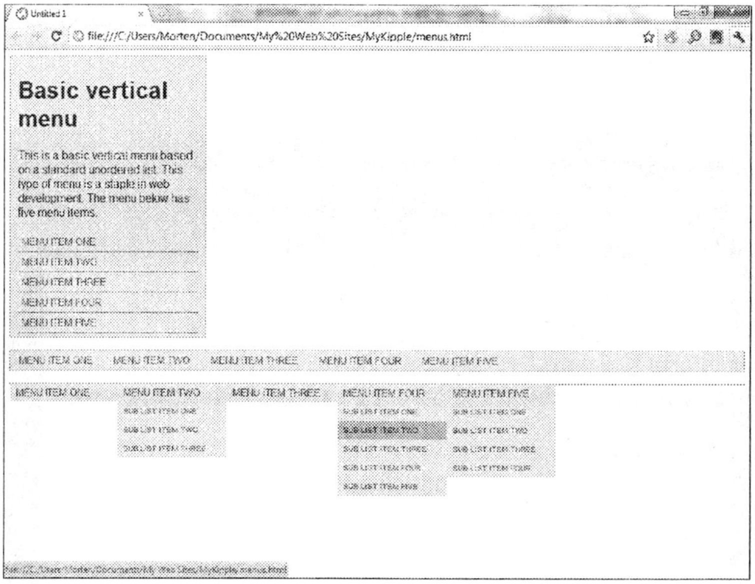

FIGURE 17.13
Although the menus line up correctly, all the submenus are visible all the time.

1. Hide the submenus so that they are invisible unless the user triggers them. To do so, create a new style with the selector #dropDownMenu ul li ul. This style affects only the unordered lists contained within a list item (that is, the submenus). Under the Layout category, set visibility to hidden. Click OK to apply the modified style. Now, the submenus are no longer visible in Design view.

2. Create a new style with the selector #dropDownMenu ul li:hover ul. This style is a pseudoclass that triggers when the visitor hovers over a main menu list item and affects any unordered list contained within that list item. Under the Layout category, set visibility to visible. Click OK to apply the new style.

3. To ensure that the drop-down menu items appear on top of and not behind content or below them on the page, open the selector #dropDownMenu, go to

Position, and set position to relative and z-index to 10. The z-index value places the entire menu in a higher level than the rest of the content on the page.

Save and preview the page in your browser; you see that the drop-down menus now work the way they should (see Figure 17.14). Furthermore, the menu is 100% CSS-based, which means it works without any code additives, such as JavaScript. However, most important, it is fully legible if the visitor uses a text-only or text-to-speech browser.

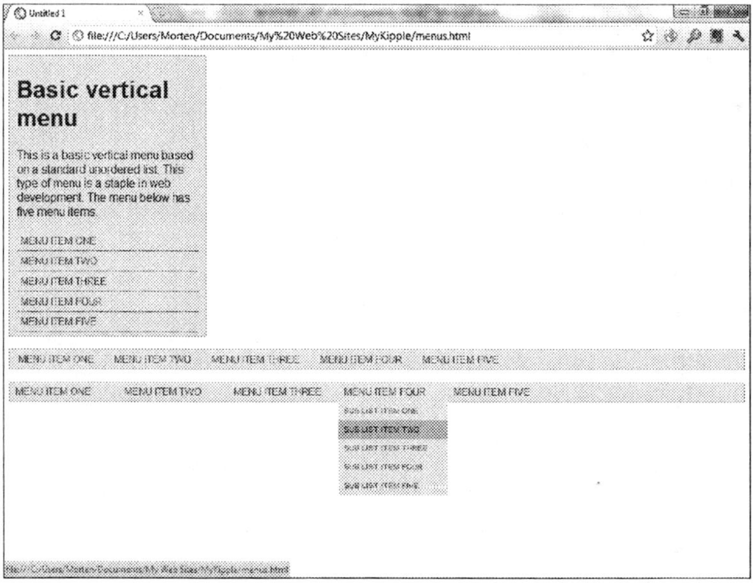

FIGURE 17.14
The pure-CSS drop-down menu now works properly in all modern browsers.

As you can see in Figure 17.15, with styles turned off, the CSS-based menus revert to their original form, which is standard unordered lists with sublists. Not only is the menu easier to read, but also the layout, and ordering is intuitive to the visitor even without styles.

Not All Browsers Like the Pure-CSS Drop-Down Menu

Watch Out!

As previously mentioned, the pure-CSS drop-down menu is not a perfect solution because not all browsers support it. For unknown reasons, Internet Explorer 6 does not support pseudoclasses attached to items other than simple anchors (a style). Because you used the li:hover style to create the drop-down effect, it will not work properly in Internet Explorer 6. To solve this problem, you have to either employ a custom JavaScript that simulates the `li:hover` pseudoclass for IE6 or create a separate menu that replaces the pure-CSS drop-down menu for IE6 users. One clever workaround is to place the pure-CSS drop-down menu in one layer and a custom IE6 menu in another, and then use the Check Browser behavior to choose what layer to show in the page based on what browser the visitor uses.

The Internet Explorer 6 compatibility issue is a diminishing one because more and more users are upgrading to newer versions of the browser (Internet Explorer 7 has been out for some time and Internet Explorer 8 was rolled out in the spring of 2009). What's more, most (if not all) other browsers support the `li:hover` property. With that said, you always have to consider the lowest common denominator and whether you should "dumb down" your sites to accommodate it.

FIGURE 17.15
With styles turned off, the CSS-based menus revert to standard unordered lists for easy reading.

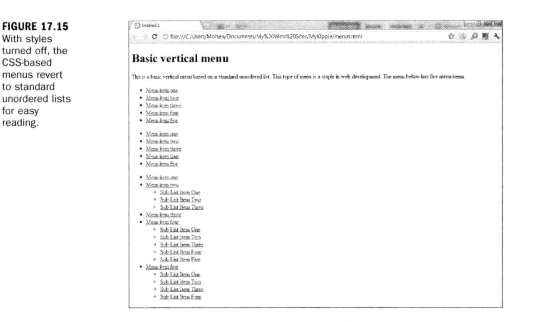

Styling the Submenus to Make Them Stand Out

Right now, there is no visual difference between the main menu items and the submenus. But, depending on the design of the site, it can sometimes be a good idea to give the visitor visual clues that separate different types of content from each other. A simple way of doing this is to give the submenu items a different set of styles than the main menu items.

1. Create a new style with the selector #dropDownMenu ul li ul li a. This style affects only the links inside list items that are housed inside another list item. Under Font, set color to #FFFFFF and under Background, set background-color to #3399FF. This gives the submenus a blue background color. Click OK to apply the new style.

2. Because of the cascade, unless you specify something different, the hover state of the submenus is styled by the #dropDownMenu ul li a:hover pseudoclass. To change the hover state, you need to create a new pseudoclass with the selector name #dropDownMenu ul li ul li a:hover. Set the color to #FFFFFF and set the background-color to #0065CA. Click OK, and save and test the page in your browser.

With the new styles applied, the submenu now has a distinct look that is different from the main menu (see Figure 17.16).

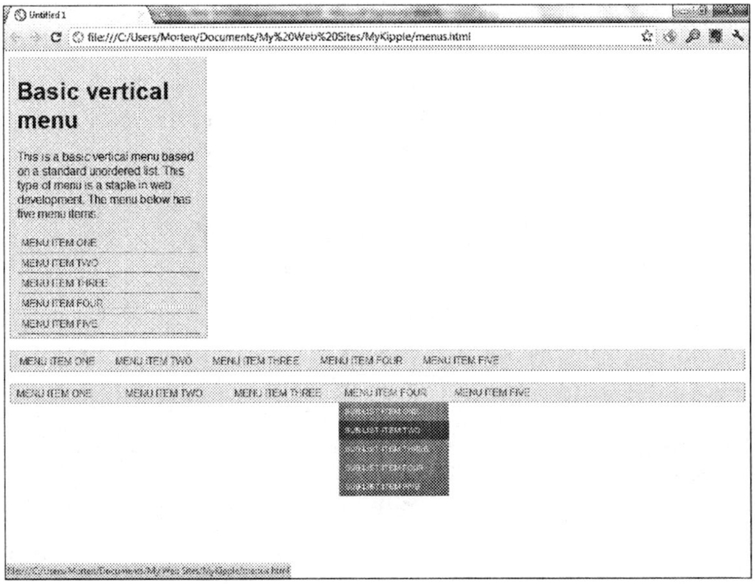

FIGURE 17.16
The submenu styling produces a visual cue that tells the visitor these buttons are different from the ones on the main menu.

Try It Yourself ▼

Create an Image-Based Menu for the MyKipple Site

Now that you know how to make a functional menu, let's apply that knowledge to the MyKipple site and, in the process, make it even more advanced by applying image-based backgrounds.

1. With the default.html file open in Split view, create a div with the ID #mainMenu and place it inside the header. In Code view, create a new unordered list with three buttons named Home, Gallery, and Contact. Make each of them a link pointing back to default.html.

2. Create a new style in kippleStyles.css and give it the selector #mainMenu ul. Set width to 100% so that the box spans the entire width of the header box.

3. Create a new style in kippleStyles.css and give it the selector #mainMenu ul li. Under Block, set line-height to 30px. Under Layout, set display to inline. This aligns the buttons on one line.

4. Create a new style in kippleStyles.css and give it the selector #mainMenu ul li a. Set color to #000000, text-align (found under Block) to center, width to 110px, height to 35px, and under Layout, set display to block and float to left.

5. Create a pseudoclass for a:hover and set color to #FFFFFF and text-decoration to none.

   At this point, you should have a basic three-item menu along the bottom left side of the #header div, as shown in Figure 17.17. The buttons work, but there are no backgrounds. Now, you assign separate graphic backgrounds to each of the three buttons using custom classes.

6. Import the three files, green.png, blue.png, and purple.png, from the lesson files for this hour and place them in the Graphics folder.

7. In kippleStyles.css, create a new style with the selector .blue. Set background-image to blue.png, background-repeat to no-repeat, and height to 35px.

8. In the Manage Styles panel, right-click the new .blue style and select New Style Copy from the pop-up menu. This creates an exact copy of the style. Rename it .green and change background-image to green.png. Click OK to save the new style, and use the exact same technique to create a third style with the selector .purple.

9. In Code view, find the anchor tag for the first of the three buttons and place your cursor directly after the letter a. Press the spacebar and type class="blue". This applies the .blue class to the first button.

FIGURE 17.17
The menu items are now styled so that they appear on a horizontal line, but they have no backgrounds and are transparent.

10. In Design view, click the second button and use the Quick Tag Selector to select the <a> tag. In the Manage Styles panel, right-click the .green style and select Apply Style from the pop-up menu.

11. In Design view, click the third button and make sure the <a> tag is highlighted in the Quick Tag Selector. In the Apply Styles panel, click the .purple style to apply it.

As you can see in Figure 17.18, you now have three buttons with three different backgrounds. If you paid attention to the earlier lessons in this hour, you noticed that the styling of this menu is the same used to create the drop-down menu, which means that if you want to, you can expand the menu to include drop-down features later!

FIGURE 17.18
The menu items now have individual colored backgrounds applied using custom classes.

Summary

Menus are important elements for navigation and design. A website with functional and well-designed menus gives the visitor a more interactive experience and the website a feeling of professionalism. For this reason and many others, it is important to know how to make different types of menus, including drop-down menus that look great and work properly across browsers and platforms.

There are many approaches to creating menus, and in this hour, you learned what I think is the best and most-solid approach: the pure CSS menu. Not only is this type of menu "standards based," but it is easy to manage and future proof (not to mention accessible).

At the end of this hour, you have three different menus: the basic vertical menu, the basic horizontal menu, and the advanced horizontal drop-down menu. All three were based on simple standards-based unordered lists and styled with fairly basic CSS. Hopefully, what you learned by following these lessons is that if you have a firm grasp of some basic CSS concepts, including the `display`, `float`, and `visibility` attributes, you can create advanced layout elements with only minimal style code.

The drop-down menu at the end of this hour is as pure and simple as I can make it. Its basis is a simple unordered list with sublists. This is done for several reasons: It makes the content of the menu accessible regardless of what type of browser the visitor is using; it keeps the styling separate from the content; and it is easy to manage because all you need to do is edit the lists themselves—the design follows automatically.

The styling you applied to the different menus in this hour was basic and can easily be expanded and elaborated to create much more advanced looks and designs. The backgrounds can be replaced by images; you can attach borders, and even classes, to make each button different from the rest. All this is made possible by the standards-based approach.

There is no right or wrong when it comes to creating menus, and there are other techniques available. You can find a tutorial on how to use layers and images to create a drop-down menu. I have deliberately taken the tutorial out of the main body of the book because I do not want you to use layers-based menus. They are not standards based; they are cumbersome; they require JavaScript support; and, most important, they are hard to modify and redesign. Nevertheless, if you want to use this type of menu or if you want to get a better understanding of how you can use layers to create some fairly advanced visibility effects, the tutorial is there for you to read.

Like I previously said, the menus you made in this hour are as clean as possible, and they are the ones I use in all the sites I design (with more advanced styling, of course). You can find a more advanced version of the pure-CSS drop-down menu that incorporates the necessary JavaScript to solve the IE6 problem by going to http://www.alistapart.com and searching for **Suckerfish menu**.

Q&A

Q. *You say that the pure-CSS drop-down menu doesn't work in Internet Explorer 6. Is that something I should worry/care about?*

A. The answer to this question depends on who your target audience is. If you assume your audience is up to date where technology is concerned and is using equipment that is less than 8 years old (that is, running Windows XP or a newer operating system), chances are they have upgraded their browser to either Internet Explorer 7, 8, or 9, in which case this really doesn't matter. However, there are certain corporations and users who for one reason or another do not upgrade their browsers, and for those people, the drop-down menu won't work. So, if you are creating a website targeted at users with old systems or a corporation that uses Internet Explorer 6, you need to add some JavaScript to your menu to make it work for your target users.

Workshop

The Workshop has quiz questions and exercises to help you put to use what you just learned. If you get stuck, the answers to the quiz questions are in the next section. But try to answer the questions first. Otherwise, you'll only be cheating yourself.

Quiz

1. What CSS attribute is used to make the items in an unordered list appear side-by-side rather than under one another?

2. If you have a menu with a submenu, what selector name do you give to the style that controls the links in the list items of the submenu?

Answers

1. `display: inline;`

2. `#menuName ul li ul li a`

Exercise

Create a new submenu for the Menu Item Five buttons. Make at least five new menu items for the submenu. Link the buttons in the different menus to random websites to see how they work.

HOUR 18

Dynamic Web Templates

What You'll Learn in This Hour:

- ▶ How to create a Dynamic Web Template
- ▶ How to create a new page from a Dynamic Web Template
- ▶ How to apply a Dynamic Web Template to an existing page
- ▶ How to edit a Dynamic Web Template and the files created from it

Most websites consist of more than a single page. The whole idea behind creating the World Wide Web was the ability to make numerous documents available and then link them together rather than presenting them all at the same time. But this causes a problem: If you have a website with multiple pages and you want to make a design change to all these pages, you have to update each page individually. If your site has only a few pages this is not a problem, but what if it has tens or even hundreds of pages?

In the past, updating large sites was a daunting task because each page contained all the styling information. As a result, webmasters rarely updated designs, and sites quickly became outdated. The introduction of Cascading Style Sheets (CSS) solved many of these problems because the designer could now put the styling code in a separate document and modify this file for sitewide changes. This was a huge step forward and paved the way for a new generation of site models, including blogs.

However, wouldn't it be great if you could take that principle one step further and set your site up so that one file controlled not just the styles but the common elements of all the pages, such as headers, footers, and main menus? This question is already answered in the form of Dynamic Web Templates (commonly known as *DWTs*).

A DWT is a special type of file built using HTML and CSS to define which areas of a page a publisher might edit and which areas are off limits to regular page building. After a DWT exists, you can use it to build new pages in which all you need to do is input new content in the predefined areas without having to worry about all the common elements present in every page. More important, when you have multiple pages built using a DWT, you can change the composition and layout of all the pages by making changes to only the DWT file. In other words, using DWTs makes global alterations to a website a snap.

In this hour, you learn how to build a DWT and create new pages based on it. You also learn how to make changes to the DWT and its children, and how to apply a DWT to an existing page. The most important lesson of this hour is that using DWTs wisely can have a huge positive impact on your workload and make updating multipage websites nearly as easy as editing a single page.

Dynamic Web Templates

When you design a website, you should always consider the following question: How do I make sure it is easy to update the look and functionality of every page within the site? Depending on the scale of the project and the kind of content you are presenting, the answer to this question is different:

▶ If you are creating a small-scale site with only a few pages (fewer than ten) and multiple different layouts and designs, you can go with straightforward HTML pages with one or several style sheets attached.

▶ If your site is (or could become) larger and you have one or two layouts to implement sitewide, creating pages based on DWTs is an effective solution.

▶ If your site has a high number of pages or constantly updated dynamic content (think an online paper or magazine, a forum, a blog, or a site with multiple authors), the best solution is to use a Content Management System (CMS) that generates pages dynamically with server-side script and a database. This option is for advanced users only.

For the large majority of sites, the second and third options are the best choice because they provide easy page construction and quick sitewide design changes.

Blogs, Forums, and Content Management Systems

If you are ready to move beyond the basics, take some time and familiarize yourself with the most common Open Source blogging platforms, forums, and CMSs. With these technologies in your toolkit, you will be well equipped to provide clients with a wide range of services and options for their websites.

One of the great things about Open Source software is that because it is developed by the users, the programs are always evolving, and someone is always out there with an answer for you when you run into a difficult problem. For this reason, the best place to start learning about these technologies is the home page of the project.

If you are new to web design, entering into the world of dynamic web technologies can be a seemingly daunting task. However, it isn't as complicated as it seems. If you want to learn about CMSs and how database-based dynamic websites work, a good place to start is actually the blogging platform WordPress.

WordPress (www.wordpress.org) was originally a basic blogging platform that over time has grown into a full-fledged publishing platform or CMS. I use it as the base of most of my clients' sites and for blogs. The benefit of using WordPress is the seemingly endless variety of plug-ins that enable you to expand the platform to do whatever you want as well. What is great about WordPress is that it is built with the user in mind, so it can be as easy or as complicated as you want it to be. Furthermore, it can work as either a blogging platform, a CMS, or both— it's totally up to you. Finally, the look and feel of WordPress is created using standards-based code and CSS, meaning that you can use the techniques learned in this book to completely redesign your WordPress-based sites.
For more information on how to do this, visit my blog at www.designisphilosophy.com.

As an added bonus, WordPress has excellent Search Engine Optimization (SEO) built in, meaning that sites built using the platform are easily found on Google and other search engines. That in itself is a huge selling point.

WordPress is not the only option available, and it might not be the platform you are looking for. Other popular platforms include PHPBB Forum (www.phpbb.com), on which the vast majority of web forums are built, and the two full-scale CMSs Joomla! (www.joomla.org) and Drupal (drupal.org), both of which also offer extensive customization and expandability.

Try It Yourself ▼

Creating a Dynamic Web Template

To get a firmer grasp on what a DWT is and how it works, you build a DWT for the MyKipple.com website based on the default.html page.

Before you begin, replace the current default.html, kippleStyles.css, and layout.css files in your site with the new ones found in the lesson files for this hour. The new files include more styling to make the overall look and feel of the pages more polished. All the changes to the files are based on the lessons you have already completed. If you take a closer look at the code in the kippleStyles.css file, you see that you can recognize most of (if not all of) the different styling elements. Also, import the two images menuBG.png and footerBG.png and place them in the Graphics folder.

1. With the new default.html page open in Design view, click File, Save As on the menu bar. In the Save As dialog, change the file type to Dynamic Web Template (.dwt) and name the new file `mykippleMaster.dwt`. This creates a new DWT.

2. With the mykippleMaster.dwt page open in Split view, delete all the text content in the `#mainContent` div (see Figure 18.1). You can do this by highlighting the text and deleting it in Design view, or by highlighting all the content between the beginning and end `<div id="mainContent">` tags and deleting it in Code view. Make sure you leave the `#centeredBG`, `#wrapper`, `#header`, `#mainMenu`, `#content`, and `#footer` divs intact.

FIGURE 18.1
After deleting the content within the #content div, you should still see the #centeredBG, #header, #menu, #content, and #footer divs in Design view.

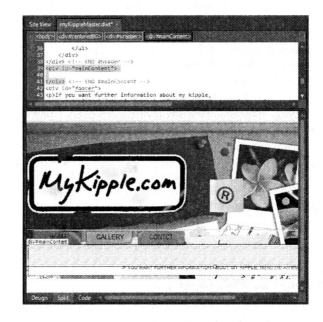

3. Place the cursor on the first line inside the `#mainContent` div, and use the Style drop-down menu from the Common toolbar to set the style of the line to Heading 2 (h2). Press Enter to create a new paragraph underneath (see Figure 18.2).

4. Place the cursor inside the first line (h2) and from the menu bar select Format, Dynamic Web Templates, Manage Editable Regions.

5. The Editable Regions dialog lets you add and remove editable regions within your DWT. Under Region Name, type **heading** and click the Add button (see Figure 18.3). This creates a new editable region called heading. Click Close to apply the changes.

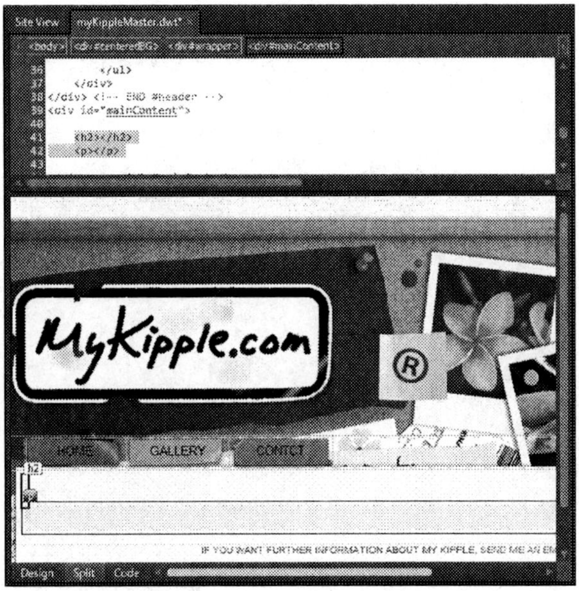

FIGURE 18.2
Add two empty text lines in the #mainContent div: the first one with the h2 style and the second one with the p style.

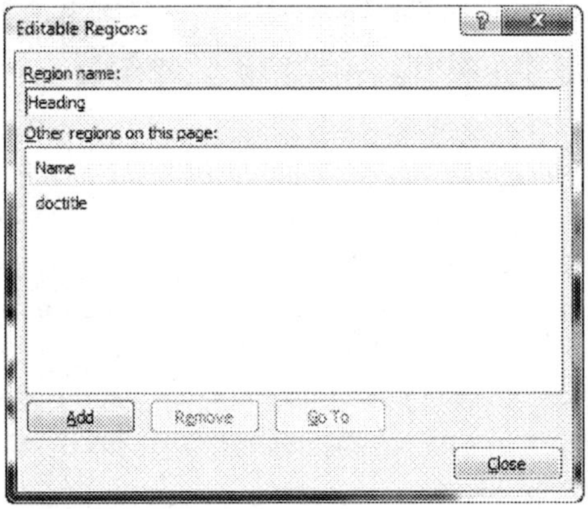

FIGURE 18.3
The Editable Regions dialog lets you add and remove editable regions.

6. Place your cursor inside the paragraph on the next line, and click the <p> tag in the Quick Tag Selector to select the entire line, including the tags. From the menu bar, select Format, Dynamic Web Template, Manage Editable Regions to open the Editable Regions dialog again.

7. Create a new editable region called content and click Close to apply the changes. You now have two regions within the page, outlined in orange in Design view (see Figure 18.4).

FIGURE 18.4
The Editable Regions heading and content are inserted into the DWT.

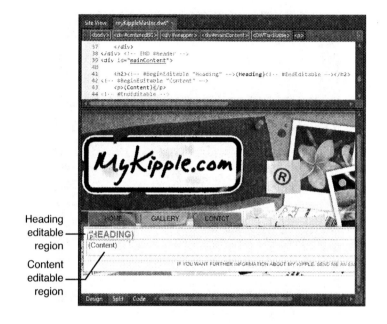

Heading editable region

Content editable region

How Dynamic Web Templates Work

Now that you have created a DWT, let's look at how it works. Looking at the page in Code view, you see that it looks pretty much the same as the original file with the exception of a few new lines of commented-out code. The new elements tell Expression Web 4 that a specific DWT controls the page. The elements are commented out because they are not HTML code but rather custom script designed specifically to work with Expression Web 4. As a result, they have no actual function when a browser displays the page. Also, like other commented content, the code is ignored. But when the application opens the page, they link the DWT and its children together.

In the body of the document are several code segments that tell Expression Web 4 which areas are locked and which areas are editable. When you create a DWT from scratch, you get a standard HTML page with two editable regions: doctitle and body. As the names suggest, the doctitle region holds the <title> tag in the head portion of the page, and the body region holds the body of the page. The same thing happened when you converted the default.html page to a DWT: Expression inserted the doctitle region into your page at the end of the <head> tag.

The beginning and end codes are commented out because they are not HTML and their sole purpose is to help Expression Web 4 to define the editable regions. For example, the doctitle editable region looks like this in Code view:

```
<!-- #BeginEditable "doctitle" -->
<!-- #EndEditable -->
```

Expression Web 4 considers anything within these two code snippets editable. Because code that is invisible to browsers defines the editable regions, you can choose how much you want to micromanage the content within them. The two editable regions you inserted in the mykippleMaster.dwt page serve as good examples of this.

If you select the heading region in Design view and look at the code, you see that the editable region is contained within the h2 tags:

```
<h2><!-- #BeginEditable "heading" -->(heading)<!-- #EndEditable --></h2>
```

That means whatever content you place inside the editable region will be styled with the h2 style. As a result, when building a page based on this DWT, the designer cannot change the style of this content. Expression Web 4 placed the editable region inside the <h2> tags because you placed the cursor inside the h1 area before inserting it.

With the paragraph, the content region is placed on the outside of the style tags, like this:

```
<!-- #BeginEditable "content" --><p>(content)</p><!-- #EndEditable -->
```

As a result, the content within the region is not yet styled and the designer can apply other tags and styles at will.

Understanding the difference between these two methods of inserting editable regions means that the designer of the DWT has almost unlimited control of the output that comes from pages created with the template.

Try It Yourself ▼

Create a New Page from a DWT

When you have a DWT, creating new pages for your project becomes much easier. The DWT contains all the common elements that all pages should feature, and all you need to do is insert the page-specific content. Because HTML is the basis for the DWT, all the CSS styling you attach to the DWT is available in your new page.

1. To create a new page from a DWT, select File, New, Create from Dynamic Web Template from the menu bar.

2. When you create a page from a DWT, the Attach Dynamic Web Template dialog opens. Select the `mykippleMaster.dwt` file and click Open (see Figure 18.5). An information box opens to report that a number of files updated; this refers to the content of the DWT populating the new file.

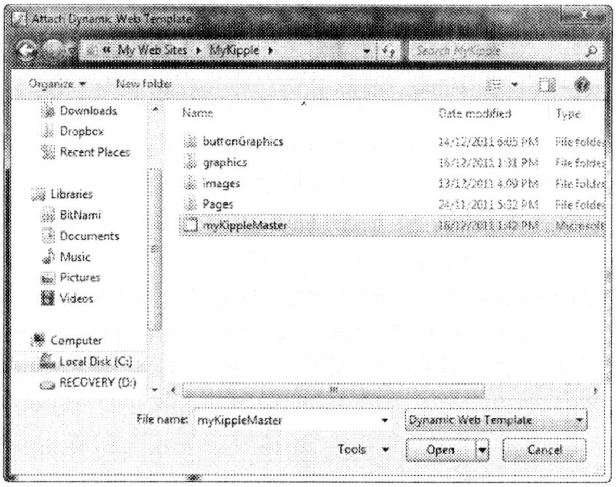

FIGURE 18.5
Select the DWT you want to base your page on in the Attach Dynamic Web Template dialog.

3. With the new page open in Design view, you now have only two clickable areas in the page: the heading and the content. If you move your cursor anywhere else, all you get is a stop sign. Place your cursor in the heading area, remove the existing text, and type **About Me** (see Figure 18.6). Expression Web 4 automatically applies the h2 style. If you press Enter to create a new line, a warning pops up to tell you that you can't make the change because a DWT is locking the code.

4. Place your cursor in the `content` region, remove the existing text, and write a short bio about yourself or insert some other content of your choice. Because this region is not contained within a tag, it is not constrained in the same way the `heading` region is. Therefore, you can add several paragraphs, images, or any other HTML content as you place and style it using the styles and classes in the attached style sheet (see Figure 18.7).

5. When you finish inserting content in the page, press Ctrl+S to save the file. In the Save As dialog, go to the Pages folder and give the new page the name **about.html**.

FIGURE 18.6
With the DWT attached to the new page, you can make changes only to the editable regions. The template locks the rest of the page.

FIGURE 18.7
The content created inside the regions can be styled with any of the styles available in the attached style sheet and new styles.

By previewing the new page in your browser, you see that, although all you did was insert the heading and main content, the page looks and works just like the default.html page, because all the common components are the same.

Understanding Dynamic Web Templates

The preceding example gives you a good idea of what happens when you create a new page from a DWT. When you attach a DWT to a new page, what actually happens is that Expression Web 4 takes the code content from the DWT and places it in your new page. However, unlike a "normal" page, the application knows that only the editable regions within the page should be available for changes, so it looks for the editable regions and blocks all the other content. After content is inserted in the editable regions, the result is the same as any other HTML page except that the code contains the commented-out code calls for the editable regions. However, because they are commented out, the browser ignores them.

▼ **Try It Yourself**

Update Your Site by Editing the DWT

The reason the editable region's code remains in the page is to give you the ability to change the DWT and by doing so to change all the pages created from it.

1. Open the mykippleMaster.dwt page in Split view. Find the unordered #mainMenu list in Code view.

2. Create a new list item before Contact to create a new button. Type **About Me** as the text, and create a hyperlink that points to the new about.html page you just created.

3. Like the three other buttons, attach a color class to the new button (see Figure 18.8).

4. Save the mykippleMaster.dwt page. An information dialog opens to tell you that there is one page attached to mykippleMaster.dwt and asks whether you want to update it now (see Figure 18.9). Click Yes. Expression Web 4 now updates all the files built based on the DWT.

5. When it finishes, another information dialog opens to tell you how many pages Expression Web 4 updated. If you check the Show Log box, the dialog expands to provide a more detailed log of the update process, including a list of what pages the application updated (see Figure 18.10).

If you test the about.html page in your browser, you see that the main menu now has an About Me button in addition to the three original ones, even though you didn't make any changes to the page.

This example showcases the true power of DWTs: By making a website where a DWT is the basis for all the pages, you can make consistent changes to the common content in every page by editing just one page.

▼

FIGURE 18.8
It is usually easier to edit lists in Code view than Design view because you have more control of how the different elements relate to one another.

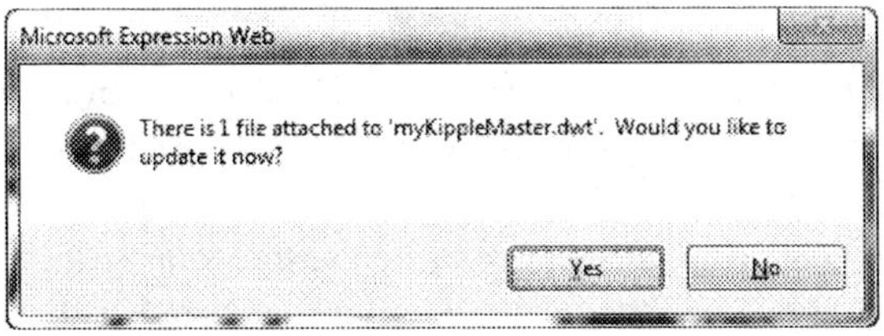

FIGURE 18.9
After updating the files connected to the DWT, Expression Web 4 opens an information dialog telling you how many files were updated and if any files were skipped.

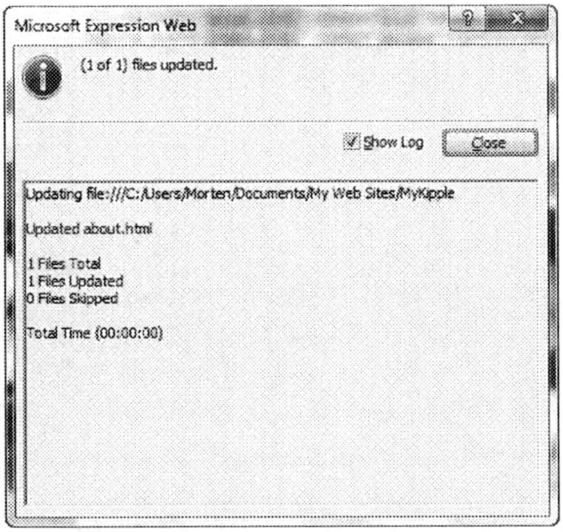

FIGURE 18.10
By changing the DWT and updating the files it attaches to, you change the contents of all the pages in the site without ever opening them.

▼

Attach a DWT to an Existing Page

Sometimes, you want to add the new DWT designs to old pages that you already
built. Your initial hunch might be to copy and paste the contents from this page
into a new one, but that is not necessary. Just as you attached a DWT to a new
page, you can also attach a DWT to an existing page. In Hour 9, "Getting Boxed In,
Part 1: Using Tables for Tabular Content," you created a page called
myCameras.html that contained a table listing all my cameras. Now, you want this
page to match the rest of the pages in the MyKipple site.

1. Open the myCameras.html file in Design view. From the menu bar, select
   Format, Dynamic Web Template, Attach Dynamic Web Template. In the
   Attach Dynamic Web Template dialog, select mykippleMaster.dwt.

2. A warning appears, telling you that content outside of the <html> tag will be
   deleted and that if you want to preserve it, you need to move it into an
   editable region or into the <head> tag. This warning is to alert designers who
   have attached code, such as a script, outside of the main content of the page.
   If that is the case, you can click No and move the script. For most situations,
   this is not necessary, so click Yes.

3. Because you did not create the myCameras.html page using the DWT, there
   are no editable regions defined within the page. Instead of just erasing the
   content not already defined in the page, Expression Web 4 makes an educated
   guess as to where you want your content and lets you correct its choices.
   When there are no matching editable regions or there is another conflict, the
   Match Editable Regions dialog opens (see Figure 18.11). From here, you can
   tell Expression Web 4 what content should go in what region. In this example,
   the <body> tag contains only one block of content, and Expression Web 4 is
   guessing that it should go in the heading region. To change this, select the list
   item by clicking it and clicking the Modify button.

4. When you click the Modify button, the Choose Editable Region for Content
   dialog appears. There, you can define which new region should receive the
   content from the old region. Use the New Region drop-down menu to select
   the content region for the <body> content (see Figure 18.12). Click OK twice to
   attach the DWT.

▼

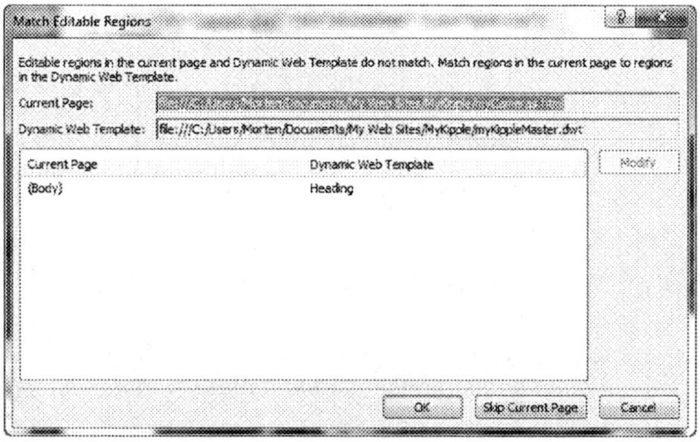

FIGURE 18.11
When the regions in the current page don't match the editable regions, Expression Web 4 lets you match them manually.

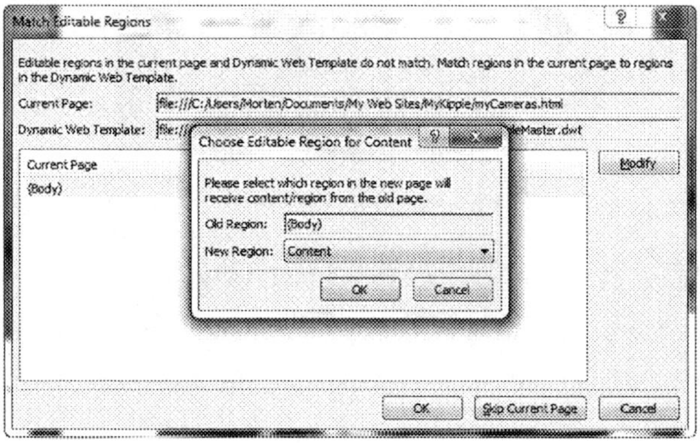

FIGURE 18.12
The Choose Editable Region for Content dialog lets you pick which editable region to put different content from the old page in.

As you can see, the conversion to the new look is not flawless. Among other things, you now have some stray divs and tags (most important, one called #wrapper0) that you need to remove, and you need to move the heading up into the heading area and delete the entire #sidebar div. All of these fixes can be done in Split view, and after some tidying up, the page will look the way it should (see Figure 18.13). Now, if you make any changes to the DWT, the myCameras.html page changes automatically, too.

FIGURE 18.13
With some tidy-
ing up, the
myCameras.html
page fits in
nicely with the
new design.

FIGURE 18.13
With some tidy-
ing up, the
myCameras.html
page fits in
nicely with the
new design.

Editable Regions Outside the Body

As mentioned in the beginning of this hour, Expression Web 4 inserts an editable region called doctitle by default in all pages attached to a DWT because the application assumes (as it should) that every page has its own distinctive title. Because the <title> tag is contained within an editable region by default, you can edit it as you normally would either through the Page Properties dialog or directly in Code view.

Using the same technique, you can also predefine other head content (editable or locked) for your pages. Moreover, you can use the editable content area in the DWT to give the page predefined common properties that you or other designers can edit, add to, or replace when building new pages.

Try It Yourself

Create Common Editable Keywords for All Pages

To make a page easier to find for people who search the Web using search engines, it should always contain keywords and a description that describes the page and its contents.

1. With the mykippleMaster.dwt page open in Split view, right-click in Design view and select Page Properties from the drop-down menu. This opens the Page Properties dialog.

2. In the Title area, enter **MyKipple.com**. In the Page Description area, enter a short description that is common to all the pages. In the Keywords area, insert the keywords **kipple, philip k dick, junk, trash, treasure** (see Figure 18.14). Click OK to apply the changes.

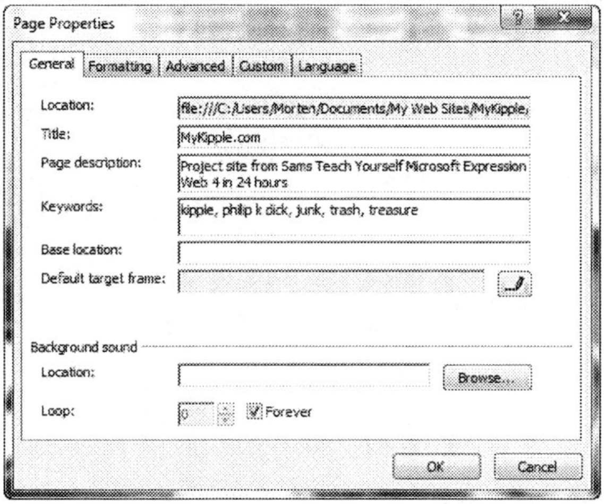

FIGURE 18.14
Inserting content in the Page Properties dialog is an easy way to create the header code.

3. Toward the top of the page in Code view (most likely around line 17) are two new lines of code that start with <meta content="".... These lines define the keywords and description for the page. In this example, you want the keywords to be editable, but not the description. To do so, place your cursor at the beginning of the first line in Code view containing the keywords and manually add the following line of code: <!-- #BeginEditable "keywords" --> (see Figure 18.15).

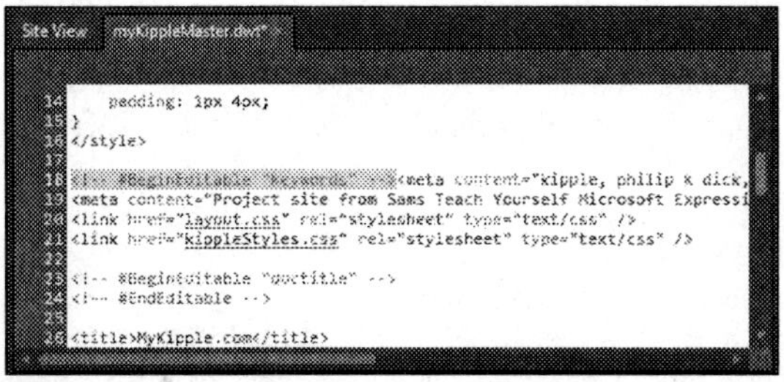

FIGURE 18.15
You need to manually add the editable regions outside of the <body> tag in Code view.

4. Press the End key or use the mouse to place the cursor at the end of the line. Add the following line of code after the last tag: <!-- #EndEditable -->.

5. Save the DWT and click Yes when asked whether you want to update the attached pages.

After applying the changes, open the about.html page, right-click, and select Page Properties from the context menu. In the Page Properties dialog, you see that the Title and Keywords areas are editable, but the Description and other areas are grayed out (see Figure 18.16). It is also important to note that even though the Keywords section remains editable, Expression Web 4 still inserts the words you added in the DWT. After the application creates the new page, you can edit, add to, or delete those words without the changes affecting the DWT or the other pages. You'll also see that the title is set to HomeGalleryContact. These are the first words on the site and Expression Web 4 has made the assumption that they are the page title. Change the title to **About Me**.

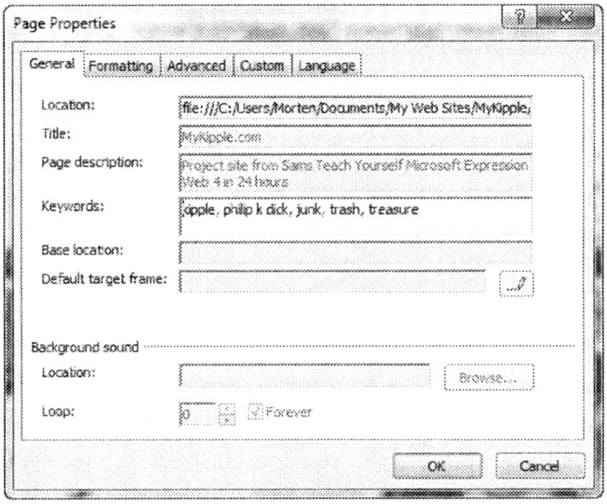

FIGURE 18.16
The Description metatag was not defined as an editable region in the DWT and is, therefore, inaccessible in the Page Properties dialog of the pages created with this DWT.

▲

Watch
Out!

You can insert and edit only the editable regions in the DWT that are outside the <body> tag in Code view. If you highlight code outside of the <body> tag and use the Manage Editable Regions dialog to add a new editable region, Expression Web 4 places the new region inside the <body> tag and wraps all the content. There is also no support for this particular code set in IntelliSense, so you have to write all the code. On the upside, there are only two variations of the editable region code: the begin editable region code (<!-- #BeginEditable "regionName" -->) and the end editable region code (<!-- #EndEditable -->). If you can't remember these two code segments, scroll down further in the document, copy the code from a different editable region, paste it where you want the editable region, and change the region name.

Editing Content Outside the Editable Regions in Individual Pages

Although I do not recommend it, you can manually change the content outside of the editable regions in individual pages. While in Design view, the only selectable areas are the editable regions. However, if you switch to Code view, you can modify the code manually.

In a page created from a DWT, Expression Web 4 highlights all the code defined by the DWT in yellow in Code view. The highlighting tells you exactly which areas the template controls externally and which areas are open for editing. Nevertheless, you can place your cursor anywhere within the code and make all the changes you want. However, if you make changes to the highlighted code, Expression Web 4 tells you that you are now changing code defined by the DWT.

When you save the file or switch back to Design view after changing the code outside the editable regions in Code view, Expression Web 4 displays an alert dialog with a warning that the changes you have made are in the code defined by the DWT (see Figure 18.17). The Dynamic Web Template Alert dialog gives you two options: either restore the noneditable content (in other words, discard any changes made to the code defined by the DWT) or keep the changes. If you choose the latter, you have the additional option of detaching the page from the DWT.

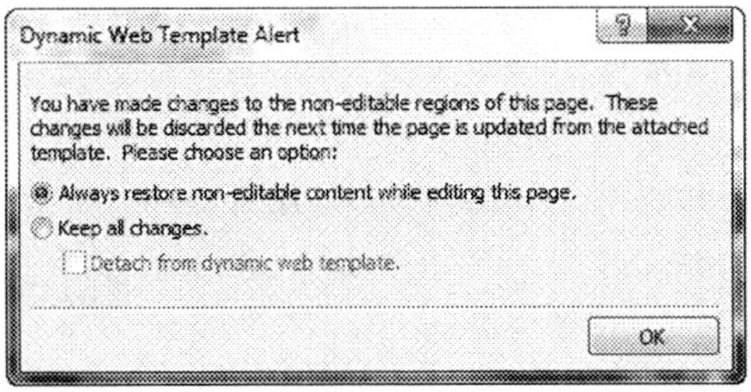

FIGURE 18.17
If you change code inserted by the DWT in your page, Expression Web 4 gives you a warning and asks you to explicitly verify that these changes are intentional.

The ability to change the code in individual pages comes with a strong warning—if later you choose to make changes to the DWT and update the files attached to it, you permanently erase the changes you made in the individual page code.

If an area within a page requires individualization for each page, it is always advisable to place this area within an editable region and place the default content in the DWT. That way, if you do nothing to the code, it remains the same across every page, but you retain the ability to change the individual pages if you choose to do so. The most obvious example of this would be if you wanted to change menu options for some pages, but not others. To do so, simply place the menu list items within an editable region called menu, and you now have the ability to change the menu in individual pages if necessary without making those changes sitewide.

Summary

One of the major challenges for web designers and developers is tackling the task of sitewide design updates. If the site's creators do not design it with this in mind, updating it could easily become a large and difficult task.

In this hour, you learned about Dynamic Web Templates and you saw how you can use them to create sites that are easy to expand and update. The DWT is a great tool if all your site's pages have common elements and only certain portions of the page have unique content.

The DWT function inside Expression Web 4 works by linking the DWT to the files it is attached to either because they were built based on the DWT or because the DWT was attached later. These pages contain small segments of code that define editable regions that are accessible to the designer or whoever is creating or editing the page. Likewise, all the content outside of the editable regions is off limits, and no one can edit it without going directly into the code. This is to ensure that when a developer updates the site by changing the DWT, none of the individual page content gets lost in the process.

After a DWT exists and creators have based a number of pages on it, a change in the DWT spreads through all the other pages, making the new changes sitewide. Rather than having to make changes to all the content in every page, you just change the DWT, and Expression Web 4 asks whether you want to update the other pages automatically.

By defining editable (and noneditable) regions within the layout, you can micro-manage the contents, both visual and nonvisual, of your pages. In addition, within the editable regions, you can add predefined content for insertion into every page and can edit the individual pages later.

A website designed using DWTs makes life easier for not only the designer, but also the client. In many cases, a client asks to have a site designed where she can add or edit the pages herself. By creating a DWT and building all the pages based on it, you give the client a set of pages in which she can edit only the informational content of the site and can't accidentally damage or destroy design elements, such as menus. This makes for a far less intimidating end-user experience because the pages have clearly marked and named regions that the client can edit using principles familiar to anyone who has worked with a word-processing application.

Q&A

Q. *I removed one of the editable regions from my Dynamic Web Template, and when I told Expression Web 4 to update the attached pages, the Match Editable Regions dialog popped up. What do I do?*

A. If you remove or rename an editable region, Expression Web 4 asks you where to place the content that used to be in that region. Whether you removed or renamed the region, you have to explicitly tell the program where to place the temporarily orphaned content. If the region has been removed and no new region has been created to take the content, select the item from the list, click Modify, and change the New Region setting to None. If you create a new region or rename the old one, change the New Region attribute to the correct region. This situation occurs because all the files that have the DWT attached have code segments calling for the old regions, and you need to redefine the code segments for the page to work properly inside Expression Web 4.

Q. *Can I open and use a DWT created in Expression Web 4 in a different web-authoring application?*

A. Yes, as long as it supports DWTs, you can open your DWT and make changes to both the template itself and its children from the other web-authoring application.

Workshop

The Workshop has quiz questions and exercises to help you put to use what you just learned. If you get stuck, the answers to the quiz questions are in the next section. But try to answer the questions first. Otherwise, you'll be cheating yourself.

Quiz

1. What is the main benefit of using a Dynamic Web Template to design your website?

2. What happens if you manually change the code outside of the editable regions in a page generated using a Dynamic Web Template?

Answers

1. By using a Dynamic Web Template as the basis for all the pages in your website, you are effectively placing all the controls of the look and functionality of your site in one file so that when you want to make sitewide changes to the layout, design, or functionality of your site, you can make those changes in one file and see them implemented throughout all the pages.

2. If you change the code outside of the editable regions, the page will work with the new code just like any other HTML page. The major concern with doing this is that if you update the page using the DWT, all the changes made outside the editable regions will be deleted and replaced by the original code in the DWT. Therefore, if you are planning to have custom code that differs from page to page, you should create an editable region to contain this code so that it won't be deleted when the site is updated.

Exercise

In the mykippleMaster.dwt file, change the Description metatag to an editable region so that you can have individual descriptions for each page.

The MyKipple project contains a number of pages that you have already built. Using what you have learned in this hour, attach the mykippleMaster.dwt template to all the pages you have created so far and give them all individual titles, keywords, and descriptions.

HOUR 19

Getting Interactive with Forms

What You'll Learn in This Hour:

▶ How to create a form
▶ How to insert and configure form controls in Design view
▶ How to change the properties of forms and form controls
▶ How to make an email form using the built-in features of Expression Web 4

The last few years have seen the emergence of the interactive web or "Web 2.0," as people like to call it. The interactive web is an evolution from one-way communication to two-way (or three- or four-way) communication, where the content becomes a conversation rather than an information session.

At the core of this evolution lies a simple group of tools introduced shortly after the World Wide Web came into existence. These tools are Hypertext Markup Language (HTML) forms, and they give the visitor the ability to input information and communicate with the site rather than just ingest the information on it.

In its most basic form, an HTML form is a group of elements that together gather information such as text or choices from the visitor and sends it off to a predetermined location for further processing. A form can be anything from a simple email generator or newsletter subscription signup tool to a fully interactive commenting feature in a blog, a posting feature in a forum, or even a checkout page for an online store. In fact, every time you input information in a web page, whether it be your address when purchasing a book or a status update in your favorite social networking site, you are using forms.

Harnessing the power of HTML forms means that you can create immersive experiences with true interactivity for the visitor and facilitate communication between the owner of the site and those who use the site.

Creating Forms in Expression Web 4

HTML defines all the different form elements and form controls. As a result, when you place these elements inside <form> tags in an HTML page, the browser automatically knows what they are and how they are supposed to behave; all you need to do is tell the browser what to do with the information gathered.

To make the creation of forms as easy as possible, Expression Web 4 provides all the available form controls in one convenient location: the Toolbox panel (see Figure 19.1). From here, you can drag and drop any of the form controls directly into either Code view or Design view without writing a single line of code.

FIGURE 19.1
All the form controls are available under the Form Controls section in the Toolbox panel.

When you hover the mouse over each form control, Expression Web 4 provides a ScreenTip with a short explanation of what each control does. These explanations are sometimes too short, so here is a more detailed explanation of each of the form controls:

Advanced Button creates a button whose actions are defined by the designer by embedding HTML code.

Drop-Down Box creates a drop-down box where you can define the different options.

Form is the outer tag that defines the form as a whole. The group of all the elements contained within the <form> tags makes up the form. A page can have multiple independent forms.

Group Box creates a separate subgroup or box within the form. You can use this control to visually separate different sections of a form and still preserve the form's integrity by keeping it together. This is a purely visual tool without any actual function.

 Input (Button) creates a standard HTML button with an onclick event that can trigger JavaScript. (Think back to Hour 16, "Using Code Snippets.") This function is most often used to create Submit, Cancel, and Reset buttons but can be used for any other purpose as well.

Input (Check Box) creates a check box. The check box lets the visitor make yes-or-no choices, such as "Send Copy of the Information to Your Own Email address?"

Input (File) creates a text box with a Browse button attached that lets the user input a location or browse for a file on her computer to submit along with the rest of the information in the form.

 Input (Hidden) creates a hidden text box that is invisible in the browser window but present in the code. This function is often used to insert extra content into a form without giving the visitor a chance to change it.

Input (Image) makes an image "click sensitive," meaning you can use it as a button. The function also collects the x and y values of where on the image you clicked. This information can be used for added interactivity.

 Input (Password) creates a text field where you can input a password. When the visitor enters text into the field, each character is replaced by an * symbol.

 Input (Radio) creates a radio button. These buttons are similar to check boxes, but rather than being standalone yes/no units, they are connected and work as multiple choice.

 Input (Reset) creates a Reset button that, when clicked, sets the value of each element in the form to its default setting.

Input (Submit) creates a Submit button that submits the form.

 Input (Text) creates a single-line text box that can collect text, such as a name or an address.

 Label associates a label with a form control, meaning that you can create a line of text, image, or other element connected to and working as a description of a specific form control. The Label can also set keyboard shortcuts for specific form controls.

Text Area creates a multiline text box for longer segments of text. You can define how many lines of text the box allows.

Because form controls are a bit cryptic in their description, it is easier to understand how they work by seeing them in action. The following exercise uses some of the form controls to make a simple email form.

▼ **Try It Yourself**

Create an Email Form

One of the most basic and most useful applications of an HTML form is to create an email form for your website. In addition to giving the user the ability to send emails to you directly from your website, an email form can also help reduce the amount of spam you receive every day. If you leave a mailto: hyperlink in your page, spam bots (computers that automatically sift through the Web looking for email addresses and then inundate them with spam) will find the address and use it. If you place an email form on the page instead, the spam bot will have a much harder time finding your address and you will most likely receive less spam.

1. Create a new page from the DWT you created in Hour 18, "Dynamic Web Templates," by selecting New, Create from Dynamic Web Template on the menu bar and then save it as contact.html.

2. Change the Heading to **Contact Me** and place the cursor in the contents editable region.

3. In Split view, remove the <p> and </p> tags in Code view. Go to the Form Controls in the Toolbox panel and find the Form control. Anything contained within this control is considered part of the same form. Double-click the Form control to place it in the editable region of the page.

4. Place the cursor inside the new form area in Design view and select Table, Insert Table on the menu bar to open the Insert Table dialog. Set Rows to 5 and Columns to 2. Under Specify Width, check the In Pixels radio button and set the width to **780** (see Figure 19.2). Click OK to insert the table.

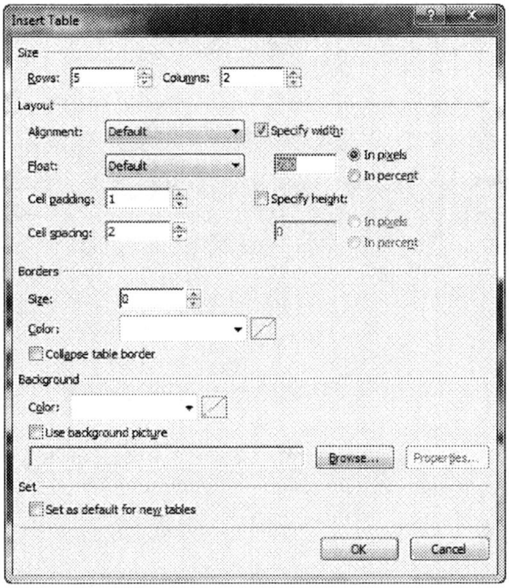

FIGURE 19.2
To keep forms structured, they are usually placed inside tables.

5. With the cursor placed in the first cell of the table, type **Your Name:**. Press the Tab key to move to the next cell.

6. Go to the Form Controls in the Toolbox panel and find the Input (Text) control. Place it in the cell either by dragging and dropping it or by double-clicking it in the Toolbox (see Figure 19.3).

7. In Design view, right-click the new form control and select Form Field Properties from the context menu. This opens the Form Field Properties dialog for this form control. Set the Name to `fullName`, the Width in Characters to 30, and the Tab Order to 1. Click OK to apply the changes (see Figure 19.4).

8. Back in Design view, place the cursor in the second left cell and type **Your E-mail Address:**. Press the Tab key to move to the next cell and insert another Input (Text) control there.

9. Open the Form Field Properties dialog for the new form control and set the Name to `email`, the Width in Characters to 30, and the Tab Order to 2 to match the first field.

FIGURE 19.3
The form controls can be inserted by dragging and dropping them into Design or Code view or by placing the cursor where you want them to be placed and double-clicking them in the Toolbox panel.

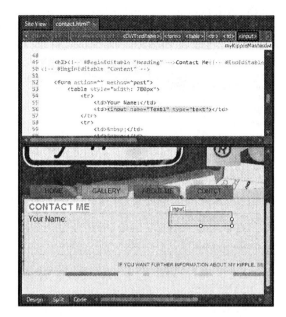

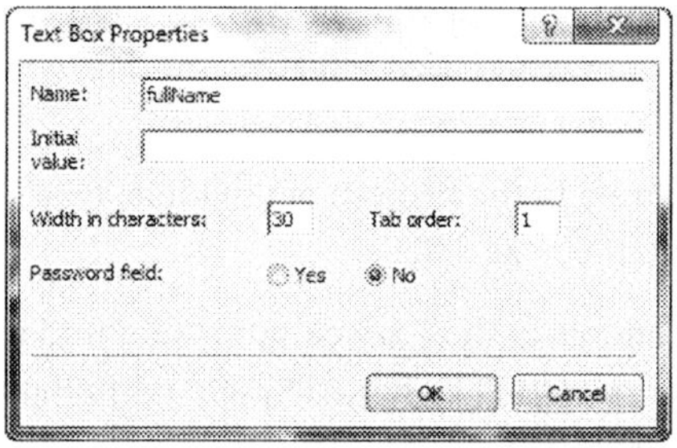

FIGURE 19.4
By right-clicking a form control and selecting Form Field Properties from the context menu, you get access to the various attributes and features provided for this particular form control.

10. Place the cursor in the third left cell and type **Type of Inquiry:**. Press the Tab key to go to the next cell and insert a Drop-Down Box control. Right-click the Drop-Down Box and select Form Field Properties from the context menu to open the Form Field Properties dialog.

11. In the Drop-Down Box Properties dialog, set Name to `options`. Click the Add button to create a new choice. In the Add Choice dialog, type **Question** as the choice and click the Selected radio button under Initial State (see Figure 19.5). Click OK to add the new choice.

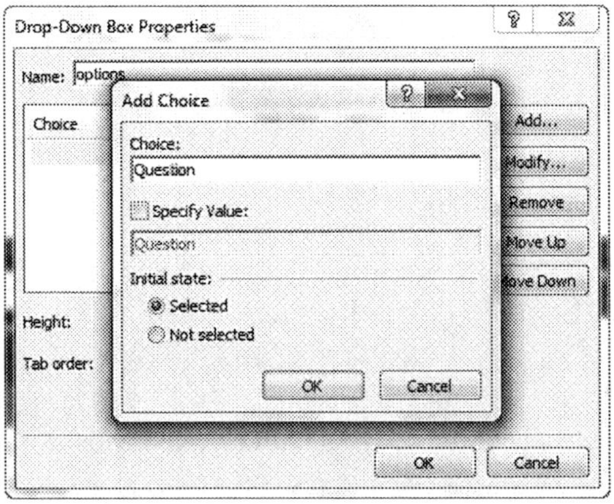

FIGURE 19.5
The Drop-Down Box Properties dialog lets you define the default choice and what choices the visitor can select from.

12. Use the Add button to create three more choices: **Comment, Suggestion,** and **Random Thought.** Set the initial state for all of them to Not Selected.

13. When all the choices are created, set the Tab Order to 3 and click OK (see Figure 19.6). The Drop-Down Box automatically resizes itself to fit the longest choice.

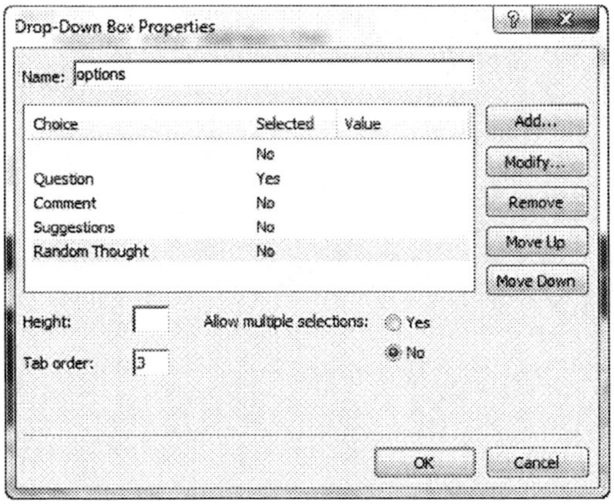

FIGURE 19.6
All the choices are added to the Drop-Down Box.

14. In the fourth left cell, type **What's On Your Mind?.** Press the Tab key to move to the next cell and insert a Text Area form control.

15. Open the Form Field Properties for the Text Area. Set the Name to comment, Width in Characters to **70,** Number of Lines to **8,** and Tab Order to **4** (see Figure 19.7). Click OK to apply the changes.

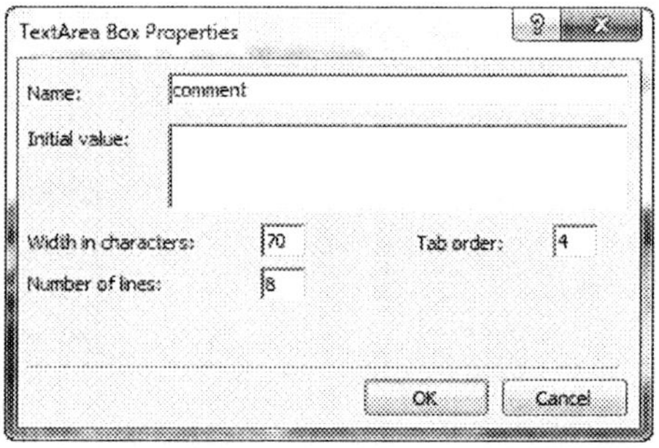

FIGURE 19.7
In the TextArea Box Properties dialog, you can set the width and height of the text area by defining the number of characters and number of lines.

16. Place the cursor in the bottom-left cell and type **Finished?**. Press the Tab key to move to the lower-right cell and insert an Input (Submit) and an Input (Reset) form control. This creates two buttons that read Submit and Reset, respectively.

17. Open the Form Field Properties for the Submit button. In the Push Button Properties, change the Name to submitButton, change the Value/Label to Submit (with an uppercase S), leave the Button Type set to Submit, and set the Tab Order to 5 (see Figure 19.8). Click OK to apply the changes.

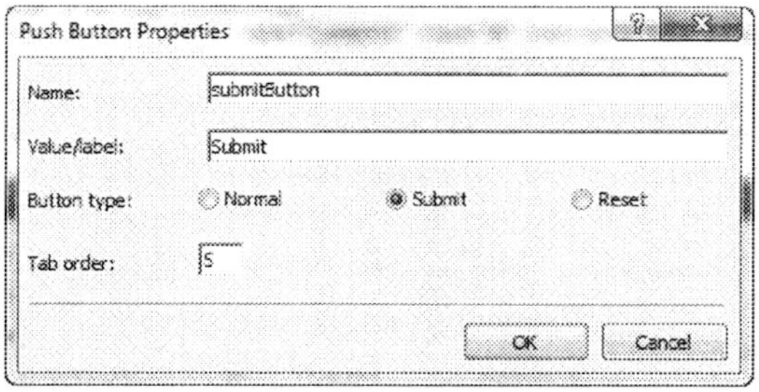

FIGURE 19.8
The Push Button Properties dialog lets you change the text that displays on the button and its function.

18. Repeat step 17 for the Reset button, but change the Name to resetButton, the Value/Label to Reset, and set the Tab Order to 6.

Now all the basic components for the email form are in place. Save the page and test it in your browser (see Figure 19.9).

FIGURE 19.9
The contact.html page with the email form as it appears in the browser.

As you can see, the form already looks pretty good, even though you haven't applied any styling to it yet. If you test the different elements, you can see that they all work properly: You can insert text into the text boxes and make a selection from the drop-down menu, and all the info resets when you click the Reset button. Because you set the tab order for each element, if you select one and press the Tab button on your keyboard, the next one is automatically selected.

However, there is still one major issue yet to be resolved: What happens to the information after you click the Submit button?

Making Use of Form Results

To make an HTML form work, you need two main components: the form itself (which you just created) and the functions that collect the info or results from the form and send them off to be processed. Although building the form is a relatively simple task, getting the form to perform the required actions is a bit more complicated.

After results are submitted from a form, the browser passes on the information to whatever process has been defined by the designer or developer. These processes are called server-side scripts, and they take the information, make the necessary alterations to it, and send it off to a file, a database, or an email account. And this is where things get complicated.

To process, or parse, the results from the form, the server that hosts the page has to perform some actions. Unfortunately, several different server languages are available, and they are for the most part mutually exclusive. As a result, a function that works perfectly on one server might generate only errors on another server. So, before you start applying functionality to your forms, you have to find out what language the hosting server speaks.

By the Way

Most web servers run one of the two main server architectures: Linux Server or Microsoft's Windows Server. Both servers support a programming language called PHP, whereas only Windows servers support the application framework called ASP.NET. If you have a Windows server, there is a good chance it has FrontPage Server extensions installed, but there is no guarantee. Therefore, it is imperative that you find out what architecture the server you plan to put your page on is running and what languages and extensions it supports. If you follow the next tutorial and upload the page to a Linux server or a Microsoft server without the FrontPage Server extensions installed, the form will not work properly.

Did you Know?

If you are hosting your page on a Linux server, you need to use PHP to create the email form functionality. Hour 21, "Beyond the Basics, Part 1: PHP in Expression Web 4," talks about PHP and has a full tutorial on how to make the email form work using this programming language.

▼   **Try It Yourself**

Send Form Results

Now that you have a basic form built in to your page, you need to connect it to the functions that make it work. Provided your server has FrontPage Server extensions installed, Expression Web 4 has built-in functions that make it easy to create forms to send results directly to a predefined email address, file, or database.

1. Right-click anywhere inside the email form and select Form Properties from the context menu. This opens the Form Properties dialog (see Figure 19.10).

2. Because you want the form to generate an email, select the Send To radio button at the top of the dialog.

3. In the Send To area, you have two options: You can enter a filename and you can enter an email address. If you enter a filename, the results of the form will be sent to a file stored on the server. The two options can be used separately or together. Saving the results to a file and sending it to an email address is an easy way to make sure the message doesn't get lost.

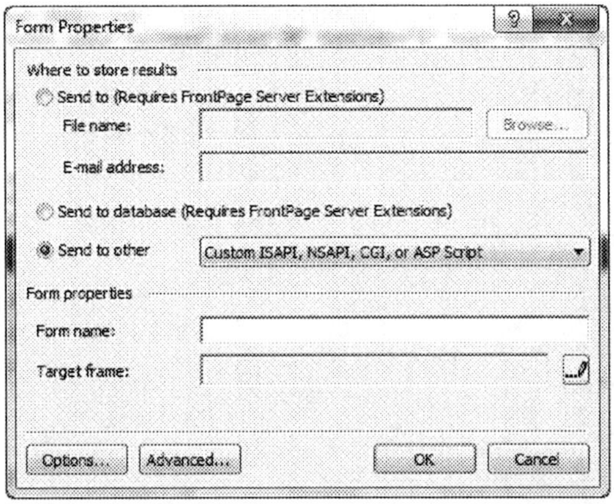

FIGURE 19.10
You can change and configure the different functions of a form from the Form Properties dialog.

Click the Browse button next to the File Name area to open the browser and create a new folder called Contact. Click Cancel and enter **Contact/emails.txt** in the File Name area.

> Step 3 asked you to use the Browse button to create a new folder without actually selecting a file inside this folder. You can use this trick to create new folders while inside a dialog without having to close the dialog.

Did you Know?

4. In the E-mail Address area, enter your own email address (see Figure 19.11).

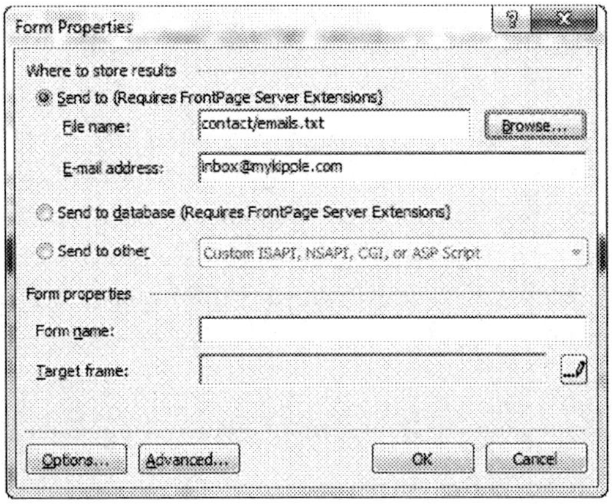

FIGURE 19.11
With the Send To function, you can choose whether to send the results of the form to a file on the server, an email address, or both.

5. To further configure the output generated by the form, click the Options button. This opens the Saving Results dialog.

6. The first tab of the Saving Results dialog deals with the file to which the content is saved (see Figure 19.12). From here, you can change the location of the file and the file format (how the content is displayed within the file). For most purposes, Formatted Text is the best option, but there are many alternatives, including HTML and XML and text database variants. Below the File Format option, you can check whether you want to include the form field names and whether you want to generate an optional second file. Leave everything as it is in this tab.

7. Under the E-mail Results tab, you can configure what the email sent by the form will look like. The email address bar is self-explanatory, and the E-mail Format menu provides the same options as the File Format menu in the prior tab. Under E-mail Message Header, you can set the Subject line and the Reply-To line for the email generated. Each of these can be set to a standard line of text or to a form field name by checking the Form Field Name box. Check the Form Field Name box for the Subject line and insert the field name options (the drop-down menu). For the Reply-to Line, check the Form Field Name box and enter the field name email. That way, the Reply-To address matches the address the visitor entered in the form (see Figure 19.13).

8. The Confirmation Page tab provides you with the option of sending the visitor to a specific page in your site after the file has been stored, email has been sent, or both. This can be any page on your site, but it is normal to create a page with a message telling the visitor the process was successful. If you do not insert a link, the server generates a page for you automatically. (However, this page does not match the rest of your site.) Even though the page does not exist yet, set the URL of Confirmation Page to **contact/confirmed.html** (see Figure 19.14). If you have inserted validation scripts in your form (such as scripts to ensure that certain fields are filled out), you can also create a custom page to redirect the visitor to if the form is not properly filled out.

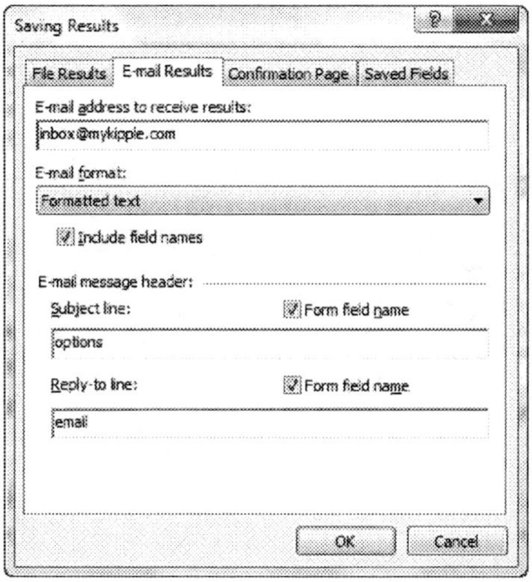

FIGURE 19.13
You can set the Subject line and Reply-To line to a predetermined line of text or get the info from one of the form fields.

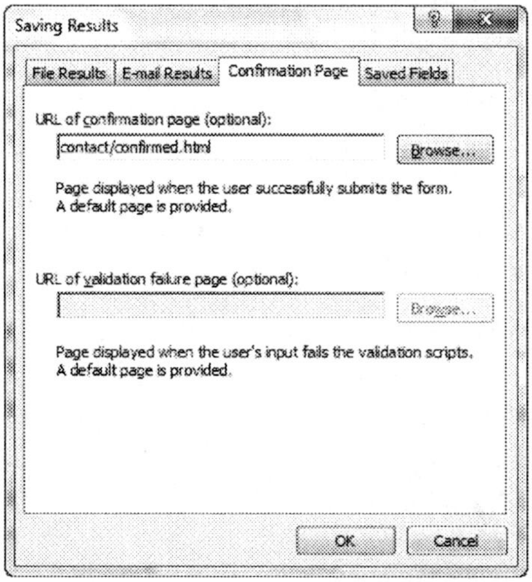

FIGURE 19.14
With the Confirmation Page option, you can send the visitor to a specific page after sending the form.

9. The last tab in the Saving Results dialog is Saved Fields. From here, you can decide what fields should be saved and submitted from the form. By default, Expression Web 4 inserts all the fields, including the Input (Submit) button. In almost every case, you want to remove this last instance because it is unnecessary. (The fact that the file has been saved or the email sent means that the

Submit button was clicked.) To remove it, simply highlight the submitButton instance in the window and delete it (see Figure 19.15). The Saved Fields tab also allows you to save the date and time of the form submission in various different formats that you can select from the drop-down menus. Finally, you can choose to save additional information about the user, including the remote computer name, username, and browser type. (Note that the username will be saved only if the user is required to log in before submitting the form.)

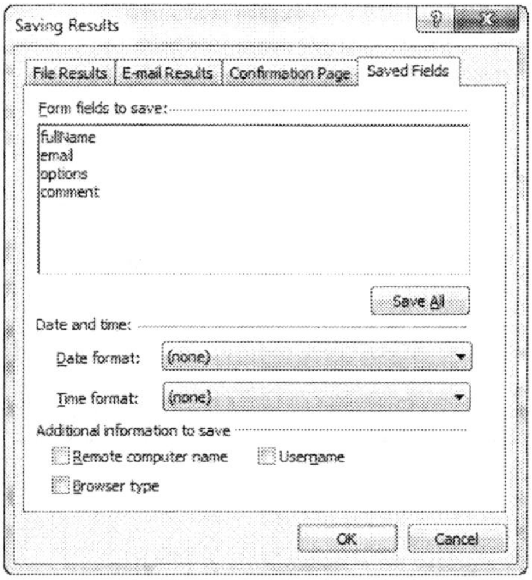

FIGURE 19.15
You can decide what fields are to be saved and submitted from the Saved Fields tab. From here, you can also include new fields that contain the date and time and information about the user.

10. When you click OK to save the changes, a warning appears and tells you that the file you are trying to link to does not exist and asks you whether you want to save the link anyway. This is because, in step 8, you entered a hyperlink to a page you have not created yet. Click Yes.

11. When you click OK in the Form Properties dialog, another warning will likely appear, telling you that this form cannot be configured to send emails because it is at a disk-based location or on a server that has not been configured to send emails. This is because the email functionality you have configured requires server-side scripting in the form of FrontPage Server extensions. Your local computer will not have these capabilities installed. The warning asks whether you want to remove the email recipient. Click No to keep the email address in the script. After the page is uploaded to a server with FrontPage Server extensions, it will work properly.

The email form with all the necessary functionality is now complete.

Other Uses for Form Results

Creating an email form using forms is just the tip of the gigantic iceberg of possibilities that are available. Forms can be used for a wide range of functions that go far beyond simple text communication.

If you open the Form Properties dialog again, notice that in addition to the Send To option, you can also select Send to Database or Send to Other Scripts. These functions let you use forms to communicate with and make alterations to databases. The databases can, in turn, manage content on a website or an online store, or even keep track of warehouse stocks for a company. The possibilities are virtually endless.

Setting up a form with a database or script connection requires both a server that supports the chosen script language and a deeper understanding of the use of databases on the Web. For this reason, it is outside the scope of this book.

Forms in Code View

As explained in the beginning of this hour, forms and form controls are simple HTML elements. To get an idea of just how simple these elements are (and through that, an understanding of why they are so heavily used), let's peek behind the curtain and look at the form in Code view.

To start, click anywhere inside the form while in Split view and look at the Quick Tag Selector. Depending on where you placed the cursor, the last few tags differ, but the main <form> tag should be the first one in the series (see Figure 19.16).

The <form> tag was the first element you inserted into the page, and all the form controls are contained within this tag. By looking at the form code in Code view, you can see that Expression Web 4 has organized it in such a way that it is easy to read.

A closer look at each form control shows you that they are all based on a basic code formula. Click the first text box as an example. The code highlighted in Code view is simple to read:

```
<input name="fullName" size="30" tabindex="1" type="text" />
```

As you can see, the form function is no different from any other HTML tag, and you insert the different attributes in the same way as any other tag. This also means that you can use the Tag Properties panel to make changes to the form functions.

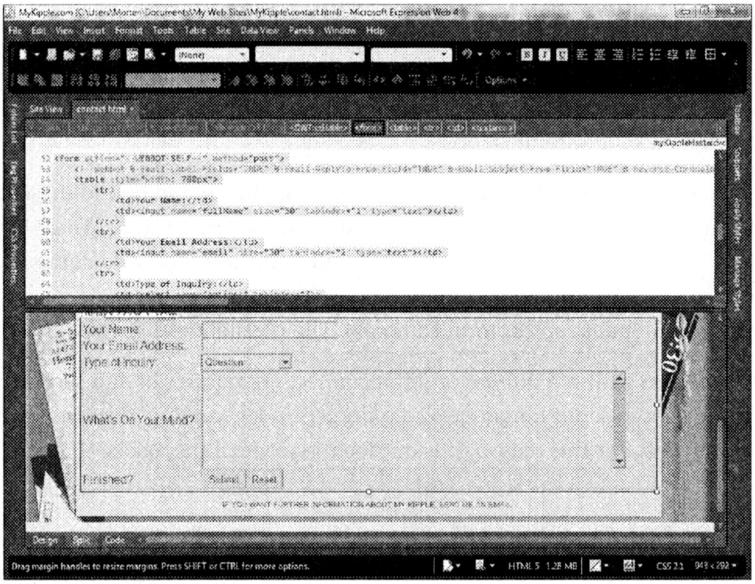

FIGURE 19.16
The <form> tag
encapsulates all
the elements
that make up
the form.

More than that, it also means you can apply CSS styles to the form controls just as
you have done with other tags throughout this book. For example, by making a
new style with the selector name form, you can set the font family, font size,
background color, box, or any number of other style attributes for the forms.
Alternately, you can set individual styles for the different form elements separately
by applying classes to them.

When you put them next to one another, you can get a clear idea of how exactly
the code for each of the form controls works:

Text box:

```
<input name="fullName" size="30" tabindex="1" type="text" />
```

Drop-down box:

```
<select name="options" tabindex="3" >
        <option selected="selected">Question</option>
        <option>Comment</option>
        <option>Suggestion</option>
        <option>Random Thought</option>
</select>
```

Text area:

```
<textarea cols="70" name="comment" rows="8" tabindex="4"></textarea>
```

Input (Submit):

```
<input name="submitButton" tabindex="5" type="submit" value="Submit" />
```

Input (Reset):

```
<input name="resetButton" tabindex="6" type="reset" value="Reset" />
```

As you can see, each tag starts with the type of function followed by the name you gave each instance, the tab index, and, if necessary, the type of control it is.

In Hour 21, when you use the same form you just built to create a PHP-based email form, you see that to unlock the true potential of HTML forms you need to have a basic understanding of the code behind form controls. This is because the Form Field Properties dialogs give you access to only a select few of the many attributes and properties available. As a result, more advanced functions have to be added manually with the help of the Tag Properties panel or IntelliSense.

Summary

Forms are key components in taking your sites from being one-way monologues to two-way dialogues. By including forms in your site, you provide the visitor with a way to interact with the site and make choices or send and receive information based on what she wants. You could go as far as saying that, without forms, there would be no search engines, social networking sites, or blogs, and the Web would be little more than a long list of boring archival material.

To get an idea of how prevalent and varied the use of form controls is throughout the Web, think about this: Every time you see a text box, check box, radio button, or any of the other main form elements, you are actually looking at a form. In fact, every time you enter a word into a search engine and click the Search button, you are using a form connected to a massive database!

In this hour, you learned how to build a simple form that lets the visitor input information that is sent to a file on the server and to your own email address. You saw that building the form itself is as easy as dragging and dropping the elements into place and using the Form Field Properties dialogs to make them do what you want them to.

You also learned that when dealing with forms, you have to take into consideration what kind of server the form will reside on. Because static HTML pages can run on any web server, the transformation of text and selections in a form on a web page into a readable file or email requires server-side scripts, and these scripts have to be written in a language the server understands and allows.

By including forms in your website, you are moving beyond the basics and into more advanced territory. That means there are more things to consider and understand, but the payoffs are also far greater. For an online vendor, the difference between providing an email address and providing the ability to ask questions or communicate with the website owner from inside the website can be the difference between a visitor dropping by and a visitor actually purchasing the services offered. In truth, something as simple as the email form you just created elevates the perceived level of professionalism many times over and makes the visitor feel like you take her seriously.

HTML forms in their most basic form are easy to build and use, and because they are HTML elements, they are not tied to any particular kind of server-side script, so they can be used for all sorts of different applications.

Q&A

Q. *I created the email form and tested it in my browser, but I am not receiving any emails. What am I doing wrong?*

A. For the actual email functionality to work, the pages have to placed on a web server that has FrontPage Server Extensions installed. Because you are testing the pages from your local hard drive through the Expression Development Server, no such extensions are running. In fact, you are testing only the form itself, not the server-side scripts. To get the form to work properly and send emails, it needs to be uploaded to a web server with FrontPage Server Extensions installed.

Workshop

The Workshop has quiz questions to help you put to use what you just learned. If you get stuck, the answers to the quiz questions are in the next section. But try to answer the questions first. Otherwise, you'll be cheating yourself.

Quiz

1. Give a brief description of what form controls are and what they do.

2. What is the number-one requirement for using the email form created using the functionalities demonstrated in this hour?

Answers

1. Form controls are a group of standard HTML components that can be inserted into any web page that gives the visitor the ability to interact with the site. Form controls come in many shapes and functionalities: from text boxes to buttons to check boxes and drop-down menus. Form controls can be grouped in a web form that, when filled out and triggered, sends information to the browser memory for further processing. Every time you input information in a web page, whether it be a search string in Google, a bid on eBay, a message on Facebook, or a blog entry, you use form controls contained in a web form.

2. For the email form you created in this hour to work, the server it is placed on has to have FrontPage Server Extensions installed. This is a requirement because all the email functionality is based on this technology. Before building and refining this form, it is imperative that you contact your web host and ensure that your hosting plan includes FrontPage Server Extensions. If not, you need to use a different technology, such as PHP, to create the email form.

HOUR 20

Working with Flash and Other Embeddable Content

What You'll Learn in This Hour:

▶ How to place a Flash movie in your web page
▶ How to configure the embedding code for Flash movies to ensure cross-browser compatibility
▶ How to embed YouTube and similar content from other sites
▶ How to build and configure an advanced Flash photo gallery

One of the major turning points in the evolution of web design was the introduction of Flash. By designing interactive components in this new animation platform, designers were no longer restricted by simple rollovers and straight page changes. All of a sudden, there was a way to make incredibly advanced animated buttons, sliding screens, and whatever else the designer could come up with.

Unlike everything else you have been introduced to so far, Flash is not a native web language. To run Flash content, visitors must have the Flash Player plug-in installed in their computer. On your end, it means that any Flash element has to be inserted into a page as a replaced item, much like an image. This puts some restrictions on how you can and should use Flash content in your pages.

For many years, Flash has been one of the only options for interactive animation in websites. With the proliferation of video-sharing sites such as YouTube, the platform has become as ubiquitous as regular television sets. But, that is changing.

The introduction of HTML5 combined with the proliferation of new devices such as smartphones and tablets has led to a sudden and fundamental shift in how advanced content such as videos and photo galleries is published and shared on the Web. As a result, Flash is being sidestepped in favor of standards-based and web-native HTML5 solutions that rely on new video codecs and JavaScript to do the heavy lifting. In the wake of this shift lies Microsoft's Silverlight framework, which as of this writing looks to be phased out within the next couple of years.

In spite of this shift, there are still instances where Flash is the preferred solution, and in this hour, you learn how to insert and configure Flash applications into your pages. As a bonus we'll also look briefly at how to include HTML5-based video applications from sites such as YouTube into web pages.

Flash: An Introduction

When you encounter Flash content in a web page, what you see is actually an external file called a Flash movie. A Flash movie is a file with the suffix .swf, and it plays through the Flash Player.

A Flash movie can be anything from a simple button with a hyperlink to a complete web experience with buttons, pages, videos, audio, dynamic content, and links to internal and external pages. All Flash movies are created using the Adobe Flash application, and they cannot be altered after they are compiled into an SWF file.

By the Way

> Flash movies were originally created and published using the Flash application from Macromedia. Adobe bought Macromedia in late 2005, so today when you speak of Flash, you refer to Adobe Flash.

Because the Flash movie itself is a static file, designers build dynamic fields much like the form fields you created in Hour 19, "Getting Interactive with Forms," that obtain data from external files. This allows otherwise static Flash content to become dynamic and interactive for the user, the designer, and content handler.

As mentioned before, Flash movies are not native web content and require a special plug-in to play. As a result, including Flash movies in your web pages requires the use of special code. The Flash movies are inserted by placing them inside special tags. There are actually two such tags: <object> and <embed>. In the past, the <object> tag worked in Internet Explorer, whereas other browsers used the <embed> tag. Both tags work in newer browsers, but because not every visitor has a newer browser, the norm is to use both tags by placing the <embed> tag inside the <object> tag. Expression Web 4 inserts only the <object> tag, so you have to insert the <embed> tag manually if you want to use both.

▼

Publish a Flash Photo Gallery

To give you an idea of how Flash movies can work with external content and to provide you with a component you can use in your design projects, the lesson files for
this hour contain a simple Flash-based photo gallery that is controlled by an external data file and that sources images from external folders. The Flash movie was
built using Macromedia Flash MX 2004 Professional, and the slideshow was based
on an excellent plug-in, SlideShowPro, that you can buy at www.slideshowpro.net.
Of course, as with all other Flash content, you need the Flash application to create
and modify the movie.

1. In the MyKipple website, create a new folder called **Gallery**.

2. Open the Import dialog by selecting File, Import, File on the menu bar.

3. Click the Add Folder button in the dialog and select the Flash folder found in
   the lesson files for this hour. When you click Open, the Import dialog lists all
   the files with their current and new location (see Figure 20.1). Click OK and
   make sure the new Flash folder ends up in the Gallery folder. If not, drag and
   drop it into the Gallery folder.

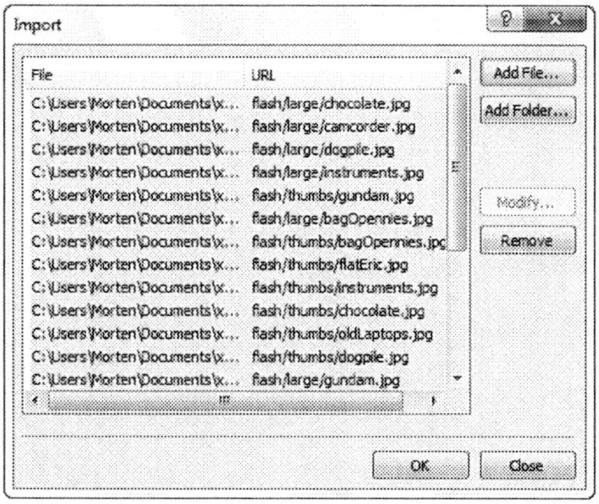

FIGURE 20.1
When you use
the Add Folder
option, the
Import dialog
lists all the files
with their cur-
rent and new
location.

4. With the Flash folder selected in the Folder List panel or the Web Site view, create a new HTML page from the myKippleMaster.dwt template by selecting
   File, New, Create from Dynamic Web Template on the menu bar. Select File,
   Save As on the menu bar and give the new page the name **flashGallery.html**
   and save it under the Flash folder (see Figure 20.2).

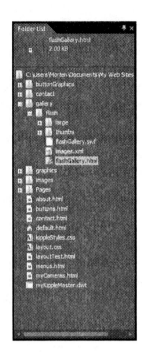

FIGURE 20.2
With the new
HTML page, the
Flash folder
should now con-
tain three files
and two folders.

5. With the new page open in Split view, give it the heading **Flash Gallery**. To insert a Flash movie into the page, you need to use the built-in media functions in Expression Web 4 that you can find in the Media submenu under Insert on the menu bar and in the Toolbox panel under Media (see Figure 20.3).

FIGURE 20.3
The Insert
Media options
enable you to
easily insert
Flash movies,
Silverlight appli-
cations, and
Windows media
files from the
Toolbox panel
and the Insert
menu.

6. The same process can be initiated by clicking the + sign next to Media in the Toolbox panel to open the media options. Click and drag the Flash Movie option into the content section of the page.

7. The Select Media File dialog opens to ask you to specify what Flash movie you
are inserting (see Figure 20.4). Select the flashGallery.swf file in the
gallery/flash folder and click Insert.

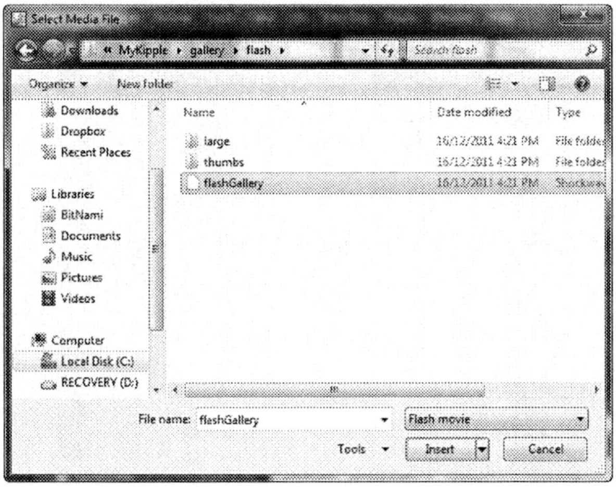

FIGURE 20.4
When inserting
a Flash movie,
you are asked
by Expression
Web 4 to
specify a file.

8. A new gray box appears in Design view with a lightning logo and the name
of the Flash movie file you just inserted. To play the Flash movie in Design
view, right-click the movie and select Play Movie in Flash Format from the
context menu (see Figure 20.5). Now, you should see a small image gallery
playing inside the box you just inserted.

Now that the Flash movie is inserted into the page, you can start working with it to
make it look the way you want. Unless otherwise specified, Flash movies resize to fit
whatever area you insert them into. Note that even though Flash movies contain
information about their intended size, Expression Web 4 insists on setting the width
and height of all inserted Flash movies to 200 by 200 pixels and scaling the content
accordingly.

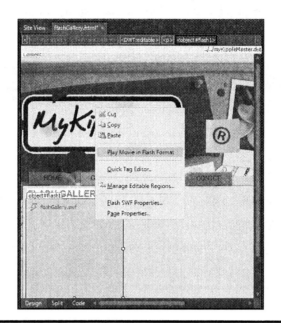

FIGURE 20.5
To play a Flash movie in Design view, you have to select Play Movie in Flash Format from the context menu. Otherwise, all you see is a gray box.

Try It Yourself

Customize the Appearance of the Flash Movie

Right now, the photo gallery is small and off to the left side of the page. To make it more appealing, you need to resize it to the intended size and center it on the page. To do this, you use the Flash properties and some Cascading Style Sheets (CSS) styling.

1. When Expression Web 4 inserted the Flash movie for you, it defaulted the width and height to 200 by 200 pixels and the photo gallery scaled itself accordingly. The Flash movie is actually 600 pixels wide and 400 pixels in height. To change the current settings, open the Flash SWF Properties dialog either by right-clicking the Flash movie and selecting Flash SWF Properties or simply by double-clicking the Flash movie.

2. From the Flash SWF Properties dialog, you can make changes to many different settings. For most purposes, the default settings (sans the sizing) are what you want. Make sure the Keep Aspect Ratio box is unchecked and change the width to 600px and the height to 400px (see Figure 20.6). Click OK to apply the changes.

The Flash movie now has the correct size, but as you can see in Design view, it is positioned to the left of the page. To make it more visually pleasing, it should be positioned in the center.

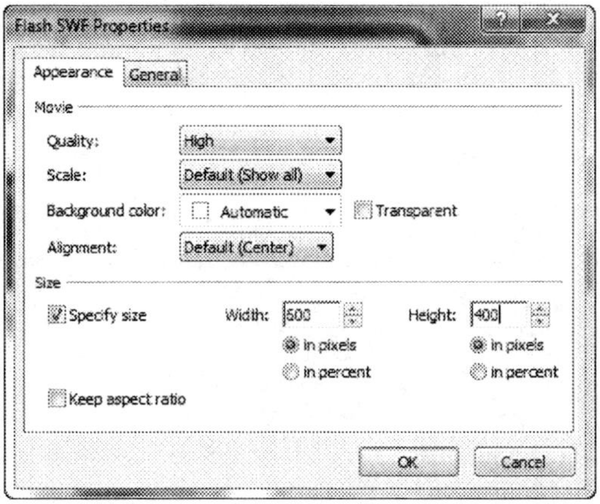

FIGURE 20.6
The Flash SWF Properties dialog gives you control of the playback functionality connected to the Flash movie, including size, position, and image quality.

3. To position the Flash movie in the center of the page, click anywhere inside the Flash movie in Design view to select the `<object>` tag and apply the `.alignCenter` class from the Apply Styles panel by clicking it.

Because Flash movies are always contained in an `<object>` tag, you can apply regular styles, classes, and IDs to this tag to further style the content. When applying styles, it might be easier to imagine the Flash movie as a simple image and apply your styles to it that way. Using CSS to position Flash content is one good example. Another is using CSS to give the Flash movie margins so that it doesn't bump up right next to the other content.

The contents inside an `<object>` tag can appear either inline or as a block, depending on how you style it. This is important to remember if you insert Flash movies commingled with the text in your page. If no styling is applied, the movie appears alongside the text content just like an image. This can cause your layout to be broken, as is often the case when bloggers insert Flash-based ads in their posts without applying styles to them first. As with images, the `.alignLeft`, `.alignCenter`, and `.alignRight` classes are lifesavers for placing Flash movies in your page without ruining the text flow in the process.

Did you Know?

Adding the <embed> Tag for Full Cross-Browser Compatibility

As you learned earlier in this hour, two tags are used to place Flash content in a page, and some older browsers (more specifically Internet Explorer 6 and lower) use only one or the other. Even though most new browsers don't have this problem, it is always a good idea to include both tags to ensure full cross-browser compatibility so that everyone can see your Flash content.

Because Expression Web 4 inserts only the <object> tag for Flash movies, you need to insert the <embed> tag manually in Code view. For a Flash movie, the <embed> tag syntax is simple to remember:

```
<embed src="flashMovie.swf" quality="high" type="application/x-shockwave-flash"
width="size in pixels" height="size in pixels" />
```

In the current case, the embed code would therefore be this:

```
<embed src="flashGallery.swf" quality="high" type="application/x-shockwave-
flash"
width="600" height="400" />
```

Watch
Out!

The <embed> Tag Doesn't Comply with Web Standards!

As explained earlier in this book, Expression Web 4 was created as an application that produces standards-based code out of the box. That means it does not insert nonstandard or deprecated code. The <embed> tag was deprecated in favor of the <object> tag and, as such, it is not supported by the World Wide Web Consortium (W3C). For that reason, when you include the <embed> tag in your code, a warning about incorrect code appears in the status bar, and if you press F9, the <embed> tag is highlighted. Even so, I recommend that you include the <embed> tag when you insert Flash movies in your page if you want to keep it accessible for as many visitors as possible.

To prevent the browser from displaying two copies of the same Flash movie, always place the <embed> tag at the end of the <object> tag on the line above the </object> end tag, as in Figure 20.7.

Site View: FlashGallery.html

FIGURE 20.7
The <embed> tag should always be placed inside the <object> tag to avoid having two consecutive Flash movies appear in browsers that support both tags.

Embedding YouTube and Other HTML5 Content

As I said in the introduction, the introduction of HTML5 and a host of new devices has completely changed the landscape where embeddable content is concerned. Nowhere is this more apparent than when you embed videos from YouTube, Vimeo, and other video-sharing services in your site. Whereas before you used a Flash-filled <object> tag to share your favorite videos with the world, today you use an iFrame that dynamically detects the type of browser currently being used and serves up the correct video format for this browser.

To understand this shift, it's a good idea to know a bit of the history of video on the Web. In the early years of the Internet, the only way you could share video on the Web was by uploading large video files that the visitor would download. This remained the case for a long time until someone figured out a workaround. By importing videos into Flash, they could share videos in a less cumbersome way. This simple realization sparked the online video revolution that saw the birth of the now ubiquitous YouTube, which, shocking as it may seem, was actually launched in 2005. The problem with Flash as a video platform is that it is notoriously inflexible and hard to work with. And to access the videos, you have to have a Flash player installed on your device. This became a problem when smartphones and tablets made their appearance in our everyday lives. Although Flash video worked well on desktop computers, the format was heavy and battery draining for these portable devices. As a result, many manufacturers, including Apple, refused to provide support for the platform.

Parallel with this development came the introduction of HTML5, which carries with it native video support. This means that, at least in theory, you can upload videos in open formats to the Web and anyone can access them. The reality is less simple because the different browser and device manufacturers use different video codecs, so any one codec will not work on all devices. The end result, which is where we are today, is that HTML5 video done right will provide an excellent video-viewing experience for all visitors on all devices. But done wrong it will exclude visitors on certain devices, certain browsers, and certain platforms. To solve this, sites such as YouTube have introduced the aforementioned iFrame solution. When you embed the iFrame code in your site, a hole is cut where a page from the service provider is displayed. This page, in turn, checks what kind of device is currently in use and what video codec that device or browser supports, and serves up the correct file format.

The bottom line is this: Embedding content from sites such as YouTube is easier and more flexible than ever before, and doing so no longer relies on Flash.

▼   **Try It Yourself**

Embed a YouTube Video in Your Page Using HTML5

To see how this brave new world of video embedding works in real life, we are going to create a new page with an embedded video from YouTube. This technique is identical across most video-sharing and other content-sharing sites:

1. In Expression Web 4, create a new HTML page from the DWT and call it **video-embed.html**.

2. Change the heading to the name of the video you want to embed.

3. I'm going to embed a time-lapse video of the setup of the 12×12 Vancouver Photo Marathon photo exhibit in 2010, found at http://www.youtube.com/watch?v=eN_U6EZiAv8. You can pick any video you like from YouTube.

4. Find the video on YouTube.com and scroll down past the video to the Share button, as in Figure 20.8. Click the Share button to open the Share dialog (see Figure 20.9). (Note that YouTube changes its layout constantly, so the page may not match what you see in the following figures exactly).

5. To get the embed code, click the Embed button. This opens the embed section of the Share dialog, as shown in Figure 20.10. From here you get a default iFrame embed code and a series of options, including player behavior and size. Because the new iFrame HTML5 embed code does not directly call the video but rather cuts a hole in the page in which the video will be displayed, you now have more options than previously. If for some reason you need to use the old <object>-based embed code, you can get this as well by checking the Use Old Embed Code box.

▼

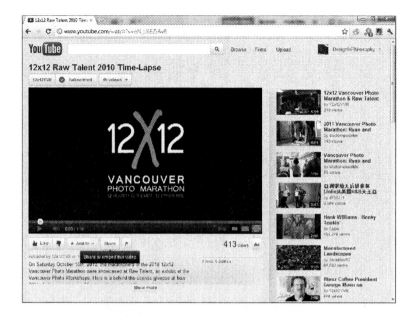

FIGURE 20.8
The Share button on YouTube can be found directly under the video.

FIGURE 20.9
The Share button on YouTube provides embedding code as well as sharing options for email and social media.

6. Change the settings to what you want (in most cases, I just use the default settings), highlight the code, and copy the embed code in the top box by pressing Ctrl+C or right-clicking and selecting Copy.

7. Back in Expression Web 4, go to Code view and place your cursor between the `<p>` and `</p>` tags. Paste in the embed code by pressing Ctrl+V on your keyboard or right-clicking and selecting Paste. Save and preview the page in your browser and you'll see the video playing in the page.

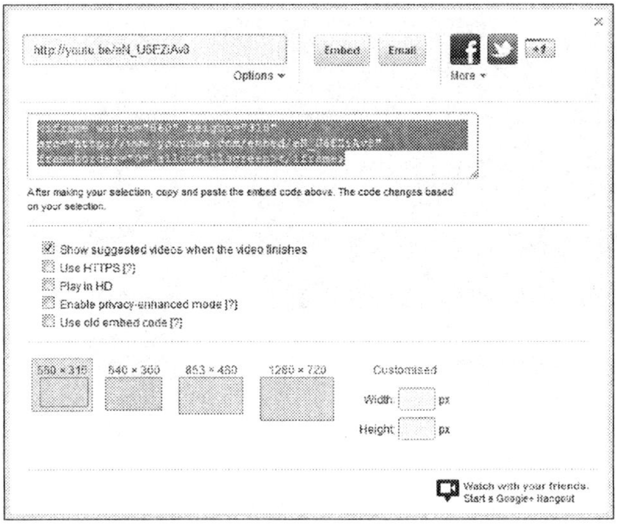

FIGURE 20.10
The new HTML5 embed code allows for more customization than previously.

Because the embedded YouTube video is contained in a simple iFrame, you can easily control its positioning and size. Just like with the `<object>` tag, you can add IDs and classes to the `<iframe>` tag. Therefore, for example, if you want to center the video, you can apply the `.alignCenter` class to the iFrame. To change the size of the video, you simply change the size of the iFrame in Code view and the video will automatically resize.

A small caveat: When you're working with iFrames, I recommend you work in Code view. The reason for this that is an iFrame is literally a hole cut in the current page, inside which is displayed a different page. So if you go to Design view and click inside the iFrame, you are no longer working on your page but rather the page displayed in the iFrame. And chances are likely, in the case of an embedded YouTube video, you don't have control over the page in the iFrame.

Bonus: Making the Flash Gallery Your Own

You can customize the Flash gallery introduced in this hour with your own images and descriptions. All the images are placed under the Flash folder: thumbnails in the thumbs folder, and the full images in the large folder. The gallery uses an XML file to define the image locations, titles, and descriptions. You can change this XML file using Expression Web 4 and make the gallery feature your own images.

The Flash image gallery is controlled by the images.xml file found in the Flash folder. The syntax of that file is simple:

```
<album
        title="Random Kipple"
        description="Some random photos of my kipple"
        lgPath="large/"
        tnPath="thumbs/"
        tn="thumbs/bagOpennies.jpg">
                <img
                        src="bagOpennies.jpg"
                        title="Bag O' Pennies"
                        caption="A small hemp bag filled with pennies" />
</album>
```

To add another image, all you need to do is add another <img> tag with the src, title, and caption attributes defined. To add another album, just create a new <album> tag and insert the new information. To add more images, simply place the large version in the large folder and the thumbnail in the thumbs folder.

One caveat: The images.xml file and image folders need to stay in the same folder as the Flash movie. Otherwise, the movie will not work.

Summary

Flash is a technology that can add an unparalleled level of visual impact and inter-activity to web pages. Flash applications, or movies, are created using Adobe Flash and inserted into your pages as finished elements.

Because Flash files are external content, Expression Web 4 is mainly used to position and style the boxes they are inserted into. Flash movies are inserted into the page using either the <object> or the <embed> tag. In most cases, you want to use both, with the <object> tag surrounding the <embed> tag, even though the <embed> tag has been deprecated. This is because many older browsers do not fully comprehend or support the <object> tag yet.

Flash movies are placed in boxes on the page, and you can apply standard CSS styling to their <object> tags to set the placement, borders, backgrounds, and what-ever else you feel like. If you ignore the Flash content, an inserted Flash movie acts just like any other replaced item (such as an image). In other words, you have full control of where the movie appears. In this hour, you learned how to embed a Flash movie into your page and use CSS to change its position and styling.

That said, Flash is no longer King of the Hill (obscure Norwegian reference, not an endorsement of the animated TV show). With the introduction of HTML5 and HTML5-powered devices such as smartphones and tablets, Flash is being replaced by HTML5, especially where video is concerned. Because of the complexities of HTML5 video and the format war between the device and browser manufacturers, most hosting providers offering up embeddable content that previously used Flash now use embeddable iFrames instead. In this hour, you learned how to get and embed such iFrame-based HTML5 YouTube videos in your pages and also how to configure these iFrames. Although the example only featured YouTube, the same technique can be used for most other video-sharing services.

Q&A

Q. When I preview the FlashGallery.html page in Internet Explorer, I get a warning that the program has restricted the website from running ActiveX controls that could access my computer. What do I do?

A. Embedded content such as a Flash movie uses ActiveX controls to play. For some reason, when you view a local web page, Internet Explorer blocks this type of content, and you actively have to tell the browser to accept it by clicking on the warning bar at the top of the page and selecting Allow Blocked Content. This happens only for local files; after the page with the Flash movie is on a web server, you no longer receive this warning.

Q. When I embed the YouTube video in my page, all I get is a black box with scroll bars in Design view. What went wrong?

A. The YouTube iFrame displays a page hosted by YouTube that detects what browser and device is currently accessing the video. Because Expression Web 4 is neither a browser nor a device, YouTube returns an empty page. The scroll bars are there because the empty page has no defined width and height, so the maximum width and height are applied.

Q. The Flash image gallery shows up, but there are no images!

A. The Flash image gallery sources its content from outside the application itself. It gets its data from the images.xml file, and the images are stored in the Flash folder under the large and thumbs folders. For the gallery to work properly, it is imperative that the folder structure described in the hour be retained. The Gallery folder should contain one folder: Flash. All the Flash files should be in the Flash folder. If your folder structure is correct and you are still not seeing anything, go to the finalized version found in the lesson files and replace your files with the ones provided.

Workshop

The Workshop has quiz questions and exercises to help you put to use what you have just learned. If you get stuck, the answers to the quiz questions are in the next section. But try to answer the questions first. Otherwise, you'll be cheating yourself.

Quiz

1. What are the two methods of embedding Flash movies in a HTML page, and which one is the correct one?

2. Why should you use the new iFrame-based HTML5 embed method when embedding videos from YouTube and other video-hosting services instead of the old Flash-based `<object>` method?

Answers

1. The two methods are using the `<object>` tag and using the `<embed>` tag. Although, technically, the `<object>` tag is the correct standards-based method, it is advisable to also place an `<embed>` tag within the `<object>` tag to account for the lack of support for the latter in older browsers such as Internet Explorer 6. Always remember to nest the `<embed>` tag inside the `<object>` tag, or you will get two instances of the Flash movie in browsers that support both.

2. Whereas the old Flash-based `<object>` embed method only works on devices that support Flash, the new iFrame-based HTML5 embed method provides the correct type of file to all devices. As a result, with the new method more people are able to access the videos.

Exercise

Use CSS positioning to change the location of the embedded Flash application. Give it a white background and a thin gray border by setting the `padding` and `border` attributes.

Embed another YouTube video into one of your pages, and use the `<iframe>` tag to resize the video so that it fits half the page. Use CSS to restyle the video and change its positioning so that the text flows around the video.

Embed a Vimeo video using the same technique you used for the YouTube video and see how the iFrame-based HTML5 embed code differs from that of YouTube.

Beyond the Basics, Part 1: PHP in Expression Web 4

What You'll Learn in This Hour:

▶ How to install PHP on your computer

▶ How to configure and use the Expression Development Server to test PHP scripts locally on your computer

▶ How to create a PHP-based email form

▶ How to use PHP to test whether form fields are filled out and that the email was successfully sent

If you have surfed the World Wide Web for any length of time, you probably noticed that not all web pages have the .html extension. When you visit more advanced sites, you often see that the filenames in the address bar end with .aspx, .php, or any number of other extensions. All these file types hint at the server-side technology that generates the pages.

Although Hypertext Markup Language (HTML) is a great code language with a variety of applications, it is capable of making only static pages. A static page is one in which the designer or developer inserts all the content, and it remains the same until someone manually edits the file. In contrast, most large websites, including news sources, blogs, social networks, and so on, consist of dynamic pages. A dynamic page is one in which the page contains only the framework, and content is gathered from other sources such as databases, other sites, or visitor input. The one thing all these dynamic pages have in common is that they all use some form of server-side scripting language to generate their content.

One of the most prevalent and popular open source server-side scripting languages is PHP, which is a direct competitor to Microsoft's application framework, ASP.NET. Until recently, they have often been mutually exclusive because the Windows Server support for PHP has been unreliable and slow, forcing many web hosts to remove the option altogether. However, with the release of Windows Server 2008, full PHP support is now available on Microsoft servers, giving you the choice to use ASP.NET or PHP. Parallel to this, Expression Web 4 was equipped with PHP support, giving designers and developers the ability to build sites and applications without looking elsewhere for their PHP scripting.

As you learned in Hour 19, "Getting Interactive with Forms," the type of server hosting your site determines what kind of server-side scripts you can use. In Hour 19, you built an email form that utilized FrontPage Server Extensions for its functionality. This form required Windows Server architecture to work. In this hour, you learn how to use the new PHP features built in to Expression Web 4 to create a PHP version of the same form that can be used in sites hosted on a Linux server.

PHP: An Introduction

PHP is a code language used to create dynamic web pages; that is, pages whose content is generated by the web server rather than stored in the pages. Advanced PHP pages are little more than frameworks with a bunch of design elements and boxes populated with content as the visitor clicks different buttons. You could say it is an advanced version of the Dynamic Web Template in which the template is the page itself and the content comes from a database or other external sources.

PHP can also perform other tasks, such as processing form results, submitting content to databases, and editing files. To get an idea of just how powerful PHP is, consider that the vast majority of the millions upon millions of blogs floating around the Internet these days run off PHP. Because of this, many new PHP applications customized for blogging are developed every day.

The power of PHP lies in its capability to work alongside standard HTML code. That means you can choose whether you want to place your PHP scripts in a separate file or place them within your HTML pages inside the HTML code. In practical terms, this means you can create an HTML page with dummy content and, when you finish with layout, you can replace the placeholder content with a PHP script that grabs the real content from an external file, database, other website, Really Simple Syndication (RSS) feed, or a form. For the file with the PHP script to work, it needs the extension .php rather than .html, but even with this extension, all the HTML code renders normally. In fact, if your site is hosted on a server with PHP installed, you can save all your HTML files as .php files without any difference in how the pages display in a browser.

What Does PHP Stand For, Anyway?

If you look up the definition of PHP, you get the following explanation: PHP is a recursive acronym for "PHP: Hypertext Processor." However, that doesn't explain anything because the long version of the acronym contains the acronym itself! This phenomenon is referred to as a *recursive acronym* and is fairly common in the geeky world of programming. More than anything, the use of recursive acronyms in programming is a tongue-in-cheek way to deal with the fact that for the most part these acronyms don't mean anything. In PHP's case, however, the acronym originally had a meaning: PHP used to stand for "Personal Home Page tools," but as the language morphed into a more advanced scripting language, this description became obsolete and the new recursive acronym was adopted in its place.

Other examples of ridiculous recursive acronyms are LAME, which stands for "LAME Ain't an MP3 Encoder" (LAME is, in fact, an MP3 encoder), and Wine, which stands for "Wine is Not an Emulator." (Likewise, Wine is an emulator that allows Windows software to run in Linux environments.) For more examples from the geeky world of recursive acronyms, look at the list found at http://en.wikipedia.org/wiki/Recursive_acronym.

Installing PHP on Your Computer to Test PHP Scripts

Because PHP is a server-side script, pages with PHP code will not work properly if you test them in your browser as you have with HTML pages. This is because, unlike HTML, which renders in the browser, PHP renders in the server, and it sends the resulting information to the browser for display. One way to work around this problem is to upload your PHP files for testing on a web server that has PHP installed and test them live, but that is a cumbersome and ineffective method requiring time, a live Internet connection, and available server space. Another way to approach the issue is to run a web server with PHP installed on your local network. This solution is common in larger companies but is not feasible (or economical) for smaller companies and those just starting out with web design.

The ideal solution would be if you could test your PHP scripts locally on your computer in the same way that you test your HTML pages. To answer this call, the Expression Development Server can be set up to include PHP as a testing environment.

The Expression Development Server can preview ASP.NET and PHP scripts, but for the PHP scripts to function properly, you first need to install PHP on your computer. PHP is free open source software that you can legally download and install on your computer.

1. In your web browser, go to http://windows.php.net/download/, as shown in Figure 21.1, to find the latest release of PHP. (As of this writing, the latest stable PHP release is version 5.3.8.)

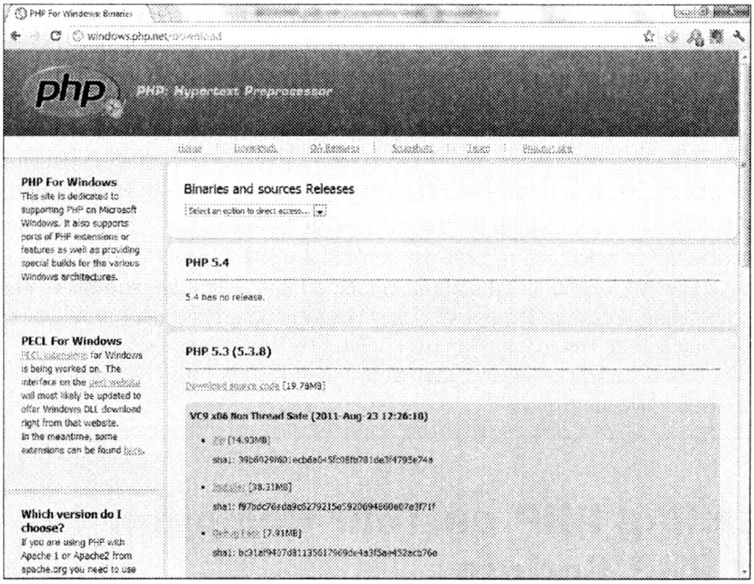

FIGURE 21.1
The PHP website found at http://windows.php.net provides new and old versions of PHP for download.

2. Download the installer and save it on your computer.

3. Run the installer and install the application to the suggested location (in my case, C:\Program Files\PHP).

4. In the Web Server Setup dialog (see Figure 21.2), you do not need to set up a web server (that's what the Expression Development Server is for), so select Do Not Set Up a Web Server unless you plan to use the web server for something else.

5. Open Expression Web 4 and select Tools, Application Options on the menu bar to open the Application Options dialog.

6. In the PHP section at the bottom of the Application Options dialog, use the Browse button to navigate to the location where you installed PHP (C:\Program Files\PHP). Select the file called php.exe (see Figure 21.3). Click OK to apply the changes.

Now PHP is installed on your computer, and when you restart Expression Web 4, it uses this installation of the program when testing PHP pages.

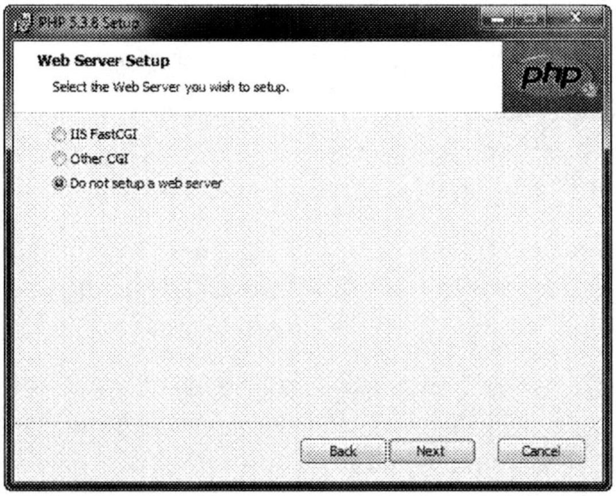

FIGURE 21.2
Unless you want to set up a web server on your computer, select Do Not Set up a Web Server when asked.

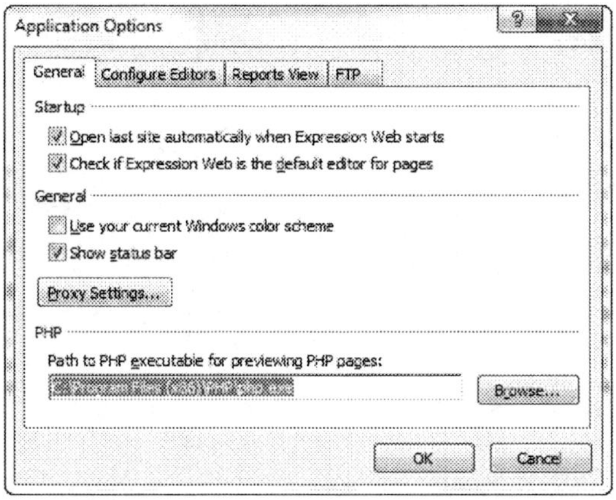

FIGURE 21.3
To be able to preview PHP scripts in your browser via the Expression Development Server, you need to tell Expression Web 4 where the php.exe file is located in the Application Settings dialog.

As you previously learned, you can place PHP script directly inside the code of an HTML page or in a dedicated file. When a browser opens a file containing PHP code, the browser looks for special PHP tags called *delimiters* that define which portion of the code is PHP and which is not. The regular HTML code then processes normally while the code inside the PHP delimiters goes to the server for interpretation.

Did you Know?

▼ **Try It Yourself**

Using PHP and HTML to Create a Contact Page

PHP is a fairly simple code language when you know how to read it. But for a novice, it can be rather intimidating. Therefore, let's create some basic examples of how you can use PHP alongside HTML to build a contact page.

1. Create a new page from the mykippleMaster.dwt Dynamic Web Template and save it in the Contact folder as PHPcontact.php, either by changing the Save As type or simply changing the file extension manually.

   All PHP code has to be contained within PHP delimiters. Unlike the regular HTML tags you previously used, all PHP content is included inside the tag itself; that is, between the < and > brackets rather than between the beginning and end tag sets. The standard syntax for PHP code is <?php ?>, with the PHP code going in the space in between.

   Expression Web 4 not only has full IntelliSense support for PHP but also has a series of common PHP scripts built in to the Insert menu for easy access and use. Many of these code segments come equipped with the beginning and end delimiters. The most basic command of any code language is the one that prints a line of text on the screen. In PHP, this command is echo. To insert a heading using PHP, you need to insert the echo command.

2. In Code view, erase the (heading) text and place the cursor in the heading editable region.

3. Select the Insert, PHP submenu on the menu bar and choose Echo (see Figure 21.4).

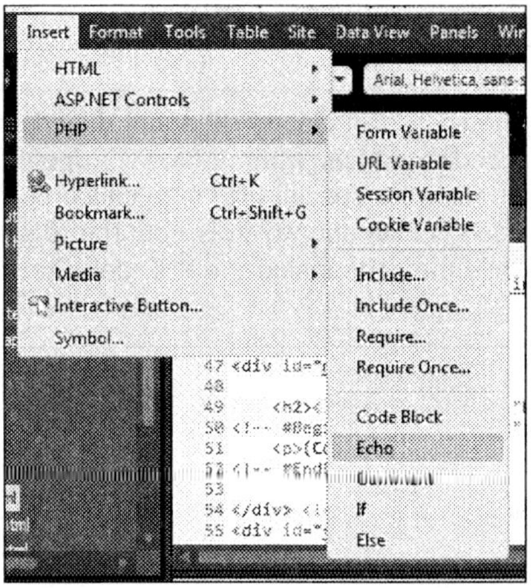

FIGURE 21.4
Expression Web 4 has a set of built-in PHP scripts accessible from the PHP submenu under Insert. This inserts the PHP delimiters and the echo command.

▼

The echo command displays any text inserted inside quotation marks as regular HTML text in a browser.

4. With the cursor placed after the echo command (in green) in Code view, type
"**Contact Me**" with the quotation marks included (see Figure 21.5).

FIGURE 21.5
You insert the
echo command
with delimiters
and a value in
Code view, but
they do not
show up in
Design view.

Save the page and press F12 to test it in your browser through the Expression
Development Server. If this is the first time you are using PHP under Expression Web
4, you get an error message telling you the php.ini file is not configured correctly and
asking if you want Expression Web to configure it for you. Click Yes. If you are using
Windows 7, you may get a second warning saying that Expression Web 4 was unable
to edit the file due to lack of access or permission. This message is irrelevant for what
you are doing, so just click OK to preview the page in your browser. If PHP is installed
and configured properly, the page appears with the text Contact Me in the header.

Using PHP, you can define variables that display using the echo command. You can
define these variables with the PHP command somewhere else on the page (such as
the head) or even in a separate file or database.

Try It Yourself

Use PHP Variables to Display Content

To define a variable, give it a name that starts with a dollar sign ($). The name
must start with a letter and can consist of only letters, numbers, and underscores. It
is also important to know that PHP is a case-sensitive language.

1. Place the cursor before the echo command in Code view and press Enter to
create a new line. Insert the following line of code:

```
$heading = 'Contact Us';
```

The first part of the code ($heading) is the name of the variable. The content
of the variable is contained within single quotation marks, and the semicolon
marks the end of the variable definition, just as in CSS.

To call a variable to display, all that's needed is to insert the variable name after the echo command.

2. Press Enter to move the echo command to a new line and delete the "Contact Me" text. In its place, insert the variable name **$heading** (see Figure 21.6).

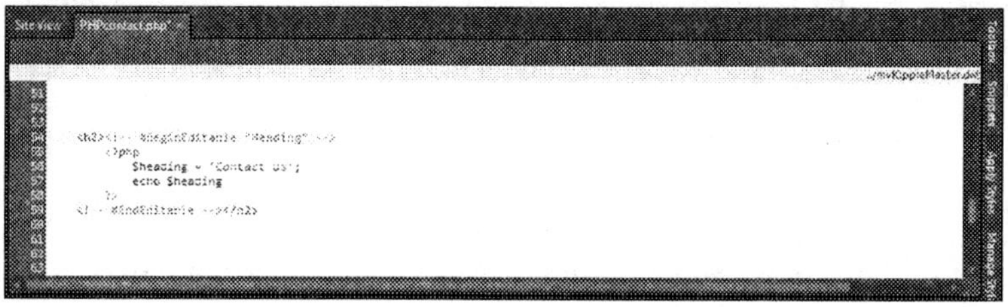

FIGURE 21.6
A variable replaces the echo text.

Save and test the page in your browser, and you see that it looks the same as before.

PHP in Design View and Snapshot

You probably have noticed by now that the results of the PHP code do not appear in Design view. This is because Design view is a web browser emulator and does not have a web server simulator connected to it. If you want to preview the output of the PHP code from inside Expression Web 4, you need to activate the Snapshot panel from the Panels option on the main menu instead of the Design view panel. Snapshot gives you a live preview from your installed browsers and thus provides the live output of PHP code.

Creating an Email Form Using PHP

In Hour 19, you created an email form using the built-in functionalities of Expression Web 4. This email form generated an email sent to a specified address by way of the FrontPage Server extensions on the web server. However, not all web servers have FrontPage Server extensions installed, and on those servers the email form generates code-only errors. If your site is hosted on a Linux server, a PHP-based email form is a rock-solid alternative.

The first step is to create a new email form for the contact page:

1. With the PHPcontact.php page in Split view, remove the <p> and </p> tags in the content editable region. Go to the Form Controls on in the Toolbox panel and insert the Form control.

2. Place the cursor inside the new form area in Design view and select Table, Insert Table on the menu bar to open the Insert Table dialog. Set Rows to 5 and Columns to 2. Under Specify Width, check the In Pixels radio button and set the width to 780.

3. Insert the names for each of the five form boxes in the left columns. From top to bottom, they are **Your Name:**, **Your E-mail Address:**, **Type of Inquiry:**, **What's On Your Mind?**, and **Finished?**.

When you click the Submit button on a form, all the form fields are sent to the browser memory. To identify which content comes from which form field, you need to give each form field a unique name. You can do that from the Tag Properties panel or with the help of IntelliSense in Code view.

4. In the first right cell, insert an Input (Text) control. Click the box to highlight it in Code view. Find the `Name` value and change it to **fullName**.

5. Use the Tag Properties panel to set the tab index to 1 and the size to 30 (see Figure 21.7).

FIGURE 21.7
You can use the Tag Properties panel to define all available variables for any form control.

6. Insert a new Input (Text) control in the next cell below, and use the Tag Properties panel to set its name to `emailAddress`, size to 30, and tab index to 2.

7. In the third right cell, insert a Drop-Down Box control. Right-click the Drop-Down Box and select Form Field Properties from the context menu to open the Form Field Properties dialog.

8. In the Drop-Down Box Properties dialog, use the Add button to create four choices: Question, Comment, Suggestion, Kipple Story, and Random Thought. Set the initial state for Question to Selected and the other choices to Not Selected.

9. Use the Tag Properties panel to set the name to `inquiryOptions` and the tab index to 3.

10. In the fourth right cell, insert a Text Area. Use the Tag Properties selector to set cols (width in characters) to 55, name to `thoughts`, rows (number of lines) to 8, and tab index to 4.

11. In the bottom-right cell, insert an Input (Submit) button and an Input (Reset) button. Use the Tag Properties selector to change their values to `Submit` and `Reset`, respectively. Set their tab index orders to 5 and 6.

You now have an email form that looks the same as the one you created in Hour 19 (see Figure 21.8). However, as with the other form, this one does nothing until you attach some functionality.

FIGURE 21.8
The email form is built.

Try It Yourself ▼

Making the Email Form Work

When the visitor clicks the Submit button in the email form you just created, four strings of text with the names fullName, emailAddress, inquiryOptions, and thoughts are created and sent to the browser. In the form in Hour 19, code inserted by Expression Web 4 intercepted the strings, and all the necessary actions performed by that code were instead done by the FrontPage Server extensions. Now, you want to re-create those same functions using PHP instead.

To perform the actions needed to send the email to the desired address, create a new PHP file that contains the code that writes and sends the email:

1. Create a new PHP file by selecting File, New on the menu bar and choosing PHP under the General option.

2. Delete all the code in the new file so that it is completely blank, and save it as emailProcessor.php in the Contact folder.

   Now you need to send the information from the contact.php file to the new file. By default, the Form control has a built-in action triggered by the onclick event attached to the Submit button. You use this action to send the contents of the form to the new file.

3. With the PHPcontact.php file open in Design view, click anywhere inside the form and select the <form> tag from the Quick Tag Selector.

4. In the Tag Properties panel, click the action tag to activate it and click the ... button. Doing so opens the Select File dialog. Navigate to the Contact folder and select the emailProcessor.php file. Click Open to set the action (see Figure 21.9). Save PHPcontact.php.

   Now you need to set up the PHP functions that generate the email.

5. Open the emailProcessor.php file in Code view. Place the cursor at the top of the page and then click Code Block in the PHP submenu options under Insert on the menu bar. Doing so inserts the PHP delimiters <?php ?>.

6. With the cursor between the delimiters, press Enter several times to create some space.

   To get a PHP script to send an email, use the mail() function. The syntax of this function is as follows:

```
mail(to,subject,message,headers,parameters)
```

▼

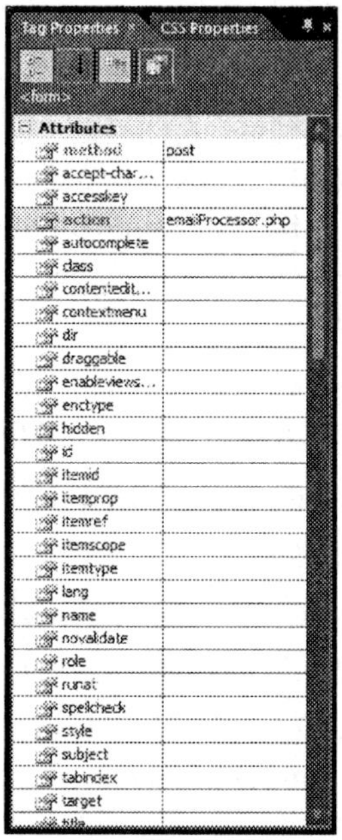

FIGURE 21.9
By setting the action attribute of the form to a file, you send the information from the form to that file.

Of these, the `to`, `subject`, and `message` variables are mandatory, whereas the `headers` and `parameters` variables are optional. For the email form you create, you use the `to`, `subject`, `message`, and `headers` variables.

To help you remember the order, IntelliSense displays a ScreenTip with the different sections as you insert them.

7. On a new line, type **mail(**. This brings up the IntelliSense ScreenTip for the `mail()` function (see Figure 21.10).

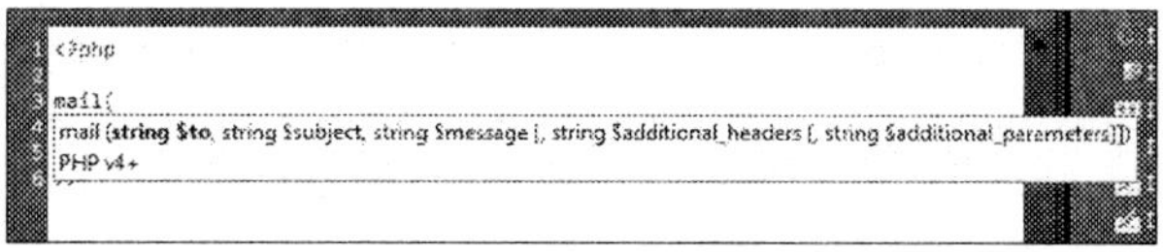

FIGURE 21.10
IntelliSense helps you keep track of the many variables necessary when using PHP functions.

8. IntelliSense asks for the names of each of the variables, but you haven't created the variables yet. To keep track of what the different variables are supposed to contain, type out the function of each variable as its name, and end the line with a parenthesis and a semicolon. When you're finished, the line of code should look like this:

```
mail($to, $subject, $message, $header, $parameter);
```

The next step is to create new variables that contain either predefined information or information received from the form.

9. You need to create a $to variable to tell the program where to send the email. Create a new line above the mail() function and type the variable name **$to** followed by your email address, like this:

```
$to = 'you@yourdomain.com';.
```

When an HTML form is submitted, all the contents are sent using a method called POST. To capture that content, you need to use a form variable. A form variable looks like this:

```
$_POST[];
```

The original variable name is inserted in single quotation marks between the two brackets.

10. Create a new line. The $subject variable should contain the choice the visitor made in the Type of Enquiry field on the form. The name of that field was inquiryOptions. To insert that content into a variable, you need to create a form variable:

```
$subject = $_POST['inquiryOptions'];.
```

Skip the $message variable for a moment. The $header variable can have several different headers, including From, Cc, and Reply-to. In this case, you want the From header to match the email address of the sender.

11. Create a new line. Set the $header variable to receive the content from the emailAddress form field: $header = $_POST['emailAddress'];.

Now all that is missing is the message, or body, of the email. Before you create the $message variable, you need to learn a few more things about PHP syntax. First, PHP enables you to mix clean text and code as much as you want. Second, to make a line break in PHP, you need to insert the line break code, which is a backslash followed by a lowercase n, like this: \n. PHP understands that this is a line break, even if it is sandwiched between two lines of text or other code without spaces.

For the emails generated from your website to make as much sense as possible, it is a good idea to space the content properly. Ideally, you want your email body to look something like this:

From: Sender Name

Sender e-mail address: sender@senderdomain.com

Regarding: The selection made from the drop-down box.

Message:

Message entered in the box goes here.

12. The $message variable will be somewhat different from the rest of the variables. Start by creating the variable: $message =" ' ; .

13. On the first line of the email body, you want the text "From:" followed by the name of the sender. Place the cursor between the two single quotes and type **From: $fullName\n**.

14. On the next line, you want the text "Sender e-mail address:" followed by the email address. The sender's email address was stored in the $header variable in step 11. Directly after the \n, without any space between, type **Sender e-mail address: $header\n**.

15. The third line of the email body should read "Regarding:" and have the selection the visitor made from the drop-down box. This information was stored in the $subject variable in step 10. Directly after the last piece of code you inserted, write **Regarding: $subject\n\n**. Note the double line shift to create a space between the sender info and the message.

16. You want the actual message to appear below the rest of the content. The text "Message:" should also appear on its own line. Directly after the last \n, type **Message:\n$thoughts\n**.

The entire variable should now read as follows:

```
$message = "From: $fullName\nSender e-mail address: $header\nRegarding:
$subject\n\nMessage:\n$thoughts\n";
```

17. To make the sender's email address appear in the From field in your email reader, you need to make a small change to the mail() function: Replace $header with "From: <$header>".

I'm Not Receiving Any Emails from the Form!

If you test the page in your browser and try to send an email to yourself, you quickly discover that nothing happens. This is because in addition to having PHP running on your computer, the email() function requires a working email server. To test this functionality, you need to upload the contact.php and emailProcessor.php files to a server with working email functionality.

18. Because you will not be using the $parameter variable, remove it from the mail() function.

The final code, as shown in Figure 21.11, generates emails laid out exactly as the earlier example from the contents of the email form.

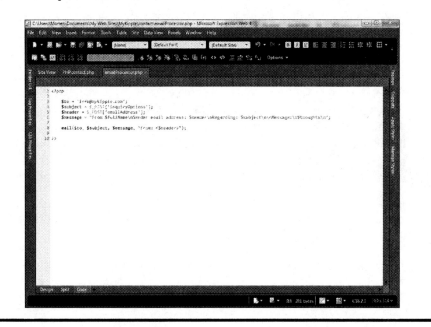

FIGURE 21.11
The finished emailProcessor .php file as it appears in Code view.

Added Functionality

There are still a couple of things to add before the email form is complete. For one, the visitor has no way to know whether the email was sent. Additionally, the form currently sends an email even if there is no information entered. You can fix both these issues by adding some simple PHP code.

Try It Yourself

Create Landing Pages for Success and Failure

As a courtesy to your visitor, you should always tell her whether the email was sent. You can do so by using "landing pages" that the browser navigates to depending on whether the email was sent.

To start, create three new HTML pages called success.html, failure.html, and error.html that have messages telling the visitor whether the email was sent, if it was not sent, or if something went technically wrong in the sending process. Place all three files into the Contact folder in your site.

PHP is actually a scripting language you can use to create small programs that behave according to your input. One of the many things you can do with PHP is define a set of conditions that have to be met for some specific action to occur and also say what happens if the conditions are not met.

1. If the email is sent successfully, you want the browser to be redirected to the success.html page. To do this, you use the echo function with an HTML metatag called Refresh to redirect the browser. Still in the emailProcessor.php file, on a new line, type **echo "<meta http-equiv=\"refresh\" content=\ "0;URL=success.html\">";**. The Refresh metatag can delay the redirection to a new page. The delay, measured in seconds, is defined by the content variable. The backslashes in front of the quotation marks tell the PHP interpreter that they are not PHP code, but HTML.

2. Likewise, if the email is not sent, you want the browser to be redirected to the failure.html page. On a new line, type **echo "<meta http-equiv=\"refresh\" content=\"0;URL=failure.html\">";**.

3. To let the server know when to say the email was sent, you first have to define what you consider a success. In the case of the email form, a success would mean that the mail() function executed properly. To define the mail() function executing properly as a success, place the cursor at the beginning of the line that has the mail() function and type $success =.

Now that you have a way to measure whether the email was sent and you have the resulting actions for what should happen in either case, you need to make a small program that tells the server when to do what. This is done by using the if and else statements. Like the names suggest, the if statement checks whether a certain condition is met. If it is, the attached action takes place. The else statement kicks in whenever the if condition is not met. In this case, you want the if condition to be the $success variable. If it is met, the success.html page should display, and if not, the failure.html page should display.

4. Create a new line above the redirect metatag that leads to the success.html page and type **if ($success){**.

5. Create a new line directly below the redirect metatag and close the curly bracket by typing }.

6. Create a new line under the last one and type **else {**. Close this curly bracket on a new line after the redirect meta tag that leads to the failure.html page.

Figure 21.12 shows the emailProcessor.php file as it appears in Code view with the new conditional redirects added. The browser now directs to either the success.html or failure.html page, depending on whether the email is sent.

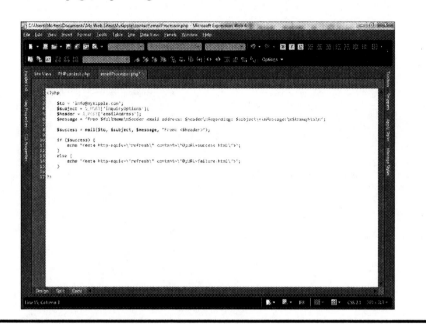

FIGURE 21.12
Add the conditional redirect tags to tell the visitor whether the email was sent.

Try It Yourself

Create a Filter to Stop Empty Messages

The easiest way to weed out nonsense emails and accidental clicks is to set up the email form so that if the visitor doesn't enter an email address, the message is not sent. To do this, you need to test whether the $header variable, which contains the contents of the emailAddress field from the form, is empty.

1. Create a new line above the $success variable. To see whether the $header variable is empty, type **if ($header =="")** {. (In programming, a single equal sign means "is the same as," whereas two equal signs mean "is identical to.")

2. If the $header variable is empty, the browser should be redirected to the error.html page in which the visitor is told to enter an email address. Create a new line and type **echo "<meta http-equiv=\"refresh\" content=\"0;URL=error.html\">";**.

3. Insert one more line and type **exit;** to stop the script from executing further. Close the curly bracket by typing }.

The final version of the emailProcessor.php file should now look like this:

```php
<?php

    $to = 'morten@pinkandyellow.com';
    $subject = $_POST['inquiryOptions'];
    $header = $_POST['emailAddress'];
    $message = "From: $fullName\nSender e-mail address: $header\nRegarding:
    $subject\n\nMessage:\n$thoughts\n";

    if ($header=="") {
        echo "<meta http-equiv=\"refresh\" content=\"0;URL=error.html\">";
        exit;
    }

    $success = mail($to, $subject, $message, "From: <$header>");

    if ($success){
        echo "<meta http-equiv=\"refresh\"
content=\"0;URL=success.html\">";
    }
    else{
        echo "<meta http-equiv=\"refresh\"
content=\"0;URL=failure.html\">";
    }

?>
```

To sum up, here is what happens step by step: When the visitor enters information into the email form and clicks the Submit button, the different variables are sent to the emailProcessor.php file. From here, each value is given a variable name and inserted in various sections of the email body. Then, the script tests to see that an email address was entered. If no email address was entered, the browser is redirected to the error.html page. Otherwise, the script continues on to send the email. If the email is successfully sent, the browser is redirected to the success.html page. If, for some reason, the email was not sent, the browser is redirected to the failure.html page.

If you test the script at this point, you'll notice that three important steps were not completed: The creation of the success.html, failure.html, and error.html pages. These three pages should contain some basic information about the success, failure, and error of the form submission and should all be stored in the Contact folder.

Summary

If you want to move beyond static pages and add dynamic content and true interactivity to your sites, you need to employ server-side scripting. And when you consider server-side scripting languages, many argue that PHP reigns supreme. Even though PHP is technically a direct competitor to Microsoft's application framework, ASP.NET,

Expression Web 4 comes equipped with an extensive range of tools to create, write, edit, and deploy PHP-based pages.

To test your PHP scripts locally on your computer, you first need to install PHP. In this hour, you learned how to install this free, open source software and set up Expression Web 4 so that it deploys when you test your scripted pages through the Expression Development Server.

One of the major benefits of PHP is that the scripts can live alongside HTML code, which means you can build your pages as you normally would and substitute your static content for dynamic content without breaking HTML. It also means that even with PHP scripts installed, you still have full control of the layout and functionality of your pages through the use of tags, CSS, and other techniques you learned by reading this book.

In this hour, you learned about basic PHP scripts and saw how a script can insert content into a page. You built an email form based on PHP that can be uploaded to a Linux server. (The form from Hour 19 works only on Microsoft servers.) Using PHP scripts, you went beyond simply generating an email and created conditional rules that sent the visitor to different pages depending on whether the email was sent. Finally, you created a conditional rule that tested whether the visitor inserted an email address before submitting the form.

PHP is an advanced coding language, and in this hour you saw only a fleeting glimpse of what can be done with it. By using the PHP tools in Expression Web 4, including the full IntelliSense support, you are well equipped to dive into the world of server-side scripting. If you want further information about PHP, including tutorials, visit the official PHP website at www.php.net or the W3C schools at www.w3schools.com/PHP/.

Q&A

Q. When I tested my PHP page in the browser after installing PHP, the address in the address bar changed to http://localhost: and some number. What happened to my original address?

A. When you run a page through the Expression Development Server, the application creates a temporary simulated server on your computer. The address changes because the page is not merely read from its original location as it is when you test an HTML page but is rendered through the server. Thus, the browser is displaying the server output, and because the server is hosted on your computer, it is a local host.

Q. When I tested the email form using the Expression Development Server, all I received was a page displaying the PHP code.

A. This problem could be caused by two different things. Either you didn't change the extension of the contact page to .php but left it as .html, in which case the Expression Development Server will not deploy, and the page will be rendered as straight HTML, or PHP is not running properly. First, check that your contact page is named contact.php. If so, make sure you followed all the steps when installing PHP on your computer.

Workshop

The Workshop has quiz questions to help you put to use what you just learned. If you get stuck, the answers to the quiz questions are in the next section. But try to answer the questions first. Otherwise, you'll be cheating yourself.

Quiz

1. What is the difference between the email form you created in this hour and the one you created in Hour 19?

2. How does the browser know what part of a PHP page is PHP code and what should be considered standard HTML?

Answers

1. The email forms you created in the two hours are virtually identical. The difference lies in how the data or information generated from the forms is handled after the visitor clicks the Submit button. In the form created in this hour, the data is sent to a PHP file that parses the information and creates an email message that is sent to the defined address. In the form from Hour 19, the data is processed by the FrontPage Server Extensions on the server and the email is generated by them. One of the biggest distinctions between the two is that whereas the PHP functions are contained in a separate file in this example, the FrontPage Server Extensions code is contained within the form code itself.

2. One of the many benefits of PHP is that it can live alongside regular HTML code without any problems. When the browser opens a PHP page, it reads all the regular HTML code as it normally would and sends only the PHP code contained within the PHP delimiters <?php and ?> to be processed by the server before being displayed. This way, the server helps out only when needed, and the browser does the rest of the work. In the extreme, this means you can create PHP pages that contain nothing but HTML, and the browser reads them as if they were HTML pages.

Test Twice, Publish Once: Professional Cross-Browser Testing with SuperPreview

What You'll Learn in This Hour:

▶ What SuperPreview is and how it came about
▶ How to use Snapshot to get instant in-browser previews of your pages
▶ How to use SuperPreview as a standalone application
▶ How to use the SuperPreview online service and remote browsers
▶ How to diagnose and fix problems uncovered by SuperPreview
▶ How to create a warning telling Internet Explorer 6 users to upgrade their browser

As previously mentioned several times in this book, cross-browser and cross-platform testing of your web pages and sites is paramount if you want to ensure that all of your visitors have the same experience. This has two reasons: First, even though the browser producers are converging on an agreement about how to interpret CSS and JavaScript (and in spite of the W3C conventions on the topics), there is still no absolute truth about how to do this; as a result, all browsers available have idiosyncrasies that can cause your pages to render improperly. This is further complicated because the same browsers running under different platforms (most notably Safari running under Mac OS and Windows) render different results. Whatever the reason, cross-browser testing is a necessary evil where web design is concerned. And it has been an annoying and time-consuming process that developers and designers alike would give a lot to go without. (So annoying, in fact, that many simply turn a blind eye to the problems and pretend they don't exist!)

The biggest hurdle for all involved has been to test against old and outdated browsers. It is a well-known fact that older versions of Internet Explorer (in particular, Internet Explorer 6) turn layouts and designs that work perfectly in pretty much every other browser into a garbled mess. The problem is that, to test for IE6, you need a working version of IE6 to test against. However, if you run an updated version of Windows XP, Windows Vista, or Windows 7, IE6 is long gone, and you can only have one version of the browser installed on your computer at one time. The only way to do proper IE6 testing would be to have an old computer running an old operating system with the browser, to run a virtual PC inside your operating system, or to use one of the many online browser screenshot services available. And even if you did somehow get to test your page against IE6, all you'd end up with would be a screenshot telling you that something is wrong. Finding out exactly what went wrong is a trial-and-error game.

Knowing the pains designers and developers went through to test their pages and sites against as many browsers as possible, the Expression Web team developed an application dedicated not only to performing proper cross-browser testing but also to providing more detailed information about what goes on behind the scenes to help in diagnosing and fixing problems. The result is Microsoft Expression Web SuperPreview—a standalone application integrated into Expression Web 4 that makes cross-browser testing a one-stop process.

With Expression Web 4 SP2, SuperPreview now carries full support for Internet Explorer 6, 7, 8, 8 in Compatibility Mode (annotated as 8→7), and 9. All these browsers are built into the application, so the output you see is the actual output that would be produced by the selected browser. In addition, SuperPreview has support for Firefox (if installed), image files, and Photoshop .psd files. Finally, SuperPreview provides support for testing of additional browsers through the new SuperPreview online service.

Having the Right Browsers

SuperPreview comes with Internet Explorer 6, 7, 8, 8 (Compatibility Mode), and 9 built in. However, to get the most out of this application, you also need to have up-to-date versions of other browsers. In particular, you need the latest version of Firefox (to get it, visit www.getfirefox.com) and Internet Explorer 9 (to get it, visit www.microsoft.com/ie).

Snapshot: Instant Browser Previews Inside Expression Web 4

SuperPreview is a powerful standalone application, but it also lends some functionality to Expression Web 4 in the form of a panel called Snapshot. With Snapshot, you get instant and up-to-date screen shots of your current page from your different browsers. The functionality is basic, but it gives you a quick-and-easy way to check whether your latest style change is current with all the necessary browsers. It is also a great tool for on-the-spot testing during the process of debugging browser problems.

Snapshot itself doesn't require a lot of explanation. To activate it, go to Panels on the main menu and select Developer (Snapshot) under Workspaces. This replaces Design view with Snapshot running the default browser (see Figure 22.1). You can also activate Snapshot manually by going to Panels on the main menu and selecting Snapshot.

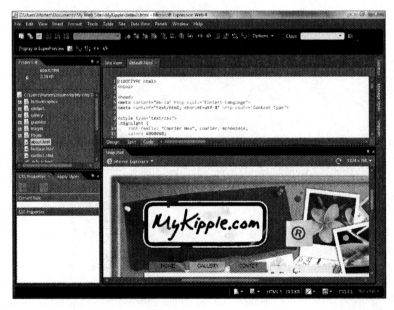

FIGURE 22.1
The Snapshot panel works alongside the Code and Design view panels. You can dock it to an area of the workspace or float it like any of the other panels.

You can cause the Snapshot panel to hover over the workspace or you can dock it to any of the panel zones by simply grabbing the top of the panel and dragging it to the desired location. As the panel hovers over potential zones, they are highlighted with a blue line. Personally, in my dual-monitor setup, I place and size the Snapshot panel to cover the entire left monitor while keeping the Expression Web 4 workspace on the right. On my laptop, I place the Snapshot panel below (or sometimes in place of) the Design view.

Snapshot Functionality

Snapshot has two drop-down menus with options: The browser menu, which lets
you pick what browser you want the snapshot to be taken from (see Figure 22.2),
and the size menu, which lets you define what size the imagined screen the snapshot is taken from should have (see Figure 22.3).

FIGURE 22.2
The browser
menu lets you
pick which
browser the
snapshot
should be taken
from.

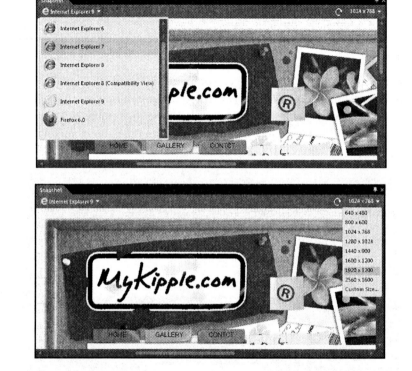

FIGURE 22.3
The size menu
lets you pick the
imagined size of
the browser win-
dow the snap-
shot should be
taken from.

The size menu requires a little further explanation: Snapshot works by passing the
page info to a browser and taking a screen grab of the output the browser generates.
To allow you to see what the page looks like in different browser window sizes, you
can define the size of the browser output. That way, even if you don't have a 30-
inch 2560×1600 pixel widescreen monitor, you can still see what the page would
look like on that monitor.

To display page output in Snapshot, you need to have a page open in Expression
Web 4. If you already have Snapshot open and you open a page, that page is displayed automatically. Depending on the content of the page and whether it is
linked to online content and so on, the actual process of taking the snapshot might
take some time, so you will probably encounter a spinning clock graphic quite
frequently.

The refresh button (circular arrow) toggles the Always Preview Active Document function on and off. With the function active, Snapshot will update every time you switch between different pages. With the function inactive, Snapshot is only updated when the currently open page is saved.

The Snapshot is just that—a snapshot or a picture of what the page looks like in the selected browser at a selected size screen. The page is nonfunctional, so you can't click to select any elements or buttons. In other words, Snapshot is in no way a replacement for Design view or viewing and interacting with your page in a web browser.

Because it is a picture of the browser output, Snapshot is not dynamically updated as you make changes to your files. To refresh Snapshot, you need to save the page to which you have made changes. This automatically triggers Snapshot to update. That means if you make a change in your CSS file only, you still need to resave the page it relates to if you want to see the change reflected in Snapshot. Another more roundabout way to refresh Snapshot is to change the browser from the browser menu. Changing the size does not trigger Snapshot to refresh, so if you want a different size you have to first change the size in the menu and then either save the page in question or change the browser.

Try It Yourself ▼

Preview default.html in Snapshot

To see how easy it is to preview pages in multiple browsers at different sizes and learn how Snapshot works, you'll preview default.html.

1. Open default.html in Code view.

2. Go to Panels on the main menu and select Snapshot. The Snapshot panel opens as a hovering panel above the workspace.

3. If the new panel floats above the workspace, grab the top of the Snapshot panel with your mouse and drag it toward the bottom of the View pane until you see a blue line appear at the bottom. Let go of the panel, and Snapshot docks underneath the View panel showing default.html as it appears in your default browser (refer to Figure 22.1).

4. Use the browser menu to change the browser to Internet Explorer 6.

5. Use the size menu to change the browser size to 1600×1200. Save the page
to refresh Snapshot.

Note that when the Snapshot panel is docked below Code view, the Design, Split,
and Code buttons shift up accordingly. This is because Snapshot is an independent
panel, not part of the View panel. So if you click the Split button, Split view appears
above the Snapshot panel.

Using SuperPreview for Cross-Browser Testing

As I said before, Snapshot is a basic version of SuperPreview that can be used from
inside Expression Web 4. The full-featured version of SuperPreview is a standalone
application that has been integrated into Expression Web 4 for ease of use. To use
SuperPreview, you can either use the SuperPreview button next to the browser preview button on the Common toolbar, as shown in Figure 22.4, or launch it from the
start menu of your operating system.

FIGURE 22.4
SuperPreview
can be launched
from the Com-
mon toolbar by
clicking the SP
button to the
left of the
browser preview
button.

Watch
Out!

Do Not Run Snapshot and SuperPreview at the Same Time!

Both Snapshot and SuperPreview are complicated applications that put a lot of
stress on your operating system. Running them simultaneously can lead to your
system getting sluggish or Expression Web 4 crashing. To avoid this problem, be
careful to use only one of the applications at one time. If you think about it, they
do the same thing, so it is superfluous to use both of them, anyway.

When you open SuperPreview, you see a menu and two preview panels, each with a
series of browser buttons (see Figure 22.5).

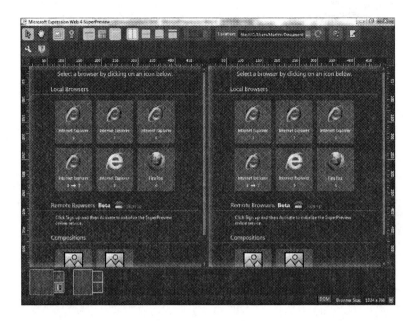

FIGURE 22.5
SuperPreview as it appears in its default state.

The easiest way to understand how the application works is to simply use it. If you haven't already done so, open the default.html page in Expression Web 4 and click the SuperPreview button on the Common toolbar. If this is the first time you've opened SuperPreview, you need to select your baseline browser and the browser you want to test against. This is done by simply clicking the appropriate browser in the two view panels. The left panel contains your baseline browser—the browser you normally test all your pages against. Mine is Internet Explorer 9, but you can choose any of the other ones if you like. The right panel contains the browser you are testing against. You can assign multiple browsers to this panel, but only one shows at a time. More on that later. As you select your baseline and testing browser, SuperPreview starts the process of creating previews for you. While SuperPreview is working, you see a spinning clock in each of the view panels (see Figure 22.6). Depending on the complexity and location of the page you load, this process can take anywhere from a couple of seconds to several minutes.

FIGURE 22.6
Creating browser previews in Super-Preview takes time, so you'll have to get used to the spinning clocks.

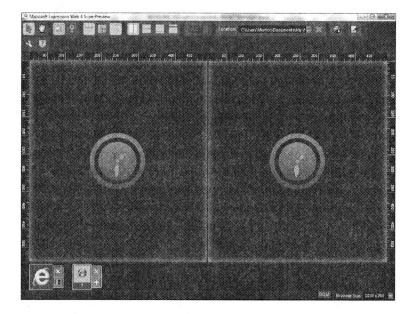

When the pages are loaded, you can start using the different functions of SuperPreview to identify and diagnose problems.

The Tools of SuperPreview

SuperPreview has a series of different tools designed to help you diagnose problems. Most of them are actually variations of the same tool, but they each have a slightly different use and purpose.

The majority of the tools are placed on the toolbar (see Figure 22.7). From here, you control what kind of information the application provides and how the application displays your page in the different browsers.

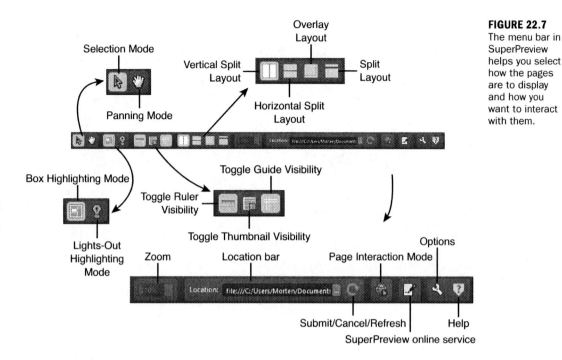

FIGURE 22.7
The menu bar in
SuperPreview
helps you select
how the pages
are to display
and how you
want to interact
with them.

▶ In Selection Mode (shortcut V), when you click an element within the page, the selected element is highlighted in your view panels.

▶ In Panning Mode (shortcut H), you can click and drag the page in the view panel. If you have two view panels open, the page in the other view panel moves in sync with the one you are moving.

▶ In Box Highlighting Mode (shortcut L), SuperPreview draws a colored and outlined box highlighting the affected area of the selected content. If both view panels are open, the box is highlighted in both panels with different colors (see Figure 22.8).

FIGURE 22.8
Box Highlighting
Mode highlights
the selected box
element with an
overlay color
and an outline.

FIGURE 22.8
Box Highlighting
Mode highlights
the selected box
element with an
overlay color
and an outline.

▶ Lights-Out Highlighting Mode (shortcut L) highlights the same area as the Box Highlighting Mode by darkening all other content surrounding it (see Figure 22.9).

FIGURE 22.9
Like the name
suggests,
Lights-Out High-
lighting Mode
highlights the
selected box
element by dark-
ening everything
not selected.

▶ Toggle Ruler Visibility (shortcut R) turns the rulers on and off.

▶ Toggle Thumbnail Visibility (shortcut T) turns the thumbnail navigator on and off (see Figure 22.10). The thumbnail navigator is a box in the bottom-right corner of each view panel that provides a thumbnail of the entire page with the currently visible area highlighted. You can use your mouse to drag the highlighted area around inside the thumbnail for quick navigation.

FIGURE 22.10
The thumbnail navigator provides a quick way to navigate inside large pages.

▶ Toggle Guide Visibility (shortcut Ctrl+;) turns guides on and off. You can place guides anywhere in the view panels by dragging and dropping them from the rulers. If you have both view panels open at the same time, a guide dragged into one panel will be duplicated in the other. The guides can be used to measure differences in size and position of elements. Note that you cannot make new guides if Toggle Ruler Visibility is turned off.

▶ Vertical Split Layout (shortcut A) is the default view panel layout in which the two browsers display side by side.

▶ In Horizontal Split Layout (shortcut S), the two view panels display one on top of the other. This display is useful if you want to compare wide elements of a page across browsers.

▶ Overlay Layout (shortcut D) is the most unusual of the layout modes. This function displays the two selected layouts one on top of the other through what is often referred to as "onion skinning," meaning you can see one shining through the other (see Figure 22.11). This function is particularly useful to identify minute changes in positioning.

FIGURE 22.11
Overlay Layout allows you to place two browser outputs one on top of another to see whether the content shifts between the two.

▶ Single Layout (shortcut F) displays only one browser at a time, giving you a full screen view of the output.

▶ Zoom (shortcut +/-) lets you zoom in and out to get a better view of details. As with the other functions, the zoom function affects both view panels identically.

▶ The Location (shortcut Ctrl+L) bar lets you enter any URL, local or external, to be previewed in SuperPreview. Because the application is standalone, there is no limit to what page you can preview: If you can visit it in your browser, you can open it in SuperPreview (as long as the website doesn't require you to log in first).

▶ The Submit/Cancel/Refresh (shortcut Ctrl+R) buttons relate to the Location bar and require no further explanation.

▶ Page Interaction Mode (Alt+I) is a new feature added with SP2 that allows you to access password-protected sites through SuperPreview. This is useful if you are testing protected Page Interaction Mode functionality or live sites that require login. When you click the Page Interaction Mode button, a new dialog opens in which you can interact with the login form like in a normal server. Once logged in, you can click the Preview button in the bottom-right corner to get back to SuperPreview in the logged-in state.

▶ The SuperPreview Online Service and Options buttons are covered later in this hour.

At the bottom of the window, two more tools are worth mentioning: the Preview Browser button and the DOM button.

The Preview Panel(s)

When you opened SuperPreview, you had to pick a baseline browser and a testing browser. But, as I said before, you can define several testing browsers. To add another browser, simply click the + symbol next to the testing browser. When you do, the testing browser view panel changes back to the browser selection page, and you can pick another browser.

Because many designers create image mock-ups of their pages, SuperPreview also enables you to test the real browser output against images. To do so, select the Open Image or Open PSD option (see Figure 22.12) and browse to the image you want to preview against. The Open Image function supports all the standard image formats (.bmp, .gif, .jpg, .png) and the Open PSD function opens Photoshop files (.psd). These image functions can also be used to import screen grabs of other browsers not supported by SuperPreview. As with the browsers, there is no limit to how many images you can test the page against (see Figure 22.13).

FIGURE 22.12
The Open Image option lets you import an image file such as an original mockup from a design application or a screen grab from another browser.

FIGURE 22.13
SuperPreview enables you to test your pages against a multitude of browsers and images at the same time.

Keep in mind that SuperPreview compares only two browsers at a time, so to switch between the different testing browsers and images, you need to actively select them.

The DOM Tree View

The final and most advanced feature of SuperPreview is the DOM Tree View, which you can open by clicking the DOM button at the bottom of the window.

Did you Know?

> Document Object Model (DOM) is the name of the code used in HTML and other web code to allow programs, applications, and scripts to access specific elements of the content and modify, style, update, or do other things to it. It sounds confusing, but the term DOM refers to the tags that contain the content inside HTML and other web documents. So, basically, if someone talks about the DOM, what that person means is literally the beginning and end tags that surround content.

When you click to select an element in your preview pages with the DOM Tree View open, SuperPreview provides a full breakdown of the entire DOM or tag structure for that element (see Figure 22.14). As a result, you can see every tag that affects the content and, if anything, what code is interpreted differently between the browsers. This is an advanced function that has limited usefulness, unless you know what you are doing. Even so, it can be a quick-and-easy way to find out why elements start behaving strangely when they are opened in different browsers. The key to using the DOM Tree View is to remember that different browsers have different DOMs, so when something goes awry, it's a fair bet that there might be something amiss in the tag tree.

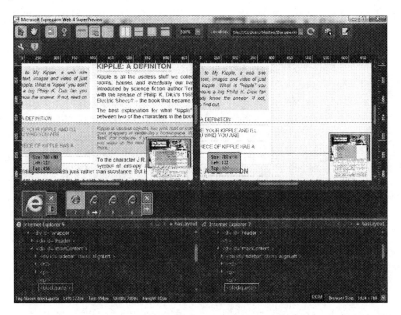

FIGURE 22.14
The DOM Tree View displays the DOM or tag tree of the selected element.

Setting Up and Using SuperPreview Online Service

You may have noticed that, in addition to the Local Browsers and Compositions options, there is a third one named Remote Browsers (see Figure 22.15). This is a new feature introduced with Expression Web 4 that lets you test your sites against browsers not on your computer through an online service. As of this writing, the service is still in beta. To utilize this new functionality, you must have a fully activated (meaning purchased) version of Expression Web 4 (the trial version does not provide this option) and a valid email address for the sign-up procedure.

> Remote Browsers **Beta** 🔵 Sign up
>
> Click Sign up and then Activate to initialize the SuperPreview online service.

FIGURE 22.15
The new Remote Browsers online service requires that you sign up.

To activate the service, click Sign Up or click the SuperPreview Online Service button in the main menu. This opens a dialog that explains the purpose of the service and provides a link to the Privacy Statement. Clicking the Sign Up button in the dialog opens a new dialog requesting your email address for the activation process (see Figure 22.16). Fill in your email address and click Next. The SuperPreview online service now sends you an email with validation information.

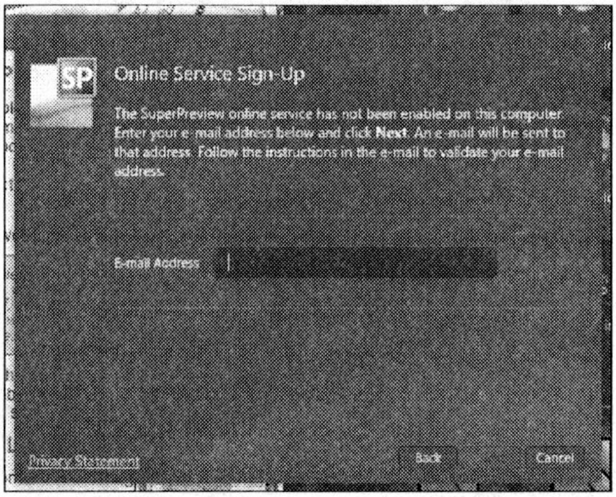

FIGURE 22.16
The SuperPreview Online Service needs a valid email account to be activated.

Once you receive the email from the SuperPreview Online Service, follow the instructions to activate your account by clicking the activation link. This opens a page in your web browser that tells you to click the Activate button in SuperPreview. Click the Activate button and SuperPreview to activate your account and change the browser selection list to include the currently available online service browsers. With the release of SP2, the list of online service browsers was increased significantly. As of this writing, remote browsers include Firefox versions 3.6.16, 4, and 5; Safari (Mac) versions 4 and 5; and Chrome. The list of available browsers will automatically update as more browsers go online.

With SuperPreview Online Service activated, you have more browser options available (see Figure 22.17). The new online browser options work exactly as the other options, but the loading time is substantially longer because the site in question has to be sent to the online service, rendered, and then sent back to SuperPreview. Most excitingly, this new function provides something previously unavailable on any PC: a proper preview of a website as it appears in Safari 4 and 5 running on a Mac.

FIGURE 22.17
With the Super-Preview Online Service acti-vated, you now have the option of previewing your sites in several other browsers, including Safari 4 and 5 running on a Mac.

SuperPreview Online Service Options

The Options button on the SuperPreview toolbar opens the SuperPreview Options dialog (see Figure 22.18). At present, it covers only SuperPreview online services. From here, you can check the server status to see if the server is online (a good idea, so you won't stare at the spinning clock indefinitely if the server is down) and acti-vate or deactivate your SuperPreview Online Service account.

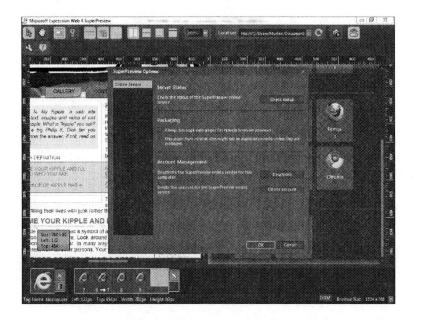

FIGURE 22.18
The SuperPre-view Options dialog lets you manage the SuperPreview Online Service.

In addition, you have the option of packaging web pages for remote browser preview. As the dialog states, this option ensures that sites running on intranets (internal networks) preview properly on the remote browsers. In layman's terms, this means if Packaging is checked, SuperPreview gathers all the relevant files for the page in question and bundles them before sending them to the remote browser. This is done because, on an internal network or intranet, you may have sites that use assets from other internal network locations that will be unavailable for the external browser. The bottom line is this: If you are working on intranet or internal network sites, Packaging should be checked. If you are not working on such sites, but manage all of your assets locally, Packaging should remain unchecked.

Watch
Out!

A Broken External Browser Preview May Be Due to Lack of Packaging

If you see a dramatic difference in the page preview from a local browser as opposed to an external browser, such as missing images, missing text, or other strange or broken elements, it is likely because the external browser could not obtain these elements. If this happens, try checking Packaging in the SuperPreview options and reload the page. More than likely, the external browser preview will now show up properly.

Identifying, Diagnosing, and Solving Cross-Browser Issues with SuperPreview

By following the lessons in this book, you have created a fully working version of the MyKipple.com site. If you followed my previous advice, you tested it against your browsers at every step along the way, and you probably have a fairly good idea of what, if any, cross-browser issues exist. However, that applies only to current browsers. For older browser versions, such as Internet Explorer 6 and 7, you don't know unless you have a fairly advanced setup, or you have deliberately avoided updating your browser for some time.

Now that the site is done, it is time to make sure it looks the same across all browsers. To do so, open default.html in SuperPreview with Internet Explorer 9 as the baseline browser and IE8, 8→7, 7, 6, Firefox, Safari for Mac, and Chrome, respectively, as the testing browsers. As you can see from clicking through the different testing browsers, and from Figure 22.19, a couple of elements look different between the browsers: Depending on the browser, the sidebar is either next to the content or the content appears below the sidebar. In addition, in IE6, everything seems slightly shifted, and the transparency is gone.

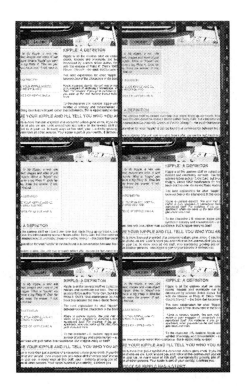

FIGURE 22.19
Default.html looks surprisingly different depending on what browser you use. From the top left: IE9, IE6, IE7, IE8, Firefox 5, and Safari (Mac) 5.

Now that you know the main issues, it is time to do some browser triage: What problems are most important and should be fixed, and what problems are either unimportant or hard to fix without a massive amount of work? This requires a bit of knowledge of the different browsers.

Technically, Firefox, IE8, and Safari (Mac) should look almost exactly the same. Any noticeable difference between them most likely means there is an actual error either in the HTML markup or CSS styles. We already know that IE6 does not support PNG transparencies without some serious JavaScript workarounds. However, apart from the transparencies and some slight shifting in the size and spacing of the text, there doesn't seem to be anything else dramatically wrong with the IE6 output. For those reasons, there is no point in trying to fix the page for IE6, but we should probably add a warning on the page telling IE6 users they should upgrade to a new version of the browser.

In SuperPreview, you can see that the heading and content appear on the right side of the sidebar in Firefox, IE8 and up, and Safari (Mac), and their positions are almost identical. (According to the position pop-ups, they are only 2 pixels apart.) However, if you click IE8 (Compatibility Mode), IE7, or IE6, the heading along with the rest of the content appears below the sidebar rather than beside it (see Figure 22.20)!

FIGURE 22.20
Small browser inconsistencies can have big consequences. In this case, the content is shifted down below the sidebar in IE7.

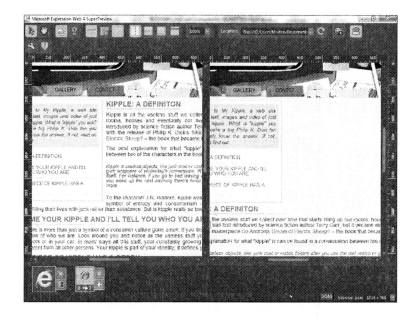

The explanation for this discrepancy lies in Hour 13, "Getting Visual, Part 3: Images as Design Elements with CSS," when you created a custom H2 style to ensure that the background image appeared behind the text rather than to the extreme left of the containing box. One of the things you did was to set the clear attribute to both to ensure that no other text appeared on the same line as the heading. Now it turns out the two older versions of Internet Explorer interpret the clear attribute a little too strictly and force the content down below the sidebar.

This is a typical situation when dealing with browser incompatibilities: To fix a problem in an older browser or one that doesn't play nice with web standards, you have to chip away at your code and remove elements that are there for a reason. So, for each such instance, you have to ask yourself a couple of questions: Is the discrepancy bad enough that I need to fix it? Is the fix going to adversely affect the design in browsers that interpret my code correctly to begin with? For this page, the answer to the first one is yes. For the second question, in most cases, you need to do some trial and error to find the answer.

Back in the default.html page in Expression Web 4, find the H2 style in the Manage Styles panel and open the Modify Styles dialog. Go to Layout and delete the clear:both attribute. Click OK, save the page, and save the attached CSS page. Save and open the page in SuperPreview.

Clicking through the different testing browsers and testing the page in your other browsers, you see that the change fixed the problem without any undesired consequences for the rest of the content in the browsers that already displayed the content properly. As an added bonus, IE6 seems to be on board as well. Unfortunately, IE7 is still not playing nice.

Troubleshooting and Fixing the Sidebar in Internet Explorer 7

With the heading issue resolved, a new and much more serious problem emerges: Part of the sidebar is now blocked in Internet Explorer 7. Because this problem is visible only in IE7, it is likely one of those idiosyncrasies I previously mentioned in which the browser doesn't interpret web standards properly. However, because IE7 is still the most prevalent version of the browser, it is a problem we have to fix. Unfortunately, because it is a web-standards-compliancy issue, the fix might result in the page looking different—in other words, we might have to "dumb it down" to work in the broken browser. Using the tools in SuperPreview to select and highlight the different sidebar elements, you can see that the content isn't merely blocked by the blockquote box, but it is cut off at the bottom. What makes this problem even stranger is that it appears only in IE7, but not IE6, which means that this is an isolated issue for that browser.

Because there is no obvious reason why the sidebar is interrupted by the blockquote, the only way to find the problem and fix it is through trial and error. Based on what you see in SuperPreview, it seems logical that the culprit is the blockquote, so let's start there:

1. In Expression Web 4, open the kippleStyles.css file in Code view and find the blockquote style.

2. Use CSS comments to disable all the styling inside the curly brackets. The syntax for a CSS comment is forward slash + star (/*) for the beginning and star + forward slash (*/) for the end. To do this quickly, highlight all the code you want to comment out and press Ctrl+J on your keyboard. This shortcut automatically wraps the highlighted content in the appropriate comment tags. To remove the comment again, press Ctrl+Shift+J. When you comment out CSS, the affected code turns gray, as shown in Figure 22.21.

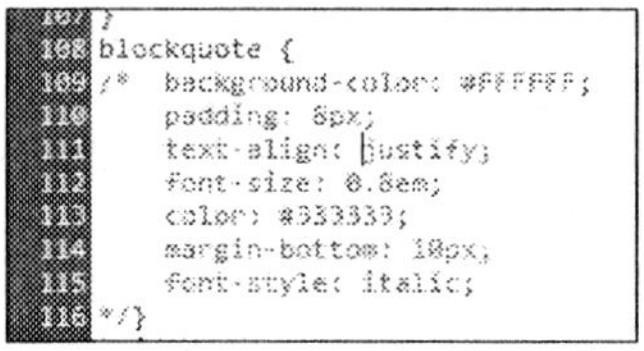

FIGURE 22.21
As in HTML, you
can use special
code to com-
ment out sec-
tions of CSS.
This is an easy
way to turn CSS
code on and
off without
deleting it.

```
107 }
108 blockquote {
109 /* background-color: #FFFFFF;
110     padding: 8px;
111     text-align: justify;
112     font-size: 0.8em;
113     color: #333333;
114     margin-bottom: 10px;
115     font-style: italic;
116 */}
```

3. Save the style sheet and reload default.html in SuperPreview. Without any of the style code, the sidebar appears as it should in IE7.

4. Back in kippleStyles.css, move the beginning comment tag down one line so that the background-color attribute becomes active. Save the style sheet and reload default.html in SuperPreview. The background color is added, but the sidebar menu is still visible.

5. Continue moving the beginning comment tag down one line, save the style sheet, and test the new style in SuperPreview until you find the style attribute that causes the problem.

Going down the list of attributes, you find that it is font-style: italic; that is the culprit. For whatever reason, it looks like IE7 doesn't like this particular style combination, and as a result, the other elements are affected. The reason why I say it doesn't like this style combination is because the problem isn't actually caused by the font-style attribute alone: If you leave the font-style attribute active and comment out the background-color attribute, the menu is also visible. So, it seems it is the combination of a background color (or a border for that matter) and italicized or oblique text that together cause the problem. That leaves you with a decision to make: What matters more to you? The background color or the italicized text? You can choose one or the other, but not both.

This, I'm afraid, is a typical browser-compatibility conundrum, and I built it in just to show you how weird things can get. Sometimes, you are forced to make choices you don't like because things don't work the way they are supposed to. There are always ways around it, but they are usually complicated and time consuming, and applying them becomes a question of whether the return on investment is good enough.

Solving IE6 Problems by Telling Visitors to Upgrade Their Browsers

As you can see by testing your site in IE6, things just don't work properly in this old browser. The problem becomes blatantly obvious when you use the Overlay Layout mode in SuperPreview: Not only are the PNG transparencies not working, but also the content positioning and text alignments are off. IE6 has been a thorn in the side of web developers and designers since day one, and there are no turnkey solutions to solve all the problems the browser creates. In many cases, designers are forced to either clutter their code with custom IE6 code (commonly known as IE hacks) or create whole separate style sheets just for this browser.

Internet Explorer 6 was released in 2001, alongside Windows XP. It was replaced by Internet Explorer 7 in 2006, and Internet Explorer 9 was released in March 2011, so you would think that people had moved on to the newer browsers. However, for myriad reasons, this has not happened. A large percentage of web-faring users are visiting your sites with this old-and-outdated dinosaur of a browser.

Since IE6's release in 2001, designers and developers have bent over backward to make their sites look and work properly in the browser. But over the past couple of years, more and more of us have decided that enough is enough and started working to educate people about why they should upgrade to a newer browser and how to do so. If you search the web for anti-IE6 campaigns, you'll find a long list. These campaigns all have the same goal in mind: to phase out IE6 for good by getting people to upgrade.

To get the world up to speed and out of the past, Microsoft has started a campaign to get everyone to upgrade their browsers. The campaign is called The Internet Explorer 6 Countdown and can be found at www.ie6countdown.com.

Try It Yourself ▼

Add the IE6 Countdown Widget to Your Site with Conditional Browser Comments

As part of the IE6 Countdown campaign, Microsoft has created a small code snippet you can add to your site to tell visitors using this old and outdated browser that they need to upgrade. The snippet uses a conditional CSS commenting technique to target and display content only in IE6 and older browsers. Because the MyKipple site doesn't look right in IE6, it is a good idea to add this snippet to the site:

1. In Expression Web 4, open myKippleMaster.dwt in Code view.

2. In your web browser, go to www.ie6countdown.com and click Join Us or Join the Cause to get to the snippet.

3. The IE6 Countdown snippet supports many different languages. Use the drop-down to select your preferred language.

4. Highlight and copy the code snippet in its entirety, as shown in Figure 22.22.

5. In Expression Web, go to Code view and place your cursor right after the beginning <body> tag.

6. Paste the code snippet in its entirety right after the <body> tag.

FIGURE 22.22
The IE6
Countdown code
snippet.

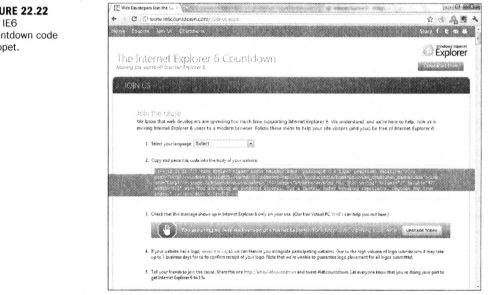

7. Save the DWT and the linked pages, and test default.html in SuperPreview.

Now when you open default.html in IE6 and IE9 in SuperPreview, you see the IE6 Countdown warning at the top of the page in IE6 but not IE9 (see Figure 22.23). This happens courtesy of the conditional browser comment that wraps the code snippet. This conditional comment works only on Internet Explorer and can be used to target any of the browsers by changing the if statement to match the browser version (5, 5.0, 5.5, 6, 7) or by setting a less than or equal (lte) or greater than (gt) value, like this: [if lte IE 6] or [if gt IE 6].

The great thing about this conditional comment trick is that there is no limit to what you can put inside the commented-out sections. And because it doesn't use JavaScript or other custom code to trigger, it works even on the most basic and stripped-down browser.

FIGURE 22.23
The IE6 Countdown warning only appears in IE6 and older browsers.

Summary

Throughout this book, I told you to keep testing your pages against as many browsers as possible to ensure that they look the same across all of them. Not only is this a cumbersome process, but it is also not 100% accurate because you need to test against old and outdated browsers you most likely don't have on your computer.

To solve this problem, Expression Web 4 comes complete with SuperPreview. SuperPreview lets you do cross-browser testing in one central location and provides you with detailed information about the elements on your page and how they interact in different browsers.

SuperPreview was a new feature with Expression Web 3 and has been improved and expanded for Expression Web 4. Because it is such an important tool in your web development toolkit, an entire hour has been devoted to helping you understand how to use it. The application actually has two components: Snapshot, which is a browser-based screen-grab panel inside Expression Web 4; and SuperPreview, which is a standalone application that works with Expression Web 4. In this hour, you learned how to use Snapshot to get instant browser previews of your current page from multiple browsers and browser versions at the click of a button. This function is a quick-and-easy way to test to make sure your code and style changes are not going to have adverse effects on your layouts and designs.

Most of this hour was spent learning how to use SuperPreview to test your pages against different browsers and browser versions and how to use the tools to identify, diagnose, and correct problems. Even though the actual operation of SuperPreview is basic, the information the application provides in terms of cross-browser issues is invaluable and can help you identify problems and make decisions on whether they are worth fixing or should be ignored.

In this hour, you learned how to use all the functions in SuperPreview, and you used the different views and tools in the application to identify and solve several cross-browser issues that you probably wouldn't have known about if it weren't for the application.

One of the things you discovered when using SuperPreview was that Internet Explorer 6 does not play nice. Unfortunately, solving IE6 issues is an uphill battle that often leads nowhere. So, rather than delving into a complicated trial-and-error process to try to fix these problems, the last part of this hour was dedicated to showing you how to warn visitors with old and outdated browsers such as IE6 that they need to upgrade.

Q&A

Q. *I have a page open in the Snapshot panel, but when I try to click the different elements to get more information, nothing happens. Why is that?*

A. Snapshot represents the most basic form of browser previewing, where all you get is a literal snapshot of what the current page will look like in a browser. The purpose of this function is to give you a quick way of testing changes in your code on-the-fly against multiple browsers instead of having to leave Expression Web to do so. To get more detailed feedback and information on individual components in your design, you need to use Expression Web SuperPreview.

Q. *When I run Snapshot and SuperPreview at the same time, my computer starts acting up, working slowly, or crashes. What am I doing wrong?*

A. The answer is actually in the question: Snapshot and SuperPreview run off the same system processes, and if you try to preview the same page in both applications at the same time, you can overload your computer. A good rule of thumb is to close Snapshot if you are going to use SuperPreview, and vice versa.

Q. *Why does my page look so different in Snapshot and Design view?*

A. Design view is not a browser but rather an approximation of a conglomerate of browsers, so it doesn't necessarily show you what the true output of a browser would be. Snapshot, on the other hand, gives you accurate renderings of what the page will look like in the real browsers.

Workshop

The Workshop has quiz questions and exercises to help you put to use what you just learned. If you get stuck, the answers to the quiz questions are in the next section. But try to answer the questions first. Otherwise, you'll be cheating yourself.

Quiz

1. Why is cross-browser testing so important?

2. Should you care if your page looks terrible in Internet Explorer 6 if it looks great in all the other browsers?

Answers

1. For whatever reason, the many different browsers available all display web content slightly differently. Cross-browser testing is essential to ensure that, if not perfect, your pages appear as similar as possible no matter what browser they are viewed in.

2. There is no correct answer to this question: The decision on whether or not to make a web page or site compliant with Internet Explorer 6 relies on what the owner of the site wants and what browsers the projected visitors of the site use. If a predominance of visitors to the site use older computers that may run IE6, the site should be designed with this compliance in mind. However, if the vast majority of visitors are using more modern

browsers, this becomes less important. A good analogy is full-screen versus widescreen TV shows: If the majority of your viewers own older full-screen TV sets, you are best suited to film and broadcast your show in 4:3 (full-screen) format. However, if the majority of your viewers have widescreen HDTV sets, you are better off filming and broadcasting the show in 16:9 (widescreen) format and leaving the few who still have full-screen TVs to either clip off the sides of the widescreen picture or watch the show with letterboxing.

Exercise

Expression Web SuperPreview is a great tool to test your own sites against multiple browsers simultaneously and check for browser incompatibilities in your scripts. However, it is also a great tool for learning about the challenges of cross-browser compatibility and for seeing that even the best designers and developers out there sometimes get things wrong. Take a moment to test some of your favorite sites in SuperPreview. All you have to do is enter the site URL in the Location bar and the site will open in the browsers you choose. I suggest testing famous sites, such as www.microsoft.com, www.cnn.com, and even the new www.whitehouse.gov. Use the different view tools to see how the content shifts around and formats differently in the various browsers.

Beyond the Basics, Part 2: Get Noticed with the New Search Engine Optimization (SEO) Checker

What You'll Learn in This Hour:

▶ What search engines are and how they work

▶ What Search Engine Optimization is and why it is important

▶ How to use the Search Engine Optimization Checker to make sure your site will be found on search engines

▶ How to troubleshoot errors and warnings from the SEO Checker

After individuals or businesses launch a website, they usually immediately ask one of two questions: "Why is no one visiting my website?" or "Why can no one find my website on Google/Bing/Yahoo!/my favorite search engine?"

The answers to these questions are as varied as they are inaccurate, but they all relate back to the science (or alchemy) of Search Engine Optimization (SEO). Basically, SEO is a series of techniques and best practices on how you format, code, and write your web pages so that the search engines list them higher in the hierarchy and you get more visits. The problem is that all the search engines are different, and all of them change on a continuing basis. Because of this, the techniques that work best for high rankings today may be useless—or even detrimental—to your rankings next week.

That said, there are some baseline best practices in place that will always work to help your SEO, and they are easy to follow once you know them. To help you stick to those guidelines and ensure that, at the least, search engines understand your content and help people find it, Expression Web 4 now has a built-in SEO Checker in the form of a new panel. In this hour, you learn how to use this new tool to optimize your site for search engines and how to write your code and content in such a way that people and search engines understand it.

One caveat, though: Following the tips and techniques in this hour and getting a perfect score (no errors) in the SEO tool in Expression Web 4 by no means guarantees that you will get tons of visitors to your site. To get visitors, you have to have great content, and that's entirely up to you.

What Is a Search Engine, Anyway?

Search engines are, by far, the most used applications on the Web, and you use them every time you are on the web, whether you know it or not. In the beginning, search engines were merely directory archives of the Internet—much like a huge phonebook for the Web—but today, they are smart, semi-intelligent content skimmers that read everything that can be found on the Web, catalogue it, and try to feed the most relevant content to users when they search for it. When you ask a search engine "What is the best recipe for apple pie?", it returns a list of the most popular and the most relevant articles on the Web pertaining to that topic.

Search engines now come in many different shapes and formats, some of which are surprising. Whereas the traditional search engines—Google, Bing, and Yahoo!—are still indexes of sorts, you now have a long line of applications that mimic search engine behavior or add a new layer to the search. Facebook is a great example of this new type of search engine. Rather than searching for a set term, you now use your friends and followers to do the searches for you. If you use Facebook as a search engine and ask, "What is the best recipe for apple pie?", you will likely get a series of answers from your friends ranging from actual recipes to links to articles on the Web. More than likely, some of these will match those from the "normal" search engines. This new kind of search can be grouped with a new type of technology, referred to as "semantic search" or "meaningful search," where the results are not merely word or sentence matches, but actual thought-through, meaningful answers.

Semantic search will become more important in the coming years, and all the traditional search engines are now falling over each other to try to leverage this type of technology in their own systems for more accurate results.

The bottom line is this: Whereas search engines used to be archives that could be tricked by putting in the right words, sentences, and keywords in your pages, today, search engines are organic semi-intelligent creatures that actually read through your content and try to match it with people looking for that content. As a result, for the best possible search engine results, both in the traditional systems and on Facebook, Twitter, and wherever else people now do searches, your best option is to make the information on your site as accurate, concise, and informative as possible. That's where we start.

Search Engine Optimization in Expression Web 4

Search Engine Optimization in Expression Web 4 is a panel function much like Find. To activate it, go to Panels on the main menu and select SEO. This opens the Search Engine Optimization panel at the bottom of the workspace (see Figure 23.1).

FIGURE 23.1
The Search Engine Optimiza-tion panel appears at the bottom of the workspace when activated.

To start the Search Engine Optimization tool, click the green arrow in the upper-left corner. This opens the SEO Checker dialog (see Figure 23.2).

FIGURE 23.2
The SEO Checker dialog lets you decide what pages to check and what to check for.

Before you actually run an SEO check of your site, click the Learn More About SEO link in the SEO Checker dialog. This takes you to a series of reference articles by the Expression Web team that explains the different elements of SEO and what the best practices are. It is a good idea to read through these articles to get a solid under-standing of what you are looking for and how things should be done. That way, when the report is generated and the errors and warnings start appearing, you know what they refer to and whether they are relevant to you.

Running an SEO Check of the MyKipple Site

With the new MyKipple site open in Folder view, open the SEO panel to run an SEO check of the site:

1. In the SEO panel, click the green arrow in the upper-left corner to open the SEO Checker dialog.

2. Under Check Where, check All Pages. Under Show, check both Errors and Warnings (refer to Figure 23.2).

3. Click the Check button. Expression Web 4 goes through all of your pages and checks them for SEO optimization. The resulting list shows all the places Expression Web 4 found something it considers to be an error or warning (see Figure 23.3).

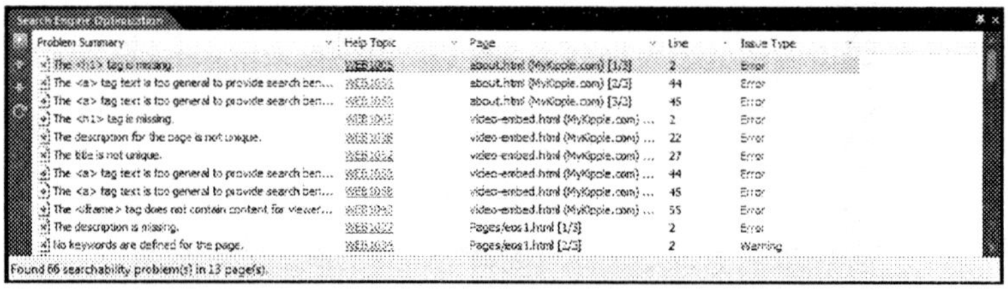

FIGURE 23.3
After the SEO Checker completes its run, the SEO panel lists all the errors and warnings it found in your page(s).

Looking at the output of the SEO Checker, you can now see how it works. On the far left, you have the Problem Summary, in which the actual problem is described in short form. To its right, you have a Help Topic link that takes you to a further description of the problem, what causes it, and how it can be fixed. Next to that is the address and name of the page the error was found on and what line the error was found on. The final column lists whether this is an error or a warning. The difference between errors and warnings is that errors are things that Expression Web 4 thinks will damage or interfere with your Search Engine Optimization, whereas warnings are things that are left out or not done properly that will increase your ranking if they are fixed.

If you hover your mouse over any of the error items, you get a ScreenTip with further information about the error (see Figure 23.4). This is a quick way of getting an explanation for what's wrong if you don't want the full breakdown from the Help link.

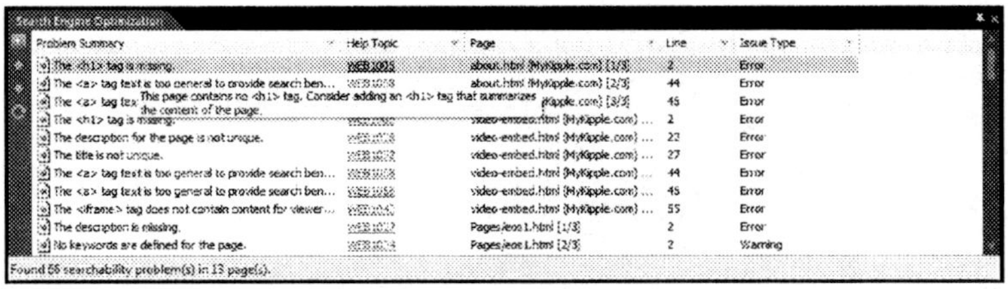

FIGURE 23.4
The SEO Checker provides a lot of information about your errors and warnings if you hover the mouse over each item.

The SEO Checker should return 66 errors from the 13 pages in your site. This sounds like a lot, but if you scroll down and actually read the errors, you'll notice that a lot of them are repeated on every page and even more are things you don't necessarily want to change. This is an important lesson learned early: The fact that Expression Web 4 and the SEO Checker consider something to be an error doesn't necessarily mean it is an error. You'll see what I mean by this shortly.

Analyzing SEO Checker Reports

As I said in the introduction to this hour, Search Engine Optimization is part science, part alchemy, and part common sense. For this reason, the output of the SEO Checker may not necessarily be something you want to follow. You have to treat each error or warning as an individual case and look at whether the particular problem Expression Web 4 found is one that should be looked into or whether it can be ignored.

The best way to see this in action is to look at some of the errors and warnings and analyze them.

The <h1> Tag Is Missing

The first error you should have is "The <h1> tag is missing" on line 2 in about.html. This error indicates that the page has no main heading for the search engines to index. The idea is that the content wrapped in the <h1> tag is the descriptive heading for the whole page and search engines will look for this tag first. If you look back to when you created the page layout for MyKipple.com, you'll remember you used the <h2> tag for headings. This is an educated choice, because faced with the lack of an <h1> tag, the search engines will look for an <h2> tag instead. Even so, it might be a good idea to make the heading an h1 instead of an h2.

Scrolling down the error list, notice that this error appears for every page. This is when you'll be happy you set up a DWT in Hour 18, "Dynamic Web Templates." To fix this problem, just change the tag in the DWT and edit the h1 style:

1. Go to the Folder list and open myKippleMaster.dwt.

2. In Code view, go to line 131 and change the <h2> beginning and end tags
to <h1> and </h1>.

3. Save the DWT and make sure it updates eight pages.

4. Open the kippleStyles.css file, which is found under the styles folder, and
find the H1 style.

5. Find the h2 style directly below and copy the background-image,
background-repeat, background-position, display, and padding-bottom
attributes up to h1, as shown in Figure 23.5. Save kippleStyles.css.

FIGURE 23.5
It is often easier
to copy CSS
code from one
style to another
in Code view
than to use
the Modify Style
dialog.

Run the SEO Checker again, and you'll see you now have only 57 errors to deal
with: All the <h1> warnings were removed in one sweep.

The <a> Tag Text Is Too General to Provide Search Benefit

With the h1 tag added to all the pages, the next errors on the list are regarding the
<a> anchor tags, more specifically that the <a> tag text is too general to provide
search benefit. Most of these errors are referring to the menu links. The error says
that the text is too generic, and this is, of course, accurate. However, to fix this error,
you have to replace the simple button words (Home, Gallery, About Me, and
Contact) with something more descriptive, and that wouldn't be functional. So, once
again, you can ignore this warning.

That said, the <a> tag warning is actually vitally important, just not in this particular instance. Search engines rank sites based on interactivity. That means the more
links you have inside your site pointing to other pages or places inside your site, the
better it will be ranked by search engines. However, at the same time, you need to

make those links descriptive so people (and search engines) understand where they are pointing. Simply setting all link texts to "link" or "click here" does nothing for your search rankings. The SEO Checker warns you about this. A better option is to use descriptive words or even full sentences as link texts.

The `<title>` Tag Contains Placeholder Content or Text That Is Too General to Provide Search Benefits

Earlier in this book, you populated the `<title>` tag for some of the pages. The `<title>` tag contains the text that appears in the browser bar, in bookmark links, and, most importantly, as the heading for search engine links. Therefore, it is important that your `<title>` tags are not only filled in, but that they provide information about the page so people understand what is to be found on that page. For this reason, simply setting the title of each page to "MyKipple.com – Home" or "MyKipple.com – About" is not ideal. Better titles are "MyKipple.com – a site about the stuff that surrounds us" and "What is MyKipple.com? Learn more about us."

In the case of most of the pages in our project, the title of all the pages is currently MyKipple.com. To change this, double-click the error in the SEO panel, and Expression Web 4 takes you to the line in question in Code view. From here, you can remove the original text and replace it with something more descriptive. Including the site name at the end of the title ensures that, if people search for a word in the title along with your site name, they are more likely to find this page.

The `<title>` tag warnings must be dealt with on an individual, page-by-page basis. Scroll through the SEO panel and fix the `<title>` tag warnings as they appear. Remember to save the pages after inserting the new descriptive titles.

The Description for the Page Is Not Unique

In addition to the `<title>` errors, the SEO panel also indicated that there is a problem with the description of some pages—more specifically, you'll find another error saying the description for the page is not unique. As you learned earlier, the `description` metatag is a short description of the contents of the page. This particular metatag is important because it is the text that appears under the main title when the page is listed on search engines. In other words, it needs to be short and descriptive so people will click it. The reason for the warning is that the descriptions of all the pages in the MyKipple site are the same.

Try It Yourself

Make Individual Descriptions for Each Page

If you think back to when you created the DWT, you'll remember that you made the
`<title>` tag and `keywords` metatag an editable region, but not the `description`. To
create individual descriptions for each page, you must first make a new editable
region for the `description` metatag in the DWT:

1. Go to the Folder list and open myKippleMaster.dwt.

2. In Code view, go to the metatag line with the name description (most likely
   line 19) and place the cursor at the beginning of the line.

3. Create a new editable region by typing
   `<!-- #BeginEditable "description" -->`.

4. Go to the end of the line and close the editable region by typing
   `<!-- #EndEditable -->`.

5. Save the DWT and make sure all pages are updated.

Now that the `description` metatag is an editable region, you can go into each
page and give it a unique description. If you don't want to make the change in
Code view, you can right-click the page in Design view, select Page Properties
from the context menu, and enter a new description in the Page Properties
dialog.

The `<img>` or `<area>` Tag Does Not Have an `alt` Attribute with Text

Ignoring the warnings we have gone through so far, you'll find a series of warnings
that the `<img>` or `<area>` tags don't have `alt` attributes attached to them. This warning refers to the image hotspots you created in Hour 7, "Getting Visual, Part 2:
Advanced Image Editing, Thumbnails, and Hotspots." Like with images, hotspots
(wrapped in `<area>` tags in HTML) need `alt` attributes to be valid. This `alt` attribute
is not only for people visiting your site with non-image browsers, but for search
engines. In fact, if you think about it, Google, Bing, and Yahoo! may be the three
most important "blind" visitors. As computers, they can't see images, and they rely
solely on the text on your site.

Clicking the `<img>` errors, you'll quickly realize why these errors are being generated:
Rather than attaching the correct `alt` attribute to the hotspots, we used the incorrect
`title` attribute. This is a common mistake that, because it doesn't immediately
cause a validation error, is easy to make. Fortunately, it's just as easy to fix. In Code
view, all you have to do is change `title` to `alt` for the four lines in question, and
the error disappears.

Summary

As you have worked your way through this book, you have learned a lot about how to write and edit valid code and what web standards are. Now, at the end of your journey, I introduce you to yet another set of rules you have to adhere to. So, is SEO really all that important? And should you care? The answer to both questions is a resounding "yes." However, that's not a bad thing.

Even though the site did generate what seemed like a lot of errors, the reality is that most of them were errors you could ignore, and those that were not were usually omissions and/or easy fixes. The reality of the situation is this: If you write 100% standards-based code (as Expression Web 4 does), and you remember to add a unique title, description, and keywords to all of your pages, you are writing a site with solid SEO. Any warnings that show up will likely be extraneous elements that don't really matter or things you simply forgot to deal with. So, caring about SEO is, in many ways, synonymous with caring about web standards. Because Expression Web 4 pretty much does that for you, you're on safe ground.

I wasn't joking when I told you in my Introduction that using Expression Web 4 puts you leaps and bounds ahead of the competition right out of the gate. For many, SEO and web standards are still a mysterious alternate reality they can't wrap their heads around. However, as you learned in this hour, it really isn't all that hard, and the rules are simple.

Q&A

Q. *The SEO Checker produced a lot of errors for the extra pages made in this book, such as menus.html. What do I do with those?*

A. The SEO Checker will check all the pages in your site unless you specify otherwise. Throughout this book we have created several demo pages that are not meant to be published to the Web. When you run the SEO Checker, you can choose to only check the pages you actually intend to publish, or you can get the demo pages up to standard by following the recommendations the Checker provides. It's up to you.

Q. *If I create a page that returns no warnings or errors from the SEO Checker, will it be listed at the top of Google searches?*

A. Sadly, the answer is no. Google and other search engines rank sites on a long list of features, including quality of content, popularity, number of other sites linking to the site, and so on. Just because your site passes inspection in the SEO Checker doesn't mean you'll be King or Queen of Google. What it does mean is the search engines will have an easier time indexing your content. And that is half the battle.

Exercise

Using the SEO Checker tool, try to get your site as close as possible to zero errors and warnings. Keep in mind that you have to accept the warnings for the menu links, but every other error or warning can be omitted by cleaning up your code.

Publishing Your Website

What You'll Learn in This Hour:

▶ What the six different publishing options are and how they differ
▶ How to set up your site for publishing using FTP
▶ How to use the Publishing view to publish and update your site
▶ How to change the publishing and HTML optimization settings

The final, and arguably most important, step to create a website is publishing it so that it is available to your intended audience, whether it is on a local network, an intranet, or the World Wide Web.

In practical terms, publishing a website means taking the files you have been working with on your computer and putting them on a server so that others can access them. There are many ways to do this, and which method works best for you depends on where the files go, what software the server runs, and several other considerations.

In the publishing phase of the website-building process, Expression Web 4 goes from being a developer and designer tool to a file-management tool. When you publish files to an external host, the application keeps track of which files were published and when they were published. That way, you can easily see whether a file has already been published, or if you have a newer version of the file on your computer that needs to be published in place of an older one.

In this hour, you learn how to use the different publishing methods to manage files on your computer and on the final location and discover how to decide which method works best for you. You also learn how to configure Expression Web 4 to automatically update new versions of your files for you and keep tabs on what you have done in the past.

A Word on Domains and Web Hosting

In most cases, a website is intended to be published on the Web for everyone to see. In that case, you need a web server connected to the Web on which to place your files and a web domain that takes the visitors to your site. The most common way to do this is to use a web-hosting service that provides both domain name registration and web hosting.

The All-Important Domain Name

Buying a domain name can be a harrowing and frustrating experience because so many names are already taken, and it is important to get an easily spelled and memorable name that reflects positively on your company or service. In addition, thousands of companies out there prey on designers looking for a specific domain name. If you're not careful, they might snap up your preferred name right before you buy it and ask for a ridiculous fee (or ransom, if you will) to release it to you. A common mistake people make when looking for a new domain name is to search for it on Google. What they don't know is that people monitor Google and other search engines for those searches. When they pop up, those people buy the domain names so that you have to pay them to get the names released. If you are looking to see whether a domain name is taken, always use a trusted Whois service, such as www.whois.net, rather than a search engine. Such services not only tell you whether a domain is taken, but if so, also who holds the rights to it and when those rights expire.

After you find a domain name you like, you can buy it from any number of vendors. The price of a domain name depends on the extension you want (.com, .ca, .net, .tv). Some domain extensions (.edu, .gov, and so on) are not available to the public. As of this writing, a .com domain should run between $10 and $20 per year. Pay any more and you are being ripped off!

Did you Know?

Most web hosts offer free or discounted domain names with the purchase of a hosting plan, but you don't need to register your domain name with your web host unless that is what you want.

After you decide on a domain name, you need to find a place to host your site. Depending on the size of your site, what primary web technology you want to use (ASP.NET or PHP, for example), and the estimated traffic your site will receive, you have many options to choose from. A small site with limited traffic will do fine with a basic shared-hosting plan, whereas a high-traffic site might need a virtual private server or even a dedicated server. In most cases, you can start with a small shared-hosting plan and upgrade when it becomes necessary.

An important thing to consider when buying hosting is what kind of applications you will run on your site. As you learned in this book, if you plan to run ASP.NET applications, you need a host that supports ASP.NET. Likewise, if you run PHP applications, such as the popular WordPress blogging software, you need a host that supports PHP. Before buying hosting anywhere, always make sure the hosting plan includes all the features you plan to use.

> A bit of research can save you lots of money! There are millions of web hosts, and their services and prices differ greatly. By doing some research and asking around, you can quickly find that the same service can be up to ten times more expensive from one host to another. And the most famous hosts are not always the best ones. I have used five different hosts, and they have been progressively cheaper yet offered better service.

Did you Know?

Six Different Publishing Options

Expression Web 4 offers several different publishing options to choose from, all with advantages and drawbacks. Which option you should use depends on where you are publishing the site to, what software the server runs, and your own personal preferences.

To select a publishing option, you need to set up your Publishing properties. This is done from the Site view (see Figure 24.1). At the bottom of the Site view are four options: Folders, Publishing, Reports, and Hyperlinks. To set up your remote website properties, click the link in the middle of the panel with the text Add a Publishing Destination.

FIGURE 24.1
Publishing set-
tings can be
accessed from
the Publishing
area under the
Site view.

This opens the Connection Settings dialog (see Figure 24.2), which gives you options of how you want to publish your files. One of the most important features is that you can set up several different publishing options for the same site, so you can publish the same site to different servers or other locations without having to change your settings every time. You can also choose which one to use each time you make a change. For this reason, the first element you need to define for your connection setting is a name. This name is just an identifier, so you can call it what-ever you want, but it is a good idea to give the connection a name that makes sense and is easily understood and identifiable.

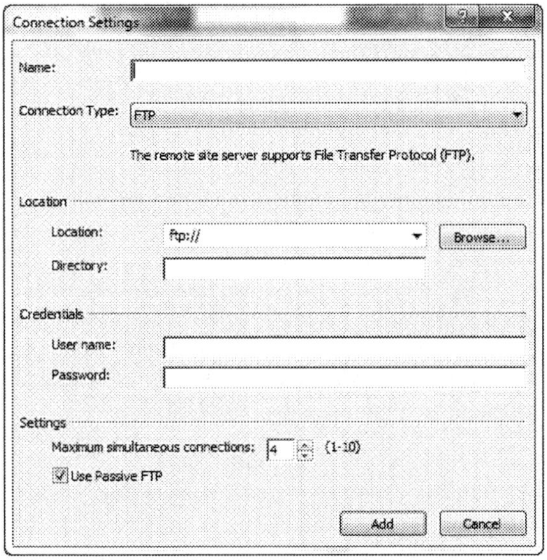

FIGURE 24.2
The Connection Settings dialog lets you define the different settings for each of your connections.

After you decide on a name, you need to select a connection type. Expression Web 4 offers six different types that all fit different scenarios:

▶ File Transfer Protocol (FTP)

▶ Secure Shell File Transfer Protocol (SFTP/SSH)

▶ File Transfer Protocol over Secure Sockets Layer (FTPS/SSL)

▶ FrontPage Server Extensions

▶ Web Distributed Authoring and Versioning (WebDAV)

▶ File System

These six methods are quite different and serve different purposes. Depending on your server, you might choose from several or be restricted to just one. Knowing the difference between them means you can make the right decision now and not run into trouble in the future.

File Transfer Protocol (FTP)

Of all the methods offered, File Transfer Protocol (FTP) is the most well known and frequently used. FTP is an old file transfer method that dates back to 1971. Because of its age, FTP is a simple protocol that is firmly rooted and supported in networking and the World Wide Web. For this reason, FTP can be considered the standard for file transfer between computers.

In spite of FTP's reliability and ubiquitous support, it has some significant drawbacks; the most important is that the protocol is not secure by default. Without using an added layer of security, it is relatively easy for outsiders to monitor an FTP connection and pick up both usernames and passwords.

When Expression Web originally appeared, the FTP performance was sporadic at best, and the many bugs associated with this feature became a major hang-up for early adopters. The release of Expression Web 2 saw significant improvements on this front, and the FTP option worked at an acceptable level. Even so, the Expression Web development team took criticism seriously, and for the release of Expression Web 3, they rewrote the entire publishing portion of the application from the ground up. As a result, the FTP options in versions 3 and 4 of the application are solid and work properly across the board.

To set up FTP as the publishing method, select FTP from the Connection Type list and insert the destination address in the Location field. With FTP, you also have the Directory option to specify a destination folder that the files will be sent to. That folder must already exist on the server.

Next, set your FTP username and password under Credentials. Your web host supplies the FTP username and password, and if you use FTP as your method for transferring files, you should change the password frequently.

In the Settings section, you can set the maximum number of simultaneous connections from 1 to 10. A higher number can speed up the time it takes to push data from your computer to the server, and vice versa, but not all Internet service providers and web hosts allow multiple connections (thus, the term "maximum connections"). Figure 24.3 shows the FTP setup for the MyKipple.com site with the username blocked out. Note that the FTP is specified in the prefix of the address, so the address starts with ftp:// instead of http://.

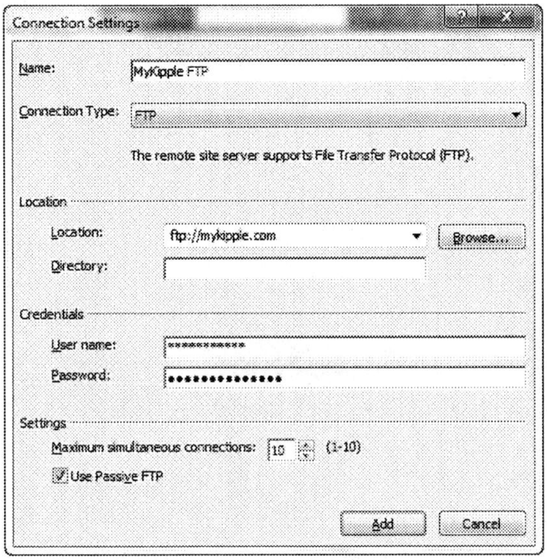

FIGURE 24.3
When selecting FTP as the publishing method, you need to insert the address with the FTP in place of the regular HTTP.

Finally, you have the option to turn on passive FTP if active FTP is not available. (Active FTP is often blocked by firewalls, but you can normally get through using passive FTP.)

Secure Shell File Transfer Protocol (SFTP/SSH)

In spite of what the name suggests, Secure Shell File Transfer Protocol is not regular FTP run under Secure Shell (SSH), but a file transfer protocol in its own right. Whereas FTP transfers all of your file content and other data (including your username and password) in plain text between your computer and the server, SFTP transfers this information under encryption, making it extremely hard to intercept or exploit. That said, for you, the user, there is no discernable difference between the two. The setup for SFTP is almost identical to that of FTP, with the exception of SFTP not having the option of using Passive FTP.

File Transfer Protocol over Secure Sockets Layer (FTPS/SSL)

FTPS is an FTP protocol that uses a Secure Sockets Layer (SSL) for added security. An oversimplified explanation of the difference between SFTP and FTPS is that SFTP encrypts the data as part of the transfer protocol, whereas FTPS adds a layer of encryption on top of the FTP transfer. Another way to think of the difference is that SFTP encrypts all the data to binary code before it is transferred, whereas FTPS sends the plain text data inside an encrypted connection that can be read only by the clients and servers that share the same authentication key.

As the name Secure Sockets Layer implies, FTPS employs a second layer of constant challenging and verification of the authenticity of the transfer between the client and the server. For this reason, FTPS works only with hosts that have a valid SSL certificate and support SSL. And, in many cases, to get this service, you have to pay extra.

Setup of an FTPS connection is identical to the setup of a regular FTP connection, because with the exception of the added secure layer, there is no difference between them.

FrontPage Server Extensions

You were briefly introduced to FrontPage Server Extensions in Hour 20, "Working with Flash and Other Embeddable Content," when you used them to create an email form. FrontPage Server Extensions is a set of small programs that run on the web server and give you the ability to add functionality (such as the ability to generate and send emails) to websites. More than that, it keeps tabs on your files both locally and on the server to ensure that elements, such as hyperlinks, are updated if a file is moved from one folder to another, and so on. FrontPage Server Extensions follows your web-authoring process to tell you what files have been altered either by yourself or someone else on your team and whether the files on your computer are newer or older than the ones on the server. As the name suggests, FrontPage Server Extensions was introduced with Microsoft's old web design program, FrontPage, and has become common throughout web servers, especially those running Microsoft Windows Server software. The name FrontPage Server Extensions might be a bit confusing because you are actually talking about many different things: the extensions that run at the heart of the server, the extensions that run independently inside your files (such as the email form functions), and the extensions that run in your authoring program keeping tabs on your files and your work.

When you check the FrontPage Server Extensions option in the Remote Web Site Properties dialog, you tell Expression Web 4 that the server you are publishing the site to has FrontPage Server Extensions installed and that you want to use this technology to communicate the files to and from the server. After setup, the application uses HTTP or HTTPS to send and receive file contents. This is the same protocol you use when you surf the Internet (the http:// prefix in front of all web addresses), which means that, even if you are on a computer behind a strong firewall, if you can surf the Internet, you can use FrontPage Server Extensions to publish content.

To set up FrontPage Server Extensions as your upload option, select the option from the list and enter your Remote Web Site location in the address box along with the username and password.

You can use FrontPage Server Extensions as your publishing method only if your web server supports this technology. If it does not, you immediately get a warning message saying the current settings will not work, and you are directed back to the Connection Settings dialog where you can make a different choice.

FrontPage Server Extensions Is on the Way Out

Despite its popularity, Microsoft has not supported FrontPage Server Extensions for some time. For this reason, there have not been any security updates to the technology for several years, and many web hosts are now stepping away and discontinuing their support for these scripts entirely. If you plan to use FrontPage Server Extensions, it is imperative that you contact your web-hosting service to make sure it is supported now and in the future.

Web Distributed Authoring and Versioning (WebDAV)

Web Distributed Authoring and Versioning (WebDAV) is an extension of the HTTP protocol that provides better security in the form of encrypted transmissions (to keep your data secure), file versioning (to prevent files from being overwritten when more than one person is working on them at the same time), and authentication. Unlike FrontPage Server Extensions, which uses add-ons, WebDAV is already built in to your operating system to handle external links to HTTP addresses.

Setting up WebDAV as the publishing method is done the same way as setting up FrontPage Server Extensions: Simply select the WebDAV option and insert the destination address, username, and password. Also, as with FrontPage Server Extensions, WebDAV has to be supported by your web server for it to work. If it is not supported or not turned on for your specific plan, you cannot access the server, and Expression Web 4 generates an error message. Unfortunately, this message causes a lot of confusion because the first item on the list of possible reasons why the connection failed is that the server does not have FrontPage Server Extensions installed (see Figure 24.4). This suggestion is misleading because WebDAV and FrontPage Server Extensions are mutually exclusive. In fact, if WebDAV fails, it could mean that FrontPage Server Extensions is installed on the server and is blocking WebDAV. If you get this message, contact your web-hosting provider and ask whether WebDAV is supported, and if so whether FrontPage Server Extensions is interfering with your connection.

Microsoft Expression Web

Unable to open 'http://mykipple.com'.
Server error: The web server at "http://mykipple.com" does not appear
to have FrontPage Server Extensions installed.

Possible causes:
1. The web server may not have the FrontPage Server Extensions
installed.
2. The web server may be temporarily out of service.
3. If you are connecting through a proxy server, the proxy settings may
be incorrect.
4. An error may have occurred in the web server.

If this server does not support the FrontPage Server Extensions,
Expression Web may still be able to publish to the server via FTP or
WebDAV. Please select one of these options and try again.

Ok

File System

The final option is to host your website in a folder on your local computer or in your
local network. That option can also be used to place your files on removable devices,
such as data discs, USB (Universal Serial Bus) keys, PDAs (Personal Data Assistants),
MP3 players, or any other storage device that can be connected to the computer.
That way, you can bring the website with you without having to lug around your
entire computer. The file system option is frequently used when publishing to local
networks and corporate intranets where the web server is on the same network as
the computer used.

If you publish to a local drive, all you need to do is insert the folder name in the
address bar. If you publish to a local network location or a mapped drive, you need
to insert the Universal Naming Code (UNC) path for this location. A UNC path looks
like this: \\myServer\sites.

Example: Publishing Content Using SFTP

You now have a basic idea of what the six different publishing methods offer and
when to use them. After you select a preferred method, the actual publishing process
is the same. The method that is most readily available and at the same time secure
is SFTP; therefore, in this example, you see how to use SFTP to publish your website
to an external web host.

1. With the MyKipple site open, in Site view, click the Add Publishing Destination link in the middle of the window, or click Publishing Settings in the top-right corner, and under the Publishing tab, click the Add button to open the Connection Settings dialog.

2. In the Connection Settings dialog, set the name to MyKipple SFTP Connection. Select SFTP; enter the destination address provided by your web-hosting service. If you publish to a specific folder, enter the folder name in the FTP Directory box.

3. Under Credentials, insert the username and password provided by your web host. Leave the Maximum Simultaneous Connections setting at 4 and click Add. If you started by opening the Publishing Settings, you need to click OK in the Publishing Settings dialog to complete the process.

When you add the new connection, the blue link in the middle of the Publishing view changes to say "Connect to the current publishing destination." Clicking this link logs into your new connection automatically. Depending on your Internet connection and your web host, this initial login procedure might take a little bit of time, and while it is working, the control bar at the top of the Site panel will be blurred out.

After successfully logging in, you are presented with a view similar to what's shown in Figure 24.5 with the local website on the left and the remote website on the right. The left column shows all the files in the folder you defined as your website project in Expression Web 4. The right column shows all the files currently at the remote location you defined in the address bar in step 2.

Expression Web 4 uses icons to tell you about the status of the files in your local and remote locations. In front of a file you can find a box with two columns, one green and one white, with either the left side green (file to be published to the remote location) or the right side green (file to be downloaded from the remote location), an exclamation point (Expression Web 4 is unsure what to do with this file), or a red circle with a slash in it (don't publish this file). Examples of all these icons are shown in Figure 24.5. When you log in to your remote location for the first time, all the files in your local view have the green and white column boxes with the green area on the left because none of the files are in the remote location yet.

How you proceed from this point depends on what you want to achieve. For example, if you publish your entire site to the remote location for the first time, all you need to do is click the blue arrow button in the middle going from left to right. This sends a copy of all your local files and folders to the remote location.

By the Way

Depending on how many files you have in your website, publishing the entire website to a remote location can take some time. And it might look like Expression Web 4 stalls in the process. In general, publishing large sites to a remote server is a test of patience, so I usually start the process and then leave the computer to work on its own to avoid getting annoyed at how long it takes.

If you have previously published files to your remote server and you have made changes to only some of your local files, Expression Web 4 inserts column icons on only the files that have been changed, and you can use the same option as before to overwrite the old files on the remote location with the new ones.

If files on the server have been changed since you last uploaded them, Expression Web 4 signifies that by attaching a column box with the right side highlighted in green to the files in the remote location. This usually happens if you or a colleague uploads new files from a different computer or if someone made changes to the file directly on the server. To transfer these files from the server to your local computer, you simply click the arrow in the middle pointing left.

In some cases, alterations have been made to both local files and remote files. If that is the case, you can use the Synchronize Files button in the middle column (the one with two arrows pointing in opposite directions). Use this function with caution because, sometimes, even though the files on the server are newer than the ones in your local folder, they might not be the ones you want to keep, and you could inadvertently overwrite important files in your local version of the site.

In addition to using the publishing options from the menu, you can also drag and drop files and folders between Local and Remote view. This is actually an effective way to perform targeted updates and give you detailed control of which files are located where.

You often find that your local folder contains many files that should not be put on the remote location for different reasons. For example, there is no reason to upload the Dynamic Web Template file to the server because it is functional only within Expression Web 4. To prevent a file or folder from being included when Expression Web 4 suggests files that should be uploaded or downloaded, right-click the file and select Exclude from Publishing from the pop-up menu (see Figure 24.6). A red balloon icon is attached to the file, and the file will be ignored in the publishing process.

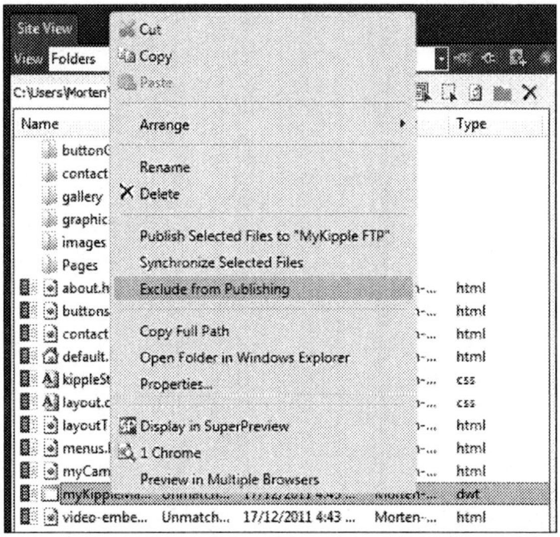

FIGURE 24.6
To prevent a file from being uploaded or downloaded, right-click it and select Exclude from Publishing from the context menu.

Publishing Open Files Without the Publishing Panel

One of my personal pet peeves with all web-publishing applications is that you always have to go to a publishing panel to actually push the files to the external server. In my work process, this is a huge time-sink because I tend to work on one or two files at a time, and I want to immediately see them live on the remote site. Now, after much hinting and suggesting from myself and other members of the Expression Web community, this is no longer an issue. Expression Web 4 introduces three new publishing methods that can be activated from anywhere inside the application. The three methods can all be found under the Site button on the main menu, and they are Publish Current File To (currently open connection), Publish Changed Files To (currently open connection), and Publish All Files To (currently open connection), as shown in Figure 24.7. The same functions can also be triggered with these keyboard shortcuts: Ctrl+Shift+U for current file, Ctrl+Shift+H for changed files, and Ctrl+Shift+A for all files.

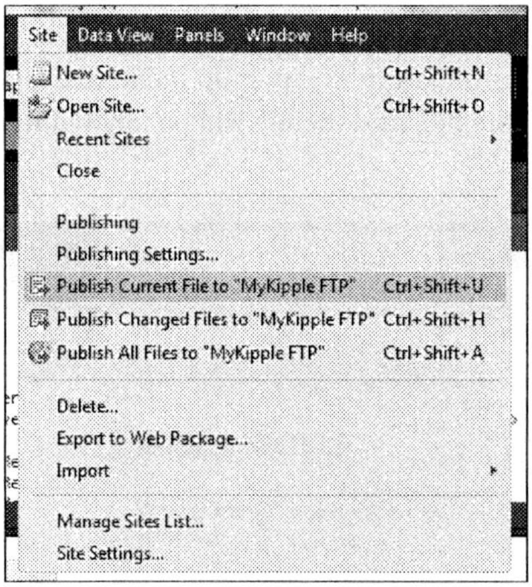

FIGURE 24.7
The new publishing functions can be found under Site on the main menu or activated with shortcuts.

As the description suggests, these three publishing functions push the current, changed, or all files to whatever publishing connection you currently have active in the Publishing panel. If no publishing connection is active, Expression Web 4 activates the default connection and pushes the file(s) there. In other words, make sure you have the correct connection active when using these functions; otherwise, your files may end up in the wrong place.

Did you Know?

These new publishing functions may seem small and unimportant, but they are huge timesavers, especially if you teach yourself the keyboard shortcuts. While I was participating in the beta testing of Expression Web 4, I got so used to the ability to push the current file I was working on directly to the server with the keyboard shortcut Ctrl+Shift+U that, when I switched back to Expression Web 3, I found myself punching in the key combination over and over and cursing under my breath because nothing was happening. This is one of those innovations you didn't really know you needed, but once it's there, you can't figure out how you managed without it.

Advanced Publishing Settings

You can change the way Expression Web 4 handles local and remote files by default and configure the application to make changes to the files as they are uploaded. This is all done from the Publishing tab in the Site Settings dialog.

Optimizing HTML

Under the Publishing tab, you have an option called Optimize HTML during publishing. If you check this option and click the Customize button that becomes available, you are taken to the HTML Optimization Settings dialog. From here, you can instruct Expression Web 4 to remove all or part of the nonfunctional code in your HTML pages (see Figure 24.8). This option is available because both designers and developers using Expression Web 4 tend to insert a lot of nonessential elements in HTML pages to make them easier to understand. Among these elements are comments explaining the different sections, Dynamic Web Template comments, and whitespace. You can also remove code generated by the application. The rationale behind removing this content is usually to either reduce the file size to improve load times (although this improvement will be negligible at best) or to make the HTML page less readable for people who take a sneak peek at the code.

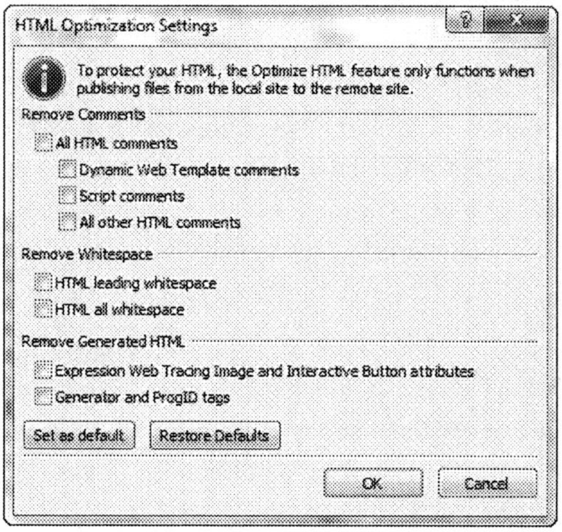

FIGURE 24.8
You can configure Expression Web 4 to remove all nonfunctional code from your HTML pages.

There are several options for HTML optimization, and when they are checked, the selected components are removed as the files are published to the remote location. Here is a quick rundown of each option:

▶ **All HTML Comments**—All HTML comments, whether inserted by Expression Web 4 or yourself, will be removed. HTML comments are ignored by the web browser and are visible only in the source code. They always start with `<!--` and end with `-->`.

▶ **Dynamic Web Template Comments**—In Hour 18, "Dynamic Web Templates," you learned that the editable regions in pages based on Dynamic Web Templates are inserted with HTML comments. These code sections relate only to Expression Web 4 and have no purpose outside the application.

▶ **Script Comments**—Expression Web 4 includes comments when inserting JavaScript and other script elements in your HTML pages. Likewise, it is common to attach comments to scripts to help remember what they do.

▶ **All Other HTML Comments**—This option covers all comments not covered by the other categories and can be used to remove only the comments you inserted without touching the comments Expression Web 4 created.

▶ **HTML Leading Whitespace**—The leading whitespace is the empty space before the first character in each line.

▶ **HTML All Whitespace**—In addition to leading whitespace, you can have inline whitespace and empty lines.

▶ **Expression Web Tracing Image and Interactive Button Attributes**—When tracing images and interactive buttons are inserted into a page, Expression Web 4 adds attributes to them for editing purposes (that is, allowing you to open and edit the interactive buttons). These attributes relate only to Expression Web 4 and have no function in a web browser.

▶ **Generator and ProgID Tags**—The Generator and ProgID tags used to be inserted in HTML pages to tell the browser what program was used to create and edit them. This is not done by Expression Web 4 but can apply to pages originally created in other web-authoring applications.

All the changes made by the Optimize HTML options are applied as the files are published to the remote location. Your local files are not changed. However, if you apply any of these options and then later overwrite your local files with ones from the remote location, all the content that was removed when the files were published will be removed locally.

The Publishing Tab

From the Publishing tab (see Figure 24.9), you can add, edit, or delete the publishing destinations for the current site. In addition, and you can tell Expression Web 4 to publish subsites and generate a log file each time it publishes content.

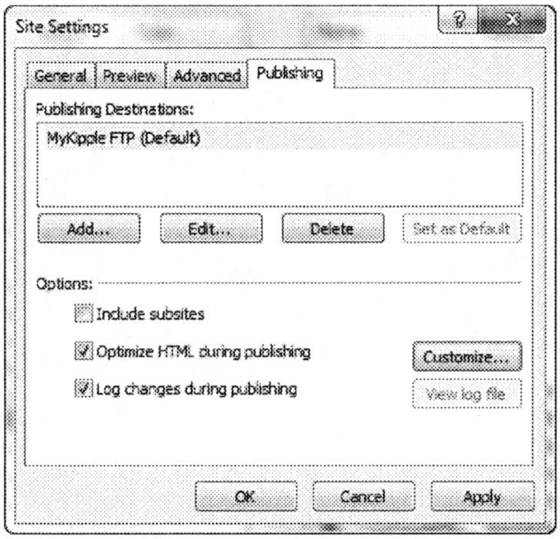

FIGURE 24.9
You can add, edit, or delete the publishing destinations for the current site.

By default, only pages and folders contained within the main site are published by Expression Web 4. However, if you have subsites defined in your project that you want published at the same time, you can check the Include Subsites option.

When you open the Publishing view of your site, Expression Web 4 makes an educated guess as to what files it thinks you want to replace in your local and remote locations. By default, it does this by comparing the modified dates of the files in both locations. However, if you work on the remote files as a team, from several different computers, or on the server itself, it can be almost impossible for Expression Web 4 to know which file is the correct one.

Finally, you can choose whether to let Expression Web 4 create a log file during publishing. If this box is checked, an HTML page is created and stored in your Temporary Internet Files folder so that you can check to see whether the publishing process went according to plan.

To view the log file after publishing a site, click the View Your Publish Log File option under Status in the Publishing view. This opens the log in your web browser for you to inspect. If you want to save the log file, select Save As under File in your browser.

At the bottom of the Publishing view panel is a section that provides information about your publishing status. This area lists the last publish status (whether files were published successfully and what problems were encountered, if any) and the last publish time as well as provides a link that says "Open destination site in Expression Web." This link opens the external site in a new instance of Expression Web 4 and sets it as the local site for that instance. That way, you can work directly on the files in the remote location as if they were on your local computer.

Summary

By following the tutorials in this book, you have created a basic website with a lot of functionality. The last step of any web design process is to publish the site so that others can access it and enjoy the results of your hard work. That is when Expression Web 4 goes from being a web design and authoring tool to becoming a file and website management tool.

When your site is completed and ready for the world to see, Expression Web 4 offers you six different methods for publishing your content, all with benefits and setbacks. Those methods are FTP, FTPS, SFTP, FrontPage Server Extensions, WebDAV, and file system. In this hour, you learned what each of these options mean and when they are used.

There is no correct answer to the question, "Which method should I use?" And, after setup, the actual publishing and file-copying processes are the same regardless of what method you choose.

Expression Web 4 keeps tabs on what you do with your files in the program and makes educated guesses about what files you want to publish to your site. Even so, you can change these options either by selecting or deselecting files for upload or changing the publishing settings. You can also use the program to strip your HTML files of nonfunctional content such as comments and whitespace. All this is done from the Remote Web Site Properties dialog.

In this hour, you learned how to set up your site in Expression Web 4 for publishing to the desired location. With that, you have reached the end of the road of the initial design and deployment process. However, this is just the beginning. When your website goes live and you start getting visitors, you'll probably want to make additions and changes to the site or build a subsite. Now that you know how to use Expression Web 4, you can apply the techniques you have acquired to build your knowledge of HTML, CSS, ASP.NET, PHP, and all the other technologies available to you and make informative and entertaining web experiences for the world to see.

Q&A

Q. *I tried uploading my site to my web host using FrontPage Server Extensions/WebDAV, but when I do, I get a warning saying that FrontPage Server Extensions is not installed on the server. What do I do?*

A. To use FrontPage Server Extensions or WebDAV as your publishing method, they need to be installed and supported by your server. Furthermore, they are mutually exclusive; so if you can use one, you cannot use the other. The warning message Expression Web 4 generates is a bit confusing because it tells you there are no FrontPage Server Extensions installed, even if you try to use WebDAV to upload your files. If you get this message using either method, contact your hosting provider and find out if either technology is supported with your plan. Most likely, it is not, and you will be forced to use FTP as your method for uploading content.

Exercise

Because this is the final hour, and you are probably tired of answering questions and doing exercises, I am giving you a challenge instead:

Take all the things you learned from reading this book and use them to create your own fantastic website. When you finish, publish your site for the world to see and send me a message on Twitter @mor10, become a fan of this book on Facebook, or leave a comment on this book's website (http://expression.pinkandyellow.com).

And, last but not least, have fun!

Index

Sams **Teach Yourself**

When you only have time
for the answers™

Whatever your need and whatever your time frame, there's a Sams **Teach Yourself** book for you. With a Sams **Teach Yourself** book as your guide, you can quickly get up to speed on just about any new product or technology—in the absolute shortest period of time possible. Guaranteed.

Learning how to do new things with your computer shouldn't be tedious or time-consuming. Sams **Teach Yourself** makes learning anything quick, easy, and even a little bit fun.

HTML and CSS in 24 Hours

Julie C. Meloni
Michael Morrison
ISBN-13: 978-0-672-33097-1

Java in 24 Hours

Rogers Cadenhead

ISBN-13: 978-0-672-33575-4

JavaScript in 24 Hours

Michael Moncur

ISBN-13: 978-0-672-32879-4

HTML, CSS, and JavaScript All in One

Julie C. Meloni

ISBN-13: 978-0-672-33332-3

PHP, MySQL, and Apache All in One

Julie C. Meloni

ISBN-13: 978-0-672-33543-3